SO-BIQ-293

Mountain Dr

Parma Park

Stanwood Dr

144

Sycamore Canyon Rd

Sycamore Canyon Rd

Eucalyptus Hill Rd

Hot Springs Rd

192

E Valley Rd

San Ysidro Rd

MONTECITO

Manning Park

Voluntario St

S Salinas St

Olive Mill Rd

Cacique St

El Camino Real

Hot Springs Rd

Coast Village Rd

Jameson Ln

Chavez

101

Andree Clark Bird Refuge

Santa Barbara Cemetery

Hill Rd

101

o Blvd

Butterfly Beach

PACIFIC OCEAN

H O M E T O W N

SANTA BARBARA

The Central Coast Book
2009 • 2010

Editor
Nancy Roberts Ransohoff

Writers
Cheryl Crabtree
Leslie Dinaberg
Zac Klobucher
Nancy Roberts Ransohoff
Starshine Roshell

Publisher
Colleen Dunn Bates

Prospect Park Books

Published by Prospect Park Books
prospectparkbooks.com

Distributed to the trade by SCB Distributors
scbdistributors.com

Special Sales
Bulk purchase (10+ copies) of *Hometown Santa Barbara* is available to companies, colleges, organizations, mail-order catalogs and nonprofits at special discounts, and large orders can be customized to suit individual needs.
  For more information, go to prospectparkbooks.com

Library of Congress Control Number: 2008930541
The following is for reference only:
  Ransohoff, Nancy Roberts
  Santa Barbara / Nancy Roberts Ransohoff.
        p.cm.
        Includes index.
ISBN 978-0-9753939-5-6
  1. Santa Barbara (Calif.) — Guidebooks 2. Los Angeles (Calif.) — Guidebooks.
I. Ransohoff, Nancy Roberts II. Title.

Production in the United States of America
Design by James Barkley
Production graphics by Kate Hillseth

Printed by Everbest Printing Co. in China

This book was printed on paper certified as sustainably produced by the Forest Stewardship Council.

First Edition

PROSPECT
·PARK·
BOOKS

Love at First Sight
by Fannie Flagg

Being a novelist by trade and therefore able to work from home, I have the happy option of living anywhere in the world. I chose Santa Barbara – or rather, it chose me. I'm not sure which.

The year was 1975. I was living in New York at the time and was in California for only a short visit (or so I thought) when friends invited me to drive up to Santa Barbara for lunch. That very afternoon I walked into a real estate office and bought a house, and I am still here.

Why? Why would someone who never had any intention of living in California do such an impetuous thing? For starters, the sheer physical beauty of Santa Barbara took my breath away. Oh sure, I had seen the Pacific Ocean before, and I had seen mountains before. I had seen magnificent architecture, beautiful flowers and lush greenery before – but never had I seen them all in one place. Secondly, everybody looked so happy. Was it any wonder I fell in love at first sight?

I've given a lot of thought as to why Santa Barbara residents, including me, are so happy, and I think the reasons are several. For one, the climate is perfect – never too hot, never too cold and, best of all for a girl raised in Alabama, it has no bugs! For another, it's the perfect size: not too big and not too small. Santa Barbara combines the friendliness and sense of community of a small town with the perks of a larger city: great restaurants, wonderful shopping, intelligent theater and art, quality colleges and interesting museums. And don't even get me started on the outdoor activities – almost any day of the year you can play tennis, golf, swim, hike, ride horses on the beach, kayak, sail, ride bikes, go deep-sea fishing … you name it.

After having traveled quite a bit, I can honestly say that Santa Barbara is one of the friendliest and most beautiful cities in the world. No matter where I go, I am always happy to come home.

Just one word of warning for you readers who are first-time visitors: Watch out for real estate offices. You never know where you might land up.

Fannie Flagg is the author of many novels, including *Fried Green Tomatoes at the Whistle Stop Cafe* (Ballantine) and her latest, *A Redbird Christmas* (Ballantine). She was nominated for an Academy Award for her screenplay of the 1991 film *Fried Green Tomatoes* and is a regular speaker at the Santa Barbara Writers Conference.

Contents

About *Hometown Santa Barbara*

This is not a guidebook. At least not in the conventional sense – that is, as a resource to guide visitors to tourist attractions, fun activities and good restaurants. Okay, okay – so maybe you will find some of that in the pages that follow. But *Hometown Santa Barbara* is something different, something more.

The *Hometown* concept began in 2006 with the publication of *Hometown Pasadena*, which was written by a team of five locals and met with immediate, and continuing, success. The goal was to reflect the community the writers knew – not just the weekend-visitor highlights, but the real community: its neighborhoods, its people, its culture, its quirks, its foibles. Based on the response, we achieved that goal. Next we did it with Santa Monica, thanks to a team of writers who were natives and/or longtime locals. Now it's Santa Barbara's turn – and what a place to celebrate! For one thing, it's a true hometown, with established neighborhoods, a walkable downtown, strong educational and cultural institutions, great architecture and an engaging history. For another, it's a damn fine place to spend a sunny day, whether you're paddling out at Rincon, shopping the Montecito farmer's market, celebrating at Fiesta or sipping a local Pinot Noir on State Street.

To create this book, we assembled a team of passionate, savvy writers. They had a wonderful time interviewing their local heroes, uncovering new favorite places and working together to produce a book that (we hope) will make locals proud and inspire visitors to go beyond the obvious and get to know the best of Santa Barbara and her sister communities.

As with any proper guidebook, you can flip and search for that one bit of information you crave: a good place for a margarita, perhaps, or a quiet beach for an evening stroll. But unlike other guidebooks, *Hometown Santa Barbara* goes inside, revealing the character of our communities and introducing you to some of the people who matter here. We hope you get to know these people, and then seek out more like them. We hope you read the Reaching Out chapter and find a way to make a difference here. And we hope you learn enough about Santa Barbara to make it your hometown, if only for a while.

Nancy Roberts Ransohoff
Editor

Colleen Dunn Bates
Publisher

P.S. The More Things Change ...

Please forgive us if a business has closed, if prices have been raised, or if your experience does not match ours. We labored mightily to verify every scrap of information in this book, but some places will close, change or misbehave, and we can't do a thing about it.

Seven Towns in Search of One

From Summerland to Montecito, Isla Vista to the Santa Ynez Valley, Santa Barbara is the nucleus of a number of smaller Central Coast communities. Each is blessed with the natural beauty and appeal of this southern stretch of the Central Coast, but each is unique. In these pages you'll get to know all of these towns: their origins and what's changed over time, their best hangouts, their famous residents and even their embarrassing secrets.

Santa Barbara
The American Riviera

The Facts
What It Is: A small city nestled between the Pacific Ocean and the Santa Ynez Mountains, about 80 miles north of Los Angeles
Population: 89,600 in the city; 400,335 in Santa Barbara County
Sister Cities: Dingle, Ireland; Puerto Vallarta, Mexico; San Juan, Philippines; Toba City, Japan; and Weihai, China
Ethnic Diversity: 74% Caucasian, 22% other ethnicities and 4% multiethnic; Latinos of any race are 35% of the population, and African-Americans and Asians are few and far between
Median Household Income: $47,498

The Look
Santa Barbara, also known as the American Riviera, is respected around the world for its respectful (rabid?) adherence to an architectural style that combines Spanish, Mediterranean and Moorish influences. The best-known characteristics of this appealing blend are the city's red-tile roofs and mission-style adobe buildings. Some of the best examples are the Santa Barbara Mission and the Santa Barbara Courthouse (don't miss the unbelievable clocktower view).

Key Players
As many as 150 Native American tribes (including the Chumash, who still reside in the Santa Ynez Valley) occupied what is now known as Santa Barbara for at least ten centuries before Sebastian Viscaino sailed into the Channel of Santa Barbara on December 4, 1602, and gave the town its name in honor of Saint Barbara. Father Junípero Serra founded the Santa Barbara Presidio in 1782, and added the mission four years later.

Telling Moments
Santa Barbara is the birthplace of the environmental movement in the United States. After a huge oil spill in 1969, several grassroots organizations (including GOO: Get Oil Out) formed to protect the environment and avoid future spills, and the late Senator Gaylord Nelson (D-Wisconsin) came upon the idea of Earth Day while in Santa Barbara to view the damage caused by the spill.

The city still prides itself on its environmentalism; it is home to more than 34,000 public trees, it ranks among the nation's top 20 counties for bicycle commuters, and it operates the nation's largest fleet of electric buses.

The Santa Barbara News-Mess
Journalistic scandal erupted in 2006 when a group of writers, editors and columnists at the *Santa Barbara News-Press* quit because they felt that gazillionaire owner Wendy McCaw had abandoned all journalistic ethics. America's press corps followed the ensuing brouhaha, which involved firings, protests, lawsuits, accusations and, most recently, the release of a documentary film called *Citizen McCaw*. Although bad news for journalism, it benefited the weekly *Independent*, which got some terrific writers out of the mess.

If It Only Had a Heart...
As the home base to approximately 600 nonprofits and 900 social and cultural programs, Santa Barbara is unofficially considered home to more nonprofits per capita than any other town in the United States.

Our Favorite
Parade: The goofy, wildly colorful Summer Solstice Parade, held downtown the first Saturday after the summer solstice (that's June 21 to you Mayan calendar adherents)
Farmer's Market: The Saturday downtown one, where Montecito mamas and Rasta surfers shop for produce, cheeses, pies, fresh seafood and more
Dog Park: Hendry's Beach (aka Arroyo Burro Beach), on the east side of the slough

Local News Personality: KEYT's Paula Lopez, a hometown girl who we trust to bring us our news

Hangout: The rose garden at the Mission is the perfect place to throw a Frisbee or watch the sunset

Park: Stevens Park is great for kids to play, and there are hiking trails and plenty of tables for barbecues and picnics

Radio Station: KCBX, 89.5 FM, the NPR affiliate in town, whose June fund-raising Live Oak Music Festivals in the Santa Ynez Valley are terrific

Hospital: Cottage Hospital, with a 24-hour trauma center, 805.569.7451

Newspaper: The *Daily Sound* and the weekly *Santa Barbara Independent* (see *News Mess*, left)

Web Sites: SBParent.com, noozhawk.com, independent.com, SantaBarbaraFree.com, edhat.com and the restaurant guide on SantaBarbara.com

What He/She Said

"Santa Barbara is a paradise; Disneyland is a paradise; the U.S. is a paradise. Paradise is just paradise. Mournful, monotonous, and superficial though it may be, it is paradise. There is no other."

– Jean Baudrillard

"It was Wednesday, the second week in April, and Santa Teresa was making a wanton display of herself. The lush green of winter, with its surfeit of magenta and salmon bougainvillea, had erupted anew in a splashy show of crocuses, hyacinths, and flowering plum trees."

– Sue Grafton, describing Kinsey Millhone's Santa Teresa, aka Santa Barbara

Hollywood North

California's first major movie studio, Flying A, arrived in Santa Barbara in 1910 and produced hundreds of silent films in the early 1900s. The town's early cinematic history included Cecil B. DeMille's *The Ten Commandments* and W.C. Fields' *The Bank Dick*. Since then, Santa Barbara has been cast in many films, from *The Graduate* to *Seabiscuit*, and was the setting of the prime-time soap opera *Santa Barbara*, from 1984 to 1993.

The Neighborhoods

Santa Barbara is rich in coveted residential neighborhoods, the best known of which is the Riviera, the hills above downtown that evoke the south of France. Other lovelies include the Upper East, a tapestry of architectural gems (Victorian, Craftsman, Mediterranean) from the 1800s and beyond, near downtown; the rustic yet refined Mission Canyon, which stretches into the foothills northeast of the Santa Barbara Mission; the tabletop bluff known as the Mesa, with its beach-casual sensibility and commanding views of the Pacific; San Roque, off of upper State Street, a traditional neighborhood of storybook cottages interlaced with more stately homes; and the ultra-posh Hope Ranch, which offers a private beach, horse trails and a Ralph-Lauren-goes-to-the-beach vibe – and yet it's still convenient to Vons and the other necessities of boring middle-class life.

Born in Santa Barbara

Motel 6
Tom Curren
Edie Sedgwick
Sambo's
Dishwalla
Anthony Edwards
Lockheed Aircraft
Balance Bar
Kathy Ireland
Big Dog Sportswear
Toad the Wet Sprocket
Egg McMuffin

And Many Top Athletes, Including:

Karch Kiraly
Dax Holdren
Terry Schroeder
Kim Herrin
Eddie Mathews
Jamaal Wilkes
Sam Cunningham
Randall Cunningham
Don Ford

Carpinteria
Tar, Avocados and the World's Safest Beach

The Facts
What It Is: Founded in 1863 and located twelve miles southeast of Santa Barbara, Carpinteria was once one of the more affordable of the Santa Barbara coastal communities. Still packing small-town charm, beautiful beaches and breathtaking mountain views, it recently shed any lingering dust by taking down the giant Santa on the now-swankier lane that still bears his name. A hint for Santa seekers: Oxnard.

Population: 14,194

Ethnic Diversity: 73.4% Caucasian, 4.4% multiethnic and the rest other ethnicities and; Latinos of any race are 43.5% of the population, and there are even fewer African-Americans here than in Santa Barbara

Median Household Income: $47,729

Best Hangouts
Long, sandy Carpinteria State Beach Park is so tranquil it's been called the "world's safest beach." In town, locals head for main drag Linden Avenue, for *the* breakfast spots in town, Cajun Kitchen and the Worker Bee, and Robitailles Candy, whose famed mints were served in red, white and blue at President Reagan's inauguration.

The Name
The first inhabitants, the Chumash, called this area Mishopshno, meaning "correspondence," because it was a center of trade. Later the Spanish named it *carpinteria* (carpentry shop), in honor of the Chumash's large canoe-building enterprise, which they located here because of the plentiful supply of naturally occurring surface tar, that they used to seal the boats. You can still see the goo seeping from cliffs. BTW, up your street cred with locals who call home "Carp," not Goo-ville.

Our Favorite
Festival: The California Avocado Festival, in early October, honoring the local avocado industry, third largest in the U.S.

Museum: Carpinteria Valley Museum of History, fave of local school groups for oh, yes, the asphaltum mining display!

Preserve: Salt Marsh Nature Park, also known as El Estuaro, is one of the most important wetlands in SoCal; docent tours on Saturdays from May to November

Neighborhood: Sandyland Road, with killer views of the Channel Islands

All Aboard! Amtrak runs daily to nearby beach cities; unstaffed station at Linden and Fifth

Lunch: Rain or shine, you will find Bill Connell and his stand, Surf Dog, at the 101 and Bailard, dishing out hot dogs and salty conversation

Beach: Rincon Point, for its park, world-famous surf break and great beach

Newspaper: *Coastal View News*

Best-kept Secret
The Harbor Seal Preserve is home to almost 100 seals, who give birth to their cubs on the Carpinteria shoreline. From December through May, the beach is closed on either side of the rookery. There's been much debate about whether to publicize the preserve; we're sure well-behaved visitors will keep a respectful distance.

Made in Carpinteria
Established in 1911, the Santa Barbara Polo & Racquet Club (located in Carpinteria) is the third-oldest polo facility in the U.S. and is renowned for its lush fields and international competition. Matches open to the public spring through fall. Good show!

Mr. Zog's Sex Wax, the leading surfboard and snowboard wax producer, is headquartered here. The wax was actually invented in Goleta in 1972 by chemist Nate Skinner and surfer Frederick Charles Herzog III, who still lives and surfs in the area.

More than sixteen varieties of potted plants and 40 varieties of cut flowers are grown in Carpinteria, home to 30-plus nurseries and a top producer of orchids.

Goleta
The Good Land

The Facts
What It Is: Incorporated in 2002, Goleta is a coastal community just north of Santa Barbara, adjoining Isla Vista and the University of California, Santa Barbara

Population: 55,204

Sister Cities: La Union, Mexico (in process)

Ethnic Diversity: 78.6% Caucasian, 1.3% African American, 6.4% Asian; Latinos of any race are 22% of the population

Median Household Income: $60,314

The Name
First called "The Good Land," Goleta was officially named for an old schooner that explorer José de la Guerra brought from Mexico in 1822.

Key Players
Euro-American homesteaders founded Goleta, which became a prominent lemon-growing region beginning in the late 19th century. It remains home to Fairview Gardens, Southern California's oldest organic farm. With the development of UCSB in neighboring Isla Vista in the 1950s and the boom in the aerospace industry in the '60s and '70s, Goleta morphed from rural-ag hamlet to high-tech haven. Now it's tech-firm central and a swank bedroom community for Santa Barbara worker bees, as well as the site of the fetching mission-style airport. But ix-nay on the airport ovation. Most of the do-re-mi goes to Santa Barbara, and Goleta, grrr, gets the congestion and noise pollution.

Our Favorite
Coffeehouse: Mojo Coffee, with slouchy couches, free WiFi and seating outside in the sun

Microbrewery: Hollister Brewing Company, a brewpub in the Camino Real Marketplace

Golf Course: The oceanview Sandpiper Golf Club is one of the top-ranked public courses in the country

Wildlife: Ellwood Mesa's butterfly preserve is an unrivaled place for a winter stroll among thousands of Monarch butterflies

Happening: A toss-up between the California Lemon Festival (fall) and the Dos Pueblos versus San Marcos High football game (Go Chargers! Go Royals!)

Restaurant: The Beachside, not so much for the food, but because it's smack-dab on the sand at Goleta Beach Park

Hey Dude, You're Famous!
Anthony Edwards (*ER, Top Gun*) and Eric Stoltz (*Mask, Pulp Fiction*) started their acting careers at San Marcos High in the late 1970s. They both got their first big movie break in *Fast Times at Ridgemont High*, costarring as Jeff Spicoli's (Sean Penn's) stoner buddies.

And Infamous...
On January 30, 2006, the Goleta postal processing facility was the locale, sadly, for the nation's worst office-place massacre by a woman.

Best-kept Secret
Unlike the Santa Barbara office, where you can wait for hours, the Department of Motor Vehicles in Goleta is almost never crowded.

Second Best-kept Secret
The world's two top (no pun intended) breast-implant companies both operate out of inconspicuous buildings in Goleta. Mentor and its longtime neighbor and so *not* breast friend, so *not* bosom buddy rival, Inamed, design and produce the vast majority of saline and silicone implants seen in Orange County women the world over.

Isla Vista & USCB
Town and Gown

The Facts
What It Is: Isla Vista is an unincorporated community adjacent to Goleta and Santa Barbara. The majority of its residents are college students at UC Santa Barbara.
Population: 18,344
Ethnic Diversity: 69% Caucasian, 2% African American and 11% Asian; Latinos of any race are 20% of the population
Median Household Income: $16,151 (kids with pizza money)

Key Player
There is but one player in town: UCSB. It is Santa Barbara County's largest employer, with almost 10,000 people on staff, and it provides at least five percent of the county's economy. *Dang.*

What was originally a small, independent teachers' college joined the University of California system in 1944 and moved from a campus on the Riviera to its current digs in 1954. Provost Clark Kuebler was charged to develop UCSB into a first-rate small, liberal arts college that could complement the enormous campuses of Berkeley and UCLA.

When post–World War II baby boomers flooded the University of California, the original vision of UCSB as a small campus was revised, and the Gauchos saddled up to mirror Berkeley and UCLA, the other two UCs at the time.

Nobody Parties Like a Nobel Laureate
The faculty of UCSB has received five Nobel Prizes since 1998, for landmark research in chemistry, physics and economics. Despite its growing reputation for academic excellence, UCSB also has a well-earned rep as a party school. Even though nobody really reads *Playboy*, in 2006 they tapped it as the No. 2 party school in the country. The student Halloween parties in Isla Vista are legendary, though the annual tradition is not as popular with school administration and local police.

Our Favorite
Coffeehouse Name: IV Drip
Burrito: Freebirds, famous for late-night-munchies-size burritos
Pizza: Woodstock's Pizza Parlor, for delivery or on-site karaoke-night pizza
Workout: The rock-climbing walls at the UCSB Recreation Center
Park: Fortuna Park, the only place in town that still has the old-fashioned spinning rides that mom swears will "rip your leg off one day"
Cultural Experience: Any of the enlightening programs put on by UCSB's Arts & Lectures (see the Smart chapter)
Unexplained Tradition: UCSB students throwing tortillas at halftime

Fun Facts
In 1970, Paul Orfalea started Kinko's as an 8-by-12-foot copy shop next to a hamburger stand in Isla Vista.

UCSB's Bren Hall laboratory received the LEED Platinum Award – the highest certification possible. Way to go green!

Famous UCSB Alums
Gwyneth Paltrow
Michael Douglas
Benjamin Bratt
Jack Johnson
Woody Harrelson

Montecito
"Little Mountain"

The Facts
What It Is: Just south of Santa Barbara, Montecito is one of the wealthiest zip codes in the country, home to celebrities, business titans and, yes, on a part-time basis, Oprah. Boutiques, restaurants, small hotels and art galleries populate Coast Village Road and the Upper Village, the two commercial sections of town.
Population: 10,000
Ethnic Diversity: Let's just say it's about the whitest place around, Oprah aside.
Median Household Income: $110,669; with 35.2% of families earning $200,000 or more (according to the 2000 U.S. Census)

The Name
Montecito means "little mountain" – an apt name for this area of winding, tree-shaded hillside lanes reminiscent of Provence. The area is known for the style and elegance of its residences, many of which are estates built at the turn of the last century by wealthy Easterners.

A Montecito Myth?
For decades, the Spanish-style Montecito Inn has trumpeted that it was built in 1928 by Charlie Chaplin; it uses an image of Chaplin in its logo, and every guidebook that has ever listed it repeats this historical claim. Which makes the folks at the Montecito Historical Society want to spit nails. They say it's total hogwash.

Famous Residents (at least part-time)

Oprah Winfrey	Troy Aikman
Carol Burnett	Steven Spielberg
Jonathan Winters	Kevin Costner
Steve Martin	Kirk Douglas
Eva Marie Saint	Dennis Miller
Tab Hunter	Julia Louis-Dreyfus
John Cleese	Ty Warner (Beanie
Rob Lowe	Baby billionaire)
Jimmy Connors	
Christopher Lloyd	

COAST VILLAGE ROAD

Our Favorite
Coffeehouse: Jeannine's Bakery & Café
Beach: Butterfly, recently named by *Travel + Leisure* as one of the "20 Great American Beaches," especially for people-watching
Breakfast: Montecito Coffee Shop
Parade: The Village Fourth of July Parade
Shops: dressed and ready, Susan Pitcher's two *très chic* boutiques
Dog Walk: La Casa de Maria Retreat Center, a place of tremendous serenity
Sandwich Spot: Pierre Lafond
Expense-account Restaurant: Lucky's
Expense-account Bar: The Four Seasons Biltmore Santa Barbara, which is actually in Montecito, both physically and spiritually
Newspaper: *Montecito Journal* (montecitojournal.com)

Most Romantic
In 1940, Sir Laurence Olivier married Vivien Leigh at the San Ysidro Ranch.

In 1955, Rock Hudson said "I do" to Phyllis Gates at the Four Seasons Biltmore.

Jack and Jackie honeymooned at the San Ysidro Ranch in 1953. Years later, Julia Roberts also honeymooned there.

More recent celebrity weddings include Sandra Bullock, Gwyneth Paltrow, Mira Sorvino, Jim Carrey, Debra Messing, Will Farrell, Heather Locklear, Halle Berry and Avril Lavigne, each with a spouse, who are people in their own right.

Don't Ever Change
Montecitans are preservation-minded. Also, quietly tasteful. And they love their gardens, from hedgerows surrounding serene cottages to the wacky grandeur of Lotusland. Come for a home and garden tour, by all means, but please, don't gawk.

On Screen
The 1981 version of *The Postman Always Rings Twice*, starring Jack Nicholson and Jessica Lange, was filmed at the currently shuttered Miramar, which at press time was awaiting its remake by developer Rick Caruso.

Santa Ynez Valley
Viticulture Valley

The Facts
What It Is: Located some 35 miles north of Santa Barbara, the Santa Ynez Valley feels like it's worlds away with its picture-book setting of rolling hills dotted with dark-green valley oaks, grazing cattle, blue skies and white clouds. Largely rural and agricultural, it is home to horse and cattle ranches, apple orchards, an ever-growing number of vineyards and wineries, and an infrastructure that supports money-spending, wine-sipping vacationers from L.A.
Population: 4,584
Ethnic Diversity: Almost 92% Caucasian and small numbers of other ethnicities
Median Household Income: $80,284

Towns & Neighborhoods
The Santa Ynez Valley includes six unique communities:

Ballard is home to a 1893 little red school-house that still accommodates the local kindergarten. Grown-ups prefer to hang out at the Ballard Inn.

Buellton is found at the intersection of the 101 and Highway 246. It's a beloved little town, not least for Pea Soup Andersen's restaurant, nor for the Hitching Post's Pinot Noirs, savored in the movie *Sideways*.

Los Alamos is known for its seven-block-long main street, historic train depot, quaint shops, restaurants and parks. It's also home to American Flatbread, purveyor of the best all-natural flatbread pizza on the planet.

Los Olivos is a slice of upscale Americana, with art galleries, an art museum, boutiques, more than a dozen wine-tasting rooms and Fess Parker's Wine Country Inn & Spa.

Santa Ynez, founded in the 1880s and named for nearby Mission Santa Inés, still serves real cowboys at the historic Maverick Saloon. Walk along Sagunto Street – where many of the original false-front buildings are preserved, though they now contain modern shops and restaurants – and you'll hear so many "morning ma'ams," you just might bop somebody all the way back to the 19th century.

Solvang, founded by Danish settlers in 1911, is a showcase of Scandinavian architecture, windmills, food, celebrations and customs. Visitors clamor for the cartloads of precious "souvenirs" here. Full-size windmills dot the city and surrounding countryside, and there's even a bronze replica of Copenhagen's Little Mermaid statue in front of the pharmacy.

Famous Faces
In 1949, Clark Gable rode onto the 10,000-acre Alisal Guest Ranch and Resort to wed Sylvia Hawkes, lucky spouse No. 4 for both.

Salad Days
Creamy Hidden Valley Ranch salad dressing is named for the Hidden Valley Ranch in the Santa Ynez Valley. Steve Henson created the dressing recipe while living in Alaska, before he moved to the valley. Cold Spring Tavern (which is still open today) was the first restaurant to serve his dressing, and before long it had became a salad-dressing craze; Henson sold the brand in 1973 for $8 million. It's now America's most popular salad dressing.

Summerland
Spookville

The Facts
What It Is: Located right on the 101 south of Santa Barbara and north of Carpinteria, Summerland is a charming little beach town on a steep slope, with a good surfing and swimming beach and a pervasive sense of serenity. A small artists' colony exists here, but Summerland today is most famous for its antiques shops, casual cafés, blufftop Lookout Park and Summerland Beach.
Population: 1,545
Ethnic Diversity: Here we go again: about 92% Caucasian, 2.4% Asian and a smattering of other ethnicities
Median Household Income: $53,964

Key Players
Harry L. Williams had originally hoped to make his living as a pig farmer when he settled here in 1885 with his wife, Katie. But he soon ran into money trouble and decided to sell off small lots from his 1,100-acre parcel, building a community of 500 around Spiritualism, a quasi-religious fad of the era. He donated land for a temple, where fellow Spiritualists and mediums gathered for séances. Rumors of bizarre goings-on spread through the area, and folks in neighboring towns took to calling Summerland "Spookville."

Ghost Story
The landmark Big Yellow House that you see as you drive into town was built in 1884 as the Williamses' personal residence. Like many original buildings in town, it is rumored to have ghosts, including a noisy fellow named Hector, who hectors from the basement to the upstairs library.

Our Favorite
Antiques Store: It's a bevy of riches, with more than a dozen shops on Lillie Avenue, but Rue de Lillie's antique birdcages and vintage fabrics make us particularly weak in the knees
Burger: Stacky's Seaside, Summerland's very own Krusty Krab
Breakfast: The Nugget, where the Clintons once noshed
Coffeehouse: Café Luna

Place to Browse: The Sacred Space, filled with Buddhas, prosperity elephants, garden art and ritual items – all for a price, of course
Park: Lookout Park, between the 101 and the sand
Workout: Walking on Summerland Beach or riding up the Ortega Hill bike path, so you can skip your spin class

On the Avenue
Highway 101 might seem like Summerland's main drag, since it bisects the tiny town, but the main artery is actually Lillie Avenue. It's a classic small-beach-town street, reminiscent of New England, with cottages and board-and-batten structures housing an inn, a couple of day spas, one old seafood diner (Stacky's), an even older bar (the Nugget), such locals' necessities as a post office and an astonishing number of fabulous antiques shops.

Oil Greases the Path
An oil boom in 1896 turned the beachside hamlet into an eyesore, with derricks and machine works all around. The beach regained its scenic beauty after the oil played out by the 1920s. (Drilling now takes place offshore – you can see several platforms out toward the horizon.) The area suffered during the Depression, reemerging in the '60s and '70s as an arts and surfing haven. The '80s brought a housing boom, but residents continue to protect the town's funky character, jealously guarding a balance between development and constraint.

Keep Your Shirt On
Despite the glorious bluffs and stunning hidden coves, there are no nude beaches in Summerland.

Fifteen Minutes of Fame
Summerland, a 2004 *The O.C.* look-alike TV show, didn't fly, even with a young Zac Efron in the cast.

Historic

Eons ago, Mother Nature set up a glorious stage for those who would play out our region's history. Isolated from the rest of the mainland by steep mountains, the Chumash lived here virtually undisturbed for thousands of years. Then the Spanish explorers and missionaries "discovered" this hidden corner of the continent and came to stay. Later, Mexican and American settlers developed the sleepy pueblo, and it grew into a sizable trading post. When wealthy kingpins from the Midwest and East came to vacation, word spread that Santa Barbara was one of the planet's most desirable places to live and play. The rest, as they say, is history.

In the Beginning

The Mountains Take a Lucky Hike

From the get-go, Santa Barbara has always marched to a different drummer. Its history really begins with a most unusual series of events that took place several million years ago. You see, most major mountain ranges run from north to south. And most of the Pacific coastline faces west. But the mountains here took a radically different path. As they erupted and stretched and poked their way ever higher, they marched from west to east. So did the peaks that emerged from the ocean just a few miles south of the mainland.

This fortuitous orientation created a near-perfect pocket of paradise. The mountains sheltered the beaches and valleys, and the islands protected the channel waters and shore. Flora, fauna and marine life flourished. During the cool Ice Age, pine forests blanketed the mountains, while oaks and fruit trees thrived in the valleys. It was as idyllic as anywhere on Earth.

The offshore islands attracted numerous types of creatures, including gigantic 20,000-pound Columbian mammoths. About 20,000 years ago, during the Pleistocene era, what we now know as the four northernmost Channel Islands were actually one big Ice Age island, Santarosae. Sea level was 300 feet lower than it is now, and the island was only about six miles from the mainland. The mammoths are believed to have swum to Santarosae from the mainland, lured by the scent of delectable dining possibilities. These behemoths evolved into more diminutive versions – a new species called the Channel Islands pygmy mammoths.

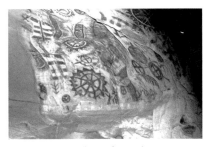

Although it has been fenced to protect it from vandals, the Painted Cave is still easy to see through the gate. This collection of natural-pigment art, some of which dates back 1,000 years, is found on Painted Cave Road off San Marcos Pass Road.

Eventually the glaciers and ice melted and caused the sea level to rise, so the peaks of Santarosae became the four islands we mainlanders see across the channel today: San Miguel, Santa Rosa, Santa Cruz and Anacapa.

Mammoths Out, Humans In

At the end of the Pleistocene, humans arrived. They originally came from Asia, crossing over islands of the Bering Strait to North America. Some scientists believe they also may have traveled by boat. Some people traveled south, and when they eventually reached the Central Coast, many stayed put. In 1959 paleontologists discovered the oldest dated human remains in North America – the Arlington Woman – near Arlington Springs on Santa Rosa Island. Recent testing indicates that this Paleoindian female lived about 15,000 years ago.

The Paleoindian settlers eventually evolved into the Chumash, whose diet consisted mainly of shellfish. By 5,000 BP the Chumash language (Samala) began to evolve, and over the next few thousand years the people developed excellent hunting and fishing skills. The land and sea provided so much bounty that the Chumash had plenty of time to devote to arts, crafts and a rich spiritual and cultural life. In fact, the Chumash are respected as some of the finest basket makers in the world. They also built *tomols*, plank canoes carved from a single tree trunk, and were widely known as makers of shell-bead money, which they would string on leather strips and use for trading. About two-thirds of the Chumash lived near the coast, in tribes with names like Sisquoc, Lompoc and Tecolote (place names still used today).

Paradise Discovered

Spain Breezes Through

Life for the Chumash remained relatively calm and peaceful – and hidden from the rest of the world – until 1542, when explorer and navigator Juan Rodriguez Cabrillo, commissioned by Spain to find a passage connecting the Pacific and Atlantic oceans, sailed his galleon in between the northern Channel Islands and the mainland. The Chumash canoed out to greet the ship, unwittingly welcoming the very people who would all but destroy their culture. Historians believe that Cabrillo landed on the beach of Siyuxtun, a village just west of the mouth of Mission Creek (near present-day Stearns Wharf) and he and his crew exchanged presents with the Chumash.

JUAN RODRIGUEZ CABRILLO

Spanish explorer Juan Rodriguez Cabrillo.

Cabrillo claimed the channel, the islands and the mainland for Spain, then headed out again, steering his galleon north toward San Francisco. A gale forced him to turn back and head south, and he purportedly disembarked at San Miguel Island. He is presumed to have died there, although neither his grave nor remains have ever been found.

Other explorers cruised by in the following decades, including Sir Francis Drake on the *Golden Hinde*, but there are no records of anyone stepping foot on shore. In early December 1602, Sebastian Vizcaino, on a Spanish expedition to seek out safe harbors in Alta California, entered the channel. A Carmelite friar on the expedition had a penchant for naming places after the particular saint whose feast day occurred on the date of the expedition's arrival at a new site. On December 4, 1602, after surviving a heavy storm the previous night, the ship found itself in calm, sparkling waters, protected by islands and mountains. The grateful friar named the channel Santa Barbara, after the patron saint of mariners, whose feast day is December 4th, the anniversary of her death.

The Quest for Real Estate

Spain didn't care much about California for nearly 170 years. But a couple of trends caused Spaniards to perk up their ears. Around 1750, Russians began coming down to the area to hunt otter and other mammals. As more trappers arrived and more English ships plied Pacific waters, the Spaniards began to worry about losing their territory. At the same time, the Roman Catholic Church was looking to expand its presence in the New World. The padres already had built a series of missions in Mexico and Baja California and were hoping to expand northward into Alta California.

El Presidio Real de Santa Barbara.

So King Charles III of Spain ordered two expeditions – one by land and one by sea. They were told to occupy sites at San Diego and Monterey and build secure garrisons from which the Spanish military could rule the land and surrounding seas. He appointed Gaspar de Portolá as the new governor of California, to be based in Monterey. Portolá, accompanied by Father Junípero Serra, led a land expedition north. The expedition arrived here in August 1769, and the group checked out the various possibilities for later settlement. On September 6, 1772, Father Serra returned to Santa Barbara with another land expedition, this time led by Pedro Fages. Both expeditions established missions along their route – but the Santa Barbara site was not among those selected in the first waves.

By 1775 the Spaniards had figured out that the missions between Monterey and San Diego needed protection, and that a fourth military outpost (after Monterey, San Francisco and San Diego) should be situated in the Santa Barbara Channel area. Governor Filipe de Neve and Father Serra formally founded El Presidio Real de Santa Barbara (the Royal Fort of Santa Barbara) on April 21, 1782, after finally settling on a site (now the corner of Santa Barbara and Canon Perdido streets). Lieutenant José Francisco Ortega became the first presidio comandante.

Mission construction, however, had to wait until the presidio was secure and staffed. It also took a while for the founding padres to settle on a mission site. Finally they decided it shouldn't be far from the presidio, and designated a spot up the hill, near a creek. In 1786 Father Fermín de Lasuén founded Mission Santa Barbara on December 4th, the feast day of Saint Barbara. Missions were soon established just north of Santa Barbara: La Purísima in Lompoc in 1787, and Santa Inés in 1802.

A Westernized Chumash couple in the late 19th century.

Bad News for the Chumash
The padres rounded up as many Chumash as they could to convert them to Catholicism – and to help with presidio and mission construction. The missions had vast parcels of land, many of which became ranches. The padres taught the natives how to raise sheep and cattle and to grow crops. Sadly, many of these native peoples contracted European diseases and died. Those who remained near the missions were forced to adapt to "civilized" mission and pueblo life, and to abandon their "heathen" customs.

When the Spaniards first settled in the Santa Barbara area, an estimated 15,000 Chumash lived in the region. In the early 1830s, when the Mexican government secularized the missions, taking control of large areas of land previously controlled by the Church, only about 3,000 Chumash remained. Most of them returned to their former tribal lands, and, sadly, many experienced difficulties reassimilating to the old Chumash way of life.

Mexico Takes Over – But Not for Long

In 1810, Mexican revolutionaries launched a rebellion against Spanish oppression. The Mexicans eventually won the rebellion, and in 1826 Santa Barbara's new Mexican town council did away with military rule and replaced it with a civil government. Under Mexican control, strict Spanish laws prohibiting foreign trade flew out the window. Soon local residents started trading tallow and hides with traders from New England.

In 1819 Captain José de la Guerra, the commander of the Royal Presidio, began construction on a sprawling adobe home for his large extended family near the city's main plaza. Completed in 1827, it was called La Casa Grande, and it soon became the social, political and economic hub of the town. Many of the townspeople turned to wealthy, influential Don José, and later his son Don Pablo, when they needed advice or assistance.

Santa Barbara quickly became known as an important trading post, and more Yankees started arriving in town, creating a whole new social scene. Some stayed, marrying young Santa Barbara *señoritas* and establishing *casas* of their own. One of these was a dashing sea captain named William Goodwin Dana. William's cousin, Richard Henry Dana, came along on one of William's voyages out west and wrote about Santa Barbara – including a three-day-long 1836 wedding celebration at Casa de la Guerra – in his classic book, *Two Years Before the Mast*.

In the Spanish period, the missions controlled a number of huge, valuable tracts of land they never used. The Mexican government took these and began to dole them out to soldiers and civil servants when they retired from government service. Some of these land grants (which numbered about 30 in all) encompassed as much as 40,000 acres. The new ranch owners planted vineyards, orchards and vegetable gardens and raised cattle for beef, hides and tallow.

By 1846 the Yankees were at war with Mexico. In August, Commodore Robert Field Stockton and a group of U.S. soldiers sailed into Santa Barbara. They marched into the presidio and hoisted the U.S. flag. The Mexicans tried to regain control over the next few months, but to no avail. In December, Colonel John Fremont arrived, and the Mexican period of our history was soon over. The Gold Rush brought many people from around the world to California, and the growth in population enabled California to become the nation's 31st state, in 1850. That same year, Santa Barbara became an American city.

The Lone Woman of San Nicolas Island

San Nicolas Island is the most remote of the eight Channel Islands off the California coast. The Nicoleños, descendants of the Tongva Indians, thrived on the island until Russian otter hunters and Aleutians decimated their population in the early 1800s. In 1835 the padres sent a schooner to fetch the remaining handful of natives and transport them to the mainland to live at the mission and pueblo. Somehow, the boat left one woman behind, for reasons unknown. Some stories say she ran back to find her child. In any event, she survived there alone for seventeen years.

A hunter and trapper named George Nidever noticed her footprints on the beach in 1851, and he returned with a crew in 1853 to look for her. They discovered her on the second day of their search: She was in remarkably good health, and a group of dogs accompanied her. Nidever took her back to the mainland, where she was given a Spanish name, Juana María. Unfortunately, she survived less than two months on the mainland. Her digestive system, accustomed to a simple diet of seal meat, roots, shellfish and other island fare, never adjusted to the rich mainlander diet. A century later, in 1961, Newbery Award–winning author Scott O'Dell wove Juana María's story into a famous novel, *Island of the Blue Dolphins*.

From Isolation to World-Class Resort

The Californio Era Ends

After a while, word about Santa Barbara's excellent growing conditions spread. Land was affordable, and farming was big, with people planting lemons, tomatoes, grapes, olives and walnuts, all of which thrived in the fertile soil and sunny climate.

Residents at the time were largely Californios – people of Spanish and Mexican descent. Most resented the influx of Americans who were flooding into town. They also resented having to learn the new official language, English, and to adjust to the Yankee culture. It was hard for people who had spoken only Spanish all their lives to switch to English, so the city reverted to using Spanish for public records, among other documents, from 1864 until 1870. Most difficult to accept was losing rights to their lands, which often were seized and sold to Americans for dirt-cheap prices. Many Californios who lived and worked in respectable neighborhoods left town or moved into other, less desirable areas.

Connecting to the World

Although the world was hearing about Santa Barbara, geography still prevented folks from getting here. Those rugged mountains were difficult to cross, and deep-water ships had nowhere to park.

Once here, riding horseback was the easiest way to get around, and most Santa Barbarans were accomplished equestrians. Also, the stagecoach traversed rickety roads to destinations north and south for more than 40 years. The first stagecoach arrived from San Francisco in 1861, and plans were made to build a road connecting the Santa Ynez Valley with coastal Santa Barbara – San Marcos Pass. A road over Casitas Pass in Carpinteria was completed in 1878.

Trading ships steamed or sailed into the waterfront area, but the water was too shallow to allow these vessels close to shore, so crew members rolled logs off the sides and floated in on them with the surf, and passengers boarded rowboats and stepped into the water when they disembarked – unless they were lucky enough to hire someone to carry them to the sand. A group of local investors built a 500-foot wharf at the end of Chapala Street in 1869, but this too stood in shallow water. However, passengers could at least stay dry when they climbed out of the rowboats onto the dock. The Chapala Wharf charged steep docking fees, but people didn't have much choice in the matter.

A local lumberyard owner, J. P. Stearns, wanted to build a larger wharf that would enable larger, deep-water ships to offload goods and passengers and compete against the Chapala Wharf monopoly. Stearns went to Colonel W. W. Hollister, who forked over $40,000 for the cause. In 1872 Stearns Wharf, which stood in 40-foot-deep water at low tide, was completed. Both shippers and businesspeople backed Stearns wholeheartedly, as the wharf effectively ended Santa Barbara's relative isolation and opened up tremendous opportunities. And Stearns Wharf charged only half of its Chapala counterparts fees to dock and unload. Wood and lumber buildings soon began to replace the old adobe construction, and the look of the former Spanish-Mexican pueblo began to look more and more American.

The Chapala monopoly was not at all happy about the spiffy new wharf up the beach. They ranted and raved and coerced the city to impose outrageously high taxes on Stearns Wharf. J. P. Stearns refused to pay them, and the city council threatened to shut down the wharf. Fate took matters in hand on January 14th, 1878, when a vicious storm hammered the channel. A barge broke loose and smashed into the Chapala Wharf, demolishing it. Another small wharf a few miles east, at Serena Point, also was destroyed.

Early Santa Barbara visitors – and residents – got around by stagecoach.

This eliminated Stearns's competition. Though his wharf also was damaged, he refused to fix it until the city promised not to levy the tax. Stearns won the political battle, and he repaired the wharf and soon reopened for business.

Meanwhile, famous New York journalist Charles Nordhoff (secretly funded by railroad tycoons who wanted to fill their new trains with passengers) traveled through California and wrote a best-selling guide praising the state's virtually unlimited attractions. He visited Santa Barbara in 1872 and described it as "the most pleasant spot" he had visited in the state, and lauded the spectacular scenery, hot springs and healthful, mild climate. The steamships hitching up at the brand-new Stearns Wharf started delivering curious visitors in droves.

With the flocks came a new set of challenges – and opportunities for development. The visitors craved cultural pursuits, and Santa Barbara responded by establishing a thriving arts community. (See the Artistic chapter.) In 1872, José Lobero opened the Lobero Theatre, the first community playhouse in the state of California. Santa Barbara also had few places for wealthy travelers to stay overnight. Most wished to stay for weeks or even months during winter to avoid snow and sleet back home. Hotels and posh rental homes began popping up everywhere. The swank, 90-room Arlington Hotel, bordered by State, Sola, Chapala and Victoria streets, opened in 1875. A host of rich and famous guests vacationed there – including U.S. presidents and royalty from around the globe – until it burned to the ground in 1909.

The Railroad Arrives
When the Southern Pacific puffed into town in 1887, residents cheered for days. Before then, they had to travel by stagecoach to get anywhere locally, either over Casitas Pass in Carpinteria toward Ojai, or along the beach between Ventura and Rincon at low tide.

Finally there was a quick connection to the rest of Southern California! Southern Pacific laid tracks as far as Goleta and Ellwood and had plans to continue north up to Santa Margarita to connect with the existing line to San Francisco. But an economic downturn delayed the completion of a 40-mile gap until 1901. Then again, residents celebrated. Instead of three long, uncomfortable days on a stagecoach, or 28 hours getting seasick on a steamship, the trip by train to San Francisco now took only eight hours! Santa Barbara's isolation from the world was over.

The arrival of the Southern Pacific in 1887 changed life in Santa Barbara forever.

Luxury Travelers

Soon thereafter, in 1903, the opulent Potter Hotel opened on a mound just steps above West Beach. The resort was a village unto itself, with nearly 600 guest rooms, a zoo, a huge rose garden, a bowling alley, lounges, shops and more. It had its own farms, which supplied the dining room with fresh meats and produce; a country club; and a theater in town. Hundreds of famous people came to stay, including President Theodore Roosevelt, and such celebrity millionaires as the Rockefellers, Armours, Carnegies and Vanderbilts. The Potter even had its own sidetracks from the main train station for people to park their private rail cars. And travelers enjoyed more convenient access when the paved coastal highway for automobiles between Ventura and Santa Barbara was completed in 1915. No more waiting for low tide!

Gradually, the affluent visitors who wintered here discovered that the Santa Barbara region won hands down when it came to climate and gorgeous scenery. They began to establish year-round roots, building mansions for themselves and guests and smaller homes for their numerous servants and employees. Soon they had filled the hills of Santa Barbara and Montecito with grand estates, many designed in a popular Spanish-Mediterranean style that paid tribute to regional history. (See the Architectural chapter.)

These wealthy new residents gave generously to the community, helping to establish hospitals, schools and cultural and artistic venues and events. (See the Artistic chapter.) One patron, Major Max C. Fleischmann (the gazillionaire yeast tycoon), had a fancy yacht and needed a safe place to anchor it. In the late 1920s he gave the city money to build a breakwater, which was the beginning of what later became Santa Barbara Harbor. In 1924 Santa Barbara created its first Old Spanish Days Fiesta, a tradition that evolved into an annual five-day celebration of the Chumash/Spanish/Mexican eras, with an equestrian parade, dancing, music and heaps of great food.

The Potter Hotel in its heyday.

Film Capital of the World

In 1912 Chicago-based American Film Company moved its production headquarters here. The Flying A Studios (the nickname stood for its winged logo) was California's first major motion-picture studio. The company chose Santa Barbara because it offered just about every type of scenery it needed for motion-picture backgrounds: ranchland for Westerns, as well as mountains, creeks, beaches and even Italianate villas. It also had rail access to the Chicago headquarters, and a fairly dry climate that wouldn't hamper production schedules. Construction of studio facilities, covering an entire block at the corner of State and Mission streets, was completed in 1913. The Flying A cranked out nearly 1,200 silent-era films in eleven years. Alas, the one thing Santa Barbara didn't have at the time was an urban setting, so the actors and producers relocated to Hollywood in 1921.

The 1925 earthquake destroyed much of downtown, including the Hotel Californian.

Earthquake of 1925

On June 29, 1925, a 6.3 earthquake damaged or demolished much of downtown, including the old courthouse. While devastating to many, it did provide the town the opportunity to create a "new" Santa Barbara look. Since the adobe era, people had built in many different styles: Victorian, Craftsman, ramshackle bungalow, you name it. After the earthquake, the city established a board that created a unified style rooted in its earlier Spanish-Mediterranean traditions. (See the Architectural chapter.) Santa Barbara effectively made lemonade out of a heap of lemons, and set the stage to become one of the world's most beautiful cities. The Spanish-Moorish County Courthouse was completed in 1929; an exquisite example of the architecture that lent character to the entire town.

Oil & the Environmental Movement

Prospectors found crude oil and natural gas deposits in Summerland in 1886, and someone struck petroleum in 1895. This marked the first offshore drilling operation in the nation. Piers sprang up all along Summerland beaches, and by 1902 more than 400 offshore wells pumped crude oil. The Summerland deposits proved smaller than anticipated, and the wells eventually closed. But in 1927 a substantial new source of petroleum was identified at the Ellwood oil field in the Santa Barbara Channel. In just the first year, production reached 86,000 barrels – making it the-fifth largest production site in California. By 1929 hundreds of wells were pumping. In 1958 Standard Oil placed the first offshore oil platform in the channel, several miles off the shores of Summerland. Other petroleum companies followed suit, establishing additional offshore wells and obtaining rights for tankers filled with oil to pass through channel waters.

On January 28, 1969, a well at Unocal's Platform A blew out, causing one of the worst oil spills in global history. (See Green chapter.) A wave of outrage swept through the community, spurring activism. Locals formed groups like GOO (Get Oil Out), and in the process gave birth to the planet's modern environmental movement – right here in Santa Barbara.

Japan Attacks the United States – in Sleepy Goleta

After Pearl Harbor, the west coast prepared for feared attacks by the Japanese, which, thankfully, were limited to only a couple of ineffective forays. One was right here in Goleta. On February 23, 1942, a Japanese submarine shelled Ellwood in Goleta. Its gunners took aim at a couple of large oil storage tanks in the oil fields. But they missed and inflicted only minor damage to the landscape and one tin shed. U.S. bombers came later that night and dropped depth charges. From 1942 through 1945 the Navy took over the harbor, along with San Miguel Island.

School Days

Santa Barbarans have placed a high value on education since the days of the padres. In 1795 the Royal Presidio started a school – the second in Alta California. The city formed a school district in 1866, and by 1887 Santa Barbara boasted five public school buildings serving students from primary grades through high school. The Anna C. Blake Sloyd School on Santa Barbara Street educated local youth in the 1880s. The school expanded and changed names over the years, and in 1908 became the Anna S. C. Blake Normal School (in those days, a "normal school" was a teacher's college). In 1909 it morphed into the coed Santa Barbara State Normal School of Manual Arts and Home Economics, which later became Santa Barbara State College, with a campus on the Riviera.

Education again took the forefront in the post–World War II baby-boomer years. Both Westmont College and Brooks Institute School of Photography were founded in 1946, and the Music Academy of the West, a summer program for up-and-coming classical musicians, followed in 1947. In 1949 State College became part of the University of California system, relocating in 1954 to a new campus in Goleta and becoming the UCSB that we know today.

The Sloyd School, a high school that later evolved into the predecessor to UCSB.

The R & D Era
From the 1950s through the '70s, the area became a research and development hub. Raytheon and other high-tech enterprises employed more than 160,000 workers. Tract homes sprouted like weeds, providing housing for the young families who came here for the new jobs and excellent climate and quality of life.

Wildfires – a Fact of Life
Wildfires, often whipped by the infamous Santa Ana winds into infernos, have always been a danger in the area. Fire is part of the local ecology; the dry chaparral is actually meant to burn naturally every 25 to 30 years. The Sycamore Fire in 1977

Lost Cannon & Other Funny Street Names
No, it's *not* supposed to be called Cañon Perdido, or Lost Canyon Street. It's actually the translation for the Spanish name for Lost Cannon Street, named for a real live lost cannon. In December 1847 the ship *Elizabeth* wrecked near what's now the harbor. A bronze, ten-foot cannon was salvaged and brought to the sand, where it was supposed to stay until it could be transported elsewhere. At the time, the American military occupied Santa Barbara.

On April 5th, 1848, five Californio teenagers borrowed oxen and a cart, which they hooked up to the cannon. They dragged it to a lagoon near what's now the foot of Laguna Street and buried it in the sand. They might have been hiding it just in case the Californios rose up in revolt. Or maybe it was just a prank. Whatever the reason, Captain Lippitt, the American commander, overreacted and alerted Governor Richard Mason in Monterey that there was going to be an uprising, and that he should respond quickly and powerfully. Instead, Mason levied a whopping fine of $500 on the town for losing the cannon.

Mason ordered Lippitt's superior, Colonel Stevenson in Los Angeles, to collect the fine. Stevenson worried that the townspeople would cause a ruckus and refuse to pay up, so with the blessing of an influential member of the De la Guerra family, he brought a regimental band up from L.A. and hosted a two-day fiesta. Santa Barbara residents enjoyed the fun and then paid the fine without protest.

Three streets were named in honor of this series of events:

Canon Perdido Street, Lost Cannon Street

Mason Street, after Governor Mason

Quinientos Street, which means 500 in Spanish, for the $500 fine

Here are a few other street names that may seem a tad unusual (and hard to pronounce):

Alameda Padre Serra, named for Junípero Serra; it is often called APS by locals

Anacapa Street points toward Anacapa Island across the channel. *Anacapa* is a Chumash word for an illusion or mirage (the island is often draped in fog)

Anapamu Street, named for a Chumash chief who ruled over many tribes in the area

Yanonali Street, named for Chief Yanonalit, who greeted the Spanish travelers on their arrival here in 1769

destroyed 195 homes, and the Painted Cave Fire in 1990 took out more than 500. In the summer of 2007, the Zaca Fire traveled south all the way from the North County to jump over the Ventura County line, and in 2008, flames closed in on Goleta. Despite the risk of wildfires (not to mention earthquakes), Santa Barbara's resilient residents choose to stay in paradise, no matter what lemons roll their way.

Vineyards now blanket the Santa Ynez Valley.

The Wine Country Takes Root

Grapevines arrived with Father Serra way back in 1782. But the wine business really didn't start booming until UC scientists identified the northern valleys of Santa Barbara County as ideal growing regions for premium wine grapes – largely due to their east-west orientation and the cooling winds from the ocean. A few visionary pioneers planted vineyards in the late 1960s and early '70s, and by the '90s, the county's wine business boomed. (See Wine Tasting.) Today the North County attracts droves of tasters who want to relax in the bucolic countryside and sample wines that are among the best in the state.

Today, Santa Barbara still looks and feels like paradise. Tourism continues to boom, and at least some newcomers manage to buy real estate, despite astonishing prices. Therein lies the biggest challenge: affordable housing. Nonprofits and governments are tackling this problem, and new developments are appearing, with rents or mortgages that "real" people can pay. Transportation is another issue, as people move to Ventura or the North County for affordable housing and commute to Santa Barbara for work. Options being explored include light rail, expanded highways and high-speed ferry services.

So far, Santa Barbara's future looks mighty bright. Better keep those shades in hand.

An Incomplete Timeline

1542	Juan Rodriguez Cabrillo sails into Santa Barbara Channel.
1602	Sebastian Vizcaino's ship arrives.
1769	Gaspar de Portolá and Junípero Serra lead an expedition north through Alta California; they reach Santa Barbara in August.
1772	Fr. Serra returns with another expedition.
1782	El Presidio Real de Santa Barbara – the fourth and last Spanish military outpost in Alta California – is founded.
1786	Father Fermín de Lasuén founds Mission Santa Barbara on December 4th, the feast day of Saint Barbara.
1787	Mission La Purísima is founded in Lompoc, north of Santa Barbara.
1802	Mission Santa Inés is founded.
1821	Mexico declares independence from Spain.
1847	The Mexican-American War ends, and the U.S. gets California.
1850	Santa Barbara becomes an official American city.
1853	George Nidever finds the Lone Woman of San Nicolas Island and brings her back to the mainland.
1861	The first stagecoach arrives from San Francisco.
1872	Stearns Wharf opens; deep-water ships dock in Santa Barbara for the first time. The Lobero Theatre opens.
1875	Posh Arlington Hotel opens.
1887	Southern Pacific railroad arrives.
1901	Southern Pacific completes the connection to the San Francisco rail line.
1902	Oil drilling in Summerland peaks with more than 400 wells.
1903	The world-class Potter Hotel opens. President Teddy Roosevelt visits.
1908	Anna S. C. Blake Normal School begins operation.
1909	Arlington Hotel burns to the ground.
1912	American Film Company builds Flying A Studios.
1920	Construction of Gibraltar Dam is completed.
1921	Potter Hotel (now called the Ambassador) burns. Archaeologists excavate prehistoric Chumash artifacts on the site.
1924	The first Old Spanish Days Fiesta takes place.
1925	A massive earthquake destroys or damages many structures; the city organizes the Architectural Board of Review to create a unified look for reconstruction.
1927	Oil is discovered in the channel waters off Ellwood, which produces 86,000 barrels that year.
1929	The County Courthouse is completed. Hundreds of wells now operate from scores of piers in Ellwood and other coastal sites.
1930	The breakwater is completed, sheltering the area's first safe harbor.
1942	Japanese submarines shell the mainland near Ellwood in Goleta; the Navy takes over Santa Barbara Harbor until 1945.
1948	The 101 freeway is constructed through the county.
1954	The University of California (formerly Santa Barbara State College) moves from the Riviera and Mesa to brand-new facilities in Goleta.
1958	The channel's first offshore oil platform, several miles off the Summerland coast, begins operation.
1969	Oil spills from a Unocal platform, contaminating the channel and beaches for months; public outrage results in activism, which in turn gives birth to the modern environmental movement.
1970	Vietnam War protestors burn a Bank of America near UCSB, and Gov. Reagan sends National Guard troops; police accidentally shoot and kill a UCSB student. Santa Barbara stages the nation's first Earth Day.
1972	The city limits building heights to four stories.
1975	The Santa Barbara City Council passes a resolution restricting the city population to 85,000.
1983	Queen Elizabeth II visits the city and meets with President and Mrs. Reagan at Rancho del Cielo, their nearby hideaway.
1987	County supervisors limit onshore oil drilling to Gaviota and Las Flores Canyon.
1990	The Painted Cave Fire, fueled by Santa Ana winds, destroys more than 500 homes in a matter of hours, but only one person dies.
1994	The Coastal Commission bans Chevron oil tankers in the channel.
1998	Fire destroys part of Stearns Wharf, closing it for months of reconstruction.
2006	Six *Santa Barbara News-Press* editors suddenly resign over what they called breaches of journalistic ethics by owner Wendy McCaw. During the ensuing turmoil, which makes news across the nation and around the world, nearly 80 employees quit or get fired, and thousands of Santa Barbarans cancel subscriptions.

History on View

Carpinteria Valley Museum of History
956 Maple Ave., Carpinteria
805.684.3112, CarpinteriaHistoricalMuseum.org
Once an important Chumash center for trade
and canoe building, the fertile Carpinteria
Valley, between Santa Barbara and Ventura,
attracted many settlers during all periods
of local history. Exhibits trace this history,
covering Chumash culture, Mexican ranching
times, Victorian home furnishings, farming and
blacksmith trades, schooling, oil and mining
industries, and more.

Carriage & Western Art Museum
129 Castillo St., Santa Barbara
805.962.2353, CarriageMuseum.org
Practically every type of horse-drawn contrap-
tion imaginable resides here – stagecoaches,
police and fire buggies, even hearses. The collection, the largest of its kind in the nation, also
includes silver saddles and gear dating back
to the Spanish and Mexican eras, as well as
famous artworks by Western painters.

The chapel at the Presidio.

El Presidio State Historic Park
Santa Barbara Trust for Historic Preservation
123 E. Canon Perdido St., Santa Barbara
805.965.0093, sbthp.org
Santa Barbara's early days as a Spanish military outpost come alive through a living-history
program in buildings restored or re-created
on the same site as the original Royal Presidio, founded in 1782. An original building, the
adobe guardhouse, El Cuartel, still stands – it's
the second oldest building in California. The
restored **La Casa de La Guerra**, just a block
from the presidio grounds at 15 East De La
Guerra Street, was the grand home of former
presidio comandante José de la Guerra. It
served as the social center of the pueblo from
1828 to 1858.

Elverhøj Museum of History & Art
1624 Elverhoy Way, Solvang
805.686.1211, elverhoj.org
This residence is one of a handful of museums
outside Denmark devoted to Danish culture and
the Danish-American experience. The hand-
crafted home looks like an 18th-century Danish
farmhouse. Rooms exhibit period pieces,
historic photographs and arts and crafts, and
docents wear authentic Danish garb.

Mission Santa Barbara
2201 Laguna St., Santa Barbara
805.682.4713, SantaBarbaraMission.org
The "Queen of the Missions" reigns from a hilly
expanse above downtown. Take a self-guided
tour to peek at Spanish-era living quarters,
gardens and the magnificent church, built in
the early 1800s. (See Architectural chapter for
more.)

Old Mission Santa Inés
1769 Mission Dr., Solvang
805.688.4815, MissionSantaInes.org
The nineteenth of the 21 California missions,
Santa Inés was founded in 1804. It occupies
a lovely spot on a bluff above the Santa Ynez
River, on the outskirts of Solvang. Self-guided
tours take you through museum exhibits, the
still-active parish church and gardens.

Old Spanish Days Fiesta
805.962.8101, OldSpanishDays-fiesta.org
For five days in early August, Santa Barbara
celebrates its history, spirit, traditions and
heritage in a big, big way (organizers boast that
it's one of the five best regional festivals in the
nation). The first festival took place in 1924.
Today's version includes one of the country's
largest equestrian parades, Chumash performers, flamenco dancing, mariachi music and
mercados where nonprofit organizations serve
fabulous food at dozens of booths lining De La
Guerra Plaza and MacKenzie Park.

Red-Tile Walking Tour
Santa Barbara Conference & Visitors Bureau
1601 Anacapa St., Santa Barbara
805.966.9222, SantaBarbaraCA.com
This easy, self-guided walking tour takes you
through twelve square blocks of the downtown
historic district. Its seventeen stops include
adobes, the old presidio buildings, museums
and Spanish-Moorish structures built after the
1925 earthquake. Maps can be found at the

The 1817 Casa Covarrubias adobe at the Historical Museum.

visitors bureau; also watch the video podcast, *Beyond the Rooftops: The Santa Barbara Red Tile Walking Tour*, hosted by TV celebrity John O'Hurley. Just visit SantaBarbaraCA.com and click on Fun Stuff, or download it to your MP3 player and take it along as your guide. You'll find more about the tour in Architectural.

Santa Barbara County Courthouse
1100 block of Anacapa St., Santa Barbara
805.962.6464, SantaBarbaraCourthouse.org
This stunning building, completed in 1929, is probably the most gorgeous public courthouse you'll ever see. With a spiral staircase, hand-painted tiles, fountains, wrought-iron embellishments and lush gardens, it reflects the Spanish-Mediterranean image that characterized the post-earthquake reconstruction of downtown. Check out the mural of Santa Barbara history on the second floor, and ride the elevator to the rooftop to gawk at the 360-degree views.

Santa Barbara Historical Museum
136 E. De La Guerra St., Santa Barbara
805.966.1601, SantaBarbaraMuseum.com
Just walking through the exhibits and grounds here gives you a fantastic overview of local history. The collections cover the various cultural influences (Chumash, Spanish, American, Chinese) and include photos, furniture, artifacts and textiles, some dating back to the 15th

century. Stroll next door to check out Casa Covarrubias (built in 1817) and the 1836 Historic Adobe. The museum's Gledhill Library holds thousands of rare documents and photographs.

Santa Barbara Maritime Museum
113 Harbor Way, Santa Barbara
805.962.8404, sbmm.org
The ocean influenced much of Santa Barbara history, and you can learn all about it through hands-on exploration in this fun, high-tech center, right in the harbor.

Santa Barbara Museum of Natural History
2559 Puesta del Sol Rd., Santa Barbara
805.682.4711, sbnature.org
Learn about Chumash history and culture via exhibits and events led by tribal members. (See the Childlike chapter for more museum information.) The most complete skeleton to date of a Channel Islands pygmy mammoth (Mammuthus exilis) was excavated on Santa Rosa Island in 1994, and a full-size cast of the mammoth is on display in the Geology/Paleontology Hall. In 2005 a rare, 750,000-year-old southern mammoth skeleton and other bones from the early Pleistocene were discovered about 60 miles south of Santa Barbara, and these extraordinary fossils were brought to this museum, which is designing a revamped and expanded hall to display both mammoths and other amazing prehistoric treasures.

Q & A: Michael Redmon

Few Santa Barbarans – if any – know more about local lore than Michael Redmon. He's worked at the Santa Barbara Historical Museum since 1981, and as director of research and publications, he's in charge of the museum's Gledhill Library and its vast collection of historical documents and photographs. He also edits the museum's journal, *Noticias*, and writes a weekly column for the *Santa Barbara Independent*. Born and raised in Northern California, Michael moved to Santa Barbara to earn a BA and MA in history at UCSB. While at UCSB, he met his wife and, following the path of many a grad, settled here.

Michael spends much of his time as a detective, sleuthing for information for other historians, writers and researchers, and for his own articles. He talked with Cheryl Crabtree at the Gledhill Library, overlooking the museum's Spanish-style courtyard and fountains.

Have you always been interested in history?
Yes, even as a kid. In high school I really liked world history and kept on that path ever since. Math was always the bane of my existence. After I earned my degrees, I taught here at City College and took oral histories for the Carpinteria Historical Society.

What's your favorite historic place?
I've always liked Meridian Studios, just next door. You step into that courtyard and it's like stepping into another time and place. It's not that old – it's from the 1920s – but it was different for its time: the purple hues on the walls and the fact they were built as artist studios, which speaks to the town's role as an important art colony since the late 1800s.

How about your favorite historical figure?
I've always been a big fan of Abraham Lincoln. I really respect him for what he had to go through and for his self-effacing sense of humor.

What about a notable local character?
I'd say John Stearns, because I think the construction of the wharf was one of the watersheds of our history. There was no train yet. And back then, the stagecoach was a teeth-rattling, eight-hour ride from Santa Barbara to Los Olivos. When the wharf was finished in 1872, it opened up Santa Barbara to the world. Deep-water ships could now come here. That really changed the look of the town, because more lumber could be used, and adobe shifted to wood construction. When the city fathers wanted to slap a tax on Stearns Wharf, John refused to pay it. He won out in the end.

Do any Santa Barbara stories in particular stand out?
I've always enjoyed the story of how the harbor was made in the late 1920s. Max Fleischmann gave the money to build it. He was a philanthropic guy, but actually, he needed a safer place to keep his yacht. He was wealthy enough to build a harbor – and how many of us can do that?

Looking toward the future, do you think the city is evolving in a positive or negative way?
It's evolving in a mostly positive way. The quality of life Santa Barbara prides itself on is still here – there are no high-rises, we're preserving some of the open space, and the density is still pretty low – but it's growing. I think we have many serious challenges ahead of us: for example, how to provide affordable housing and keep the middle class here.

Beachy

For centuries, the Chumash spent their days near the shore and canoeing out to sea in their *tomols* to catch fish. Tourists, lured by the same stunning beachfront and balmy weather, began flocking to Santa Barbara's beaches in the 1870s. And, today, with nearly 100 miles of coastline, there are white-sand family hangouts, world-class surf breaks, solitary beaches and humongous sand dunes. Out at sea, the Channel Islands provide incredible diving and snorkeling, not to mention pristine beaches and coves. This beach life has produced legends in the world-wide surf and skateboard communities, as well as beloved surf and skateboard shops. Santa Barbara was, is, and always will be a beach town at heart.

Up & Down the Coast

From Rincon to Point Sal, the Santa Barbara coastline and its offshore waters are home to countless idyllic habitats for thousands of species of fish, birds, plants, mammals and other wildlife – including the human sunbather. Wherever you choose to experience ocean life in the region, you can count on a lovely scenic backdrop. From southeast to northwest, here is a sampling of our favorite beaches. The list is not complete – that's a book in itself – but it should whet your appetite and provide a starting point for further explorations of other local beaches, coves and seaside hideaways.

Rincon Point

In the surfing world Rincon Point is recognized as "The Queen of the Coast." When a swell hits here, and those classic waves roll through, board riders, photographers and filmmakers commune to catch the action. Rincon Point straddles the Santa Barbara/Ventura county line, which is delineated by Rincon Creek. Technically, Rincon Point lies on the Ventura County side of the creek, where you'll find a small bay and a short stretch of rocky beach, with tide pools and (typically) crowds of surfers. The state park system provides a parking lot and restroom facilities. To reach the point, exit Highway 101 at Bates Road and head toward the ocean. Look for the state park parking lot on the left and follow the access trail to the beach.

Rincon Beach County Park

If you take the same Bates Road exit, and head toward the ocean and take a right up the hill on the Santa Barbara County side of the line, you'll discover Rincon Beach Park, one of our favorite places to spend a day with the family. Eucalyptus and pine tree groves pepper the bluffs, and the ocean and island views while picnicking at tables near the grassy park entrance are heavenly. A stairway leads from the bluffs down to a serene, white-sand beach perfect for strolling and tide pooling. The waves here are usually more suitable for beginner and intermediate surfers, as the shore isn't as rocky.

Even on a flat day, the rights peel off of Rincon Point.

Carpinteria State Beach.

The Rincon Classic

Roger Nance and the Surf-n-Wear crew founded the Rincon Classic surf contest in 1979, and it quickly became a hallmark event in our local surfing world. The all-ages event, which is open to area residents, celebrates the sport and the spirit of aloha within our community. For seventeen consecutive years the county's top surfers congregated at the "Queen of the Coast" to showcase their skills, but in 1995 Nance and crew, deciding to lay the Classic down to rest, said their final alohas.

However, thanks to Chris Keet, founder and owner of Surf Happens surf school (805.966.3613, surfhappens.com), the Classic was brought back to life in 2001, with lots of advice and support from the original founders. With age divisions from 8-and-under to 55-and-over, the popular Classic unites the SB extended family of local surfers and draws more than 500 spectators to Rincon's fabled cobblestone point. Sometimes three generations of a surfing family compete in the same event. A portion of all proceeds is donated to local charities, including Heal the Ocean, Hugs for Cubs and the Teddy Bear Foundation. Plus, the Classic has grown into a green event, and hand-crafted items like guitars, drums, ukeleles and driftwood carvings are awarded as trophies.

Carpinteria State Beach

Carpinteria State Beach encompasses a mile-long swath of wide, sandy beach and dunes near downtown Carpinteria. A natural offshore reef often dilutes riptides and softens heavy surf; these gentle waves are ideal for younger or less experienced swimmers and surfers. More than 800,000 visitors come here every year to hike the trails through wooded groves, picnic, fish, swim and camp. Wildlife viewing here can't be beat, especially in the numerous tide pools, home to starfish, sea anemones, crabs and sea urchins. In the winter and spring, seals and sea lions pup in the adjacent city-owned harbor seal rookery. Thus, the beach is closed from 750 feet east and west of the Casitas Pier from December 1 through May 31. You can watch the mammals (but not disturb them) in their sanctuary from the cliffs above (contact Carpinteria Sealwatch at 805.684.2247).

A major Chumash village and trading center once occupied the site – largely due to the oozing black asphaltum (aka tar) that seeped up naturally from the earth into bulging mounds on the bluffs and sand. Chumash boat-builders capitalized on the liquid gold by using it to caulk their canoes, and later, residents mined the asphaltum to pave the county's first roads. You can view evidence of these operations at the southeastern section of the park: a nature center, snack bar, picnic area, 216 family campsites and visitor center, with an indoor tide pool and interpretive displays.

Sunrise on Miramar Beach, looking east from Hammond's.

To get to the state beach, exit Highway 101 at Casitas Pass Road and head toward the coast. Turn right on Carpinteria Avenue, then left on Palm Avenue, which dead-ends at the park entrance.

Carpinteria City Beach

This broad expanse of soft, glistening white sand extends west from the state beach toward Santa Barbara. It's great for swimming and surfing, fishing, bird watching and tide pooling and is the site of city recreational programs — from surfing and kayaking to the popular summer Junior Lifeguard program. In the summer months, you can rent kayaks and purchase snacks and lunch right on the beach.

Summerland Beach/Lookout County Park

At Lookout, a four-acre county park perched on the cliffs above the sand in the tiny village of Summerland, you can hike the trails along the bluffs, barbecue on grills and play beach volleyball or horseshoes. Spectacular views of ocean, islands and mountains unfold from nearly every vantage point, with daily sunrises and sunsets and seasonal whale-migration "shows" as the stunning highlights. There's a restroom and kids' playground, as well as a ramp down to the glorious beach below. Parking is free.

Hammond's Beach

Many a Santa Barbara surfer catches his or her first wave at Hammond's Reef, the surf break near this smallish, pretty, mostly locals' beach tucked into a peaceful cove just east of the Coral Casino Country Club in Montecito. This spot was once the site of an ancient Chumash village called Shalawa, and a sandstone marker in the Sea Meadows area above the beach commemorates these early inhabitants. To get there these days, walk westward from the grassy expanse at the end of Eucalyptus Lane in Montecito along the public access trail.

Butterfly Beach

The posh Santa Barbara Biltmore Hotel (now a Four Seasons property) was built in 1927, right across the street from gorgeous Butterfly Beach. At the time, the beach was wide and the hotel set up cabanas in the sand for its guests. Unfortunately, after the breakwater was built, the beach diminished due to shifting sand deposits. To keep its guests happy, in 1937 the hotel acquired an adjacent estate's beachfront gardens and transformed them into the Coral Casino Beach and Cabana Club. Though slimmer than its former self, Butterfly Beach attracts an eclectic mix of celebrity locals and visitors, people-watchers and down-home locals. Low tides are particularly glorious for long-walkers.

East Beach

With its soft, golden sand that stretches nearly a mile to Stearns Wharf, Santa Barbara's East Beach often receives media kudos as one of the nation's best all-around beaches. It's sports action central, especially in the summer months. The dozen or so sand volleyball courts at the east end play host to AVP tour events as well as to VB tournaments for amateurs of all ages and levels. The beach also serves as home base for triathlons, lifeguard championships and other competitions. Packs of red-suited youth run and swim along the beach, participating in the city's popular – and challenging – Junior Lifeguard program. The Cabrillo Pavilion Bathhouse is open to the public and has a weight room, warm showers and lockers; and you also can rent beach equipment, including umbrellas, volleyballs and wheelchairs. There's a playground adjacent to the bathhouse, and anyone can rinse off salt and sand in the cold outdoor showers, and take a break from sun and surf on the East Beach Grill's patio (see Hungry & Thirsty). Grassy, palm-lined Chase Palm Park, a popular place to walk, jog or cruise on a bike, parallels the beach from the bathhouse to the pier.

West Beach

West Beach lies (you guessed it) west of Stearns Wharf, right at the harbor entrance. With eleven acres of glistening sand and a generally flat ocean due to the sheltering breakwater, it's a wonderful place to swim, kayak and watch boats enter and exit the harbor. Outrigger canoe clubs launch their canoes from here, and from April through September the Sea Shells youth sailors practice their tacks and jibes in the sheltered cove between the beach and the sandspit that extends from the end of the harbor's breakwater. A number of large public special events take place at West Beach, including a 4th of July celebration. A public wading pool, 50-meter pool (Los Baños del Mar), and a playground are located at the west end of the beach. To access West Beach, enter the Santa Barbara Harbor parking lot and drive to the east end, near Sea Landing and the boat-launch ramp.

A playground is just one of the many amenities on East Beach.

Grass and sand at Leadbetter Beach.

Healthy Surf

In 1995, during a period of heavy rains, Santa Barbara's Environmental Health Services began testing a few local beaches for bacteria. The high levels found in our creek and ocean waters pointed to the probable culprit: storm-water runoff. The next year, Environmental Health Services established a regular ocean-water monitoring program, which today samples twenty beaches every week, and distributes the results to the media and interested groups.

It appears that the program's efforts, along with those of environmental groups like Heal the Ocean, have made some great cleaning-up progress in the last decade. Santa Monica–based Heal the Bay's May 2008 Beach Report Card gave very good to excellent rankings to all twenty Santa Barbara beaches that were tested weekly for water quality during the dry months, when most folks swim at the beach. On the down side, water quality slipped significantly in the wet season, especially after storms. We still have work to do, but at least you can count on healthy surf most of the year.

In light of this data, we recommend a few tips from Heal the Bay regarding when and where to take to the sea:

- Wait 72 hours after a rainstorm to swim
- Avoid flowing storm drains and swim at least 100 yards from where storm-drain flow enters the surf
- Check the weekly Beach Report Card at healthebay.org (more local info at sbcphd.org/ehs/ocean.htm; or call the Ocean Water Quality Hotline at 805.681.4949)

Leadbetter Beach

Families flock to this busy expanse of sandy beach and grassy parkland across from City College for many good reasons: barbecue stands and picnic tables in a palm-studded park, beach volleyball courts, restrooms and cold showers, and gentle waves perfect for young and novice surfers and boogie boarders. When the wind picks up, "Led's" attracts kite boarders, wind surfers and catamaran sailors. Shoreline Beach Café offers both sit-down service and quick to-go orders. On Wednesday summer evenings, the popular Nite Moves ocean swim and 5K walk/jog events end here, followed by food and entertainment. Nice.

Mesa Lane Beach

Quiet, residential, blufftop Mesa Lane ends at a steep set of 241 steps that were built in 1923. This is one of our favorite local beaches: it's private, peaceful, and there's that good heart-healthy workout coming back up the stairs, which provide the only public beach access for a mile in either direction. (These steps are sometimes confused with Thousand Steps, another, longer set at the end of Santa Cruz Boulevard, about a mile to the east.)

Arroyo Burro Beach County Park

Locals call this county park and adjacent beach "Hendry's," or "Henry's" (the d got dropped at some point), or the Pit, depending on how long they've lived here. It is one of the most popular local hangouts in town – you can catch a quick surf session at lunch or after school or work. It's also a favorite venue for walkers and joggers, since you can often walk all the way to Goleta or Santa Barbara at low tide. The rocky shoreline makes for excellent tide pooling, and dolphin, seals and whales (during migration season) are often spotted just offshore. In the summer months, families with small children tend to camp out right in front of the lifeguard tower, beachside restaurant, restrooms and outdoor showers. A small, grassy park area near the restaurant provides barbecue grills and picnic tables. For more privacy, just head east or west about 200 yards. You can bring your dog here, but he must be on a leash no longer than six feet. To find Arroyo Burro, take Las Positas Road south to Cliff Drive, and turn right. The park entrance is just a block away on your left.

Lifeguards & Beachy Tidbits

From Memorial Day through Labor Day and weekends in May and September, lifeguards vigilantly watch over many of the region's beaches. The general rules that protect and preserve our beaches include: No bottles or open fires on city beaches, and no dogs (even on a leash, except the stretch of beach east of Arroyo Burro Creek) on city beaches, but you can walk Fido at county beaches as long as he's on a leash. Day-use fees at state beaches are usually $8 per vehicle. Most city waterfront parking lots charge fees, while most county beaches provide free parking or charge a nominal fee. For more details on facilities and fees at specific locations, visit sbparksandrecreation.com (city beaches), sbparks.gov (county beaches), or parks.ca.gov (state beaches).

Goleta Beach County Park

This 29-acre gem right next to UCSB has everything you need for a full-on beach day: superb sunbathing, swimming, boogie boarding and sandcastle building. You can barbecue and picnic on the palm-lined grassy expanse, which also includes a fun play structure, restrooms and showers, volleyball courts and a horseshoe pit. Or walk out onto the pier to fish or gaze at the scenery. Hunger pangs suddenly strike? Duck into the Beachside Bar and Café, with interior or al fresco dining. Artists and birders like to hang out at the east end of the park, overlooking the Goleta Slough wildlife preserve. Directions: take Highway 217 toward UCSB, exit at Sandspit Road and follow the signs to the park. Parking is free.

North County State Beaches

The spectacular Gaviota coastline, with some of the last remaining parcels of undeveloped open space in Southern California, stretches for nearly 40 miles from Santa Barbara westward to Point Conception. It's home to the following three state beach parks, each unbelievably gorgeous in settings nestled between mountains and sea. For more information: parks.ca.gov. (For information on camping at El Capitan and Refugio, see the Outdoorsy chapter.) Day-use fees at each park are $8 per vehicle.

Goleta Beach.

El Capitan State Beach

To reach this vast sandy beach, a dune-lined sanctuary for marine mammals and rocky tide pools, exit Highway 101 just 17 miles west of Santa Barbara. The bike trail connects El Cap with Refugio State Beach 2.5 miles away.

Refugio State Beach

Refugio Creek empties into a sparkling, palm-lined cove, an excellent spot for diving, snorkeling and fishing that resembles a tropical island. Bring a picnic or buy snacks at the park's convenience store. Directions: exit Highway 101 at Refugio Road and follow the signs.

Mussel Rock and the Guadalupe Dunes.

Gaviota State Park
Gaviota hugs the coastal mountains just west of Highway 101, 33 miles west of Santa Barbara, as it curves north toward Santa Ynez and inland valleys. Gaviota ("seagull" in Spanish), which was named by the 1769 Portola expedition soldiers while camping here, is a perfect place to stop for a picnic and swimming break while touring the California coast. Anglers fish in the surf and off Gaviota Pier, surfers and scuba divers launch their boats from the pier's hoist (gaviotahoist@parks.ca.gov), and hikers who trek along the trails in the rugged upland areas of the park reap great rewards, including Gaviota Hot Springs and Gaviota Peak. Because Point Conception sits just a few miles to the west, the place can get a bit windy at times. Camping is available April through September.

Rancho Guadalupe Dunes Preserve/ Guadalupe-Nipomo Dunes Preserve
Dunes, dunes and more dunes – the collective eighteen miles of majestic shoreline preserves between Guadalupe and Pismo Beach look a bit like the desert scenes of *Lawrence of Arabia*. That's probably why so many films have been shot here. More significantly, the preserves provide a protected habitat for more than 1,400 species of flora and fauna, including sea otters, black bear and deer, and more than 200 species of birds. The highest beach dune in the western United States, Mussel Rock, rises 1,500 feet up into the sky. In certain areas near the shore, kids and kids-at-heart love to slip and slide down the sandy slopes of the otherworldly dunes.

Surf Legends

Santa Barbara is a major player in the international surf scene, and you can learn all about it at the Marilyn S. Tennity *Surf's Up! Santa Barbara* exhibit at the Santa Barbara Maritime Museum in the harbor (sbmm.org). The permanent multimedia exhibit highlights local surfers, innovators and surf spots that have impacted surf culture worldwide. Works include the camera and casing George Greenough used to film *The Innermost Limits of Pure Fun*, and photos and video interviews with surfing legends like Renny Yater, Al Merrick, Tom Curren, Chris Brown and Bobby Martinez. Upstairs from the museum, the Endless Summer Bar-Café displays memorabilia from Bruce Brown's timeless surf films.

George Greenough

George grew up in Montecito and surfed Rincon, Hammond's and all the great breaks up and down the South Coast. In the 1960s he played a leading role in designing, testing and perfecting the lightweight shortboard, which has three fins (its predecessor, the longboard, is heavier and single-finned). The now-ubiquitous fast, maneuverable shortboard, which has enabled riders to get closer to the curl of a wave and cut back and forth, changed the style of surfing forever.

Professional Champs

Tom Curren developed his surfing skills right here, and in 1980 won the World Amateur Surfing Championships. He did it again in 1985, 1986 and 1990. Meanwhile, his former Santa Barbara High School classmate Kim Mearig (see the Q & A in this chapter) took the 1983 Women's World Championship and toured the world as a pro for a decade. Curren and Mearig both rode Channel Islands Surfboards designed by Al Merrick, and the CIS name rode to world renown with them.

Mr. Zog

Surfboards sure get slippery when wet, so it was inevitable that some clever surfer would come up with a way to create traction. A local guy, Frederick Herzog III (aka Mr. Zog), invented the surfing world's leading variety of the sticky stuff: Mr. Zog's Sex Wax.

Renny Yater and one of his boards.

Reynolds "Renny" Yater

Renny Yater, one of the region's first real commercial surfboard builders, helped put the sport of surfing on the map – and not just here in Santa Barbara, but around the world. Renny began shaping and fiberglassing his own boards in the early 1950s. In the fall of 1959 he opened Yater Surfboards on Anacapa Street, where he established the famous Santa Barbara Surf Shop logo. Throughout his career, he's experimented with new materials and technologies and continually produced innovative boards. During the 1960s he came up with two wildly popular models: the Yater Spoon, a longboard, and the Pocket Rocket, a shortboard. In those days, surfing's heyday, many legends rode Yater boards, including Bruce Brown, John Severson, Joey Cabell and Gordon Clark. Today, Renny remains a leader in the surf world.

Channel Islands

Congress established Channel Islands National Park in 1980. Eight Channel Islands lie off the coast; the five northernmost islands – Anacapa, Santa Cruz, Santa Rosa, San Miguel and tiny, one-square-mile Santa Barbara Island – and a mile of surrounding seas make up the park. Beyond the national park boundary, Channel Islands National Marine Sanctuary protects the waters out to six nautical miles surrounding the islands. The sanctuary is managed jointly by the National Park Service and the National Marine Sanctuary. More than 2,000 species of plants and animals thrive there – and 145 are exclusive to these waters. Offshore, more than 30 species of whales, seals, sea lions, dolphins and other marine mammals play in this sparkling ocean sanctuary. The park's 175 miles of pristine coastline include long stretches of white-sand beaches, craggy cliffs and one of the world's largest sea caves.

These magnificent islands are not far away – just 14 to 26 miles from the mainland – but strangely, crossing the channel is daunting to many people. Approximately 620,000 visitors check in at the mainland visitor center annually, but only a tiny fraction of those actually travel out to the islands. We strongly encourage you to get out there in your lifetime, because few places on the planet are as beautiful and contain such an abundance of protected natural scenery and wildlife. High-speed boats take visitors to the "North American Galapagos" for a half or full day of hiking, or for multiday camping adventures. Don't wait. Just do it.

Frenchys Cove on Anacapa Island.

Elephant seals, some as large as 8,000 pounds, breed on San Miguel Island.

Channel Islands National Park Robert J. Lagomarsino Visitor Center

1901 Spinnaker Dr., Ventura Harbor
805.658.5730, nps.gov/chis
Whether you head out to the islands or not, we highly recommend visiting this information-packed center in Ventura Harbor. Technically, it lies a bit outside the geographic boundaries of this book, but it's too important to leave out. As headquarters for Channel Islands National Park, it's open daily and houses a museum, bookstore and island exhibits.

Island Views

Anacapa Island is actually a series of three narrow islets edged by soaring cliffs, sea caves and rich kelp forests. Only fourteen miles from Ventura Harbor, Anacapa is your best bet for a quick island adventure. **Santa Cruz** is the largest island in the chain and the largest island off the California coast. The national park manages the eastern 25 percent of the island, where it maintains an extensive trail network and several campgrounds. It's a popular destination for kayakers and hikers. **Santa Rosa** also has excellent hiking trails, particularly to its rare grove of Torrey pines, as well as spectacular beaches and canyons. More than 30,000 pinnipeds haul out of the ocean every year at rugged, windswept **San Miguel**, the outermost island. **Santa Barbara Island** is known for its excellent wildlife viewing and crystal-clear water for once-in-a-lifetime diving, snorkeling and kayaking adventures.

Getting There Is Half the Fun

The channel is teeming with life, and chances are good that seals, dolphins, birds and other assorted curious creatures will greet your boat as you cross the channel. Truth Aquatics (see On the Water section page 44), the official transportation concessionaire, out of Santa Barbara Harbor, offers limited multiday hiking trips via its live-aboard dive-boat fleet. Other main transportation options include:

Channel Islands Aviation

305 Durley Ave., Camarillo
805.987.1301, flycia.com
Air service from Camarillo out to Santa Rosa Island for half-day excursions, camper transportation and surf-fishing adventures.

Island Packers

1691 Spinnaker Dr., Ventura Harbor
805.642.1393, islandpackers.com
The Ventura area's official concessionaire for the national park provides boat transportation to Anacapa and East Santa Cruz islands year-round on its two high-speed catamarans. Its trips to Santa Barbara, Santa Rosa and San Miguel islands run regularly from April through November.

On the Water

To get out on the water, the place to start is the Santa Barbara Waterfront, from Stearns Wharf to the Santa Barbara Harbor, where there's access to sailing, motoring, kayaking, fishing and scuba diving. About 28,000 gray whales pass by on their annual 13,000-mile round-trip from Siberian-Alaskan seas to Baja lagoons, where they deliver their calves. Humpback, minke, orca and blue whales also visit in spring and summer to feast in the nutrient-rich channel. Sea lions and dolphins frolic year-round. Here are some good on-the-water outfits.

Lil' Toot chugging through Santa Barbara waters.

SEA Landing (805.963.3564, sealanding.net), next to the boat-launch ramp in the Santa Barbara Harbor, is a one-stop access point for oceanic outings and rents out kayaks and jet skis and dive equipment. Several boat operations call this home base. **Truth Aquatics** (805.962.1127, truthaquatics.com) runs a fleet of well-equipped dive boats that takes divers, kayakers, snorkelers and hikers to the Channel Islands. The 75-foot high-speed catamaran *Condor Express* (805.882.0088 or 888.77WHALE, condorcruises.com) goes on whale-watching trips year-round – winter and spring, following gray whales; spring and summer, out to the islands looking for blues and humpbacks. On-board naturalists explain what you're seeing. The 65-foot *Stardust* (stardust-sportfishing.com) operates fishing excursions year-round and twilight trips in the summer.

Santa Barbara Sailing Center (805.962.2826, sbsail.com), adjacent to the harbor boat-launch ramp, is a certified sailing school and boat-rental outfit. Summer sailing and kayak camps for kids fill up fast.

Captain Don's (805.969.5217, captdon.com), based at Stearns Wharf, goes a step further with its pirate-themed whale-watching and harbor and sunset coastal cruises.

Sunset Kidd's Sailing Cruises (805.962.8222, sunsetkidd.com) are aboard a 41-foot, eighteen-passenger ketch – with a salon, two staterooms, restrooms with showers and a bar – that zips out to the channel on sunset and whale-watching cruises.

Paddle Sports of Santa Barbara (805.899.4925, 888.254.2094, kayaksb.com) is a kayak, canoe, outrigger and water-sports center. It operates out of two sites: a small one in the the harbor and a new store at 3825 Santa Claus Lane in Carpinteria. The harbor location carries a full inventory of kayaks, gear, accessories and clothing; the Carpinteria store houses even more. Both offer kayak trips with guides, including daily beach trips along the Gaviota coast. A favorite is the Santa Cruz Island day trip through sea caves and coves.

Other companies that lead kayak trips along the Santa Barbara coastal region and out to Channel Islands National Park include **Aquasports** (800.773.2309, caladventures. com/Aquasports), **Santa Barbara Adventure Company** (805.898.0671, sbadventureco.com) and **Captain Jack's Santa Barbara Tours** (888.810.8687, captainjackstours.com).

The Land Shark (805.683.7600, Out2seeSB. com), a funny-looking amphibious boat-bus, chugs through town and the harbor. The 90-minute narrated land-and-sea adventure, which takes off from Stearns Wharf and drives through downtown and the waterfront before plunging into the harbor, is a touristy hoot.

The pet of the sea, the **Santa Barbara Water Taxi** (805.896.6900, sbwatertaxi.com) is a cute little tugboat called *Lil' Toot*. A green machine, it runs on biodiesel and shuttles passengers between the harbor and Stearns Wharf.

For scuba equipment, contact these full-service dive centers: **Anacapa Dive Center** (805.963.8917, anacapadivecenter.com) and **Santa Barbara Aquatics** (805.967.4456).

Fun on the Waterfront

The Santa Barbara waterfront, home to Stearns Wharf, the harbor, a skatepark and the main beaches, buzzes with activity all year long. Our Outdoorsy chapter describes a few excellent walking tours on and near the waterfront, but if you don't feel like hoofing it, you can tour around on a bike or kayak, or hop on the battery-electric shuttles that cruise along Cabrillo Boulevard and State Street.

Cabrillo Bike Lane
The mostly flat 3.2 miles of two-lane path stretches from Leadbetter Beach through the harbor, along West and East beaches to the Andree Clark Bird Refuge. You can rent bikes, surrey cycles, skates and even electric cars and scooters at **Wheel Fun Rentals** (805.966.2282, wheelfunrentalssb.com). Its three locations: 23 East Cabrillo Boulevard, 22 State Street (electric cars and scooters), and 633 Cabrillo Boulevard (Fess Parker's Doubletree Resort). Bike-path walkers, beware. Technically, you're not supposed to use the bike path, but so many do. Just stick to the edges and be ready to jump out of the way.

Chase Palm Park
This superscenic 35-acre grassy park lines both sides of Cabrillo Boulevard. On the beach side, a narrow strip of palm-lined grass park stretches all the way from Stearns Wharf to East Beach. The bike path runs through it, and on fair-weather Sundays and some holidays, artists display their works at the Arts and Crafts Show. On the opposite side, from Garden Street to Milpas, the park centers on Shipwreck Playground and houses a carousel, fountains, creeks, a lagoon and a snack bar. In the summer, there are free concerts in the large grassy area next to the playground.

Santa Barbara Harbor
Home to more than a thousand boats, the Santa Barbara Yacht Club, restaurants, a fish market and marine-related shops, the harbor is the maritime hub of the town. Trace the region's ocean-related history at the **Santa Barbara Maritime Museum** (805.965.8864, sbmm.org), where you can view a hand-crafted Chumash *tomol*, one of the oldest known diving helmets and model ships and try your hand at virtual sportfishing. Up on the fourth floor, the **Outdoors Santa Barbara Visitor Center** (805.884.1475, outdoorsb.noaa.gov) dispenses information on several local national protected

areas: Channel Islands National Park, Channel Islands National Marine Sanctuary and the Los Padres National Forest.

Skater's Point
Our kids love this place – a 14,600-square-foot paradise for skateboarders and roller and in-line skaters, right next to the beach on Cabrillo Boulevard near Garden Street. Even if you don't skate, it's a good time watching skaters ollie the volcano, rip up and down the taco bowl, and fly up the pyramid. If you're inexperienced and/or young, try to skate on weekends before noon, when the big skaters begin to congregate. Helmets, elbow and kneepads are required.

Stearns Wharf
Built in 1872 by John P. Stearns (see Historic), this is Santa Barbara's most visible and visited landmark (stearnswharf.org). Locals and tourists flock here for the fishing, restaurants, wine-tasting rooms and shops. You can't beat the 90 minutes of free parking (with merchant validation) on the wharf and in certain waterfront lots. On summer weekends you can hop on the free Wharf Woody electric shuttle. At the **Ty Warner Sea Center** (805.962.2526, sbnature. org), owned and operated by the Santa Barbara Museum of Natural History, budding marine biologists learn about marine life through interactive exhibits, a 1,500-gallon surge tank and water-sampling stations.

Stearns Wharf.

Surf & Skate Shops We Love

A few of the stores outfitting our surfers with boards and gear have been around for decades. Some names, like Channel Islands Surfboards and the Beach House (for Surfboards by Yater), are known throughout the surfing world. After all, our waves have served as testing grounds for innovative designs, and they continue to spawn new surf-related creations and budding surf legends. Skateboard culture also has thrived in SB for decades, and a couple of shops are dedicated exclusively to selling gear for serious riders. Here are our favorite surf and skate stores, where you can find just about everything you need to pursue your passion for the sports, or at least look like you do.

A-Frame Surf Shop
3785 Santa Claus Lane, Carpinteria
805.684.8803, aframesurf.com
This shop sits right next to the beach, at the west edge of town. Best known for friendly service and a fun, happy-go-lucky, down-home surfer vibe, A-Frame sponsors a surfing team and arranges lessons for all surf levels. It also sells a wide range of clothes, wetsuits and accessories, and rents boards and gear.

Backdoor Boardshop
1693 Mission Dr., Solvang
805.686.5886, bdboardshop.com
If you're up in the Santa Ynez Valley, this is your one-stop-shopping venue for all things related to boarding adventures in the surf, snow and skate park: clothing, equipment and accessories. It's also a great place to find out about North County surf and skateboard spots.

The Beach House
10 State St., Santa Barbara
805.963.1281, surfnwear.com
Legendary board shaper Renny Yater started Surf-n-Wear in 1962 in Summerland. He moved his retail operation into this State Street storefront in 1991 and called it the Beach House. Nearly four decades later, many of the same surfers who originally shopped at the Summerland site – along with their kids and grandkids – still come here to get their beach and surf clothes, gear and collectibles. The Beach House also is the home of Santa Barbara Surf Shop, and is the exclusive local dealer of Surfboards by Yater.

Channel Islands Surfboards
36 Anacapa St., Santa Barbara
805.966.7213, cisurfboards.com
CIS is synonymous with custom, high-quality boards used by many pros on the touring circuit. Designer/shaper Al Merrick founded CIS in 1969 as a local grass-roots operation, and it grew rapidly as surfers demanded ever-higher-performing boards that gave them an edge. So Al developed them. Today CIS is a larger operation but is still known for its innovative design and quality. Burton Corporation acquired CIS in 2006. The manufacturing facility has moved near Rincon; you can shop for gear and surf attire at the retail store just a couple of blocks north of Cabrillo Boulevard.

The house of skateboard worship.

Carpinteria's surf central, Rincon Designs.

Rincon Designs
659 Linden Ave., Carpinteria
805.684.2413, rincondesigns.net
Born and raised on the beach in Carpinteria, Matt Moore has been shaping and selling surfboards since the 1970s (he's shaped about 20,000 of them). Many great surfers have ridden his custom creations, including three-time world champion and local claim-to-famer Tom Curren. Pop into Matt's fun, colorful shop in downtown Carpinteria to check out his famous designs and browse through all the latest gear, clothing, accessories and gifts.

Santa Barbara Skate Shop
16 Helena Ave., Santa Barbara
805.899.8669
Keep up with the local skateboard news at this small, friendly, family-owned shop just a half-block north of Cabrillo Boulevard near Skater's Point. It's a great place to assemble a custom skateboard, hang out with other skateboarders, and add to your clothing and gear collections.

Surf Country
5668 Calle Real, Goleta
805.683.4450, surfcountry.net
Tucked in a strip mall not far from UCSB, Goleta's only full-service surf and skate shop carries all the essentials for boarding enthusiasts of all types. It sells skateboards, shortboards, longboards, skim boards, boogie boards, parts and accessories. It also handles surfboard and wetsuit rentals, repairs and lessons, plus sales of the latest surf and skate fashions.

Church of Skatan
26 E. Gutierrez St., Santa Barbara
805.899.1586, churchofskatan.com
Housed in a former church a half-block from State Street, this cool place is the answer to skateboarders' prayers for one-stop shopping: quality skateboards (buy all the parts separately and assemble it here), clothing, shoes, DVDs, even snacks and sodas. The stained-glass windows shower colorful beams of light around at certain times of the day.

SkateOne/Powell Peralta
George Powell, who earned an engineering degree at Stanford, likes to tinker with skateboard designs. He came up with winning recipes for skateboard wheels, and moved from Los Angeles to Santa Barbara in 1976 to found Powell Corporation and start manufacturing and selling his creations: Bones Wheels. These and other subsequent designs sent George on a high-flying stardom ollie in the skating world. In 1978 he teamed up with Stacy Peralta, and the pair began to produce skateboard videos. Today, George's factory is still busy testing and building high-quality skateboards and components. SkateOne Corporation is not a retail outlet, but once or twice a year it holds warehouse sales, and skaters line up *early* in the morning to score discounted skate stuff.

Q & A: Kim Mearig

Former world champion Kim Mearig, one of the best surfers to have ever ripped our local waves, made her mark at a time when few women surfed. She has inspired a generation of young girls to wax up their own boards and hit the water.

Kim's family moved to Santa Barbara in 1963 when she was just 6 months old. Her first rides were on the family surf mat; while in elementary school, she rode on the Santa Barbara Skateboards team and got on a surfboard at 11. By the time she was 14, she was traveling and competing as an amateur. Kim won the NSSA Nationals when she was 16, was selected for the NSSA national team, and went on to take the West Coast and U.S. Championships. After high school she turned pro, signing a deal with Ocean Pacific that made her the highest-paid female surfer on record. Kim retired in 1994 to spend more time at home in Carpinteria with her husband and two children. She met up with Cheryl Crabtree on a glorious South Coast beach day.

How did you get into surfing?
I was about 11 years old and my uncle, who surfed, took me to the beach. I stood up on the board and rode it in. That was it. I was hooked. I used to leave my stuff at Leadbetter, and I'd take my bike, skateboard or ride the bus to the beach. We had to be creative about our transportation. After Leadbetter and Sandspit, I moved up to surfing Hammond's. Once I saw Rincon, that was it. I stayed there.

How did you get to know Tom Curren?
We went to Santa Barbara High together – he was a year behind me in school. When I was 16 and 17 we were on the same NSSA team for two years. Tom and I turned pro around the same time. I was 18.

How long did you compete on the pro circuit?
I surfed professionally for about ten years. I traveled a lot. Sometimes my husband would join me. We went to the Great Barrier Reef, New Zealand, Bali, France, Spain, Portugal, South Africa, lots of places. But after ten years, I wanted to start a family, so I retired when I was 28.

Do you still surf much?
I'm a mom, so I can't go out as much as I used to. But I surf as much as I can. My son, who's 16, surfs with me all the time; my daughter's not really into it.

What other sports and activities do you pursue?
As a family, we go wakeboarding and waterskiing. We go inland to places like Nacimiento, Shasta, Trinity, Lake Powell.

What is your favorite surf break?
Rincon, hands down. It can be crowded, but it's some of the best waves – not just in Santa Barbara – in the world.

Can you imagine not living on the South Coast?
I really can't. This is the ultimate setup, with the mountains in the back, the ocean, the islands. You don't realize how pretty it is until you've seen the rest of the world.

Architectural

The mere mention of the name Santa Barbara conjures up images of red-tile roofs, creamy stucco walls, arched entryways and wrought-iron gates. Few cities can claim such a distinctive architectural identity – the pleasing blend of Moorish, Spanish Baroque, Spanish and Portuguese Colonial, Andalusian and other Mediterranean styles. And beyond the red-tile roofs are exquisite examples of California's most revered architectural styles, from beach bungalows and Cape Cod cottages to Victorian grande dames and risk-taking postmodern structures.

The Architecture of Santa Barbara

The first homebuilders in the Santa Barbara area, the Chumash, lived in peaceful simplicity in bent-willow huts along the shoreline. But when talking about the evolution of architectural styles in Santa Barbara and its surrounding towns, the discussion begins where all discussions about California architecture begin: the Spanish and Mexican influences, from the 18th century and the first missions through the 19th-century ranchos.

In 1786 the first Mission Santa Barbara, which would later reign as the "Queen of the Missions," was constructed on a site overlooking the fledgling town of Santa Barbara, with the Santa Ynez Mountains as its backdrop. The Spanish padres obviously knew the value of location. The original mission, however, was composed of several log-and-mud structures built mainly by the Chumash. Altered and restored over the years, it looked nothing like it does today. By the 1840s the area between the Mission and the beach was studded with whitewashed adobe houses, some with the familiar red-tile roofs. The Presidio (1782–1797) served as the nucleus around which these adobes were clustered. Several of them have stood the test of time and are on view in the Red-Tile Walking Tour (see Beyond the Rooftops later in this chapter).

On a Mission
La Purisima Mission (2295 Purisima Road, Lompoc, 805.733.3713, lapurisima-mission.org) is the most fully restored of all California's missions. It was founded in 1787, but the 1812 earthquake destroyed many of its structures; it was rebuilt on its present site in 1813. Today, ten of the mission's original buildings, along with the historic aqueduct and water system, are surrounded by a sprawling 1,928-acre state park. This is one school field trip

The Presidio, on Canon Perdido in central Santa Barbara.

we always sign up for – our faves are the weaving room, five-acre garden, livestock and hiking trails. Self-guided tours run from 9 a.m. to 5 p.m. daily except on Thanksgiving, Christmas and New Year's Day; there is a free guided tour daily (except during special events) at 1 p.m. Private vehicle entry fee is $4.

The most visited landmark in the city, the old **Mission Santa Barbara** (2201 Laguna Street, 805.682.4713, santabarbaramission.org) was founded in 1786 as the tenth of 21 Franciscan missions in California. It also has the distinction of being the only one that has been continuously occupied by the Franciscan order since its founding. The current stunner on the lovely hilltop setting is the third incarnation of the "Old" Mission. Built largely by the Chumash, the original small chapel and living quarters for missionaries and Chumash was nearly leveled in the 1812 earthquake. The present pink sandstone church was built around the old chapel, but with only one bell tower, and was dedicated in 1820. (The second bell tower was added about ten years later.) When the ground shook again in 1925, the living quarters and towers had to be repaired and reinforced. The gradual deterioration of the building forced complete reconstruction of the façade in the early 1950s.

Mission Santa Barbara from the back side, looking through the gardens.

Father Antonio Ripoll, who designed the "Queen of the Missions" in 1812, chose a Greco-Roman architectural style featuring columns and statuary on the cornice. The famous sandstone façade is based on a drawing of a church designed by Roman architect M. Vitruvius Polion dating to 27 B.C., and is distinguished by twin bell towers, which no other California mission has. With its thick adobe walls, open courtyards and red-tile roof, the Mission helped to set the tone for architectural style in Santa Barbara.

Visitors can attend Mass on Sundays and take a self-guided tour through the museum, the cloister gardens, the courtyards, the chapel and the cemetery, where 4,000 Chumash are buried. It's open daily (except on Thanksgiving, Christmas and Easter) from 9 a.m. to 5 p.m. Admission is adults $5, seniors $4, kids 6 to 15 $1, and kids under 6 free.

Easterners & Midwesterners, Oh My!

It wasn't until the United States annexed California in 1848 that, architecturally speaking, things began to change in Santa Barbara. While Spanish neoclassicism was still revered (and flourishes to this day), the adobe building method used by Mexican and Native American workers was soon replaced by fired-brick-and-wood-frame construction, a style preferred by the new settlers from back east who had begun pouring in by the thousands. But even as Easterners and Midwesterners made their presence known, the Spanish influence prevailed.

Symmetry at La Purisima Mission.

Charles Nordhoff, New York journalist and enthusiastic California supporter, noted: "The old Spanish part of the town is an agreeable novelty to strangers." And it remains that to this day.

Of course, the sun-deprived newcomers needed places to stay and thaw out. The posh Arlington Hotel, the first of the grand resort hotels on the west coast, was built in 1875, designed by Peter J. Barber, Santa Barbara's first resident architect.

The Arlington, Santa Barbara's first resort hotel.

Many of the Easterners who vacationed in Santa Barbara decided, but of course, to build homes and stay year-round. At first, they favored the then-fashionable late Queen Anne, Shingle and Colonial Revival styles, centering on the Upper East and Montecito areas. Brick-and-wood commercial buildings in a jumble of Italianate and other neoclassical styles fronted the main street of town. Side streets were lined with Victorian, Gothic, Italianate, American Colonial, California Craftsman, Queen Anne and Stick-Eastlake houses. One of the most stunning streets to browse today is Brinkerhoff Avenue, which is packed with colorful Victorian homes-turned-antiques shops. The charming one-block street is an historic district.

One of the gems of this era, the Italianate-style Upham Hotel (originally called the Lincoln House), built in 1872 at 1404 De La Vina Street, is the oldest hotel in continual use in Southern California. Santa Barbara still boasts many wood Victorian houses and a few masonry buildings from this time, but most didn't survive the 1925 earthquake.

Despite the influx of other architectural influences, residents of the 1890s and early 1900s remained fascinated with the area's Spanish heritage. By 1910 Santa Barbara, like many other California communities, was establishing itself as a Mission Revival city. The huge, and hugely popular, Potter Hotel, designed by John Austin, opened in 1902 and reflected this trend (and, alas, burned down in 1921). In 1905 Southern Pacific Railroad built the inviting Mission Revival train depot (now the Amtrak station at 209 State Street), designed by Francis W. Wilson, for the convenience of guests of the Potter Hotel, which stood just a few hundred yards from the station.

The Victorian-Italianate Upham, the oldest hotel in continual use in Southern California.

By the 1920s the infatuation with Mission Revival style had expanded to include Mediterranean and Spanish-Colonial Revivals in both Santa Barbara and Montecito. By this time, Bertram G. Goodhue had designed the Montecito Country Club (920 Summit Road), with its characteristic tower; Myron Hunt had done the fetching shopping and office arcade, La Arcada (1100 State Street); and James Osborne Craig had designed El Paseo (812 State Street), a grouping of shops, studios and offices set up to resemble a Spanish village. (The Anacapa annex to the Paseo was finished by Mary Craig and Carleton Winslow, Sr. after Craig's death in 1922.)

Mr. Smith Goes to Santa Barbara

It's a story of Pennsylvania boy makes good, although George Washington Smith took a circuitous route to his successful career as an architect. He did attend the Harvard School of Architecture in 1894, but was forced to drop out for financial reasons, and eventually became a stocks and bonds trader in Philadelphia. He married and, until the outbreak of World War I, traveled in Europe and studied painting in Paris. While pursuing a short but award-winning painting career, Smith visited friends from Philadelphia who had moved to Montecito. He never left. The Smiths bought land in Montecito, where G. W. designed and built a home and studio in the style of farmhouses he had seen in Andalusia, Spain. A house he built in 1917, called Casa Dracaena, was a big hit, and Smith quickly found that his neighbors wanted to live in houses like the house that G. W. built. No fool, he promptly put down his paintbrush and became one of the most sought-after architects in the country, with articles about his homes appearing in leading magazines. Smith is sometimes referred to as the father of the Spanish-Colonial Revival style in the United States, although he worked in other styles as well.

By the time Smith died in 1930, he had designed more than 80 homes in Santa Barbara County. One of his best known is Casa del Herrero (House of the Blacksmith), built for St. Louis industrialist George Steedman in 1922 and now open for tours (by reservation). The exterior is a pleasing blend of Mediterranean, Moorish and Spanish Revival elements; the house and impeccable grounds took three years to finish. The house was ready for occupancy on the day of the 1925 earthquake, and it survived unscathed. Other renowned G. W. Smith designs include Meridian Court (112–116 East De La Guerra Street), a charming dappled-stucco and brick studio grouping, and the Lobero Theatre (33 East Canon Perdido Street), which was completely rebuilt to Smith's design in 1924.

Earthquake!

On June 29, 1925, a 6.3-magnitude earthquake leveled much of the downtown commercial district. The loss of life was tragic, but from the pile of rubble rose a lemonade-from-lemons story: The city and its sage leaders seized the opportunity to establish an architectural board of review to create a unified look for reconstruction. Along with a stricter building code, the board required commercial buildings along State Street to conform to a Spanish-Moorish style.

Pioneering SB architect Lutah Maria Riggs.

Given this clean slate, many talented architects rolled up their sleeves and got to work. George Washington Smith (see Mr. Smith Goes to Santa Barbara, above) was busy leaving his graceful architectural mark on residences and public buildings all over Santa Barbara and Montecito. Architect Lutah Maria Riggs applied her ample skills to projects including a library addition (1929–1933) to the Mediterranean, Moorish and Spanish Revival–style Steedman House, known as Casa del Herrero, on East Valley Road in Montecito. Joseph Plunkett, with his knack for quick sketching, also played a big part in the rebuilding of Santa Barbara after the earthquake. He partnered with William Edwards to design residences in Hope Ranch and Montecito, as well as public buildings such as the Santa Barbara Airport Terminal Building and the iconic Arlington Theatre on State Street. Los Angeles architect Reginald Johnson got into the act with various projects, including the 1926 Biltmore Hotel, a Spanish Colonial treasure at 1260 Channel Drive in Montecito overlooking Butterfly Beach. These visionary architects, and their inspired peers, created a distinct Santa Barbara style.

Reginald Johnson's Biltmore Hotel.

The post–World War II years witnessed a scattering of modern-architecture projects, including the 1948 Tremaine House by Richard Neutra and Riggs's Irving House (1953), both in Montecito, along with the later UCSB Faculty Club, the only work in the area designed by Charles W. Moore. In 1960 the city asserted more controls by establishing the El Pueblo Viejo District downtown, which left no doubt that the Spanish-Colonial Revival style would continue. And just in case anyone should get the crazy notion to slap up a skyscraper, in 1972 the city limited building heights to four stories.

Edgy Edifices

All this architecture talk is not to say that Santa Barbara is swimming in a sea of red tile – you'll find edgier edifices if you just look for them. For instance, at UCSB are Robert A. M. Stern's colorful postmodern Physical Science Buildings (North and South, 1994), along with Michael Graves's Kohn Hall (1994), with its circular tower and classical pediments, which houses the Kavli Institute for Theoretical Physics.

Today's local architects are leading the charge for the new era, addressing the urgent issues of climate change, pollution and energy shortages, along with affordable workforce housing. They're designing buildings that are rich in natural light and fresh air but light on energy and water consumption. UCSB's cutting-edge Bren Hall, which houses the Donald Bren School of Environmental Science & Management, has won many awards, including the U.S. Green Building Council's LEED Platinum Award – the highest certification possible – and recognition as the nation's greenest laboratory building. It's a stunning example of the next generation of green building, which is keeping Santa Barbara and its neighbors at the forefront of innovative design.

If you're interested in more reading (and photos) on the subject, get your hands on *Santa Barbara Architecture*, by Herb Andree, Noel Young and Patricia Halloran (with an introduction by David Gebhard), and published by Capra Press, a local publisher.

Architect Jeff Shelton's Gaudi-inspired Ablitt House on West Haley Street pays homage to downtown's red-tile aesthetic, but takes it to a new era – as well as to the small-is-beautiful movement. It sits on a lot that's just twenty by twenty feet.

Preservationists with a Purpose

Imagine Santa Barbara with high-rise hotels lining the beach, billboard-plastered roadways and blinking neon signs. This aesthetic nightmare might have been reality if not for hometown visionaries like Pearl Chase, Dwight Murphy and other forward-thinking folks who worked like fiends during Santa Barbara's formative years.

Pearl Chase, the patron saint of Santa Barbara preservationists.

During the 70 years between Pearl Chase's graduation from Berkeley in 1909 and her death in 1979 at the age of 90, she was actively involved in helping to develop Santa Barbara's distinctive architectural character. Although she never held public office, she was a dynamo in the areas of historic preservation, commercial development and conservation. She left her lasting, positive mark on architecture, health and building codes, historic landmarks, parks and even Old Spanish Days events. As a member of the city's Plans and Planting Committee, she joined forces with the newly formed Architectural Board of Review following the 1925 earthquake to help create well-defined standards for a cohesive Spanish-Mediterranean "Santa Barbara style" of architecture, along with stringent building codes.

Chase was a strong advocate for building-height limits and a ban on billboards. She even went to bat against Standard Oil, which was planning to chop down the now-famed Moreton Bay fig tree at Highway 101 and Chapala Street. It's no wonder that in 1956 Chase was voted Santa Barbara's first "Woman of the Year." The unstoppable, formidable Chase also started the still-vibrant Santa Barbara Beautiful and Santa Barbara Trust for Historic Preservation, which presents the annual Pearl Chase Historic Preservation and Conservation Award to a community member or organization dedicated to the values Pearl Chase stood for. The Pearl Chase Society is still going strong as a nonprofit committed to preserving sites of enduring community value. The lovely Chase Palm Park along East Cabrillo Boulevard is named in her honor.

Another force to be reckoned with, Dwight Murphy arrived in Santa Barbara from St. Louis in 1905 and immediately recognized great potential in this place of physical beauty and perfect climate. But he also saw a town being overtaken by decay and unplanned growth. The powerful combination of Murphy's managerial skills, humanitarianism and personal wealth was just the shot in the arm Santa Barbara needed. In his own quiet way, Murphy set about making changes. He led the trio that included *Santa Barbara News-Press* editor and publisher Thomas More Storke and yeast king Max Fleischmann in orchestrating a renaissance of post-quake Santa Barbara. For example, often working behind the scenes, Murphy led the charge to acquire and preserve the city's stunning waterfront; construct the breakwater, which created the harbor and Leadbetter Beach; and develop its abundant parks system. Murphy also organized efforts to turn the old Salt Pond – a dried-up, smelly eyesore during the summer months – into the Andree Clark Bird Refuge across from East Beach. He helped rebuild the Mission twice, and was instrumental in the construction of Bradbury Dam and Lake Cachuma, even though it entailed the loss of some of his own prized ranch land. In 1953 Murphy was named Santa Barbara's Man of the Year, and in his 1968 obituary the *Santa Barbara News-Press* dubbed him "Man of the Century."

Beyond the Rooftops: Red-Tile Walking Tour

One of the easiest ways to sample the city's architecture, this popular self-guided tour is now available as a video podcast, which can be viewed or downloaded at SantaBarbaraCa.com (click on "Fun Stuff" and select the tab titled "Podcasts"). Download the companion map from the site or pick it up at the Visitors' Center (Garden Street at Cabrillo Boulevard) or at one of the tour's several locations. Narrated by John O'Hurley – best known for his turn as catalog king J. Peterman on *Seinfeld* – the sixteen-minute podcast takes you through twelve small, easily navigated blocks, making seventeen stops along the way and visiting 22 adobes dating from the late 1700s through the 1800s, plus many of the structures built in the Spanish Revival and Moorish styles mandated by community leaders after the 1925 earthquake. It's a flat walk, the distances between stops are short, and because everything is either on State Street or just off it, a restorative snack or iced mocha is never far away. Here are some of our favorite stops on the tour.

The **Santa Barbara County Courthouse** (Anacapa Street at Anapamu Street), which is listed on the National Registry of Historic Places, serves as the starting point. The stunning Spanish-Moorish courthouse was designed by William Mooser III and completed in 1929. Don't miss the famous Sunken Gardens (see Horticultural chapter), which served as a bullring in colonial times; the Moorish mosaic-tiled stairway to the second floor; and the recently restored paintings in the second-floor Mural Room that depict county history and were created by Dan Sayre Groesbeck, a background painter for film director Cecil B. DeMille. For a seagull's-eye view of the city, mountains and ocean, climb to the top of the 80-foot bell tower.

The **Santa Barbara Public Library** (40 East Anapamu Street) is an eclectic yet graceful Spanish Revival–style building with decorative murals.

The **Santa Barbara Museum of Art** (1130 State Street) is a former post office, built in 1914 and remodeled in 1941 with a Spanish flair and an interior patio in a semi-Regency style. The museum is home to *Portrait of Mexico Today* (1932), the only intact mural in the United States by renowned artist David Alfaro Siqueiros, on view at the front entry steps.

Santa Barbara County Courthouse.

La Arcada Court (1100 block of State Street) dates to 1926 and was designed by Myron Hunt, who also designed Pasadena's Rose Bowl and San Marino's Huntington Library. Carefully restored by former owner Hugh Petersen, the complex is framed by tall Spanish Revival buildings and lined with shops and galleries; the narrow lane conjures up images of Spain.

Just a hint of the tilework gracing the Santa Barbara County Courthouse.

El Paseo (15 East De La Guerra Street) was one of the first "shopping malls" in California. Built in 1924 in the Spanish-Colonial Revival style and partially encompassing Casa de la Guerra, it's a delightful collection of shops, galleries and restaurants linked by cobbled passageways surrounding a courtyard with a bubbling fountain. This "Street in Spain" is a perfect spot to take a breather – lunch at the Wine Cask, anyone? A margarita at El Paseo?

Casa de la Guerra (15 East De La Guerra Street), the home of presidio commander José de la Guerra and his family, was completed in 1827 and is among the most coveted remnants of Santa Barbara's Spanish-Mexican heritage. The U-shaped adobe was remodeled in 1923 and today is a museum reflecting the period from 1828 to 1858, when de la Guerra lived in the casa and was the go-to guy for all things political, financial and social.

Plaza de la Guerra (across from Casa de la Guerra) has been a park since 1855, but before that was a bullring. The bloodletting continues, as it's now home to City Hall and the *Santa Barbara News-Press*.

Presidio Avenue is the oldest street in Santa Barbara. At the corner of Presidio Avenue and De La Guerra Street, a plaque commemorates the Guard's House, which was built around 1840.

The colorful and elegant **Lugo Adobe** (114 East De La Guerra Street) is set behind filigreed iron gates in the picturesque Meridian Studios courtyard. Next door is **Santiago de la Guerra Adobe** (110 East De La Guerra Street), which dates to 1812 and is one of the city's oldest structures.

A complex of adobe structures, the **Santa Barbara Historical Museum** (136 East De La Guerra Street) has been restored and crafted into a serene museum space by the Santa Barbara Historical Society. Behind the museum are two adobes: the 1817 L-shaped **Casa de Covarrubias**

(715 Santa Barbara Street) and the adjoining 1836 **Historic Adobe**. The **Rochin Adobe** (820 Santa Barbara Street) was built in 1855 with bricks salvaged from the presidio walls and is a top-notch example of an American-period adobe.

El Presidio de Santa Barbara State Historic Park (123 East Canon Perdido Street) is the site of the presidio's founding in 1782 as part of the last Spanish military outpost in California. The fifteen-minute slide show provides a good overview of its storied past. Comprising a space of about four city blocks, the original whitewashed buildings were constructed of sun-dried adobe bricks laid upon foundations of sandstone boulders, and timbers from the Los Padres forest supported red-tile roofs. The landmark Presidio Chapel, the largest of the El Presidio buildings, was Santa Barbara's first church, and recently was reconstructed on the original stone foundation and houses the padres' and commandants' quarters. Ghoulish kids on field trips are fascinated by the fact that under the chapel's floor is a cemetery for the town's erstwhile influential citizens.

El Cuartel, part of the Presidio Park, is the oldest existing adobe in Santa Barbara and the second oldest in the state.

Reginald Johnson designed the 1937 Santa Barbara main **Post Office** (836 Anacapa Street) in the Spanish-Colonial style, with decorative motifs derived from the then-popular moderne style.

Italian immigrant José Lobero built the **Lobero Theatre** (33 East Canon Perdido Street) in 1873 as an opera house. It was rebuilt entirely in the Spanish Revival style in 1924 by George Washington Smith and Lutah Maria Riggs, and today is California's oldest continuously operating theater. (It survived the 1925 earthquake without skipping a note.)

A work of wrought-iron beauty at the Meridian Studios.

The Show Goes On

The Arlington Theatre (1317 State Street, 805.963.4408, thearlingtontheatre.com), or more formally, the Arlington Center for the Performing Arts, is the kind of theater you remember – as in, "Oh yeah, I saw *E.T.* there when it came out." One of the most striking of Santa Barbara's downtown structures, the theater was built on the site of the former Arlington Hotel. The first hotel burned down in 1909; it was rebuilt, then heavily damaged in the 1925 earthquake and demolished. In 1931, Fox West Coast Theatres hired the architectural firm of Edwards, Plunkett and Howell to design a showcase movie house. And it was restored and expanded in the mid-1970s by Metropolitan Theatres Corporation. Built in a combination of Spanish architectural styles, the Arlington's whitewashed exterior features some Andalusian touches, with a spectacular tower, a tiled courtyard entrance with gurgling fountains and, of course, a red-tile roof. Inside, the sweeping glazed-tile-lined staircases and wrought-iron chandeliers in the lobby hint that this is not your typi-

The beloved Arlington Theatre.

cal multiplex. The theater itself feels like a Spanish plaza – a mock village runs along its walls, complete with red-tile roofed buildings with balconies and lighted windows, and to cap it off, stars twinkle overhead in the concave ceiling.

This unique performing arts venue is home to everything from Santa Barbara International Film Festival events and screenings to music gigs, UCSB Arts & Lectures talks and blockbuster movie premieres. No tours are offered, and the theater is open only during events, so get there early to get a good look around before the lights go down and the "stars" come up.

Fresh from a $50-million-plus renovation, the **Granada** (1216 State Street, 805.899.3000, granadasb.org) is now taking bows as the grande dame of Santa Barbara theaters. This eight-story "skyscraper," designed by architect A. B. Rosenthal and constructed by Charles Urton, was built in 1924 (well before the city enacted height limits). For decades, the theater was owned by Metropolitan Theaters and was home to the Santa Barbara Symphony, Civic Light Opera and the State Street Ballet. The balcony was walled off, and the place was converted to a triplex movie theater, with films screened during the opera and ballet's off-seasons.

Over the years, the grand theater gradually lost its luster, and in 2003, the Santa Barbara Center for the Performing Arts embarked on an ambitious campaign to give the old dame a massive face-lift. Local philanthropists donated millions, and after years of construction, the curtain went up in spring 2008 to present a spiffed-up state-of-the-art theater. The original chandelier, stored for decades in the closed-off balcony, was fully restored, and outside the theater, a new replica of the original 1920s marquee now welcomes guests. A hybrid of 1920s architectural styles, the façade's ultra-Baroque decorative motifs were preserved intact, and this old flapper is dancing like she's young again.

Out of Town

Architecture & *Abelskivers*

If you're driving north of Santa Barbara and happen upon what looks like a European village, don't worry, you haven't had one too many at the last tasting room. This is the quaint (if kitschy) tourist town of Solvang. It dates to 1911, when intrepid Danish-Americans escaped, er, traveled from Iowa to settle in sunny California. They purchased 9,000 oak-studded acres of the former Spanish land grant Rancho San Carlos de Jonata next to Old Mission Santa Inés. The Danes built a folk school and church (the building now houses Bit O' Denmark Restaurant, 473 Alisal Road), followed by Atterdag College, now the site of the Solvang Lutheran Home (636 Atterdag Road).

Adorableness incarnate in Solvang; the center brown-roofed building is Bit O' Denmark.

After Solvang was featured in a 1946 article in *The Saturday Evening Post*, tourists poured in, eating up its ambience like so much Danish pastry. The architecture of many of the buildings is based on traditional Danish/German style and is a virtual smorgasbord of half-timbered houses, cobblestone sidewalks and windmills. Don't miss the replica of Copenhagen's famous Little Mermaid statue, as well as the bust of Danish fairy tale writer Hans Christian Andersen. The 1804 Old Mission Santa Inés (1760 Mission Drive, 805.688.4815;missionsantaines.org), known as the "Hidden Gem of the Missions," is located near the center of town at the junction of Highway 246 and Alisal Road.

And by the way, *abelskivers* are addictive pancake balls, usually smothered in powdered sugar and jam ... betcha can't eat just one.

Beachy Bungalows & Seaside Spiritualists

From the 101 in Carpinteria you'll see greenhouses galore, but there's more to this easygoing beach town. Stroll through the quiet streets and you'll notice well-maintained bungalows dating to the late 1800s and early 1900s scattered about like so many pretty seashells on the sand. The bungalow was well suited to beach-town life – it didn't use much agricultural land, it was low maintenance, and it used available materials (many were built of redwood). Most have porches for enjoying sea breezes. Today, a group of survivors on Olive Avenue stands as good examples of beach bungalow style – basically a boxlike frame with a hip roof and a small porch. Built by the Southern Pacific Railroad for its Chinese workers, the houses were moved in 1918 from a trackside spot to their present location.

Easterners and Midwesterners brought their housing preferences with them to Carpinteria. For example, the Victorian Andrews-Tubbs-Sears home at 8th Street and Oak Avenue was built by the Andrews family in 1889 at Maple Avenue and Carpinteria Avenue. When Seaside Oil bought the property to develop a gas station in 1940, the Hebel family moved it to its present location. This is a private home – please don't disturb the residents. The earliest known structure in the Carpinteria Valley is the Heath Adobe, built by state legislator and walnut farmer Russell Heath in 1858. Portions of the walls of the original two-story adobe have been preserved as a Carpinteria Historical Landmark at Heath Ranch Park on Eucalyptus Street off El Carro Lane.

Meanwhile, in the tiny Spiritualist haven of Summerland, similar bungalows and Victorians were being built, but many were torn down during 1925 and 1951 highway-reconstruction projects. One that has survived is the Galen Clark home (2355 Shelby Street), an 1891 house on the middle of the hill. It was built for Galen Clark, the "Guardian of Yosemite" for 21 years. When he retired, he lived in the house, occupying the lower floor while the upper floor housed a museum of Yosemite flora and fauna. The Big Yellow House, former home of Summerland founder Harry L. Williams, was built in 1884, and later became a restaurant (now shuttered but still yellow) that remains that familiar just-off-the-freeway landmark.

Sneak a Peek: Home Tours & Walks

Architectural Foundation Walking Tours
Various locations
805.965.6307, afsb.org
$10 donation, kids under 12 free
These 90-minute walking tours are among
the best bargains in town. Docents guide you
through adobes, architecturally distinctive
buildings and hidden courtyards downtown
while relating tales of local lore. The Sabado
(Saturday) tour leaves from De La Guerra Plaza
(look for the friendly docent with the sign) at
10 a.m. The Domingo (Sunday) tour leaves
from the entrance of the public library at 10
a.m. Reservations are required only for private
groups and the physically challenged.

Built Green Expo, Conference & Tour
Various locations
BuiltGreenExpo.com
This free annual tour of green residential and
commercial buildings is one component of Built
Green, Santa Barbara's mission to encourage
building owners, builders and architects to
incorporate green-building practices.

Casa del Herrero
1387 E. Valley Rd., Montecito
805.565.5653, CasadelHerrero.com
Tours Wed. & Sat. 10 a.m. & 2 p.m. Feb.-Nov.
$20, reservations required
One of Montecito's hidden gems, Casa del
Herrero is an eleven-acre estate with a home
designed by George Washington Smith in a
combination of Moorish, Mediterranean and
Spanish Revival styles. Built in 1925 and listed
in the National Register of Historic Places, the
property is now a living museum comprising not
only the house but also its elaborate Moorish
gardens and a treasure trove of European paintings and decorative arts and antiques. Dazzling
Mediterranean tile work, Spanish doors and
shutters and a ceiling from a 15th-century
Spanish convent are some of its highlights.

Fernald Mansion
414 W. Montecito St., Santa Barbara
805.966.1601, santabarbaramuseum.com
Tours Sat. 1 & 2 p.m.
Adults $5, kids under 12 $1
One of only a few remaining Victorians in town,
this fourteen-room mansion is a lovely example
of the traditional Queen Anne style. Built in
1826 by Judge Charles Fernald for his wife,
Hannah, the house is a museum operated by
the Santa Barbara Historical Society.

Pearl Chase Society's Historic Homes Tour
Various locations
805.961.3938, pearlchasesociety.org
This annual spring tour varies in focus from
year to year but always offers glimpses into historically and architecturally interesting homes.
Proceeds support this nonprofit conservancy.

Stow House
304 N. Los Carneros Rd., Goleta
805.964.4407
Open Sat.-Sun. 2-4 p.m.; 30-minute tours at 2
& 3 p.m.; closed Jan.
$3 donation, kids under 12 free
This beautifully restored two-story Victorian
built in 1872 by Goleta pioneer Sherman P.
Stow is the oldest frame home in Goleta.
Stocked with period furniture, clothing and
kitchenware, it's particularly lovely when
decked out for the holidays. Don't miss the
grounds, including Lake Los Carneros. Next
door is the South Coast Railroad Museum and
Goleta Depot (goletadepot.org), a 1901 building
housing railroad memorabilia, a model railroad,
and a miniature train that circles the grounds.

Stow House.

Trussell-Winchester Adobe
412 W. Montecito St., Santa Barbara
805.966.1601, santabarbaramuseum.com
Tours Sat. 1 & 2 p.m.
Adults $5, kids under 12 $1
Next door to the Fernald Mansion, this adobe
marks the transition from Mexican to American
rule. It's also an example of early recycling:
In 1853 the steamer *Winfield Scott* sank off
Anacapa Island. Horatio Trussell, the ship's
enterprising captain, salvaged a ridgepole from
its mast, along with other timber and brass, and
combined them with adobe bricks to build his
home, which is now a museum decorated with
period furnishings and details.

Q & A: Barry Berkus

Renowned architect Barry Berkus has been designing buildings for more than four decades – with the world as his stage. His creations are as diverse in their designs as they are pleasing to the eye and the spirit. The prolific founder of B3 Architects & Planners and Berkus Design Studio, he and his teams have won more than 400 design and planning awards for their projects. In his spare time, Barry is a contemporary-art collector, philanthropist, longstanding trustee of the UCSB Foundation, educator and involved community member. Among his local projects have been homes for Kenny Loggins and Jeff Bridges, the Santa Barbara Maritime Museum interior, Hospice on the Riviera and UCSB's Mosher Alumni House. Nancy Ransohoff caught up with Barry at his office in the former Ebbets Hall on the old UCSB campus, now called the Riviera Research Park.

Did you always know you wanted to be an architect?
I started out studying economics at UCSB, then later took the law boards at USC, but I always loved to draw. I knew I wanted to pursue something in that arena. I grew up in Pasadena among the Greene & Greene and Frank Lloyd Wright houses.... I guess it was embedded in me.

You have an international practice – you could live anywhere. Why Santa Barbara?
My wife and I knew that we wanted to live in a place that had culture – where we could live in proximity to a downtown area with core values we were interested in. We were very involved in the arts, and we also wanted to be near the ocean (I was sailing a lot then) and in a place of beauty. I had gone to school here, so it was like coming home.

What do you think is the most interesting building in Santa Barbara?
By far the most interesting building is the Courthouse – it's brave. It has stood the test of time and become the mark of Santa Barbara. There are also a lot of gems about town: La Arcada, El Paseo, Meridian Studios and beautiful 1920s and '30s courtyards, paseos and connections from one place to another – these are stellar in their use of patterning and light.

You've been practicing here for more than four decades. What changes have you seen?
The changes I've seen are all for the good. In 1955 I lived on the Child Estate in a Victorian that was the Delta Tau Delta fraternity house. It's now the zoo – I guess it was probably a zoo then, too! We commuted to the then-new UCSB campus in Isla Vista. The town had billboards and the 101 running through it. It was a town that was beginning to find itself. Pearl Chase had gotten the path to Spanish Revival started in the mid-1920s.

What changes do you see coming in the local architectural arena?
The next changes will be around the green movement – not so much in the façades as in the way solar angles are respected and in the materials used. Also, people are moving back into the city. And other changes are in encouraging people to leave their automobiles and rediscover the city as pedestrians and bicyclists.

Horticultural

Horticulture has a happy history on the Central Coast ... and why wouldn't it? The area is tucked between ocean and mountains (the visitor's bureau doesn't call it the American Riviera for nothing), with a temperate climate that bestows abundant sunshine, low humidity and just enough rain to make plants grow like Chia Pets on steroids. As a result, Santa Barbara boasts 900 plant species, some of which were brought here by 19th-century horticulturists like Francesco Franceschi; 57 parks and open spaces; and 32,000 public trees. From the greenhouses and growing fields of Carpinteria to the manicured private gardens gracing multimillion-dollar estates in Montecito to the lavender and live-oak-studded Santa Ynez Valley, Central Coast horticulture is alive, well and thriving.

Dynamic Duo:
The Botanic Garden & Lotusland

Wilderness meets the manicured garden in this meadow at the Santa Barbara Botanic Garden.

The Santa Barbara Botanic Garden
1212 Mission Canyon Rd., Santa Barbara
805.682.4726, sbbg.org
Daily March-Oct. 9 a.m.-6 p.m., Nov.-Feb. 9 a.m.-5 p.m.; members free, adults $8, seniors, students, teens & military $6; kids $4, kids under 2 free; guided tours weekdays 2 p.m., weekends 11 a.m. & 2 p.m.

It's hard not to lose yourself in the beauty and tranquility of these spectacular 65 acres of gardens framed by the vistas of the Santa Ynez Mountains to the north and Channel Islands (on a fog-free day, that is) to the south. It's an almost obligatory visit for guests, and is deeply beloved by Santa Barbarans. Here some 1,000 species of rare indigenous plants are displayed in beautifully landscaped natural settings, and with 5.5 miles of hiking trails, the gardens provide something new to see on every visit.

But the botanic garden is more than a beautiful spot to visit; it's a true community center that offers lectures and workshops for amateur gardeners and classes for everyone from children to serious students of botany. Researchers can pore over the more than 15,000 books and journals in the library. Along with wildflower hikes, there are field trips and family nature camps. And then there's that great garden shop....

The garden was originally conceived in 1925 as a joint project of the Santa Barbara Museum of Natural History and the Carnegie Institution. Over the years its mission has evolved from being a botanical showplace to actively preserving endangered plant species of the Central Coast. You can take one of the informative docent-led tours, but if you prefer going on your own, be sure to stop for a brochure at the entrance. Don't miss the carved-stone dog bowl, where Fido can have a drink (yes, dogs are allowed, if kept on a short leash), then continue past the pond to the showy California native-orchid area.

The meadow to your right is representative California grassland, where in spring California poppies and salvias add a riot of color. From here, stone steps lead into the canyon and dam area where spectacular, towering coast redwoods (the oldest planted in 1930) and sycamores provide a cool, shady sanctuary on a hot day. Built in 1807 by Native Americans working for the Franciscans, the stone dam and aqueduct are part of the system that delivered water 1.5 miles down to the Santa Barbara Mission.

The picturesque Pritchett Path continues through natural chaparral and oak. There's a lot more to see – don't miss the Discovery Garden, which includes signage geared toward children, and the Home Demonstration Garden.

The Botanic Garden even has its own redwood miniforest.

If all this garden gazing gives you a yen to shop, have no fear – the shop stocks crafts, books and gifts for nature lovers of all ages. The nursery sells California natives as well as drought-tolerant plants from Mediterranean climes around the world (members receive a discount in both the shop and the nursery); it also operates the Master Gardener Helpline (805.682.4726, extension 117) in conjunction with the University of California Cooperative Extension.

Buddha in a blaze of maple glory at Lotusland.

Ganna Walska Lotusland
Cold Springs Rd. Santa Barbara
805.969.3767, 805.969.9990,
lotusland.org
Reservations required; docent-led tours Wed.-Sat. mid-Feb.-mid-Nov. 10 a.m. & 1:30 p.m.; adults $35, kids 5-18 $10, kids under 5 free

If you can visit just one garden while you're in the Santa Barbara area, this is the one. But you'll need to plan ahead. Because Lotusland is in a residential neighborhood, the number of visitors is limited and advance reservations are required. Happily, it's far less difficult to snag a reservation today than it has been in the past.

The 37-acre estate and botanical garden reflects the colorful, larger-than-life personality of its creator, Polish opera singer Madame Ganna Walska. Madame Walska bought the Montecito estate in 1941, intending it to be a retreat for Tibetan monks. The monks never materialized

Lotusland's garden clock is an actual working timepiece.

(their loss), and over the ensuing 43 years until her death, Walska poured her considerable energy and resources into creating a botanical garden full of striking and whimsical images. Lotusland opened to the public in 1993.

Walking tours take about two hours (only members can walk unguided). Docents are so knowledgeable you get the impression they could lead you around all day without repeating any information. And that's no easy feat: More than 3,000 species are represented in fifteen gardens, each with its own distinct personality. You can walk through the stunning Australian tea-tree arbor, then visit the serene Japanese garden, with its koi pond, lanterns and Shinto shrine. The aloe garden has 170 varieties of aloe – some of which look downright Seussian – and a kidney-shape pond with fountains cascading down giant clamshells. The water garden, built around the estate's old swimming pool, features lotus and water lilies as well as water-loving plants like taro. Madame Walska had the help of landscape designers and master gardeners, but her personality prevails throughout.

It's said she sold jewelry to finance the cycad garden, her final project, and horticulturalists have been thanking her ever since. This is thought to be one of the most complete collections of cycads – prehistoric cone-bearing plants, including the sago palm – in any public garden in the United States. Other gardens include cacti, butterfly and one showcasing blue-gray plants amid paths lined with marine blue glass. We wish we could describe all the gardens – topiaries, a dancing pig, giant chess pieces and so much more – but trust us, you'll just have to see for yourself.

Don't miss the garden shop at the visitor center, which has a small but well-chosen selection of books, notecards, plants, hats and decorative items, many created for Lotusland. Members receive discounts on all purchases, as well as other privileges.

An audience of gnomes and other creatures awaits a performance in Lotusland's Theatre Garden.

Moreton Bay Fig Tree
Montecito & Chapala streets
More than 130 years old, this Australian immigrant is believed to be the largest of its kind in the United States. A young girl who had been given the seedling by a sailor fresh off the boat from Australia planted the tree in1876. When the girl moved away a year later, she gave the little tree to a friend, who planted it in its current location. During the 1930s the tree came close to being cut down to make way for a gas station, but its life was spared by preservationist Pearl Chase. Today, at 80 feet tall, the tree has a 176-foot average crown spread — that's a lot of shade – with massive gnarled roots that sit on the ground like dinosaur claws. It's been a magnet for tree climbers, initial carvers, snoozing transients and photo-snapping tourists over the years, so a chain fence now protects it. You'll find the tree at the bottom of Chapala Street on the south side of Highway 101; you have to take State Street under the 101 to reach it.

Gnarly! The Moreton Bay Fig Tree.

Secret Gardens of the Central Coast

Lawns, roses and mountains beyond at the A. C. Postel garden.

A. C. Postel Memorial Rose Garden

Los Olivos St. & Laguna St., Santa Barbara
805.564.5418, sbparksandrecreation.com
Sunrise-1/2 hour after sunset
This kid-in-a-candy-store experience for rose lovers occupies an eight-acre parcel, with city and mountain views, just across the street from Mission Santa Barbara. The 1,600 lovingly tended roses are a mix of heritage and modern hybrids. At all times of the day, you'll find camera-toting visitors alongside locals who love to hang out on the nearby lawns, toss a Frisbee, have a picnic or just relax and, yes, smell the roses. The All-America Rose Selections Committee has accredited the garden, so it receives each year's award-winning rose one year before it's available to the public. A popular recent addition is the butter-gold Julia Child rose, a grouping of which is found in an oval in the garden's center. Try to visit during the growing season, from April through November. An army of devoted volunteers, as well as the Santa Barbara Rose Society and the city parks department, capably tend the garden. The annual January pruning is a friendly affair in which volunteers are asked to show up, no experience necessary (rosarians are on hand to demonstrate proper technique), in work clothes, with leather gloves and hand pruners.

Alameda Park

1400 Santa Barbara St., Santa Barbara
805.564.5418, sbparksandrecreation.com
One of the city's oldest parks, Alameda is best known today as the site of Kids' World (see Childlike chapter), a way-cool, 8,000-square-foot paradise of a playground that has a castle, swings and slides. But the two-block Alameda also boasts a unique collection of more than 70 species of trees, along with a bandstand and acres of grass.

Alice Keck Park Memorial Gardens

1500 Santa Barbara St., Santa Barbara
805.564.5418, sbparksandrecreation.com
Daily sunrise-10 p.m.
Before we wax poetic about the gardens, let's set the record straight: This horticultural oasis is named after benefactor Alice Keck Park – so, rather than call it Alice Keck Park Park, it's the Alice Keck Park Memorial Gardens. Often called the "crown jewel" of Santa Barbara parks, this downtown favorite occupies an entire city block bounded by Santa Barbara, Micheltorena, Garden and Arrellaga streets.

Its 4.5 acres were the center of a tug of war between developers and preservationists before philanthropist and Superior Oil heiress Alice Keck Park bought it and established the gardens; donated the parcel to the city in 1975. "Alice Keck," as it's known, is now one of the most-visited parks in the city — and if you happen by toward sundown on certain Saturdays in May, you'll see clusters of parents snapping photos of their prom-going progeny, as well as brides scoping out the most picturesque spots. (A wisteria arbor is a popular wedding site.)

The park is home to a large, well-marked botanical collection of about 75 different tree and plant species; koi pond complete with resident turtles; sensory garden with audio posts and interpretive Braille signs; water-stingy demonstration garden; picnic areas; and a gazebo. Plants, some native and some ornamental, were chosen specifically for their tolerance for the low-rainfall Santa Barbara climate. Seasonal highlights are the wisterias, columbines and spectacular yellow Tabebuia trees (spring); jacarandas and magnolias (spring and summer); and red-leafed cigar box trees and colorful cassias (fall and winter).

Clairmont Farms
2480 Roblar Ave., Los Olivos
805.688.7505, clairmontfarms.com
Daily 10 a.m.-6 p.m.; admission free
Feel like taking a trip to Provence but can't quite swing it? Check out this family-owned lavender farm in the Santa Ynez Valley. The farm has five acres of Grosso-variety lavender, touted for its healing properties. Three-hundred-year-old oak trees dot the grounds, and the driveway is lined with olive trees planted by missionaries more than 175 years ago. Visitors are welcome to stroll through the fields, sit for a picnic and shop for essential oil or lavender-based soap in the boutique.

Four Seasons Biltmore Self-Guided Tour
1260 Channel Dr., Montecito
805.969.2261, fourseasons.com
Using the map provided in rooms or from the concierge, stroll along beautiful red brick walkways on a walking tour of 44 of the Biltmore's

Lavender and oaks at Clairmont Farms.

Valley of Flowers

Lompoc is known as "The Valley of Flowers," and for good reason. Starting in April, wildflowers break out in a riot of color, blanketing hillsides with purple-blue lupine and golden California poppies. For the best viewing, drive on West Ocean Avenue west of Lompoc into the rural areas. The bloom time varies depending on rainfall, but the Lompoc Valley Chamber of Commerce and Visitors Bureau (805.736.4567) lists locations and provides a downloadable map on its web site, lompoc.com. The town celebrates its floral bounty for five days around the end of June at the Lompoc Valley Flower Festival. Visit flowerfestival.org for more information on events, which include a parade, carnival and crafts show. The area also is home to lots of flower growers, so there's eye candy year-round.

Poppies run rampant through the Santa Ynez Valley and Lompoc in spring.

rarest plants and most exceptional horticultural treasures. Some 2,000 specimens grace the historic grounds, including 75 types of palms and Santa Barbara's second largest tree, a Moreton Bay Fig dating back to the 1800s.

Franceschi Park

1510 Mission Ridge Rd., Santa Barbara
805.564.5418, sbparksandrecreation.com
Sunrise-1/2 hour after sunset
Originally the home of pioneering 19th-century horticulturalist Francesco Franceschi, the Mediterranean-style palazzo and grounds offer a panoramic view of the city and the ocean. The eighteen-acre park encompasses part of a nursery that Franceschi owned until 1925. He brought some of the rare plants, including cape pittosporum, tipu, floss silk and naked coral trees, to California. Plans are under way to restore the house and grounds, so stay tuned.

Orpet Park

Alameda Padre Serra & Moreno Rd., Santa
Barbara
805.564.5418, sbparksandrecreation.com
Sunrise-10 p.m.

Park Superintendent E.O. Orpet established
this four-acre, two-parcel park as a horticultural
showplace in 1921 and enlisted the famed Olm-
sted brothers to draw up the plans. Perched
on the Riviera, the park is blessed with ocean
views, rare plants and trees, picnic tables and
walking paths. It's a wonderfully quiet place for
birding in the fall and spring.

Rose Story Farm

Carpinteria
805.566.4885, rosestoryfarm.com
Reservations required; tours Wed. 11:30 a.m.
& Sat. 11 a.m. mid-April-Nov.; tours $38, May
"first bloom" tours $45

In 1998 Danielle and Bill Hahn decided to make
a change from growing avocados and lemons
on their fifteen-acre Carpinteria Valley farm.
They were attracted to the romance, charm and
fragrance of old-world roses and wanted to
grow varieties that people rarely see outside of
private gardens. Well, grow them they did, and
Rose Story Farm now produces more than 180
varieties – almost exclusively old roses, European varieties and pre-1950 American hybrid teas.
You'll see 20,000 individual roses, along with a
newly developed White Tranquility Garden composed of more than 1,000 white roses bordered
by white companion plants. This rosey paradise
has been featured in *Martha Stewart Living*, *O*
and *Veranda* magazines, and the roses are sold
online. Tours are followed by a catered gourmet
lunch in the garden with farm-made dessert
and iced tea blended with (what else) rose
petals. Be sure to call ahead for a reservation
– tour schedules vary as, need we say, this is a
popular wedding spot.

Santa Barbara County Courthouse
Sunken Gardens

1100 Anacapa St., Santa Barbara
805.962.6464, santabarbaracourthouse.org

Okay, so they're not secret, but they are
sunken, which is close enough. The grass
expanse behind the Courthouse plays host to
many a gathering, including the Santa Barbara
Symphony's 4th of July free concert, Earth
Day festivities and Las Noches de Ronda, a

program of Spanish music, singing and dancing during Fiesta. But the gardens themselves
also deserve applause. Plantings around this
magnificent 1929 Spanish-Moorish courthouse
include an outstanding collection of palms
and exotics from more than 25 countries. You
can stand under Paradise Palms and Umbrella
Palms that are otherwise found only on a single
small island in the South Pacific. Or check out
the rare Franceschi Palm that is extinct in its
native Mexico. Others are noteworthy specimens because of their age, size and/or rarity.
You'll also frequently see the not-so-rare but
nonetheless beautiful Santa Barbara bride and
groom having their wedding photos taken here.

Santa Barbara Zoological Gardens

500 Niños Dr., Santa Barbara
805.962.6310, sbzoo.org
Daily 10 a.m.-5 p.m.; closed Christmas Day &
at 3 p.m. on Thanksgiving

As you can tell by the name, this is a zoo that
loves plants almost as much as animals. The
zoo is on the site of the former Child Estate,
and several of the formal plantings from that

A Chilean wine palm in the Courthouse's palm
garden.

era, such as the palm garden, are still on view. Look for an unusual Dr. Doolittle–sounding bunya bunya tree, also called the monkey puzzle tree, located at the top of Olive Road. You'll also see many species of coral, and don't miss the South American–native silk floss trees that grace the anteater exhibit. One of them took a 45-degree turn after a young llama bit off its top. A large wisteria vine – glorious in the spring – grows on the pergola leading up to the hilltop.

Water-wise succulents at Seaside Gardens.

Seaside Gardens
3700 Via Real, Carpinteria
805.684.6001, seaside-gardens.com
Mon.-Sat. 9 a.m.-5 p.m., Sun. 10 a.m.-4 p.m.
When we're looking for garden inspiration (which is frequently), we always stop in at Seaside Gardens. The four-acre property is set up so you can stroll "around the world" through spectacular gardens created by twelve acclaimed landscape designers, each representing different countries or climates. The garden shop and retail nursery has a huge selection, including rare and exotic plants from around the world. Happy travels!

Orchid Paradise or Orchid Mania?
Santa Barbara County produces more orchids than any other region in the United States. Producers include Gallup & Stribling, Starbek Farm, Stewart Orchids and Westerlay Orchids in Carpinteria, Chaotic Exotics in Lompoc and Cal-Orchids in Santa Barbara.

Santa Barbara International Orchid Show
Location varies
805.969.5746, sborchidshow.com
Adults $10, seniors & students $8, kids 12 & under free
Going strong after 60-some years, the Santa Barbara International Orchid Show seems to just keep getting bigger and more spectacular. Held annually in March (often under the golden rotunda at "The Earl Warren," but the location may change), the show features more than 60 exhibitors from around the world. Free workshops are led by experts, and Santa Barbara-area orchid nurseries host open houses. If you're planning to stay overnight, be sure to book your hotel early – this event attracts orchid addicts by the thousands.

Santa Barbara Orchid Estate
1250 Orchid Dr. (actually S. Patterson Ave.), Santa Barbara
805.967.1284
Mon.-Sat. 8 a.m.-4:30 p.m., Sun. 11 a.m.-4 p.m.
This seaside orchid haven lives at the bottom of South Patterson Avenue, down a long palm-lined driveway, and since 1957 it's been known locally as the place to find all things orchid. With one of the largest collections of species and hybrids (more than 2,000 varieties), the estate offers everything for sale – and it's happy to ship flowers (wouldn't Aunt Ethel in Cleveland love to get an orchid in the middle of winter?). For the past 28 years, the estate has hosted an orchid fair in July, when more than 50 growers from around the world gather to show and tell ... and sell.

Nurseries We Love

Eye of the Day Garden Design Center
4620 Carpinteria Ave., Carpinteria
805.566.0778, eyeofthedaygdc.com
Closed Mon.-Tues.
This gorgeous garden oasis is an easy stop just off the 101. From high-end designers outfitting Montecito estates to green thumbs picking up a pot for the front porch, everybody has a good time here. Hand-crafted pots and containers, French and Italian limestone fountains and English stone birdbaths are displayed along with garden furniture. Although these are mostly high-ticket items, you can score some American-made reproductions for a bit less.

Island Seed & Feed
29 S. Fairview Ave., Goleta
805.967.5262, islandseed.com
Since 1988 this has been the mecca for people passionate about seeking a sustainable lifestyle. Tucked in an industrial area, Island carries organic garden and farm supplies, seeds, drought-tolerant plants and natural pet products. The staff is knowledgeable, enthusiastic and happy to special-order anything. It's a great place to feel like you're helping the planet in your own small, green-thumbed way.

Island View
3376 Foothill Rd., Carpinteria
805.684.0324, islandviewnursery.com
Spread over ten acres of greenhouse and outdoor space, Island View offers artful displays of plants and furnishings. You'll find pots and con-

A few of the treats at Eye of the Day.

So Many Nurseries, So Little Time …
Here are a few more venues that provide the goods and the expertise to help you with an afternoon's planting project.

Doug Knapp Nursery
909 Carlo Dr., Goleta
805.681.1151
A no-frills nursery with reasonably priced, terrifically healthy plants, and lots of 'em.

Foothill Nursery
5355 Foothill Rd., Carpinteria
805.684.6171, carpinteriafoothillnursery.com
A real plantsman's place, stocked with dependable and sturdy shrubs and plants.

Seven Day Nursery
3301 State St., Santa Barbara
805.687.8036, 7daynursery.com
A great north-side resource for plants, pots, flowers, garden-themed gifts and advice.

Turk Hessellund Nursery
1255 Coast Village Rd., Montecito
805.969.5871
In spite of being located on posh Coast Village Road, this is a low-key nursery with a sign that's time-worn and overgrown with vines, so you have to look carefully to find it.

tainers, fountains, furniture, garden art, supplies and gifts. Workshops, speakers and events happen the first Saturday of the month.

La Sumida Nursery
165 S. Patterson Ave., Goleta
805.964.9944, lasumida.com
The Sumida family has run the South Coast's largest nursery since 1958. They have more than an acre of eye-popping roses, along with plenty of gardening products and tools. The web site is also rich with advice, from monthly planting lists to what to do about garden pests.

Terra Sol Garden Center
5320 Overpass Rd., Santa Barbara
805.964.7811, terrasolgardencenter.com
The sign says that Terra Sol provides information and inspiration, and you'll find that in spades … and you'll find spades, too. It's all here: every kind of plant your garden-loving heart desires, including exotics, succulents and bonsai, all labeled with helpful descriptions. The staff is eager to assist. There's also some lovely pottery, statuary, garden art and fountains.

Q & A: Dan Bifano

Perhaps it was destiny: The Montecito house in which Dan Bifano grew up had 100 rose bushes. Now a landscape designer who specializes in roses, Dan is in great demand for his artistic eye and his well-tuned nose. "Dan the Rose Man," as Oprah fondly refers to him, has designed several gardens for her Montecito estate. (She's also had him on her show.) Other Hollywood-heavyweight clients include Barbra Streisand, Michael Eisner and Ivan Reitman. For the past 25 years or so, Dan has been a key player in the development, design and maintenance of the A. C. Postel Memorial Rose Garden across from the Santa Barbara Mission. He took a break from yard work to sit down with Nancy Ransohoff in the garden to talk about, well, roses.

How did you get started in roses?
When I was young my parents moved from Detroit to Montecito and bought a house with a one-and-a-half-acre garden. I guess I've always liked plants – I used to jump the fence at Lotusland (we lived in the neighborhood) and Ganna Walska would chase me away. When I got my first house I bought five rose bushes. I stumbled into a Santa Barbara Rose Society meeting, and the next thing I knew I was helping maintain this property!

What advice do you have for the home rose gardener?
With roses, it's all about location. They need full sun, good air circulation and excellent drainage. Hybridizers are currently putting out disease-resistant roses – look for newer varieties.

What is the thorn in your side about people's perception of roses?
When people say that they're too much work. They're really not, compared to how much you get out of them – they bloom for nine months. Now, how many plants will give you so much satisfaction for that amount of work?

What is your favorite rose variety?
Color Magic – it's an incredibly popular rose from 1978. The fragrance is exactly what I want. I also love the Barbra Streisand rose, and now I love Legends, which is new for the spring 2009 planting season. It's perfect for Santa Barbara – it's a rich red, and every petal is ruffled like a Spanish dancer's dress.

You were instrumental in developing the A. C. Postel Memorial Rose Garden. Can you imagine it being anywhere else?
I don't think there is a more beautiful spot for a rose garden – you have the Queen of the Missions with the backdrop of the Santa Ynez Mountains…. I truly believe this is the best place in the country, possibly in the world, for growing roses.

Smart

Dad always said that the easiest way to tell if a man is stupid is by how loudly he tells you he's smart. So, we're going to whisper this to you – Santa Barbara is kind of smart – like how Angelina Jolie is kind of cute. It's home to more than half a dozen colleges, a bunch of museums and libraries and a thriving tech industry. People who come to college here don't want to leave, and if they actually figure out a way to stay – well, then, they must be pretty brilliant.

The College Tour

Is it possible to study and learn when there are waves to be surfed, trails to be hiked, and bodies to be tanned? If you can't decide on your own, then see what two of our Nobel laureates said (at the end of the chapter).

University of California, Santa Barbara
Isla Vista
805.893.8000, UCSB.edu

UCSB is slipping. Oh sure, five of its professors have received Nobel Prizes since 1998, it was ranked thirteenth among all public universities in the country in the *U.S. News & World Report* guide, "America's Best Colleges," its soccer team won the 2006 NCAA national title, and it's been named one of America's "hottest colleges" twice in the past five years by the popular Newsweek/Kaplan guide. But we're worried that it might not be maintaining the all-important No. 2 spot it achieved on the 2006 *Playboy* list of top party schools.

Brains, brawn *and* beauty? We're going back to college.

Straddling almost 1,000 acres on a peninsula alongside a lagoon on the edge of the Pacific Ocean, the university is so infused with natural beauty that it gets to use words like "peninsula" and "lagoon" to describe itself. Originally a small teachers' college, it joined the University of California system in 1944 and is now home to about 20,000 students.

UCSB has its very own college town in the form of Isla Vista. Populated mostly with college students, as well as a few hardy locals, it easily has the highest population density of any Santa Barbara community, with more than 13,000 seasonal residents in a little over half a square mile. Given the campus and the youthful population, both Isla Vista and UCSB are home to close to 30 billion bicycles and enough bike paths to make walking just a little bit dangerous.

Not surprisingly, UCSB boasts a top-notch marine biology program, but you'll also find an excellent school of engineering and materials, as well as both a nanofabrication facility and the brand-new Nanotechnology in Society center. The Kavli Institute of Theoretical Physics, which is partially funded by the National Science Foundation, brings together physicists and other scientists in cross-disciplinary study. In fact, UCSB is such a big fan of interdisciplinary studies that if someone wanted to use exotic materials to invent nanoscopic fish who like to read Thoreau, this would be the place.

With real estate like this, plus a vaunted roster of professors and programs, it's no wonder that UCSB turns away tens of thousands of applicants each year.

Brooks Institute

801 Alston Rd., Santa Barbara
805.585.8000, brooks.edu
Because of Brooks, there are always students somewhere in town with professional camera equipment doing photo shoots, making Santa Barbara feel just that much more glamorous.

Spread over four small campuses, which between them hold 30 studios and six digital labs, the school offers bachelors of art degrees in photography, filmmaking, photojournalism and graphic design, and it's designed around the educational philosophy that there's nothing like learning by doing. Brooks graduates include Isidore Mankofsky (cinematography for *The Muppet Movie* and *Somewhere in Time*); Dominick Palmer (cinematography on the TV series *M*A*S*H*); and Robert Legato, Academy Award winner for Best Effects (Digital Domain) on the movie *Titanic*. This may be the only school in the country where Yearbook is mandatory.

Fielding Graduate University

2112 Santa Barbara St., Santa Barbara
800.340.1099, fielding.edu
A graduate school with a focus on adult learners and midcareer professional education, Fielding has three divisions: the School of Psychology, the School of Educational Leadership and Change, and the School of Human and Organization Development. It is predicated on the notion that adults seeking education midcareer are going to be more excited about lifelong learning, and that mature adults learn in different ways than young adults do. More self-directed learning – less finger painting.

Music Academy of the West

1070 Fairway Rd., Santa Barbara
805.969.4726, MusicAcademy.org
Okay, it's not really a college, it's really a summer school – run by Marilyn Horne.

Among the nation's preeminent summer schools and festivals for gifted young classical musicians, the Music Academy of the West is an unusual gem in a city the size of Santa Barbara. The eight-week program brings 150 musicians from around the country together to participate in a remarkable series of private lessons, chamber coaching and master classes. The program provides extensive performing opportunities – including chamber ensemble,

Brooks Institute's Cota Street Campus.

solo performance, orchestra and opera – which leads to terrific entertainment opportunities for the classical music lover. The setting of many of the performances and of the nine-acre campus itself is stunning: an estate named Miraflores, which was donated by an early admirer of the school.

Students are admitted solely on merit, and all are awarded full fellowships that cover tuition and room and board. Many of the students go on to populate the world's finest orchestras and operas; alumni include Burt Bacharach and Marilyn Horne (who currently runs the vocal program).

If you're in town during the summer, make sure you catch one of the academy's 175 performances. Audiences can watch master classes, chamber concerts, recitals, orchestra concerts, a fully staged opera, dress rehearsals and vocal and concerto competitions.

Overheard on campus: "This one time, at band camp...."

Pacifica Graduate Institute

249 Lambert Rd., Carpinteria
805.969.3626, pacifica.edu
Either Santa Barbarans are really smart or really stupid – in any case, they certainly seem to like to keep going to school. Another graduate school offering only advanced degrees, Pacifica has programs in psychology, the humanities and mythological studies, and it is a very fine training ground for therapists, counselors and

Pacifica Graduate Institute.

clinical psychologists. The school is set up for the working professional, with either monthly three-day learning sessions supplemented with individual study, or two on-campus weeks in residence supplemented with online distance learning. The two campuses are on estates in Montecito, and one of them houses the Joseph Campbell Archives and Library.

Santa Barbara City College

721 Cliff Dr., Santa Barbara
805.965.0581, sbcc.edu
What a surprise – yet another stunningly gorgeous beachfront college campus. Locals jokingly call it Stanford by the Sea or Harvard on the Hill; it is, in fact, a beautiful facility on a hill by the sea that also happens to be one of the best two-year colleges in the country. Students who maintain a certain GPA and complete enough credits are guaranteed admission into the UC system.

SBCC is a community college that is truly integrated into the community – not only does it have classes for kids who are fresh out of high school, it also offers a huge assortment of adult-education classes. With more than 90 programs, many of which provide vocational training or technical certification, SBCC is a local treasure that gets heavily used. Its most popular programs include early-childhood education, business, environmental horticulture and health technologies.

Hot tip: One of the best-kept-secret gourmet spots in Santa Barbara is the dining room for the Culinary Arts and Hotel Management program. For a relatively low price, you get to be a happy guinea pig for chefs-in-training.

Westmont College

955 La Paz Rd., Santa Barbara
805.565.6000, westmont.edu
Have you always wanted to live in Montecito but don't have enough in your piggy bank to buy Oprah's place? Westmont College might be the solution.

A Christian, liberal-arts college, Westmont is located in the heart of Montecito in what feels like the middle of fairy-tale woodlands, with pathways, stone bridges and gardens typical of neighboring Montecito estates. The college moved from Los Angeles in 1945 to the 125-acre Dwight Murphy estate, and it has built a good reputation for such specialties as education, business, communications and, of course, religious studies. It's a pretty conservative place, and you won't find any Muslim, Buddhist or atheist kids in the student body.

Westmont is recognized as one of the nation's top 100 colleges committed to character development, but around town it's mostly known for its decades-long planning meetings with angry Montecito neighbors every time it wants to add a stop sign or paint a building.

High School Academies

The local high schools rank high as far as test scores are concerned – but the school system is smart enough to look far beyond testing. So our high schools also provide students with practical skills. The district offers a number of academies, or "schools within schools," that combine core academic programs with a career focus. Many of the courses fulfill University of California entrance requirements, and some allow students to earn college credits. Here are a few examples of the academies.

Dos Pueblos High School
Engineering Academy: In this hands-on, college-prep science academy, kids can apply theoretical knowledge to tangible, project-based engineering problems. A superb example is the robotics team – in April 2008, the team earned a second-place ranking out of 85 teams in their division of the international FIRST Robotics Championships, held in the Georgia Dome in Atlanta.
International Baccalaureate Program: Students interested in the humanities earn an internationally recognized secondary diploma by pursuing a rigorous liberal-arts curriculum.

San Marcos High School
Construction Academy: Students develop skills and experience in design and building.
Health Careers Academy : This academy prepares participants for possible careers in the health field. Courses include medical terminology, anatomy, physiology and sports medicine; it also arranges for nursing-assistant internships.

Santa Barbara High School
Green Academy: How very Santa Barbara! This academy focuses on sustainable horticultural methods, combining theory and practice to help students become stewards of the environment.
Multimedia Arts & Design Academy (MAD): Students combine challenging academic studies with simultaneous training in media arts and technology.
Visual Arts & Design Academy (VADA): Designed for students who have a strong interest in the arts. The small classes are project-oriented, and the curriculum includes field trips, guest speakers, artists-in-residence, job shadowing and mentorship/internship opportunities.

On the Outskirts

Allan Hancock College
800 S. College Dr., Santa Maria
805.922.6966, HancockCollege.edu
A two-year community college in Santa Maria, about an hour north of Santa Barbara, this place is a bit unusual in that students can actually complete bachelor's degrees in association with other colleges (UCSB, CSU Bakersfield and others) right on its campus. The highly regarded Pacific Conservatory of the Performing Arts (PCPA) is part of the college, and it's the only two-year community-college theater program of its kind in the country. Allan Hancock also offers two programs that are perfect for the area: Viticulture/Enology, with its own on-campus vineyard, and Ornamental Iron, which extends traditional welding into an art form. Double majors in winemaking and welding are strongly discouraged.

Cal State University Channel Islands
One University Dr., Camarillo
805.437.8400, csuci.edu
Opened in 2002, CSUCI is the 23rd and newest in the state university system. Despite its name, it is not on the Channel Islands, but rather inland in Camarillo, which is about an hour south of Santa Barbara. While the university is still searching for a clear identity, it does already have a couple of unique programs: the Center for International Affairs, which brings a global perspective to academic programs, and the Lifelong Learning Institute, for local residents 50 or older. The school's mascot is the dolphin, which has a bit of a commute, since the Pacific is five miles away.

Libraries & Lectures

The onetime residence that houses the Montecito Library is a home away from home for the community.

Check Out the Libraries

Karpeles Manuscript Library
21 W. Anapamu St., Santa Barbara
805.962.5322, rain.org/~karpeles
With nine locations across the country, this library preserves the largest private collection of original manuscripts in the world. Founded by a local real estate investor, the branch in Santa Barbara displays a somewhat random but fascinating mixture of historical documents, artwork and wonders of modern technology. Traveling exhibitions have included the Magna Carta, the Moon Landing and the Abolition of the French Monarchy & the Execution of Marie Antoinette. It's a little like the hyper-upscale version of that eccentric bookseller guy at the swap meet. The library is open daily to the public, and it's always fun to visit.

Santa Barbara Public Library
Central Branch, 40 E. Anapamu St., Santa Barbara
805.962.7653, SBPlibrary.org
Miss Sara Plummer founded the very first library in Santa Barbara in 1870 on State Street. As soon as she got married (perhaps the husband wasn't fond of book larnin'), she sold the library to the Odd Fellows, who moved it to their lodge on the corner of State and Haley. Finally, the library became public and free when the Odd Fellows donated the collection to the city upon the enactment of the California Municipal Library Law.

The Spanish Revival Central Branch downtown was built in 1917 and reconstructed after the big 1925 earthquake. The Faulkner art and music wing was added in 1930, with a much later round of major remodeling completed in 1980. Not only is it a lovely library, it also offers year-round art exhibitions, events and lectures in the Faulkner gallery, as well as several fine special collections, including historic photos of Santa Barbara, choral scores, local history and Spanish-language publications.

The library today operates a number of branches; see sidebar listings (below) for details.

UCSB Library
University of California, Santa Barbara
805.893.2478, library.UCSB.edu
The UCSB Library is an excellent resource for research and study, with more than 2.7 million volumes and 315,000 audio recordings. Its special collections include the Sciences and Engineering Library, the Ethnic and Gender Studies Library and the Map and Imagery Laboratory, which has a stunning collection of more than 467,000 maps.

But really, the best thing about the UCSB library is that it's eight stories tall, which makes it one of the few buildings in town where it's legitimate to want to take the elevator.

Branch Library Locations

Carpinteria
5141 Carpinteria Ave.
805.684.4314
Closed Sun.

Eastside
1102 E. Montecito St.
805.963.3727
Closed Sun.

Goleta
500 N. Fairview Rd.
805.964.7878
Open daily

Los Olivos
Grange Hall, 2374 Alamo Pintado Ave.
No phone
Open Sat. 10 a.m.-1 p.m.

Montecito
1469 E. Valley Rd.
805.969.5063
Closed Sun.

Santa Ynez
3598 Sagunto
No phone
Open Sat. 2-5 p.m.

Solvang
1745 Mission Dr.
805.688.4214
Closed Mon. morning and Sun.

City college or country club? It's hard to tell at Santa Barbara City College.

Lectures

KITP Public Lecture Series
UC Santa Barbara, Santa Barbara
805.893.4111, kitp.ucsb.edu
Each year the Kavli Institute for Theoretical Physics (KITP) hosts several public lectures given by some of the preeminent scientists in their fields. Known by some as Nerdapalooza, these talks are not always for the faint of mind – but they are always stimulating and enlightening, even if not entirely easy to follow. Previous lectures have included the pleasantly quirky "Welcome to Your Brain," "Einstein's Blunder Undone" and "Putting Weirdness to Work."

Mind & Supermind
Santa Barbara City College
805.964.6853, ce.sbcc.edu
This series of lectures purports to stretch minds to their untapped potential, to delve into the world of dreams, to explore realms beyond the imagination, and to ponder the mysteries of life. And then on Tuesday....

Some seasons there's a theme, like the recent Expanding the Limits of Consciousness, and other seasons it will just be a collection of speakers with something worthwhile to say, like eco-philosopher Joanna Macy or Dr. Kenneth R. Pelletier, author of *Mind as Healer, Mind as Slayer*. The lectures are held at various locations around town, and you must register in advance. But because they're hosted by SBCC, they're all free. How smart is that?

Speaking of Stories
Lobero Theatre, 33 E. Canon Perdido St., Santa Barbara
805.966.3875, speakingofstories.org
Speaking of Stories is a delightful marriage of literature and acting – superb short stories, written by local and famous authors, are read by actors. T. C. Boyle has read many of his own works here, and Christopher Lloyd, Joe Spano, Annabeth Gish, Jay Thomas and Robert Guillame have all lent their excellent voices to telling the entertaining tales.

UCSB Arts & Lectures
UC Santa Barbara, Santa Barbara
805.893.3535, artsandlectures.ucsb.edu
This program, put on annually by UCSB for the last five decades, brings a stellar array of writers, artists, scientists, performers and public figures to town. A recent season presented Salman Rushdie with Pico Iyer, Stephen Sondheim with Frank Rich, Queen Latifah, Philip Glass and Tom Brokaw. Held at venues throughout Santa Barbara, these programs bring much more sophistication and culture to the town than one would think was necessary.

Q & A: Alan Heger & Walter Kohn

UCSB has five homegrown Nobel laureates (not one was poached!), making it a research institution with some serious *bona fides*. With two laureates in physics, two in chemistry and one in economics, the school has enough to field an entire smart basketball team. Zak Klobucher asked 40 percent of the local laureates a few silly questions. As one of the basic laws of physics predicts, he got a few silly answers.

Alan Heger
Alan Heger won the Nobel Prize in chemistry in 2000 for the discovery and development of conductive polymers. His current research is in the area of transport in semiconducting polymers and light emission from semiconducting polymers (both photoluminescence and electroluminescence) – whatever that means.

I remember touring a UCSB science lab in elementary school in the '70s and seeing a laser beam create a red, holographic image of a pair of dice. Can you guys still do anything that cool?
Yes, and many more cool things, too. The science and engineering departments and faculty at UCSB are among the top in the world. There's remarkable innovation here.

Which is better: semiconductors or superconductors?
They are both remarkable classes of materials. Semiconductors are the basis of all modern electronics, with new visions continuing in the laboratories. Superconductivity is one of the most remarkable phenomena in science – zero resistance to the flow of current. There's been a resurgence of superconductivity research in recent years after the discovery of high-temperature superconductors – which allows for superconductivity above 100 degrees kelvin.

Is too much sunshine, surf and natural beauty a help or a hindrance for thinking big thoughts?
I have often wondered about that – but in fact I see no evidence of it being a hindrance. People work hard here. The wonderful weather and the beautiful surroundings seem to enable them to focus on their work.

Walter Kohn
Walter Kohn won the Nobel Prize in chemistry in 1998 for his development of the density-functional theory. This theory revolutionized scientists' approach to the electronic structure of atoms, molecules and solid materials in physics, chemistry and materials science. Walter is not a chatty man.

Have you ever successfully explained your density-functional theory at a cocktail party?
Yes, easily.

As the founding director of the Institute for Theoretical Physics (later named the Kavli Institute), are you pleased with its current iteration?
Yes, I am.

Is too much sunshine, surf and natural beauty a help or a hindrance for thinking big thoughts?
Think ancient Greece.

Famous

Michael Jackson. Oprah Winfrey. Ronald Reagan. Michael Douglas. Never heard of 'em, right? Santa Barbara's celeb-to-normal-person ratio is shockingly high for a town of this size. You can't toss an autograph book here without hitting a major player in the high-profile worlds of music, movies, TV, sports and politics.

Hollywood North

Cinematic Capital of the World?

Back before Hollywood was Hollywood, Santa Barbara was poised to become the cinematic capital of the world.

Movies had only just been invented when the Chicago-based American Film Co. opened a studio in 1910 on the site of an old ostrich farm at the corner of Mission and Chapala streets. Flying A Studios, as it came to be called, proved hugely popular with up-and-coming filmmakers (to be fair, they were *all* up-and-coming at that point), who poured into the surrounding hills to shoot the popular Westerns of the day.

Hardly a trace remains of Flying A Studios, which cranked out a few films a week at its downtown Santa Barbara lot in the silent-picture days.

By 1913, Flying A was wrapping a silent film every few days and rivaling burgeoning Paramount and Universal Studios in movie production. Over the next decade, it produced more than 1,200 pictures, attracting such talents as actor Lon Chaney and director Victor Fleming, who went on to make a couple of little-known flicks, *The Wizard of Oz* and *Gone With the Wind*.

By the time the Depression hit, Los Angeles had established itself as *the* moviemaking mecca, and Flying A faded to black.

But if Santa Barbara couldn't be where movie stars worked, it was destined to be where they play. Considered a romantic escape from the fast pace of Tinseltown, the area drew silent film stars Charlie Chaplin and Buster Keaton, who used to enjoy the steaks and swimming pool at Rancho Oso guest ranch, where they are said to have staged impromptu skits for kicks. Charlie and Oona Chaplin honeymooned in Montecito, and the Montecito Inn claims that Chaplin built the place, or at least funded it, although evidence of this is scant, and the Montecito Historical Society doesn't believe the claim is true.

After actor Ronald Colman bought the San Ysidro Ranch in the 1930s, the posh hideaway drew guests from Audrey Hepburn to Bing Crosby to Groucho Marx. John Huston once stayed for three months, while finishing his *African Queen* script.

The lovelorn heroes of *Sideways* sat in front of this wall o' wine at the Los Olivos Café, and fans of the movie often ask the waiters to snap their photos here.

Tipsy on *Sideways*

From the moment the first trailers rolled into wine country, you could say Santa Barbara was drunk on *Sideways*. Starring Paul Giamatti and Thomas Haden Church, the quirky, Academy Award–winning comedy about two buddies on a wine-tasting trip was set in the vineyards, hotels and restaurants of the Santa Ynez Valley and shot at upward of 50 locations from Santa Barbara to Santa Maria.

From golf courses and tasting rooms and down bucolic country roads to farmer's markets and, um, bowling alleys, the 2004 road-trip movie seemingly exposed the area's every picturesque nook and down-home cranny to theatergoers throughout the country.

The film's success — and its focus on real, locally produced wines — popped the area's tourism cork. Since then, wine lovers have poured into town to taste the Pinot Noirs touted in the film; they can even buy a *Sideways* map and revisit the places seen in the movie.

Detritus from the filming of *The Ten Commandments* still can be found at Nipomo-Guadalupe Dunes in northern Santa Barbara County.

Lights, Camera, Action!

Santa Barbara may no longer have its own studio, but it's a hugely popular filming location. TV shows from *Baywatch* to The *X-Files* have filmed on our offshore oil rigs, and visitors to the Union Hotel and Victorian Mansion in Los Alamos may recognize it as the setting for the music video for Paul McCartney and Michael Jackson's 1983 duet, "Say Say Say." But it's the silver screen that loves Santa Barbara best. Here are twenty movies that shot here:

The Ten Commandments, 1923, Guadalupe Dunes (pieces of the set are still buried beneath the sand)

The Best Years of Our Lives, 1946, Santa Maria Airport

The Graduate, 1967, Gaviota tunnel

Friday the 13th, 1980, Zaca Lake

The Postman Always Rings Twice, 1981, Zaca Lake and Cachuma Lake

Scarface, 1983, a Montecito mansion

The Rocketeer, 1991, Santa Maria Airport

Of Mice and Men, 1992, Gaviota train ride, Lompoc fields

The Pelican Brief, 1993, State Street downtown

How to Make an American Quilt, 1995, Red Rock swimming hole

Steal Big, Steal Little, 1995, County Courthouse, De la Guerra Plaza, Solstice Parade

Face/Off, 1997, offshore oil platforms

G.I. Jane, 1997, Guadalupe Beach

Star Trek: Insurrection, 1998, Sedgwick Ranch, Santa Ynez

Adaptation, 2002, Earl Warren Showgrounds

Seabiscuit, 2003, La Purisima Mission, a Los Alamos ranch, Paradise Road

Flight of the Phoenix, 2004, offshore oil rig

Hidalgo, 2004, Guadalupe Dunes

Alpha Dog, 2007, Carpinteria State Beach

Pirates of the Caribbean: At World's End, 2007, Guadalupe Dunes

Notable Neighbors

You don't have to be a superstar to fall in love with Santa Barbara. But the town's got two things that make it especially appealing to celebrities: First, it's close enough to L.A. that they can zip down for script meetings. Second, it's laid-back enough that residents don't hound them for autographs – and perhaps there's a certain comfort in knowing that no matter how high you rank on Hollywood's A-list, there's probably somebody more famous than you at the next table.

Star-spotting
We've seen John Cleese checking out the meat at Costco. We've seen Oprah in line at the market. We've even seen David Crosby on the downtown trolley. Considering the number of famous folks who call Santa Barbara home, the best advice for celeb-seekers is simply: Open your eyes. To increase your odds, frequent these hot-shot hangouts:

In Santa Barbara:
Blue Bee stores on
  State Street
Chaucer's Books
Metro Theatres
Farmer's markets
Four Seasons
  Biltmore Hotel
Santa Barbara Bowl

In Montecito:
Friday farmer's market
Lucky's
Montecito Village
  Grocery
Pierre Lafond Market
  & Café
Tre Lune
Vons

Most-sighted Star by Far
Dennis Franz (*NYPD Blue*)

Raised in Santa Barbara
Anthony Edwards
Eric Stoltz
Michael Douglas
  (graduated UCSB)
Kathy Ireland
Andrew Firestone
Taylor Hackford
Edie Sedgwick
Karch Kiraly
David Crosby
Martha Graham
Randall Cunningham

Eddie Matthews
Jamaal Wilkes

VIP Transplants
Oprah Winfrey
Arnold Schwarze-
  negger
Michael Jackson
Kevin Costner
Jeff Bridges
Julia Child
Jane Fonda
Ronald Reagan
Rob Lowe
John Cleese
"Dr." Laura
  Schlessinger
Paul Hogan (*Crocodile Dundee*)

Fess Parker
Tab Hunter
Ty Warner
Bo Derek
Christopher Lloyd
Kenny Loggins
Fannie Flagg
Julia Louis-Dreyfus
Kirk Douglas
Robert Zemeckis
Ivan Reitman
Steve Martin
Cheryl Ladd
Jack Canfield
Karla Bonoff
Jackson Browne
Bernie Taupin
Dennis Miller
Jason Gedrick
Andy Granatelli
Martin Gore (Depeche
  Mode)
Tim Matheson
Jonathan Winters
T.C. Boyle
Peter Noone
  (Herman's Hermits)
Noah Wyle

Bands Born Here
Dishwalla
Toad the Wet Sprocket
Sugarcult
Nerfherder
Lagwagon
Snot

From left, Rodney Cravens, J.R. Richards and Jim Wood of the homegrown band Dishwalla.

Did You Know the McMuffin Man?

In 2008, Santa Barbara said goodbye to one of its most beloved residents, Herb Peterson, inventor of the Egg McMuffin. Originally a Chicago ad man working on the McDonald's account (where he came up with the Ronald McDonald character), Peterson and his family moved to Santa Barbara in 1968 when Ray Kroc gave him the chance to become a franchisee; Peterson eventually owned six local franchises and was the first to hire women. The eggs Benedict fan spent much of 1971 working on a new food product, and when he heard that Kroc was spending Christmas at his Santa Ynez ranch, he invited him to taste his new creation. Although Kroc had just finished lunch, he inhaled two of Peterson's molded-egg creations, and before long, they were in every McDonald's in the nation. Peterson died at age 89 after a robust life, which included tremendous support of local charities and the donation of an elephant to the Santa Barbara Zoo.

Romance on the Radar

Though the Montecito wedding between Jennifer Lopez and Ben Affleck was canceled before the paparazzi could raise their lenses, many a major-league marriage has blossomed in Santa Barbara's sunshine. Vivien Leigh and Sir Laurence Olivier exchanged vows at the San Ysidro Ranch. So did Gwyneth Paltrow and Coldplay frontman Chris Martin. John and Jackie Kennedy honeymooned there, as did Julia Roberts and Danny Moder.

Seaside ranches are popular nuptials sites, too. Clark Gable said "I do" on a rustic local ranch. So did actress Sandra Bullock and *Superman Returns* actor Brandon Routh (but not to each other). More recently, the Bacara Resort has become the hot knot-tying spot for big-shot brides and grooms. Among the celebrities who walked away newlyweds: *Access Hollywood* anchor Nancy O'Dell, *Dancing with the Stars* alum John O'Hurley, and *Baywatch* babe Yasmine Bleeth. *Will and Grace* star Debra Messing honeymooned there.

For a couple of generations, this giant Santa sat atop a roof above Santa Claus Lane in Carpinteria, causing kids to wave hello while parents wondered what the possible connection could be between the North Pole resident and the sunny surf beach. When the day came for Santa to be demolished a few years back, a group of Oxnard folks raised money and moved him to a new home on the inland side of the 101 in Oxnard. Lately Santa's been wearing sunglasses.

This lifesize cow has been perched on top of the building that now houses Cities BBQ for many years; it first appeared when it was a dairy, then was bought by McConnell's ice cream shop. From time to time Cities sponsors a popular Decorate the Cow contest.

Santa Barbara is... **Famous**

Moments of Infamy

Airing from 1984 to 1993, the NBC soap opera *Santa Barbara* showed the world a fictionalized, blood-and-thunder version of our town, where well-lit and carefully coiffed members of blue-blood families got kidnapped, hypnotized, blackmailed, tried for murder, poisoned and left for dead.

Things here aren't quite as bad as all that. But Santa Barbara certainly has had its share of drama.

The 1969 oil spill required a massive cleanup effort and resulted in a new national awareness of the environment.

Offshore Oil Spill
In January 1969, a Union Oil platform ruptured six miles off the Summerland shore, sending 200,000 gallons of thick, black crude into local waters. The blowout spewed for eleven days, spreading over 35 miles of coastline and onto both mainland and Channel Islands beaches. It killed seals, dolphins and more than 3,600 sea birds. But some say that out of their gruesome demise, the environmental movement was born: The first Earth Day took place in Santa Barbara a few months after the spill. As President Richard Nixon said at the time, "The Santa Barbara incident has frankly touched the conscience of the American people."

Isla Vista Uprising
What began as a protest over the firing of a beloved UCSB professor spun into three days of Isla Vista rioting in February 1970. Fed up with the Vietnam War and intimidation by the local police, students broke windows and hurled rocks at the cops. They set fire to trash cans,

patrol cars and eventually the Bank of America building — a brick-and-glass symbol of the Establishment. It burned to the ground before Governor Ronald Reagan sent in the National Guard with tear gas and helicopters to subdue the protesters, whom he called "cowardly little bums."

An American Family
You could say reality TV had its start right here in Santa Barbara when the PBS documentary *An American Family* began airing in 1973. The twelve-episode series followed the real lives of the Louds, a local family with five children. The oldest, 20-year-old Lance, is credited as the first gay character on television. The parents, Bill and Pat, separated and divorced while the series was taping, adding to the show's controversy. More than ten million viewers tuned in to watch the Louds, whose family photo made the cover of *Newsweek* magazine. PBS revisited the family 30 years later to chronicle the death of Lance from hepatitis C.

Death of Linda McCartney

Reporters from gossip tabs the world over jetted to town in April, 1998 after it was announced that Linda McCartney, longtime wife of Sir Paul, had died of breast cancer while on vacation in Santa Barbara. But when the county coroner failed to receive official notice of her passing, it was revealed to be a decoy to keep the media at bay while the family grieved in peace. It's believed that the former Beatle's missus actually died at a family ranch outside Tucson, Arizona. She was 56.

Nick Markowitz Murder

This story defied logic in so many ways. In August of 2000, L.A. pot dealer Jesse James Hollywood and his posse went to settle a score with a client who owed James money. They didn't find the guy — so they kidnapped his younger brother, Nicholas Markowitz, instead. They drove Nick to Santa Barbara, where they spent several days partying at friends' houses and a motel. The abducted teen was nicknamed "stolen boy" and invited to play video games and take drugs with the crew until Hollywood ordered him killed. They drove Nick to the hills above Goleta, bound him, shot him and left him in a shallow grave — where hikers discovered his body days later. Hollywood's four young henchmen were tried and sent to prison; the ringleader himself was captured in Brazil five years later, and is scheduled to be tried in 2008.

The story of Markowitz' abduction and murder was made into a feature film called *Alpha Dog* in 2006.

David Attias Rampage

The streets of Isla Vista have always been wild: scantily clad girls, loud rock bands, drunken revelers. But until February 23, 2001, they hadn't been deadly. That night, UCSB student David Attias sped through the village, crashing his Saab into five young pedestrians and killing four: Nicholas Bourdakis, 20; Christopher Divis, 20; Ruth Levy, 20; and Elie Israel, 27. Attias, who was known for erratic behavior and had drugs in his system at the time, was reported to have leapt from his car after the incident and shouted, "I am the angel of death!" before fighting with onlookers. He was later convicted of second-degree murder, but found to be insane at the time.

Michael Jackson Trial

In 2005, singer Michael Jackson stood trial for charges of child molestation – and the world watched in fascination. The King of Pop owns a sprawling Santa Ynez property called Neverland Ranch, which includes a mansion, zoo and amusement park. But no circus could rival the entertainment factor of this fourteen-week trial, which included testimony from Macaulay Culkin. The Gloved One didn't testify, but he did show up late to court one day wearing pajamas and slippers. Prosecutors said Jackson had engaged in lewd conduct with, and given alcohol to, a young boy visiting his ranch. The defense argued that the boy's family was merely trying to bilk the eccentric celeb with false accusations. The singer was found not guilty.

The serene beauty of the *News-Press* building belies the turmoil it has housed over the last few years.

Santa Barbara News-Press Meltdown

A community-wide furor erupted after six newsroom editors resigned from the *Santa Barbara News-Press* in July 2006 over what they called breaches of journalistic ethics by the paper's owner, billionaire divorcée Wendy McCaw. Reported in *Vanity Fair*, the *New York Times* and a documentary film called *Citizen McCaw*, the story had everything a newshound loves: a drunk-driving arrest swept under the rug, front-page accusations of child pornography and the controversial publication of TV star Rob Lowe's home address. Before the outrage had settled down, upward of 80 employees of the Pulitzer Prize–winning newspaper had quit or been fired, and the paper had lost thousands of once-loyal subscribers.

Q & A: Kathy Ireland

Supermodel-turned-supermom Kathy Ireland has been making women jealous for decades. First it was the bikini bod; the hometown girl set a record with thirteen appearances in *Sports Illustrated*'s swimsuit issues. Now she has a line of clothing, housewares and exercise videos. She's also written three children's books and helps out at the Santa Barbara Rescue Mission, the Dream Foundation and the Unity Shoppe. Did we mention that she teaches Sunday school? Ireland lives in Montecito with her husband, an emergency-room physician, and their three kids, ages 4, 9 and 13.

Is it true you had a paper route as a kid?
I was kind of a tomboy. I worked for the News-Press *for three years. It was a great job.*

How did you get into modeling?
As a gift, my parents gave me a course in modeling, with the hope that I might learn to be more ladylike or something. I went, never thinking of it as a career. A scout came to class one day and asked if I'd like to go to New York for the summer. I was caught completely off guard. It was eye-opening. Before that, my world extended as far as I could pedal my bike around Santa Barbara.

You've traveled the globe. What inspired you to return to your hometown?
There's no place like home. I've got roots here. And the beauty! There's an abundance of inspiration in this town. I have never been bored one day in Santa Barbara.

How did you meet your husband?
I was having lunch with my mom, who was a nurse at Cottage Hospital. This cute guy walked by and caught me checking him out. So we met.

There are so many celebrities here. Do you ever get starstruck yourself?
My husband was at the grocery store and he saw Oprah, and he got really excited and called me and said, "Guess who's in front of me in line?!" It was at the Montecito Village market. She had some chicken and onions in her cart.

As a kid, you worked at Petrini's Italian restaurant. Did you ever go back?
I've been taking our daughter and her friend there for lunch sometimes on the way to her tennis lessons.

Do you ever get time to yourself?
I love to hike up in the hills. That's great for me to have a little alone time. I think it helps us to be better moms, better people, when we take care of ourselves, too.

Most decadent Santa Barbara dessert?
That's my weakness: I love desserts. My mom became a health nut when I was a kid, so on my 18th birthday, I just felt this freedom to indulge. There's this tiny café down by the harbor, and on my birthday, for breakfast, I had a big hot fudge sundae and french fries.

Artistic

Beauty inspires art. Some of the world's best-known art havens are also the most picturesque cities: Paris, Florence, Athens. Scan Santa Barbara's landscape — the grape hue of its mountains, the rich red-roof tiles, the gentle curve of its coastline — and you'll see why painters, sculptors and photographers have long leapt at the chance to use their brushes, chisels and cameras here.

3 Great Museums

Santa Barbara Contemporary Arts Forum
653 Paseo Nuevo, Santa Barbara
805.966.5373, sbcaf.org
Tues.-Sat. 11 a.m.-5 p.m., Sun. noon-5 p.m.; admission free

It's not unusual for this ultramodern gallery space in a traditional Santa Barbara Spanish setting to present an artist "working with a palette of garter belts, eggs, pearls, taxidermic models, nylon and resin." The leading presenter of contemporary art in central California, the 30-year-old forum dedicates itself to brand-new work that frequently surprises, and challenges, viewers. Recently, the curators created an exhibit based on the cardboard shipping tubes typically used to mail artwork. They housed an installation documenting a Danish artist's participation in a Chinese arms fair. And they commissioned a romantic-gothic artist to design pink and purple flags to fly up and down State Street for one week ... just because. In addition to more than fifteen annual exhibitions, the forum hosts some of the most entertaining events in town, from its Valentine's Day art auction, to its Speakeasy poker tournament, to its million-dollar home raffle.

Cutting-edge modern art lives behind this classic Spanish façade.

Park in the Paseo Nuevo lot below the mall. The small part-gallery, part-museum is located in the arts balcony above the mall.

Downtown's Santa Barbara Museum of Art is of a piece with the city's Spanish-Mediterranean architecture.

Santa Barbara Museum of Art
1130 State St., Santa Barbara
805.963.4364, sbmuseart.org
Tues.-Sun. 11 a.m.-5 p.m.; admission $9; children, seniors & students with ID $6; free on Sun.

The two-story entrance courtyard inside the Santa Barbara Museum of Art is a stately chamber appointed with ancient sculpture. The room is dead-silent — except for the frequent echo of a tourist exclaiming, "Holy ... ! What's a museum like this doing in a city this size?" On walls and pedestals throughout the galleries are works by Monet, Matisse, Picasso, Dalí, O'Keeffe — not exactly small-town names.

Founded in 1941 after a group of young artists banded together to claim an old post office as their gallery, this is now one of the nation's top ten regional art museums. In recent years, it has brought some dazzling exhibitions to town: from Chinese silks of the Qing dynasty to Ansel Adams photographs, from Renaissance and Rococo drawings to video art sculpture by Nam June Paik. But it's best known for its impressive permanent collection, which includes art spanning 4,000 years.

Rivaled in the western U.S. only by the Getty, the museum's antiquities collection is truly something at which to marvel. Check out the 2,000-year-old marble Lansdowne Hermes, Greek pottery from 500 B.C. and the 19th-dynasty Egyptian limestone relief of Ramses' son. From Tibetan mandalas to works on paper by Christo and Jasper Johns, the museum keeps impressive Asian and American collections, too. (We like its turn-of-the-century posters featuring work by Maxfield Parrish, Gustave Klimt and Alphonse Mucha.) But it's with works by name-dropping European artists that the museum claimed its clout. Don't miss Auguste Rodin's *Walking Man*, Marc Chagall's *Young Girl in Pursuit* and Wassily Kandinsky's *Linie-Fleck*. Outside the museum's front entrance, take a moment to appreciate the social-realist mural *Portrait of Mexico Today*. It's the only surviving mural in the nation by renowned Mexican muralist David Siqueiros, who painted the work in Los Angeles while in political exile from his native country.

Get the back story on each canvas and carving during daily docent-led tours at noon and 1 p.m. And check the web site for upcoming events, because artists and scholars frequently show up to give gallery talks, and there are regular concerts.

In addition to being a repository of priceless art, the museum is one of the town's great cultural hubs. On the third Thursday of summer months it plays host to "Nights," a see-and-be-seen cocktail party with live music and such activities as henna tattooing and craft making. And doors are flung open on the first Thursday of every month, when guests are admitted free — and when the museum stays open until 8 p.m. — as part of 1st Thursday, the Downtown Organization's community arts event.

We don't know about you, but something about perusing art makes us feel like shopping. And the museum's gift store is a treasure trove far beyond the usual notecards-and-post-ers vendor. Open daily, the shop can trap art lovers for hours with its dazzling art glass, one-of-a-kind jewelry and clothing, and artistic housewares. For the museum or the store, park in City Lot 7 off Ana-pamu or Figueroa streets.

Claude Monet's *Villas a Bordighera* (1884) is among the works at the Santa Barbara Museum of Art.

University Art Museum
University of California, Santa Barbara,
Ocean Rd., Goleta
805.893.2951, uam.ucsb.edu
Wed.-Sun. noon-5 p.m.; admission free

Perched at the edge of UCSB's peace-ful lagoon, this museum draws in cam-pus denizens with edgy exhibitions of psychedelic concert posters from the 1960s and photographic essays of the Black Panthers. It also boasts Old Master paintings, Renais-sance metals and early-20th-century American Realist prints. But its crown jewel is the Architecture and Design Collection, an archive of more than 750,000 three-dimensional models and architectural documents — including photos, scrapbooks and sketchbooks — from more than 350 designers over the last century. Comparable in size to the Library of Congress's architectural collection, this one inspires fascinating and fun exhibits. One memorable show focused on theme park design. Another displayed a standardized ship-ping container that architects had transformed into a fully functional portable living space. (And they say dorm rooms are small....) The books, catalogs and posters in the small store reflect the museum's focus.

Parking can be tricky. Aim for Lot 22 and buy a visitor permit from an automated pay sta-tion in the lot. Walk along the pathway toward Storke Tower; the museum is on the right.

Artists in Paradise

From the Chumash Indians creating colorful cave paintings to the contemporary artists now working in the waterfront lofts of the "Funk Zone," Santa Barbara has long been an artist's anchorage. Today's art scene was launched at the turn of the 20th century, when painter and illustrator Alexander Harmer opened a complex of studios in town to encourage artists to interact with art buyers.

After the great San Francisco quake of 1906, a wave of artists fled south, landing in Santa Barbara. One was Fernand Lungren, a *Harper's* illustrator who became famous for his scenes of Native American life. By 1914, Lungren had announced that "as a field for artistic endeavor, it would be impossible to find a spot more favored than Santa Barbara." A member of the Community Arts Association, he founded the Santa Barbara School of the Arts in 1920.

By then the town was awash with noted artists who lived among the very landscapes they became famous for painting. Architect George Washington Smith came to Santa Barbara to paint the scenery and wound up staying. Will Rogers' pal Ed Borein, a cowboy etcher and watercolorist, also called the area home. So did Monet-influenced John Gamble, Western painter Carl Oscar Borg, portraitist Albert Herter, Thomas "Yellowstone" Moran and father-and-son painters DeWitt and Douglass Parshall. Parshall the younger helped establish the Santa Barbara Art Association in 1952. Today the group has more than 500 jury-admitted members who show their work at the cooperative Gallery 113.

If Santa Barbara is known for any one style of art, it is plein air painting, an impressionistic form of landscape painting undertaken outdoors — at the scene of the scene, as it were — rather than in a stuffy old studio. Local foothills, meadows and cliffs have alighted in countless plein air paintings, none more famous than those of Ray Strong. A native of Oregon, Strong studied in San Francisco and New York before moving to Santa Barbara in 1960 to paint the diorama backgrounds at the Santa Barbara Museum of Natural History. He, too, stayed until his death in 2006 at age 101, and helped lead a local collective of preservationist painters called The Oak Group.

Created in 1986 as a club for folks who like to paint outdoors, the Oak Group quickly established itself as a conservation entity when it discovered that one of its favorite seaside landscapes, Loon Point, was about to be developed as condominiums. They held an exhibition of their paintings and donated half of the proceeds to maintain the land as open space. More than two decades later, the group is still painting and preserving, having raised more than $1 million to protect natural areas both in Santa Barbara and elsewhere along the California coast.

The Oak Group gathered at the Sedgwick Ranch in Santa Ynez in 1997 to honor the 92nd birthday of painter Ray Strong. The artists had just finished helping the ranch, which had once been home to two large Chumash villages, become a protected reserve. Front row, from left: Larry Iwerks, Don Archer, Ed Hammerberg, Ray Strong, Arturo Tello, John Comer and Hank Pitcher; back row, from left: Skip Smith, Manny Lopez, Marcia Burtt, Whitney Abbott, Meredith Abbott, Glenna Hartmann, Thomas Van Stein, Karen Gruszka, Karen Foster, Bjorn Rye, Erika Edwards, Sarah Vedder, Chris Chapman and John Iwerks.

Going Public: Outdoor Art

The biggest challenge our museums and galleries face is the weather: Who wants to be indoors when it's sunny? (And it's almost always sunny.) Those who love art *and* a gorgeous day can have it both, thanks to these outdoor works of art.

Chromatic Gate
Locals call it the "Rainbow Arch," but Herbert Bayer called his sculpture the *Chromatic Gate*. Bayer, who studied under Kandinsky and was art director for *Vogue*'s Berlin office, died in 1985 after spending his last decade in Santa Barbara. He was the last master of the Bauhaus, and his 21-foot, 12.5-ton rectangular rainbow reflects that movement's affinity for geometry. Said to have been inspired by a Chumash legend, the steel arch was built in the '80s and erected in its current location — in front of Fess Parker's Doubletree — in 1991.

The Dolphin Fountain
Standing playfully at the foot of Stearns Wharf where State Street meets the beach, this iconic, cast-bronze sculpture is — to the chagrin of resident art snobs — the best-known public sculpture in Santa Barbara. Local artist James "Bud" Bottoms created it, and he has since installed similar fountains in Puerta Vallarta and at the Long Beach Aquarium.

It Is Raining
It's worth a trip to view longtime local artist and teacher Marge Dunlap's cool, quirky fountain *It Is Raining*, in the courtyard of the Las Aves business complex on Los Patos Way at Channel Drive. The sculpture is not only historically significant — it was the first piece of contemporary art to pass the city's review process – but it's also sweet and striking, with ceramic hands, faces and broken bits of plates and teacups embedded in its plaster. The words "it's raining" are etched in 39 languages on the piece, whose message, the late Ms. Dunlap once said, is that rain falls indiscriminately on us all.

Mosaic Boulders
You're driving around town when a gleam of sunlight glints on the roadside. It's a giant boulder blanketed in polished tiles and it's just sitting there for no apparent reason. These curious objects are the work of mosaic artist Dan Chrynko, who incorporates stained glass, shells and even meteoric rock into his whimsical pieces. Chrynko's boulders are found outside Borders downtown and the Coffee Bean & Tea Leaf at State and De La Vina. There's even a neat mosaic totem pole at 107 East Micheltorena Street. Our favorites are the two mosaic alligators, Ethel and Harry, who appear to slither along the creek in Mission Canyon's Rocky Nook Park. We like to think of them as *rep*tiles.

The details on the vivid *It Is Raining* ask that visitors spend some time with it.

La Arcada Sculptures
You'll find more playful sculptures along the charming brick pathways through La Arcada courtyard (1114 State Street) than at any other public venue in town. Three lifelike sculptures by J. Seward Johnson — including a window-washer — fool passersby into thinking they're real people. A bronze Ben Franklin kicks back on a bench. Kids love to "ride" on a pair of bronze dolphins by Bud Bottoms, and Bonifatius Stirnberg's *Mozart Trio* lets viewers move the musicians' arms around willy-nilly.

Lompoc Murals
The little agricultural town of Lompoc is known for three things: its prison, its spectacular flower fields and its murals. The self-proclaimed "City of Murals in the Valley of Flowers" boasts 100 murals depicting moments in the town's surprisingly interesting history — from mission life to coastal shipwrecks to the temperance movement. Maps are available at the Lompoc Chamber of Commerce, 805.736.4567.

Our Favorite Galleries

More than 60 galleries live in Santa Barbara County. Some preen beside designer boutiques and big-name coffeehouses on popular pedestrian thoroughfares. Others are tucked between thrift shops and hardware stores on secret side streets. They all outfit the walls and mantles of Montecito's best-dressed mansions and Hope Ranch's impeccably appointed estates.

Atkinson Gallery
Santa Barbara City College, 721 Cliff Dr., Santa Barbara
805.965.0581, ext. 2411, gallery.sbcc.edu
Mon.-Thurs. 10 a.m.-7 p.m., Fri.-Sat. 10 a.m.-4 p.m.
The Atkinson wins the award for Most Breathtaking View from a Gallery. Once you recover from the scenery, though, there are treats to be had here. Six annual exhibitions of contemporary art include a student show in the spring, a "small images" show in the fall and national and international artists in between.

Brooks Institute, Cota Street Gallery
27 E. Cota St., Santa Barbara
888.304.3456, brooks.edu
Mon.-Fri. 8 a.m.-9 p.m., Sat.-Sun. 10 a.m.-9 p.m.
Students, faculty and alumni of the prestigious Brooks Institute of Photography can show their work at this cool downtown space, one of the city's largest galleries. With a bright, open, industrial design, the room also functions as a classroom and screening room. Check out the "Brookstore," which sells prints and books by and about Brooks faculty and students.

Easton Gallery
557 Hot Springs Rd., Montecito
805.969.5781, EastonGallery.com
Sat.-Sun. 1-5 p.m. & by appt.
Tucked in a residence on a bucolic road, this gallery specializes in contemporary landscapes, many by members of the preservationist Oak Group. Shows highlight oil paintings, pastels and graphite sketches of local bluffs from the Cachuma cliffs to curving coastline. The gallery also sells books that it has published.

Edward Cella Art + Architecture
10 E. Figueroa St., Ste. 3, Santa Barbara
805.962.5900, EdwardCella.com
Tues.-Sun. 11 a.m.-5 p.m.
The local name most dropped by major artists is Edward Cella, who collects and sells work by

Gallery space at Edward Cella.

emerging and established artists and architects, mostly post-WWII and contemporary paintings and drawings. Included in his collection are signed intaglios by Jasper Johns, as well as Frank Gehry's illustrations and his ten-print portfolio of Walt Disney Concert Hall.

855 at the Art Center
855 Linden Ave., Carpinteria
805.684.2164, ArtsCarp.org
Hours vary; check web site for shows & events
On the main drag of sleepy Carpinteria, this new gallery is operated by the Carpinteria Valley Arts Council, a nonprofit that supports arts of all sorts. Residents raised money to create this center, which hosts exhibits and presents poetry readings and art workshops year-round. (And the council gets our "sitting" ovation for painting the pretty bus benches in Carpinteria.)

The Frameworks & Caruso Woods Gallery
813 Anacapa St., Santa Barbara
805.965.1812, CarusoWoods.com
Tues.-Fri. 10 a.m.-5 p.m., Sat. 11 a.m.-3 p.m.
Run by a cool couple, the spacious Frameworks supports local contemporary artists by hosting free, BYOB soirées. The popular events, which include live music and dancing, inspired the Downtown Organization to launch its 1st Thursday program (see Art Happenings). Expect to see color photos of Cuba while listening to improvisational Afro-Caribbean beats, or abstract paintings paired with a live DJ.

For up-to-date information about art events and exhibits, go to sbva.org, 805.564.6828.

Los Olivos: The Art of Small-town Living
In the heart of Santa Barbara wine country sits a quaint village whose short blocks are lined with tasting rooms, gourmet cafés, boutiques and galleries. While exploring the area, don't miss the **Wildling Art Museum**, a must-see for fans of the great outdoors. The collection of images of America's wilderness aims to promote preservation of endangered species and open spaces from Antarctica to the Everglades. It occupies a historic house at 2329 Jonata Street (805.688.1082, wildlingmuseum.org).

The **Judith Hale Gallery** houses Western and traditional artwork, from paintings, to stone sculpture, to Native American jewelry. You'll find it at 2890 Grand Avenue (805.688.1222, judithhalegallery.com).

The bucolic Wildling Art Museum.

More than 40 regional artists collectively own and operate the spacious **Gallery Los Olivos**, showing — and occasionally demonstrating — their watercolor, acrylic, photography and ceramic work. The Artists Guild of the Santa Ynez Valley also maintains a showroom within the gallery, which is located at 2920 Grand Avenue (805.688.7517, gallerylosolivos.com).

Gallery 113
La Arcada, 1114 State St., Santa Barbara
805.965.6611, sbartassoc.org
Mon.-Sat. 11 a.m.-4 p.m., Sun. 1-4 p.m.
In the shaded, sculpture-lined courtyard of La Arcada, Gallery 113 serves one purpose: to exhibit work by the 500 artists of the Santa Barbara Art Association. The exhibiting artists operate the gallery themselves.

Marcia Burtt Studio
517 Laguna St., Santa Barbara
805.962.5588, artlacuna.com
Sat.-Sun. 11 a.m.-5 p.m. & by appt.
A lovely, light-filled space, this studio makes you feel as if you're in a talented artist friend's loft. The specialty is landscape paintings by contemporary California artists, including Robert Abbott, Marcia Burtt and Patricia Doyle.

Peregrine Galleries
1133 Coast Village Rd., Montecito
805.969.9673, PeregrineGalleriesInc.com
Tues.-Sat. noon-7 p.m., Sun.-Mon. noon-5 p.m.
In addition to plein air paintings by major artists, Peregrine owners Jim and Marlene Vitanza have an impressive collection of antique silverwork and early Bakelite jewelry. A second, smaller location at 508 Brinkerhoff Avenue in Santa Barbara (805.963.3134) specializes in American Indian artifacts and jewelry, Western art, rugs, Chelsea clocks and art pottery.

Reynolds Gallery
Westmont College, 955 La Paz Rd., Montecito
805.565.6162, westmont.edu/reynolds_gallery
Mon.-Fri. 10 a.m.-4 p.m., Sat. 11 a.m.-5 p.m.
On the woodsy Westmont campus, this is a prime showcase for not just faculty and students but artists from the community. Exhibits have included the work of children's book illustrators and the Views and Visions series, in which it presents a theme — such as "shoe" — and asks artists to create a work that "best exemplifies the quintessence" of that theme.

Sullivan Goss – An American Gallery
7 E. Anapamu St., Santa Barbara
805.730.1460, SullivanGoss.com
1266 Coast Village Rd., Montecito
805.969.5112
Daily 10 a.m.-5:30 p.m.
With an inventory of more than 6,000 works, Frank Goss and Patricia Sullivan Goss have been collecting 19th-, 20th- and 21st-century American art for more than two decades. The downtown location is the flagship, with fifteen exhibitions every year, both solo shows for contemporary artists and curated historical exhibitions. The range is what makes this gallery special. Aficionados will find everything from pastel landscapes of the 1800s to photography examining the tattoo as fine art. Hungry browsers take note: The Arts & Letters Café in the back courtyard is an exquisite place to enjoy an al fresco duck confit salad on a sunny day.

An Artistic Community

Happenings

1st Thursday

Downtown Santa Barbara
805.962.2098, santabarbaradowntown.com/go
Downtown Santa Barbara devotes the first
Thursday of every month to a public — and utterly free — celebration of the arts. From 5 to 8
p.m., galleries fling open their doors, and some
serve drinks and nibbles. Strollers can stop to
watch street performers, from karaoke singers
to Irish clog dancers, or pop into a theater to
see a lecture, poetry reading or scene from an
opera. For schedules, check the web site.

I Madonnari

Santa Barbara Mission
imadonnarifestival.com
On Memorial Day weekend, artists transform
the plaza surrounding the magnificent Santa
Barbara Mission into a patchwork of 200 big,
bright chalk drawings. About 25,000 people
come to see 400 artists on their knees, creating
giant works of art on the asphalt over a three-
day period. Modeled after similar festivals that
have been taking place in Italy for centuries, the
event is named after that country's *madonnari*,
or chalk artists, who typically drew images of
the Madonna. Here, you'll see re-creations of
art by Diego Rivera, Da Vinci and Dr. Seuss,
plus bold, beautiful original work. Kids love the
area that's set aside especially for them, where
they can let their imaginations and their chalk
run wild. The temporary tableaux fade with
each breeze and disappear entirely with the first
summer shower. The event is a fund-raiser for
the Children's Creative Project, an arts education program of the Santa Barbara County
Education Office.

Santa Barbara Art Walk

Santa Barbara Museum of Natural History
805.682.4711, sbnature.org/artwalk
In the fall, the Art Walk attracts more than
200 artists to show and sell their work on the
oak-shaded, creekside grounds of the Santa
Barbara Museum of Natural History. The event
features live music, artist demonstrations and
food. Proceeds from the art sales benefit the
museum's programs.

Art under the sun at the Sunday Arts & Crafts
Show.

Santa Barbara Arts & Crafts Show

Cabrillo Blvd., Santa Barbara
805.897.1982, sbaacs.com
Inspired by the sidewalk art shows of Europe and Mexico City's Jardin del Arte, Santa
Barbara boasts its own weekly marketplace
for local arts. Every weekend for more than 40
years, hundreds of vendors have been peddling
their pottery, paintings, photography and crafts
along oceanfront Cabrillo Boulevard. From 10
a.m. to dusk on all fair-weather Sundays and
some holidays, visitors can stroll the shoreline
from State Street east, while perusing the handmade housewares and jewelry and stopping to
talk to artists — or watch them work.

Santa Barbara Studio Artists Tour

805.899.8854, SantaBarbaraStudioArtists.com
Each Labor Day weekend, the more than 50
professional artists in the Santa Barbara Studio
Artists group open their doors for three days.
Visitors buy tickets beforehand (proceeds
benefit global aid organization Direct Relief
International), then follow a map and brochure
for a self-guided tour — and rare peek — into
the artists' workspaces.

Classes & Workshops

Art from Scrap
302 E. Cota St., Santa Barbara
805.884.0459, ArtFromScrap.org
Each year, this innovative nonprofit keeps thousands of pounds of materials out of landfills by recycling it as art supplies. Corks, tiles, beads, rope, mirrors, cellophane and circuit boards are among the eclectic reusables donated by local businesses for your sculpting and collaging pleasure. Creative types can shop the store for must-have doodads, or come to a $6 workshop (every Saturday from 10 a.m. to noon), where guest artists guide kids age 6 and up in creating masterpieces from recycled feathers, frames and plastic tubing. Workshop themes vary from portraits to jewelry to celebrations of Van Gogh's birthday.

Santa Barbara City College Continuing Education
Alice F. Schott Center, 310 W. Padre St., Santa Barbara
805.687.0812, ce.sbcc.edu
Always wanted to learn calligraphy? Wish you could "paint like the Renaissance masters"? Nearly 50,000 people sign up each year for what locals call "adult ed," a diverse spate of classes that let you hone a skill or explore a new hobby. Dozens of art and craft classes are offered every quarter, from bronze casting and stone carving to basket weaving and book binding. Throw on a potter's wheel, weave on a floor loom or learn the art of Japanese embroidery, known as Bunka Shishu. Enrollment in most classes is free, although some — especially the art classes — have nominal materials fees.

Santa Barbara Contemporary Arts Forum
653 Paseo Nuevo, Santa Barbara
805.966.5373, sbcaf.org
Six times a year, this gallery-on-the-edge invites parents and kids to a hands-on art-making workshop called FAMILY+. Sometimes they make music, other times it involves photography or video. Once they made shadow puppets, traced them onto paper, cut them out and made a soundtrack for the characters. Best of all: It's free!

Santa Barbara Museum of Art
1130 State St., Santa Barbara
805.963.4364, sbmuseart.org
On the second Saturday of each month, the museum invites kids age 6 and up to discuss a work of art and create a project under the guidance of an art teacher. Classes are $20, and advance registration is required. Up the street at the museum's Ridley-Tree Education Center at McCormick House (1600 Santa Barbara Street), kids from ages 3 to 5 can partake in child-parent art classes; the After School ArtVentures are geared to kids age 6 and up. ArtVenture Camps are offered over spring, summer and winter school breaks.

Santa Barbara Scrapbooks
918 Chapala St., Santa Barbara
805.962.5099, sbscrapbooks.com
Card-makers, stamp fanatics and diehard scrapbookers will swoon with a single step into this bright retail space brimming with 10,000 paper-craft products, from heirloom-quality photo albums to reproductions of antique perfume bottle labels. The shop holds regular workshops on all kinds of folding, cutting and gluing tricks. But the most popular event is its Friday Fun Nites, when, for just $20, up to eight scrapbookers get to spread out on the store's broad boardroom tables and kick back in cush leather chairs, munching pizza and dessert while cropping photos and shopping for ribbon from 4 p.m. until midnight.

2000 degrees
1206 State St., Santa Barbara
805.882.1817
This ceramics workshop in the heart of downtown's cultural arts district invites novices and experts alike to come in and paint pottery and glass, or create a tile mosaic, while listening to cool tunes on the stereo. Pick from a vast assortment of shapes — frames, pitchers, candelabra — and plop down at a tall table with the paint palette of your choice. When you're done creating your work of art, the studio will fire it for you in one of three onsite kilns. It will ship it, or you can pick up your masterpiece five days later. You pay for the item you paint, plus a $5 workshop fee per person, but you can stay and work for as long as you like.

Q & A: Hank Pitcher

Santa Barbara has changed a lot since Hank Pitcher was growing up here. "It is more crowded and less bohemian," says the artist, who studied art — and now teaches it — at UCSB. A member of the preservationist painters club called the Oak Group, he is drawn to the local coastline both as an artist and a surfer. Perhaps Pitcher's most iconic work is his series of bright, simply rendered surfboards sticking straight up out of the Santa Barbara sand. He chatted with Starshine Roshell about light, lemons and landscapes.

What's your fondest memory of growing up here?
Warm nights when the smell of citrus blossoms from the lemon orchards covering most of western Santa Barbara was so strong that you could smell it on the beach. Surfing with a few friends on Christmas morning.

Why, as an artist, are you drawn to surfboards?
Surfboards represent science, hope and tribal affiliation. Plus, I like the way they reflect

sunlight. Painting all these dimensions at once is challenging and engaging, and I put a lot of effort into making it look simple. In the same way that a good surfboard harmonizes many complex hydro-dynamic principles to make it glide, I want to give people who look at my paintings a good ride.

What makes Santa Barbara so particularly paintable?
The beaches run east-west, which makes the sunlight and shadows run parallel to the shore.

What's your favorite work of public art in town?
Jeff Shelton's Ablitt House. Also the County Courthouse. Inside and out, the rooms, façades and landscaping are delightful, graceful and inspiring.

What's an unlikely place to see art in town?
The interior of the Arlington Theatre. I like the stars in the ceiling. I like the sandstone walls throughout Santa Barbara. Every one is different. One of my favorites is the retaining wall on Mission Ridge that starts at Los Olivos and follows the road up the hill.

Favorite local haunt?
The Paradise Café, and my wife's store, dressed. She has amazing pieces by the best designers in the world, and smart and beautiful women hang out there.

When you're not working, what are you doing?
I like going out with my wife and surfing and playing basketball with my sons. There are a lot of interesting people in this town, and I enjoy meals and conversation with them, at home or out at the great variety of restaurants.

If not Santa Barbara, where would you live … and paint?
I've looked, but I haven't found a place I like better.

Literary

Perhaps it is the call of the Santa Ynez Mountains, or perhaps it is the whisper of the Pacific Ocean. Whatever the reason, creative folks are called to Santa Barbara to write. This "community of voices" has long been a haven for wordsmiths, and those who love to write also love to read, as you'll see in the pages that follow.

The Words

All sorts of writers have been inspired by Santa Barbara over the years. Here are some of their words.

It was a peaceful, windless morning steeped in sun. The mingled smell of pines and low tide drifted across the street, and was replaced by the pervading faint fragrance of ceanothus, blooming in shades of blue and white along Mr. Palmer's walk.

> – *The Women on the Wall*
> Wallace Stegner, 1981

The first time I set foot in the state, in 1964, at the age of 7, the little town of Santa Barbara was presented to us as "the Athens of the West." Staring up from a row of eucalyptus trees, the ocean stretching out below – farther than the widest expanses of Oxford, England — the skies an exultant blue, everyone around with a light in his eyes, the hope that had brought him here, we could easily believe it.

> – Introduction to *My California*
> Pico Iyer, 2004

Where I live now in Santa Barbara it's mainly genre writers. Almost all, because no one else can afford to live there. I'm just lucky that I am the literary writer who can afford it. (Laughs) They sell a hundred books for every one I sell. I have something that they don't have, which they crave. Which is respect. But on the other hand, they never get reviewed or rarely, and they never get attacked. So they can just make their millions and be happy.

> – *Identity Theory* (literary magazine)
> T. C. Boyle, 2003

I watch the blue flanks of the Santa Ynez Mountains rise in the distance from the brush-covered hills as I drive through alternating swaths of sunshine and shade. But again that awful squint, and the scarlet words, WILL WORK FOR FOOD.

> – *Yardwork*
> Sheila Golburgh Johnson, 1998

Santa Barbara is a paradise; Disneyland is a paradise; the U.S. is a paradise. Paradise is just paradise. Mournful, monotonous, and superficial though it may be, it is paradise. There is no other.

> – *America*
> Jean Baudrillard, 1986

The Fountainblue Hotel and Apartments distinguished itself from the rest of the apartment courts in Isla Vista – a town composed almost entirely of students at UC Santa Barbara – by the fact that it had housed the San Francisco 49ers during their summer training the year before. The team had practiced on the enormous brown field nearby (brown except for several lush spots of bright green, where the recessed water sprinklers leaked continuously); but apparently had also rehearsed at least some of their plays in their rooms at the Fountainblue, for after they had left (in two air-conditioned buses), Mrs. Warner, the manager, found many enigmatic dents and lesions in the walls, which seemed to have been created by blunt instruments such as shoulder pads or elbows.

> – "K. 590," from *Best American Short Stories 1982*
> Nicholson Baker, 1982

Santa Barbara is a hard place to cover women in a film festival. You have to walk past lingerie and bikini stores to even get there.

> – *Off Our Backs*
> Batya Weinbaum, 2007

"Viva la Fiesta!" calls Rudy. "Viva la nalga!"

"Estoy bombo," grins Parrando, and blushes, pleased with himself. Parrando is up only a month, they call him El Canon because he has such a big one.

"They got the floats all line up," says Rudy. "All them little girls ready to march. Ay de mi!" He smacks his lips.

> – "Old Spanish Days," from *The Anarchist's Convention and Other Stories*
> John Sayles, 2005

To the right of me, the ocean was pounding at the beach, a muted thunder as restful as the sound of rain. Seagulls were screeching as they wheeled above the surf. The Pacific was the color of liquid steel, the waves a foamy mass of aluminum and chrome. The sand became a mirror where the water receded, reflecting the softness of the morning sky. The horizon turned a salmon pink as the sun crept into view. Long arms of coral light stretched out along the horizon, where clouds were beginning to mass from the promised storm front. The air was cold and richly scented with salt spray and seaweed.

> – *"H" is for Homicide*
> Sue Grafton, 1990

The blue-white dazzle of sun, sand and surf was like an arc-furnace. But I felt some breeze from the water when we got out of the car. A few languid clouds moved inland over our heads. A little high plane was gamboling among them like a terrier in a henyard.

> – "Find the Woman," from *The Name Is Archer*
> Ross MacDonald, 1950

Santa Barbara is both a universal and particular place. An American small town of class and race and neighborhood divisions, a Chinese box full of hidden parts, little compartments and surprises.

> – *Tales of Santa Barbara*
> Dean Stewart, 1994

I was moving frenetically from bedroom to living room packing for a road trip with my best friend, Jack Cole. We were headed to the Santa Ynez Valley and a week of wine tasting before he was to be married the following Sunday. Though I couldn't afford this impromptu excursion, I desperately needed to get out of L.A.

> – *Sideways: A Novel*
> Rex Pickett, 2004

The large islands some fifteen miles out seemed close enough to touch. Brown pelicans skimmed low above the sea. Small boats sailed offshore even in March. The girl in white played volleyball up the beach. Boys all blond and quick. Girls in bikinis, their thighs too heavy.

The sun moved down toward evening. In New York the sun set to the west over the land. This sun was also setting over the land. That was wrong. The sun should set far out over the sea. The sun was in the wrong place. Or the sea.

> – *The Girl in White*
> Dennis Lynds, 1982

Summer is the best time on the Island of the Blue Dolphins. The sun is warm then and the winds blow milder out of the west.... It was during these days that the ship might return and now I spent most of my time on the rock, looking out from the high headland into the east, toward the country where my people had gone, across the sea that was never-ending.

Once while I watched I saw a small object which I took to be the ship, but I knew that it was a whale spouting. During those summer days I saw nothing else.

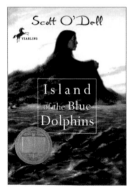

> – *Island of the Blue Dolphins*
> (the fictional name for San Nicolas, one of the Channel Islands)
> Scott O'Dell, 1960

The Literary Life

Santa Barbara has always been a haven for writers. British Nobel Prize–winner John Galsworthy wrote part of his epic trilogy, *The Forsyte Saga*, while staying at the San Ysidro Ranch in the 1920s. In 1951, also at the San Ysidro Ranch, novelist James Agee holed up with John Huston to work on the screenplay for *The African Queen*. Sinclair Lewis lived downtown during the 1940s; the great short story writer Raymond Carver taught at UCSB in the 1970s; and in the 1960s, Santa Barbara's most famous husband-and-wife writing team, Ken (Ross Macdonald) and Margaret Millar were often seen prowling around the courthouse seeking information and inspiration for their mystery novels.

These days, hometown writer Sue Grafton has become one of the nation's top mystery writers by spinning tales about private eye Kinsey Millhone and her hometown of Santa Teresa, which everyone knows is really Santa Barbara. Many other writers, including Fannie Flagg, Pico Iyer, T. C. Boyle, Alan Folsom, Gayle Lynds and Audrey Woods, call this area home, as do a host of screenwriters, who retreat to Santa Barbara from the business of Hollywood to focus on the task of bringing their stories and characters to life.

It's no surprise that along with this vibrant writing community comes a gaggle of writing- and book-related events. Here are some of our favorites.

CALM Celebrity Authors' Luncheon
Calm4Kids.org
Even with dozens of commendable charity events to choose from in Santa Barbara, the Child Abuse Listening & Mediation (CALM) Celebrity Authors' Luncheon is a perennial standout. For more than twenty years, the CALM Auxiliary has joined forces with the town's literati and glitterati to put on a luncheon to raise money to help prevent, assess and treat child abuse. Chaired by the dynamic duo of Sharon Bifano and Stephanie Ortale every year since its inception in 1987, this springtime gathering at Fess Parker's Double Tree Resort celebrates both the love of books and the good work done by CALM.

The luncheon has staged interviews with more than 70 authors and celebrities over the years, including Lisa See, Sue Grafton, Jane Russell, Barnaby Conrad, Michael Crichton, Julia Child, Ray Bradbury, Fannie Flagg, Maria Shriver and Jonathan Winters. In addition to the featured authors, local writers also participate, sticking around all day to chat and sign books, with all the profits going to support this worthy organization.

Creative Writing Program at Santa Barbara City College
CreativeWriting.sbcc.edu
Launched in fall of 2007, the Santa Barbara City College Creative Writing Certificate program is the first of its type in this area. It offers advanced courses in writing fiction, drama, poetry and nonfiction for a very low price.

Santa Barbara Book & Author Festival
SBBookFestival.org
Held in the fall, this literary festival presents to the community a weekend-long celebration of books. Each year it draws larger audiences and attracts a greater variety of panelists, along with nearly 100 booths offering books, author appearances and information on nonprofits. The Family Stage hosts entertainment for children and families, including readings from students of the California Poets in the Schools program. You'll also find readings and author panels.

Local gal Fannie Flagg speaking to her writing compatriots at the Santa Barbara Writers Conference.

Santa Barbara Writers Conference
SBWriters.com
Every June more than 400 writers gather at the Santa Barbara Writers Conference for five days of meeting their peers, hearing from successful authors and interacting with publishing professionals. Guest writers have included Joseph Wambaugh, Carolyn See, Joan Didion, T. C. Boyle, Jane Smiley, Erica Jong and Pico Iyer; Ray Bradbury has opened every conference since its founding in the 1970s. The conference also sponsors a March poetry event, an annual "café" at which unpublished writers are invited to read their works, and year-round weekend intensives for advanced writers.

South Coast Writing Project Young Writers Camp
kady.education.ucsb.edu
Held every summer at UCSB, this camp offers students in grades two to nine the opportunity to try all kinds of writing, regardless of their skill levels. Teachers build campers' confidence, inspire creative thinking and teach specific writing skills.

Speaking of Stories
SpeakingofStories.org
Speaking of Stories has a core theatrical group that presents a lively series of readings of short stories by prominent authors. The series also includes guest appearances by such writers as David Sedaris and Tobias Wolff, as well as readings by actors like Jay Thomas and Joe Spano. The organization operates Word Up!, an educational outreach program geared to at-risk youth, which uses spoken-word performances to improve literacy and self-confidence.

Women's Literary Festival
WomensLiteraryFestival.com
A relatively new event on the scene, inaugurated in 2006, this festival works with the Santa Barbara Public Library to celebrate women authors. Past participating writers have included Alisa Valdes-Rodriguez, Rebecca Walker, Gail Tsukiyama and poet Sojourner Kincaid Rolle. The festival emphasizes diversity, literacy and social justice.

Bookstores to Prowl

Titles for the seeker at the Bookstore at the Vedanta Temple.

Barnes & Noble
Paseo Nuevo, 829 State St., Santa Barbara
805.962.8509, bn.com
As far as Barnes & Noble stores go, this one is
on the smaller side, but it does stock a respectable variety of popular books and periodicals,
with a good-size children's-and-teen section,
as well as a Starbucks from which you can take
in the parade of Paseo shoppers.

The Book Den
11 E. Anapamu St., Santa Barbara
805.962.3321, bookden.com
Half a block off State Street, the Book Den has
been a Santa Barbara favorite for nearly 70
years. It stocks tens of thousands of new, used
and out-of-print titles in a clean, bright and
well-organized store. It's a wonderful place to
browse.

The Book Loft
1680 Mission Dr., Solvang
805.688.6010, bookloftsolvang.com
This full-service bookstore has a separate upstairs store, the Solvang Book Company, which
sells used and antiquarian books, with a focus
on titles from the Scandinavian countries. The
Book Loft hosts signings and readings, boasts
an extensive children's section, and owns the
neighboring Bulldog Café, where readers can

refuel with coffee and snacks. Looking for
works by local writers? This is the place to go.

The Bookstore at the Vedanta Temple
925 Ladera Lane, Montecito
805.969.5697, vedanta.org/vssc/centers/
sb.html
Located next to the lovely and peaceful South
Indian temple, this store is well stocked with
religious classics and hard-to-find books on
the major religions of the world. The store also
carries incense, religious statues, music and
imported gifts.

Borders Books & Music
900 State St., Santa Barbara
805.899.3668
7000 Marketplace Dr., Goleta
805.968.1370, bordersstores.com
Yes, it's a huge chain, but unlike the big-box
stores that sell books, Borders does a good
job of supporting the community by promoting local authors and giving to a multitude of
literacy-related causes. Both the downtown
Santa Barbara and Goleta locations stock a
diverse range of books and magazines, as well
as the usual cafés, which are popular spots for
reading, studying and hanging out.

Books to the ceiling, books to the floor… Chaucer's Books.

Chaucer's Books
Loreto Plaza, 3321 State St., Santa Barbara
805.682.6787, chaucers.booksense.com
With an extensive children's section staffed by knowledgeable book lovers and an incredible variety of adult titles, covering a very wide range of topics, Chaucer's is one of the last of the old-fashioned, locally owned bookstores. It's crammed floor to ceiling with books – more than 150,000 titles – and a warm, well-informed cast of characters stands ready to help you choose just the right book. If they don't have it, they'll order it, and it's usually there within a few days. Chaucer's motto is "No music or coffee machines, just lots of great books and great people." But if you need a caffeine fix to cozy up to your new book, take it a few doors over to Renaud's for a memorable croissant or tart and an excellent cappuccino.

Isla Vista Bookstore
6553 Pardall Rd., Goleta
805.968.3600, ivbooks.com
Smart students have been saving money on new and used textbooks here since 1965. Located a block from the UCSB campus, Isla Vista Bookstore perpetually stocks more than 75,000 titles previously used in classes at UCSB, as well as Gaucho clothing and memorabilia and products from local artists.

Paperback Alley Used Books
5840 Hollister Ave., Goleta
805.967.1051
Deceptively larger than it looks from the street, Paperback Alley is a great place to find used books on just about every subject you can think of. The books are reasonably priced (about half the cover price if they're in good condition), and you'll find particularly good collections of best sellers and genre fiction: romance, mysteries and science fiction.

Paperback Exchange
1838 Cliff Dr., Santa Barbara
805.966.3725
It may be small, but Paperback Exchange has more than 13,000 books crammed into its strip-mall storefront on the Mesa. If you're looking for a book on your way to the beach, this is the perfect place to stop. You can even exchange it for something else when you finish.

Tecolote Book Shop
1470 E. Valley Rd., Montecito
805.969.4977
Closed Sun.
The famous and not so famous come through these charming doors to purchase, sign and sell their books. With a lovely grassy area out front to complement its 1,400 square feet of shelf space, Tecolote has hosted signings by such authors as Sue Grafton, T. C. Boyle, Barnaby Conrad and Jonathan Winters – but it's as accessible to local self-published authors as it is to famous ones. This independent shop contains about 12,000 titles, and its helpful staff is always willing to go the extra mile to order a book, including tracking down hard-to-find and out-of-print titles.

Thrasher Books
827 Santa Barbara St., Santa Barbara
805.568.1936
Sandwiched between C'est Cheese and Our Daily Bread bakery, this used-book shop is a great place to browse before or after picking up your comestibles. Opened in 1997 by Karen Thrasher, the place is packed with a worthwhile selection of fiction, nonfiction and children's books.

Montecito's literary hub, Tecolote.

Bring Your Laptop: Where to Write

What makes a place good for writing? Good coffee, a congenial staff, enough space to hang out, a laid-back atmosphere and the presence of other lingerers. Along with a writer-friendly vibe, you'll also find free wireless internet access – unless otherwise noted – at these locations.

Borders Books & Music
900 State St., Santa Barbara
805.899.3668
7000 Marketplace Dr., Goleta
805.968.1370, bordersstores.com
Both locations have plenty of sunlight and lots of seating, making them comfortable places to set up shop and write for a while. You have to pay (T-Mobile) for the WiFi.

Coffee Cat
1201 Anacapa St., Santa Barbara
805.962.7164
Located catty-corner from the courthouse and right across the street from the county staff offices, this place is always hopping. It's a great spot to pick up the local buzz before it hits the newspapers.

The Daily Grind
2001 De La Vina St., Santa Barbara
805.687.4966
Lots of indoor and outdoor seating make this a fine coffeehouse for writing – plus, the sandwiches are delicious and big enough to split. It also makes really good soups (don't miss the chicken-and-dumpling).

Goleta Coffee Company
177 S. Turnpike Rd., Santa Barbara
805.964.8344
It has the same menu and coffee as the Daily Grind, but the San Marcos High School crowd and strip-mall location gives it a totally different vibe. When the kids are in class, the place is almost empty, making it a great place to write.

Good Cup
1819 Cliff Dr., Santa Barbara
805.963.8699
This coffeehouse reflects its upscale, healthy, family-oriented Mesa neighborhood. In addition to great coffee and a nice vibe, it has a cool selection of cards and gifts, with a bit of a new age/feminist bent. The WiFi is free after 4 p.m.

Java Station
4447 Hollister Ave., Santa Barbara
805.681.0202
Lots of comfy couches and seating make this a fine place to cozy up to your laptop. In fact, this chapter was written over a number of nonfat lattes with extra foam at Java Station. It's

The Call of the Great Outdoors
Who needs to plug in when there's inspiration all around you? Here are some of our favorite outdoor spots to write.

Chase Palm Park
Cabrillo Blvd., Santa Barbara
sbparksandrecreation.com
This charming park offers plenty of spots for quiet contemplation alongside its creek.

East Beach Grill
1118 E. Cabrillo Blvd., Santa Barbara
805.965.8805
Breathe in that ocean air, watch the seagulls fly by and absorb the sounds of the pounding waves. Act one, scene one: "It was a beautiful day in Santa Barbara, and I felt inspired."

Santa Barbara Botanic Garden
1212 Mission Canyon Rd., Santa Barbara
805.682.4726, sbbg.org
You couldn't ask for a more beautiful spot in which to commune with nature. Plus, there are plenty of benches on which you can plant yourself and your notebook when inspiration strikes.

Santa Barbara Zoo
500 Niños Dr., Santa Barbara
805.962.5339, santabarbarazoo.org
Park yourself on the lawn near the giraffes. What better ways to spark your muse than listening to the sounds of children playing and taking in this incredible ocean view?

Stevens Neighborhood Park
258 Canon Dr., Santa Barbara
Sitting at a Stevens Park picnic table provides a wonderful view of the canyon reaching up San Roque to the Santa Ynez range.

packed in the morning but settles down a bit later in the day.

Mojo Coffee
7127 Hollister Ave., Goleta
805.571.7070
You'll find lots of university students studying at Mojo, so the atmosphere is relatively quiet – and the service is the friendliest in town.

Muddy Waters Coffee House
508 E. Haley St., Santa Barbara
805.966.9328, personal.linkline.com/muddy-waters
The service is "pierced and tattooed with attitude," and the décor is straight outta Santa Cruz, but the lattes and the people-watching are first-rate.

NorthStar Coffee Company
918 State St., Santa Barbara
805.965.5593, northstarcoffee.com
Located in the heart of downtown, this place makes gorgeous lattes. It's hard to concentrate on your writing at the sidewalk tables because of the passing State Street parade, but if you can find a table by the fireplace inside, you'll be a happy scribbler indeed.

Peet's Coffee & Tea
3905 State St., Santa Barbara
805.687.9952, peets.com
This Bay Area-rooted chain is known for its robust coffee and careful approach to brewing tea, and it attracts your more intellectual sorts of foodies. No WiFi, but there are lots of plugs around for your laptop.

Red's
211 Helena St., Santa Barbara
805.966.5906, redssb.com
The "anti-Starbucks" in the heart of the Funk Zone, this place gets an A+ for its artsy-smart ambience and friendly staff.

Starbucks
1046 Coast Village Rd., Montecito
805.565.1935, starbucks.com
Most of the local Starbucks are soulless and crowded, and they all charge for wireless access, so we're not fans. But in this one, you can simultaneously see producers gossiping about the latest hot screenplay with the same passion with which Westmont students discuss "the Word." Looking for character inspiration? This place has it in spades.

Quiet tables and natural light are plentiful at the Santa Barbara Central Library.

Santa Barbara Public Libraries
sbplibrary.org
Okay, there's no food or drink allowed in the library, but there are cubicles aplenty, as well as nice, friendly staff members on hand when you need help with research.

Carpinteria Branch Library
5141 Carpinteria Ave., Carpinteria
805.684.4314

Goleta Branch Library
500 N. Fairview Ave., Goleta
805.964.7878

Central Library
40 E. Anapamu St., Santa Barbara
805.962.7653

Montecito Branch Library
1469 E. Valley Rd., Montecito
805.969.5063

Eastside Branch Library
1102 E. Montecito St., Santa Barbara
805.963.3727

Solvang Branch Library
1745 Mission Dr., Solvang
805.688.4214

Vices & Spices
3558 State St., Santa Barbara
805.687.7196
One of the oldest coffee and tea joints in town, this is a great place to run into old friends and find out the latest scuttlebutt. People still play checkers, read books and write in journals, instead of talking on their cell phones and scanning the online headlines. No WiFi, so you'll have to work offline, but isn't it easier to concentrate without the distraction of e-mail?

Q & A: Marcia Meier

Owner/director Marcia Meier poured her heart and soul – along with her bank account – into the challenge of retaining the legacy of excellence that the Santa Barbara Writers Conference has enjoyed for the past 36 years. She continues to refine the offerings, having added a poetry conference, a young-writers' program and master classes for professional writers. Marcia spoke with Leslie Dinaberg about living the literary life in Santa Barbara.

What's your favorite part of the conference?
Orientation, which is the first day, and on the other end of the week, the awards banquet. When people come for orientation, there is so much excitement and energy, as well as a lot of trepidation on the part of the newbies. You see the people who have come before embrace the new people and give them a hand. I get to be the master of ceremonies. Then at the end of the week, it's so great to see the awards given out, and the writing that's been done, and the tears and the emotion and the people. It's really fulfilling.

Do you ever take a laptop and write around town?
I have a MacBook and I love it, but it's almost too cumbersome for me. I can't write poetry on the computer anyway – I have to write longhand. I also have written some short stories longhand in coffee shops in Santa Ynez. I think there's something about the slowing down that allows you to go deep into yourself, and that's where my poetry comes from. I have to take the time to slow down and allow it to come through the pen.

You've got a diverse background as a reporter, an editor, a journalism teacher and an author. What's your favorite kind of writing?
I'm doing a lot of nonfiction assignments now, but I think what feeds me most is my poetry and my fiction writing. I also have a children's book that I've been working on for a number of years that's almost ready. I've written more poetry in the last few years, and I think I'm going to pull it together as a collection and call it Parking Lot Poetry, *because most of them I wrote while sitting in a parking lot waiting for my daughter.*

You wrote a coffee-table book about Santa Barbara (*Santa Barbara: Paradise on the Pacific*). What are some of your favorite local spots?
I spend a lot of time at Hendry's Beach, because I have two dogs and we walk every day. I watch for the low tides and time it so we can walk as far as possible. I also love Ellwood. I love to go up to the mountains. Santa Ynez Valley is also one of my favorite places. And on weekend evenings, I love to go downtown – I go to the movies and then hang out at Borders and have coffee and look at the books. I really love to do that.

If you could be invisible anywhere in Santa Barbara, where would it be and what would you do?
(Laughing) I would probably run naked down State Street!

Reaching Out

Few places in the country can rival the number of nonprofits and philanthropists harbored behind Santa Barbara's stunning Mediterranean exteriors. It may, in fact, hold the U.S. record for nonprofits per capita – with more than 1,500 charitable, religious, social and cultural programs. And it's home to a remarkable quantity of philanthropists, who not only pull out their checkbooks but happily roll up their sleeves. Not bad for a seemingly sleepy beach town!

Nonprofits That Matter

Assistance League of Santa Barbara
1249 Veronica Springs Rd., Santa Barbara
805.687.9717, assistanceleaguesb.org
This branch of the national volunteer organization has about 300 members who devote more than 34,000 hours yearly to supporting needy children through scholarships, tutoring, mentoring and provisions, from books to clothing. They also work extensively with senior citizens and the disabled. The Assisteens program introduces teenagers to the concept of giving, and the auxiliary, Las Aletas (Little Wings), offers busy women the chance to help without the same hefty hourly participation as the Assistance League volunteers.

Casa Esperanza Homeless Center
816 Cacique St., Santa Barbara
805.884.8481
Casa Esperanza's aim is to assist the homeless in getting back on their feet and to find them permanent housing. The shelter is open year-round to participants in recovery programs, and a day center offers counseling. During the winter months a 200-bed center provides shelter from the elements.

Child Abuse Listening & Mediation (CALM)
1236 Chapala St., Santa Barbara
805.965.2376, calm4kids.org
Founded in 1970 by Santa Barbara nurse Claire Miles as a way to prevent child abuse before it happens, CALM focuses its energies on counseling and education for parents, as well as support and therapy for abused and endangered children.

Children's Creative Project
4400 Cathedral Oaks Rd., Santa Barbara
805.964.4711, sbceo.org/ccp/index.shtml
This arts-education organization brings young people together with professional artists. The programs include workshops with resident artists and performances by professional touring artists. Not to be missed is the annual fundraiser, I Madonnari, a chalk-painting festival held at the Mission on Memorial Day weekend.

Citizens Planning Association & Foundation
916 Anacapa St., Santa Barbara
805.966.3979, citizensplanning.org
One of the reasons you don't see massive buildings, flashing lights and view-blocking billboards in Santa Barbara is the Citizens

Girls Inc. girls suit up for an after-school gymnastics class.

Planning Association, which works to manage development and protect the area's natural assets and quality of life.

Court Appointed Special Advocates (CASA)
402 E. Gutierrez St., Santa Barbara
805.879.1735, sbcasa.org
The goal of CASA of Santa Barbara County is to prevent abused, neglected and abandoned children from becoming lost in the Juvenile Dependency system and to find them safe, permanent homes as quickly as possible. CASA volunteers are advocates for children; they work to assist them through the judicial and social services system. It always needs smart, focused volunteer advocates to help kids, and no, you don't need to be a lawyer.

Direct Relief International
27 S. La Patera Lane, Santa Barbara
805.964.4767, directrelief.org
Founded in Santa Barbara in 1948, Direct Relief provides medical assistance and disaster relief, both domestically and internationally, as well as medicine, supplies and equipment to clinics and organizations that help the poor exclusively in the United States.

Domestic Violence Solutions
Santa Barbara: 805.964.5245
Lompoc: 805.736.0965
Santa Maria: 805.925.2160
Santa Ynez: 805.686.4390
dvsolutions.org
This worthy organization offers shelter, counseling and support for battered women and women in crisis. The group also educates the

community to help prevent violence against women, sometimes in collaboration with other groups dedicated to social change and the protection of women's rights.

Girls Inc. of Greater Santa Barbara
P.O. Box 236, Santa Barbara
girlsincsb.org
Championed by high-powered locals like Oprah Winfrey, this branch of the national group Girls Inc. runs an extensive after-school and summer-camp program for local girls that includes a range of activities from art to cooking to gymnastics, all designed to build skills, confidence, self-reliance and a positive body image. Girls Inc. always needs volunteers.

Heal the Ocean
735 State St., Ste. 201, Santa Barbara
805.965.7570, healtheocean.org
Heal the Ocean follows a simple philosophy: The ocean can no longer be used as a dump. Instead of lobbying the government to take action, this science-based nonprofit and its staff and volunteers take the reins and study the issues themselves, then present practical solutions for preventing, and reversing, ocean pollution.

Junior League of Santa Barbara
229 E. Victoria St., Santa Barbara
805.963.2704, jlsantabarbara.org
This blue-blood women's organization is dedicated to promoting volunteerism. The focus in recent years has been youth literacy, and as part of that the Junior Leaguers have taken on remodeling the children's area at the main public library downtown. The gals also sponsor the terrific annual Literacy Ball, as well as the very popular American Girl fashion show.

National Charity League
nclsb.org/Santa_Barbara/Default.asp
The National Charity League is a mother-daughter organization committed to community service, leadership development and cultural experiences. The mothers – referred to as Patronesses – and the daughters – called Ticktockers – work together on a variety of charitable projects, most notably hands-on work at Cottage Hospital. It's a great way to get teens connected and helping.

Orfalea Foundations
1283 Coast Village Circle, Montecito
805.565.7550, orfaleafoundations.org
Kinko's founder and former UCSB student Paul Orfalea and his family created the Orfalea Foundations – the Orfalea Fund and the Orfalea Family Foundation – to aid nonprofit programs in Santa Barbara, Ventura and San Luis Obispo counties. Their generosity runs the gamut, but it is focused primarily in the areas of early child-care, education and learning disabilities.

Santa Barbara Athletic Round Table
P.O. Box 3813, Santa Barbara
805.705.4949, sbart.org
It's been more than 30 years since Jerry Harwin, Caesar Uyesaka and Bill Bertka got together to create this all-volunteer organization dedicated to supporting student athletes. It has grown into a beloved community organization, with weekly luncheons that encourage and recognize athletes and coaches at all levels; it also provides scholarships to help students achieve their scholastic and athletic dreams.

Santa Barbara Foundation
15 E. Carrillo St., Santa Barbara
805.963.1873, sbfoundation.org
Established in 1928 as one of the first community foundations in the United States, this is Santa Barbara County's largest private source of funding for nonprofit agencies. In 2006 it awarded $23 million to area nonprofits and $2.3 million to local students. The Santa Barbara Foundation invests in a diverse range of programs: education, health, human services, culture, recreation and the environment.

Santa Barbara Performing Arts League
805.563.8068, sbperformingartsleague.org
Just about every performance-arts organization in town belongs to the Performing Arts League, an effective cooperative that fosters appreciation and awareness of the high quality and variety of performances presented in Santa Barbara. It has successfully expanded audiences for theater, dance and music.

Santa Ynez Valley Therapeutic Riding Program

195 Refugio Rd., Santa Ynez
805.688.9534

Horses are a way of life in the valley, and the Santa Ynez Valley Therapeutic Riding Program gives people with disabilities an opportunity to learn horseback riding in a safe environment.

Scholarship Foundation of Santa Barbara

2253 Las Positas Rd., Santa Barbara
805.687.6065, sbscholarship.org

This fine hometown foundation offers scholarships, no-interest loans and free financial aid advice to students headed for college, graduate school or vocational programs. It's given more than 21,000 students aid since its founding in 1962.

Inside the Unity Shoppe.

Teddy Bear Cancer Foundation

133 E. De La Guerra St., Santa Barbara
805.962.7466, teddybearcancerfoundation.org

Founded by Nikki Simon-Katz after she saw what a friend went through when her child had cancer, this worthy organization assists families of children with cancer. It provides parents with financial assistance, money-management advice and support groups, as well as activities for children and their family members.

United Boys & Girls Clubs

632 E. Canon Perdido St., Santa Barbara
805.962.2382, unitedbg.org

Working with Santa Barbara's youth since 1945, this group now has four clubhouses that offer day care, summer camps and sports, art, academics and leadership-development programs. The Boys & Girls Clubs fulfill an unquestionable need for local youth and their families: a way to keep children off the streets, out of trouble and in a positive learning environment after school and during school vacations. It relies on a professional staff but always needs financial support.

Unity Shoppe, Inc.

1219 State St., Santa Barbara
805.965.4122, unityshoppe.org

The Unity Shoppe serves Santa Barbara County as a central distribution center for food, clothing and basic necessities for more than 14,000 low-income people a year. The annual Unity Telethon fund-raiser was born in 1987 when Kenny Loggins joined forces with the Unity Shoppe to raise money for toys and essentials for local kids. Loggins remains an annual performer, and now he's joined by a host of celebrities, including such locals as Jeff Bridges, Bo Derek, the Red Hot Chili Peppers, Toad the Wet Sprocket, Jimmy Messina and Dennis Miller. Want to help? It can always use more sorters, pressers, grant writers, drivers and shop clerks.

Women's Fund of Santa Barbara

c/o Santa Barbara Foundation, 15 E. Carrillo St., Santa Barbara
805.963.1873, ext. 116, womensfundsb.org

No volunteer time, no fund-raising, no expensive-to-put-on events and no tables to fill – this fund simply accepts donations and then gives grants that make a significant difference in the community. In just four years of existence, the Women's Fund already has donated $1,425,000 to nonprofit projects that benefit thousands of women, children and families in the greater Santa Barbara area.

Griffin Saxon hands out a stocked backpack as part of FUND's Project Healthy Neighbors.

One Kid Helping

Adults aren't the only ones who get in on the charitable action in Santa Barbara. In 2003 Ken Saxon and Craig Zimmerman created a group called FUND (Families Uniting to Nurture Dreams) to help teach their children about the importance of giving back to the community. Ken's 13-year-old son, Griffin Saxon, talked to Leslie Dinaberg about his volunteer work.

What do you think about FUND?
At first I didn't really know much, I just went to the occasional meetings. But as I got older, I began to understand more. I started donating to nonprofits on my own in third grade.

What's been your most memorable experience?
Probably working at Project Healthy Neighbors, which is a health fair for homeless people. These people were getting shots, tests, and a lot of things they don't like – our job was to give the "trophy" when they got through it. The "trophy" was a backpack, a survival kit with food, clothing, basic stuff and a handwritten card made by a kid in FUND.

How did you feel coming face-to-face with homeless people?
Well, at first a lot of them looked scary. Though, as people say, you can't judge a book by its cover. Most of them weren't as scary as I thought. They were really sweet. It was great to see some of their reactions when they saw the cards. I think they realized that someone cares. One thing I noticed was that these weren't scary runaway kids; these were older people. Since they have been on the streets longer, they know each other. I loved seeing people saying hello to each other, because it made me think, Maybe they don't have homes, or families, but they have each other.

What a nice thought.
At the health fair a man showed us a photo and said, "This is what I looked like before I was home-less." It was an old passport photo of a well-dressed man. I could barely see the resemblance. Then he showed us a photo of a girl and said, "This was my wife, but when she passed away, it went downhill, and I started drinking." I realized that these people aren't big criminals, or bad guys, so when you pass them on the street, you don't have to give them money, you could just smile at them.

14 Spiritual Centers

All Saints-by-the-Sea Episcopal Church
83 Eucalyptus Lane, Montecito
805.969.4771, allsaintsbythesea.org
All Saints is a thriving community that attracts members from as far as Carpinteria in the south and Goleta in the north. Worshippers gather in the stunning Montecito Craftsman-style church, which is known for its family, youth and senior ministries, its choir and a well-regarded preschool program.

Calvary Chapel Santa Barbara
1 N. Calle Cesar Chavez, Santa Barbara
805.730.1400, calvarychapelsb.com
This Christian church offers English and Hispanic services and has just acquired a radio station. It has many youth ministries, starting with infant care during services, moving on to vacation bible school for grade schoolers and going up to outings for high schoolers. And this being Santa Barbara, there's a surf ministry.

Church of Jesus Christ of Latter-Day Saints
2107 Santa Barbara St. (First Ward, Spanish Ward, Genealogical Library)
805.687.9129, lds.org
478 Cambridge Dr., Goleta (Second and Third Ward)
805.967.4812
524 Cordoba Rd., Goleta (University Ward)
805.968.4111
1501 Linden Ave., Carpinteria (Carpinteria Ward)
Santa Barbara has a large and vibrant Mormon community, with meetinghouses from Carpinteria to Goleta. The primary family worship services (sacrament meetings) welcome visitors. For schedule information on all local services and wards call 805.967.4812.

The storybook All Saints-by-the-Sea.

Congregation B'nai B'rith
1000 San Antonio Creek Rd., Santa Barbara
805.964.7869, cbbsb.org
The largest synagogue in Santa Barbara, Congregation B'nai B'rith is a center for the Reform Jewish community. In addition to religious education for adults and children, the synagogue runs a preschool. Led by Rabbi Steve Cohen, who has a large following from his former position at UCSB's Hillel, B'nai B'rith runs a host of social programs, as well as lectures and performances by visiting writers and artists.

El Montecito Presbyterian Church
1455 E. Valley Rd., Montecito
805.969.5041, elmopres.org
Located in the heart of Montecito, "Elmo," as locals call it, has approximately 500 members and a popular and well-regarded Christian-oriented school for preschool through eighth-graders (elmoschool.com).

First United Methodist Church
305 E. Anapamu St., Santa Barbara
805.963.3579, fumcsb.org
This downtown Santa Barbara church has roots that go back to 1854, when Methodist minister Adam Bland arrived as the first Protestant to visit then-Catholic Santa Barbara. Today the church is still going strong, with children's programs, a choir, a women's group and service efforts, including helping to rebuild Southern black churches that have been victims of arson.

Immaculate Heart Center for Spiritual Renewal
888 San Ysidro Lane, Montecito
805.969.2474, immaculateheartcenter.org
Formerly a Catholic novitiate, this peaceful Montecito getaway is now an interfaith retreat center offering everything from group activities to an environment conducive to quiet contemplation and prayer. It's located in a historic estate house on 26 breathtaking acres, which it shares with La Casa de Maria (see below).

La Casa de Maria Retreat & Conference Center
800 El Bosque Rd., Montecito
805.969.5031, lacasademaria.org
People of all faiths are invited to hold day, overnight or weeklong retreats at this dreamy spot in the Montecito foothills. Director Stephanie Glatt says the center has four goals: "One is to deepen spirituality, one is to promote the

common good of our community, one is to nurture a culture of peace and social justice, and the fourth is to work for the renewal of the Earth. All of the programs that we offer and all of the groups that use our facilities fall into one of those four categories, which makes it a great place to be, because that's what everybody here is about."

La Casa de Maria.

Mount Cavalry Benedictine Retreat House & Monastery

P.O. Box 1296, Santa Barbara
805.962.9855, mount-calvary.org
This Benedictine monastery welcomes guests who come for everything from short, individual stays to organized retreats, group meetings and conferences. Visitors rave about the beauty of the main Spanish-Colonial house, which occupies a ridge 1,250 feet above the city with sweeping views of the ocean. Guest rooms, including meals, are $75 per person on weeknights and $175 for the entire weekend.

St. Barbara Greek Orthodox Church

1205 San Antonio Creek Rd., Santa Barbara
805.683.4492,
Roman Catholic missionaries may have named Santa Barbara, but in fact Saint Barbara is the martyr and key figure in the Greek Orthodox and Eastern Orthodox faiths. With its religious and social life centered on a spectacular white church in the green foothills, this is a friendly parish, with bible study, youth activities and Byzantine music. The annual summer Greek Festival is a terrific event known for its tasty food, music and good cheer.

St. Barbara Parish at the Old Mission

2201 Laguna St., Santa Barbara
805.682.4713, sbmission.org
This Catholic church is located in the historic Mission Santa Barbara, the tenth of the California missions, founded by the Spanish Franciscans in 1786. Besides being an active parish, with masses, community outreach, a choir and CCD classes, it's also a center for

the larger community, as the home of many of Santa Barbara's most beloved events and festivals. The Old Mission is also open for daily self-guided tours between 9 a.m. and 5 p.m.; call 805.682.4149 for details.

San Lorenzo Seminary

1802 Sky Dr., Santa Ynez
805.688.5630, sanlorenzo.org
This seminary run by Capuchin Franciscans in a bucolic area of the Santa Ynez Valley gives lay people the opportunity for individual or group retreats. A two-night retreat including meals is $140 per person, and instruction is available.

Unitarian Society of Santa Barbara

1535 Santa Barbara St., Santa Barbara
805.965.4583, ussb.org
Like all good Unitarian communities, Santa Barbara's is socially active and extremely inclusive. Some of the programs include morning meditation, family fun nights, yoga, intergenerational coming-of-age services, congregational town meetings and classes in transcendental meditation. It also hosts worthwhile concerts that are open to the public.

Vedanta Temple in Montecito.

Vedanta Temple

927 Ladera Lane, Montecito
805.969.2903, vedanta.org
In 1959 this 45-acre Montecito temple became the first place in the U.S. to offer *sannyas*, or final monastic vows, for women entering the Ramakrishna Order of India. Run today by nine nuns, it hosts lectures and classes as well as meditation, daily vespers and Sunday services. Located next to the temple, the Bookstore at the Vedanta Temple is stocked with religious classics and hard-to-find books on the major religions of the world.

Q & A: Thomas Tighe

Since Thomas Tighe arrived in Santa Barbara in 2000 to head Direct Relief International, the nonprofit humanitarian medical organization has made cash grants of more than $30 million and furnished more than $850 million worth of essential medicines, equipment and supplies to organizations providing health care for low-income people in 88 developing countries and all 50 U.S. states. Thomas spoke with Leslie Dinaberg about thinking – and acting – both globally and locally.

Yours is an incredibly successful global organization, yet it is located in a warehouse near the train tracks in Santa Barbara. Does it feel like Direct Relief could be anywhere other than where it is?

I don't think if you were going to start it today you would start it here, because this is not the hub of global health or pharmaceutical development. But one of the many good things about Santa Barbara is that it is an intersection of interesting people who have an incredible depth of experience and insight. There is no company in the U.S. that wouldn't want to have our board of directors. These folks have achieved remarkable success in their professional lives in all sorts of walks of life. Having so much talent in such a small place is extraordinary, and for that reason we've really benefited from the location.Besides, it's a great place to have meetings, because people will actually come!

Looking at Santa Barbara through a relief-worker's lens, what do you think is our biggest challenge?

It is in a vulnerable physical position … fire, earthquake, flooding or all three happening simultaneously present the kinds of scenarios that could make it inaccessible. The south Central Coast is singular, because it has limited access to roads. Fortunately, we have great public servants, including the smart people who developed some of the disaster-relief systems that are now used nationally, like the incident command system.

I don't think people realize that.

Almost any community in the world would be lucky to have the quality of thinking, talent and resources we have in this town, not to mention the planning that goes into local events, both at the governmental and private levels. That's another benefit of being in Santa Barbara: It's a small city, but thanks to the university, it's just big and sophisticated enough. There's a lot of complexity involved in running such a large university in such a fragile environment. They have to run through all sorts of disaster scenarios, and they are really good at it.

What else do you like about Santa Barbara?

That people love their city. There's a pride of residency that's unusual. It's not Texas-like pride, which is great in its own way. The Santa Barbara version is more understated, even elegant, but it is just as deeply rooted. People really think it's a special place, and so many of them work to make sure that on their watch, the good parts are maintained and even improved, while the bad parts are eliminated. These people are such terrific resources – and I say this as a relative newcomer who lacks the right to say it!

Santa Barbara is...

Green

The Santa Barbara region is one of the developed world's greenest places. The modern environmental movement was born right here, and residents have worked hard to make sure their paradise stays a paradise for generations to come. We're quickly becoming a global model for sustainable living. We think green, live green and teach green – and visitors can feel good about touring here without leaving much of a footprint, unless you're talking about footprints in the sand.

Birthplace of the Environmental Movement

How green are Santa Barbarans? So green that they are largely responsible for the birth of the modern environmental movement – and that's not just Al Gore blowing greenhouse gases.

On January 28, 1969, out in the middle of the Santa Barbara Channel, Union Oil's Platform A had a massive blowout. With highly flammable natural gas and mud spewing 90 feet into the air, the platform's workers activated their final defense, and slammed two giant steel rams over the well to seal it shut. Even though the well stayed capped, enormous pressure built up under the ocean floor, and five different ruptures popped in an east-west fault on the ocean floor, spewing crude oil and natural gas into the water.

One-Click Green Research
Green Santa Barbara.com
Local (but internationally famous) eco-company Simple Shoes teamed up with the Santa Barbara Conference & Visitors Bureau and Film Commission to create a one-stop web site on all things green: GreenSantaBarbara.com. It includes sections for tourists and residents, activities, suggestions for eco-friendly practices at home and work and a business section with green-minded enterprises. It's full of links to green organizations, stores and ideas.

Over the next eleven days, more than three million gallons of crude oil bubbled up, blackening an 800-square-mile area of the ocean's surface. Thirty-five miles of coastline were covered in thick tar, and the heavy crude muted the sound of the waves. Seals and dolphins were poisoned, gray whales avoided their normal migratory route through the channel, and thousands of birds were killed.

Fred L. Hartley, president of Union Oil, said, "I don't like to call it a disaster, because there has been no loss of human life. I am amazed at the publicity for the loss of a few birds."

It was that very statement that helped feed nascent environmentalism, giving it the impetus to become a full-blown movement. President Richard Nixon toured the disaster site, saying, "It is sad that it was necessary that Santa Barbara should be the example that had to bring it to the attention of the American people.... The Santa Barbara incident has frankly touched the conscience of the American people."

Radicalized Santa Barbarans of all political persuasions held huge rallies and protests, and the government responded. Legislators enacted clean-air and water acts and passed the 1970 National Environmental Policy Act (NEPA). NEPA required the federal government to hold open hearings and allow public comment on any planned development that might impact the environment. Also as a direct result of the spill, President Nixon established the Environmental Protection Agency.

The California Coastal Commission was formed, and the State Land Commission banned offshore drilling for sixteen years, until the Reagan Administration took office. The very first Earth Day occurred in 1970, and a number of local and national environmental groups were founded, including GOO (Get Oil Out) and the Environmental Defense Center. UCSB created an environmental studies program that morphed into today's Donald Bren School of Environmental Science & Management.

Santa Barbara's disaster helped spark a nationwide awareness of and movement toward fixing environmental problems. Today, that movement is finally opening its eyes to the international issue of global warming. We may look like we don't have a care in the world, but really, we have every care for the world.

Earth Day

communityenvironmentalcouncil.org

The idea for an annual Earth Day celebration originated right here in Santa Barbara. Wisconsin Senator Gaylord Nelson came in 1969 to check out the effects of the oil spill. The devastation horrified him. When he returned to D.C., he convinced Congress to pass a bill designating April 22 National Earth Day, devoted to educating the public about environmental protection.

About 20 million Americans in cities across the nation – including Santa Barbara – celebrated the first Earth Day in 1970. In 1990 the Community Environmental Council took over running the festival; that year, 30,000 people gathered to hear Jackson Browne and David Crosby sing for the cause.

Today, Santa Barbara's Earth Day festivities draw huge crowds to the County Courthouse Sunken Gardens. Presented by the Community Environmental Council and the UCSB Donald Bren School of Environmental Science & Management, it brings nearly 200 exhibitors to show how we can take steps to preserve the planet.

Kids learn how much energy it takes to power an incandescent bulb as compared to a compact fluorescent by pedaling a modified bike on Earth Day.

There's a fun children's activity area, entertainment on a solar-powered stage, a green-car show and advanced transportation marketplace, an energy village devoted to things like solar energy and wind turbines, green architects and builders, and landscapers who are committed to using fewer fossil fuels. For that day, the Santa Barbara MTD invites passengers to ride all its buses and electric shuttles for free.

UCSB Donald Bren School of Environmental Science & Management

2400 Bren Hall, UCSB, Santa Barbara
805.893.5892, bren.ucsb.edu

Given Santa Barbara's history as the birthplace of the modern environmental movement, you might assume that's why the University of California Regents decided to locate a cutting-edge environmental think tank at UCSB in the mid-1990s. But that wasn't the reason. They chose the campus because the new school would emphasize interdisciplinary studies – for example, environmental issues overlapping with economics, law and policy – and

The ultra-green Bren Hall.

UCSB is a leader in this arena. The school built the green-as-green-can-get building in 2002, and it won many awards, including the U.S. Green Building Council's LEED Platinum Award – the highest certification possible – and recognition as the nation's greenest laboratory building. It's also recognized as being one of the top graduate programs in environmental management and science. World experts on climate change and other issues convene here regularly to work on finding solutions for the planet's survival.

The Green Resident – and Visitor

Eco-conscious Santa Barbarans have lots of ways to make a difference. Many ride the bus or a bike or both, since many buses are equipped with bike racks. If you're a visitor, you'll find that it's easy to explore Santa Barbara in an eco-friendly fashion. And when you stay in city lodgings, know that you're making a contribution. In the late 1990s, residents approved a two-percent increase to the hotel tax, which goes toward restoring urban creeks and improving water quality.

Here are some of our suggestions for getting here, and once here, getting around, in guilt-free style.

Amtrak
800.USA-RAIL, amtrakcalifornia.com
You can ride the train to Santa Barbara from just about anywhere in the continental United States. It's a great way to beat highway gridlock – and once you get here, you have many car-free options for getting around.

Livingreen
218 Helena Ave., Santa Barbara
866.966.1319, livingreen.com
1275 Coast Village Rd., Montecito
805.565.4103, livingreen.com
A decade ago, while creating a walrus habitat, museum exhibit designer Ellen Strickland found that it was hard to get building materials that wouldn't harm animals and humans. That set her on a new path, and she opened a store in the Funk Zone near Stearns Wharf where people could find healthy, sustainable building materials, finishes and home furnishings. Via the showrooms and web site, you can find low-VOC paints, recycled teak tables, denim insulation, paperstone countertops, green cleaning products, you name it.

Lucky Cab
805.968.5020
Get Lucky to do the driving around town, in hybrid, eco-friendly taxis with shamrock logos. Three Santa Barbara cab drivers came up with this brilliant idea and launched Lucky in 2007 – and the company's growing like clover.

Move Green
805.845.6600, WeMoveGreen.com
Moving to a new home? Call these guys for carbon-free moving. They'll send you paperless contracts, pack your things using recycled and/or sustainable moving materials and drive them to your new digs in low-emission trucks. After the move, they'll plant ten trees to mitigate your move's environmental impact.

Santa Barbara Airbus
805.964.7759, sbairbus.com
Snooze in a clean, comfy bus from LAX directly to Santa Barbara. The Airbus makes fourteen trips daily, with stops in Goleta and Carpinteria.

Santa Barbara Bicycle Coalition
sbbike.org
This volunteer-run advocacy organization works to improve bicycling opportunities and conditions throughout the county. Its web site provides links, a free bike map and information on bike shops, rental locations, suggested rides and commercial tours and bicycle commuting.

Santa Barbara Car Free Project
805.696.1100, SantaBarbaraCarFree.org
Take a vacation from your car and save money, not to mention the planet. This cooperative partnership encourages car-free transportation. The Santa Barbara County Air Pollution Control District leads the project, with support from more than 100 agencies, organizations, associations, businesses and individuals, including the City of Santa Barbara and Amtrak. The web site has loads of information on transportation, from biking and walking to using buses and electric shuttles. It also has downloadable maps and suggested itineraries. Hotels, restaurants and activity partners offer "Discover Santa Barbara Car Free" packages with discounts, while Amtrak offers discounted tickets.

One of the city's fleet of quiet, clean hybrid buses.

Central Coast farmers raise a tremendous amount of organic produce, so one of the greenest things you can do is buy locally grown organic fruits and vegetables.

Santa Barbara Metropolitan Transit District
805.683.3702, sbmtd.gov
The MTD system is one of the easiest ways to get around town while reducing your carbon footprint. It operates the largest fleet of electric vehicles in the nation; hybrid buses using biodiesel and electric power traverse 35 routes around the area. Electric shuttles run through the downtown and waterfront areas, as well as through Carpinteria's neighborhoods and beaches, and the fare is just 25 cents. On weekends during the summer, you can hop on a free Wharf Woody electric shuttle that goes up and down Stearns Wharf.

Segway of Santa Barbara
16 Helena Ave., Santa Barbara
805.963.7672, segwayofsb.com
They might look, well … dorky, but the Segway Human Transporter (HT) is a great way to zip around town. It's an electric-powered scooter that emulates human balance using gyroscopes and tilt sensors. After a half-hour training (lean forward to move forward, lean back to move back) a guide leads you on an eco-friendly tour of old Santa Barbara, Butterfly Beach or the Mission, or on a Gaviota Coast picnic or sunset special. You also can rent, by the hour, day or week, an HT to tool around on your own.

Simple Shoes
SimpleShoes.com
Around here it's hip to wear sandals and shoes called Toe Foo, U.F. Toe and other funny names. They're all made by Simple Shoes, one of three lines distributed by Deckers, a home-grown business established in 1973 by UCSB student Doug Otto. (You're probably waaay familiar with the other two lines, UGG and Teva.) Simple Shoes uses planet-sustaining manu-

facturing practices, describing itself as "the nice little shoe company getting in touch with its inner hippie." All the products, from sneaks to sandals to bags, are made with 100-percent sustainable materials like hemp, recycled car tires, crepe, jute, cork and bamboo.

Sustainable Vine Wine Tours
805.698.3911, SustainableVine.com
This outfit is committed to minimizing its environmental footprint. A biodiesel-powered van picks you up, and your driver and guide take you on a daylong wine-country adventure that starts in the eastern Santa Ynez Valley and typically winds westward to the Santa Rita Hills. Visit organic and biodynamic vineyards, tour eco-friendly wineries, feast on a gourmet organic picnic lunch and, of course, taste the wines. Tours teach you such things as the difference between organic wine and wine made from organic grapes.

Fun Cycling Fact
Nearly 5,000 Santa Barbara County residents ride bikes to work, making this one of the nation's top-twenty bicycle-commuting counties.

Traffic Solutions
260 N. San Antonio Rd., Santa Barbara
805.963.SAVE, TrafficSolutions.info
Want to know more about car-free and ride-sharing options for your daily commute? Traffic Solutions promotes and encourages alternatives to driving alone. The folks here will give you information on walking, carpooling, vanpooling, commuter bus services, ridesharing, bicycle commuting, telecommuting and a whole lot more. It also has a free county bike map.

Wheel Fun Rentals
23 E. Cabrillo Blvd. & 22 State St., Santa Barbara
805.966.2282, wheelfunrentalssb.com
Choose from a full menu of people-powered contraptions, from road, mountain, cruiser and tandem bikes to small tricycle-style coupes for one or two people. Or rent an electric bike-board, scooter or car for quicker touring. A third outlet, at Fess Parker's Doubletree Resort, carries many, but not all, of the same models.

Local Preservation Leaders

The small city of Santa Barbara has 57 parks and open spaces and more than 32,000 public trees – more open space per capita than any other city in the nation. This is just one example of the results earned by residents who fight to preserve as much precious open space as they can. Many organizations work together on preservationist causes. Here we'll tell you about some of the major players.

Community Environmental Council
805.963.0583, cecsb.org, FossilFreeBy33.org, GetEnergized.org

The nonprofit CEC – one of the area's most active environmental groups – has helped "green" Santa Barbara since 1970. It started with a series of community gardens, experimenting with organic horticulture, solar energy, municipal-scale composting and bio-gas use. It also galvanized the community to address land-use concerns, and it opened the first nonprofit recycling center in the state.

Over the years the CEC created recycling centers and drop-off locations, plus a household hazardous-waste collection facility. It also opened the Watershed Resource Center, which educates the public about South Coast creeks and oceans, to ensure they remain safe for humans and wildlife. Today the CEC focuses exclusively on energy efficiency, renewable energy sources, alternative transportation and climate change. One of its main missions is lofty, but in the staff's view, achievable in a single generation: To end our region's dependency on fossil fuels by 2033 ("Fossil Free by '33").

Environmental Defense Center
906 Garden St., Santa Barbara
805.963.1622, edcnet.org

In the 1970s, the nascent environmental movement spawned a tangled web of regulations, and polluters soon found ways to get around them. This called for some sharp legal expertise. So the nonprofit EDC was created in 1977, to protect and enhance the South Coast through education, advocacy and legal action. Since then, the EDC has helped negotiate many historic cases and establish legal precedents. It stopped ARCO from installing three new platforms off the coast near UCSB, preserved open space and trails, and ensured the closure of the Casmalia toxic waste dump. Today it is focusing on water quality, biodiversity, watershed protection, environmental health, offshore oil and gas development, and access to public lands. Santa Barbara owes a lot to the EDC.

Heal the Ocean
735 State St., Santa Barbara
805.965.7570, HealTheOcean.org

Santa Barbarans received a huge wake-up call in 1998 when several beaches were closed due to high bacteria counts. Thanks to Heal the Ocean, which was founded because of those closures, our waters have a better chance of staying clean enough to swim in for generations to come. The organization conducts scientific studies to pinpoint sources of pollution, and then recommends practical solutions. Its goals are: Zero pathogens in sewage discharges,

The Biggest Deal Ever
In 1969, following the oil spill, environmentalists and oil companies never could have imagined being on the same page nearly 40 years later. But that's exactly what happened in 2008, with an unprecedented agreement with Houston-based Plains Exploration & Production Company (PXP). PXP wanted permission to expand its operations from an existing well in the Santa Barbara Channel, Platform Irene, to tap into state-owned underwater lands. It was so eager to get access to these oil stores that it offered to make many, many concessions – which will preserve a huge swath of the wild coast forever.

The agreement contains many complex elements. But in a nutshell, PXP will transfer almost 3,900 acres to the Trust for Public Land, which in turn will eventually transfer it to state agencies for permanent protection. This includes nearly 200 acres of prime Gaviota coast land, plus 3,700 inland acres near Lompoc. PXP also has agreed to stop drilling at a certain date, and to phase out other offshore and onshore operations to reduce emissions. Groups involved in the deal include the Environmental Defense Center (EDC), the Trust for Public Land, Get Oil Out (GOO) and the Citizens Planning Association of Santa Barbara (CPA). At press time, PXP still needed to complete the county and state permitting procedures.

Ellwood Mesa, part of the Sperling Preserve, was saved partly through the efforts of the Trust for Public Land.

a significant reduction in the use of septic systems, reduced storm-water contamination, the elimination of ocean dumping, and curbing polluted runoff from coastal landfills.

Land Trust for Santa Barbara County
805.966.4520, sblandtrust.org
Since 1985, the Land Trust for Santa Barbara County has protected and enhanced open space, wildlife habitats, farms and ranches. So far it has helped to preserve more than 18,500 acres in the region, including the Arroyo Hondo Preserve, Sedgwick Reserve, Carpinteria Bluffs, Coronado Butterfly Preserve, Point Sal, Carpinteria Salt Marsh and several ranches on the Gaviota Coast. Its web site has detailed information on these preserves. The following two preserves require advance planning to visit.

Arroyo Hondo Preserve, 805.567.1115. Rich in history, natural beauty and spectacular coastal and mountain views, the 782-acre Arroyo Hondo Preserve stretches along a canyon between Refugio State Beach and Gaviota State Park. It's home to thousands of plant and animal species, some endangered. You can come here to visit, hike and picnic, but you need to make reservations. The preserve is open the first and third weekends of each month.

Sedgwick Reserve, 3566 Brinkerhof Avenue, Santa Ynez, 805.686.1941, sedgwick@lifesci.ucsb.edu. Set in the heart of the Santa Ynez Valley, this 5,883-acre preserve is an amazing place. It looks and feels like the region must have back when only the Chumash and wild critters lived here. It's rich with oaks, grasses and creeks, and the original Rancho La Laguna headquarters, bunkhouses and barns date to the Mexican rancho days. Archaeologists have cataloged Chumash burial sites over

2,000 years old. Today the property belongs to UCSB and is used for research and arts and education programs. The reserve offers guided interpretive hikes; call for dates and times.

Trust for Public Land
tpl.org
This national organization specializes in conservation real estate. Since 1972, TPL has helped protect more than four million acres across the nation, and it turned its attention to Santa Barbara County in 1997. Since then, it has helped local groups and civic leaders save more than 6,000 acres right here in our own backyard. You can thank TPL in particular for helping save the following rare blufftop properties, where trails lead through woodlands to stunning views of the ocean and islands.

Douglas Family Preserve. This 70-acre gem, whose trails crisscross eucalyptus groves high above the beach, was the last undeveloped coastal bluff within the Santa Barbara city limits. Local groups and more than 6,000 private donors, including actor Michael Douglas, kicked in the funds to preserve the land. This is one of the few places in the city where you can walk your dog off leash.

Sperling Preserve (Ellwood Mesa). It took nearly three decades, a $5 million pledge from Stephanie and Peter Sperling, and a heck of a lot of grassroots fund-raising to come up with more than $20 million, but this mesa west of UCSB is now safe from development forever. Now owned by the city of Goleta, it is a truly magical place where you can hike, jog or bike and access long stretches of serene beach. It's next to the Coronado Butterfly Preserve (see the Outdoorsy chapter), where thousands of monarch butterflies spend the winter.

Q & A: Hillary Hauser

Hillary Hauser is executive director of Heal the Ocean, a Santa Barbara–based nonprofit citizen's action group that's cleaning up near-shore pollution. A former journalist, still-prolific writer, accomplished pianist and avid surfer and boogie boarder, Hillary is synonymous with local activism. Since she cofounded Heal the Ocean a decade ago, she has worked tirelessly to get rid of pollution sources (like improperly placed septic tanks) that send bacteria into the water. She met with Cheryl Crabtree at her downtown office.

How did you become a Santa Barbara beach person?
I'm a California girl. I was born in Palo Alto, and my family moved to Miramar Beach when I was about 10. I've been a diver since 1966. That's when I plunged into all things oceanic. I'm a body boarder nowadays.

What do you remember about the beaches back when you were a kid?
I remember the tide pools at Hammond's, sea anemones and lots of sea creatures. Now they're all gone. Underwater, there used to be a lot of types of sea grass, it was really lush. Now the reef looks more like a desert. That's why we're working hard to reverse the situation.

What does the ocean mean to you now?
The ocean is my friend. I talk to it often, one on one. It's my therapy. I usually go to a private spot.

Why and when did you found Heal the Ocean?
In August 1998, when the beaches started being closed, I went ballistic. It was like seeing your mother bleeding on the ground. I turned in a 23-page editorial to the News-Press, and they ran every word. My phone rang off the hook. People were crying, saying they wanted to help. I heard there was a demonstration planned, and I was asked to start a public pressure group. I went to the ocean, of course, to think about starting an organization, and I decided to do it. I called up my friend Jeff Young, an attorney who had an oyster farm until it was polluted out of business, and asked if he would help. We quickly came up with our platform, printed up bumper stickers, got a phone and called the media about the rally. More than 200 people showed up, Jeff and I announced the birth of Heal the Ocean, and we have been working on it ever since. I never planned to get into politics, but here I am.

Where is Heal the Ocean headed?
We're making progress, bit by bit. The focus is, "How would we fix it?" We do cost-feasibility studies and help figure out solutions. You can't stop the dumping, but there has to be a better way to do it. We just got a $330,000 grant from the Proposition 50 Clean Beaches Initiative to study a sewer outfall. This is a great breakthrough because it gets us closer to changing our attitude about how we use the ocean to dilute our waste – which is a complete and total crime.

Tell me about your most memorable moment with the ocean.
It was probably the evening I rode waves in the Rincon cove alone. I'd been teaching piano all day, so I couldn't go out until after the sun had already set. I paddled out, and just as I took off on a dark, glassy wave, a full moon rose above the mountains – and riding that wave was like riding moonbeams.

Hungry & Thirsty

There are worse fates than finding yourself hungry or thirsty in Santa Barbara. In fact, many regular visitors pine for just such a fate. This American Riviera town is blessed with famed farmer's markets and world-class wines, as well as casual-chic Cal-Mediterranean bistros, sunny beach cafés, hip coffeehouses, great taquerias, lively bars, bakeries both rustic and refined and just plain good food.

A User's Guide to Food & Drink

Price chart

Price symbols are based on the range of most dinner entrees, as follows (for one dinner main dish, or lunch if dinner isn't offered):

$ Less than $14

$$ $15-20

$$$ $21-29

$$$$ $30-up

A Note About Chains

Other than a few exceptions, we don't tell you about the chains in the pages that follow, because chances are you already know them. Just be aware that if you're craving Baja Fresh, California Pizza Kitchen, Ruth's Chris, Pollo Loco or In 'N Out, we've got 'em. And if it's Starbucks you want, just throw a rock and you'll hit one. (But please consider trying one of our fine independent coffeehouses instead.)

The Greatest Hits

We recommend every place in this chapter, but if you don't have time to try them all, here are our don't-miss favorites in all sorts of categories:

Bakery: Andersen's, pg. 152

Bar menu: Endless Summer Bar-Café, pg. 134

Burger: The Habit, pg. 150

California cuisine: Downey's, pg. 133

Cocktail lounge: Ty Lounge, pg. 160

Coffeehouse: Vices & Spices, pg. 163

Farm stand: Fairview Gardens, pg. 156

French: Cabernet Bistro, pg. 132

Happy hour: Elements, pg. 161

Lunch: Fresco, pg. 134

Lunch (secret spot): Arts & Letters Café at Sullivan Goss, pg. 144

Italian: Olio e Limone, pg. 137

Market: Los Olivos Grocery, pg. 154

Mexican: Carlito's, pg. 132

Oceanview, high-end: Bella Vista, pg. 130

Oceanview, low-end: Santa Barbara Shellfish Co., pg. 146

Old Santa Barbara: Harry's, pg. 135

Outdoor café: Via Vai Trattoria, pg. 141

Pizza: Giovanni's, pg. 147

Pub: Dargan's, pg. 159

Romantic: Stonehouse, pg. 140, Blue Agave, pg. 159

Sandwiches: South Coast Deli, pg. 146

Seafood: Hungry Cat, pg. 135

Southern: The Palace, pg. 138, Tupelo Junction, pg. 141

Star-gazing: Lucky's, pg. 136

Sushi: Ahi Sushi, pg. 130

Taqueria: La Super-Rica, pg. 150

Thai: Zen Yai Thai Cuisine, pg. 143

Vegetarian/vegan: Sojourner Café, pg. 140

Wine country: Ballard Inn, pg. 130

Good Values

The following may not charge fast-food prices, but they give good bang for the buck in their category.

Brophy Bros., pg. 131

Cajun Kitchen, pg. 144

Flavor of India, pg. 142

Fresco, pg. 134

Giannfranco's Trattoria, pg. 135

La Super-Rica, pg. 150

Los Arroyos, pg. 136

Montecito Coffee Shop, pg. 145

The Natural Café, pg. 137

Paula's Pancake House, pg. 145

Rincon Alteno Taqueria, pg. 151

Roy, pg. 139

Saigon Noodle House, pg. 142

Sambo's, pg. 146

Santa Barbara Chicken Ranch, pg. 147

Santa Barbara Shellfish Co., pg. 146

Shoreline Beach Café, pg. 139

Sojourner Café, pg. 140

South Coast Deli, pg. 146

On the Waterfront

It's the eternal question, asked of every California restaurant writer for decades: Where can we get a really good dinner with a view of the ocean? The answer has typically been: Nowhere! But that old dining-out axiom – great view = bad food – is only true sometimes along the the Santa Barbara coast. Here are our favorite oceanview restaurants in various categories:

Tables sit right on the sand at the Shoreline Beach Café.

For a lively special occasion
Santa Barbara Fishouse. Crowded, convivial and located just across Cabrillo from the beach, the Fishouse is the catch of the day with first-rate seafood. See page 139.

To propose marriage
Bella Vista. This elegant, recently remodeled dining room at the swank Four Seasons Biltmore boasts brilliant California cuisine and impeccable service, just across from Butterfly Beach. See page 130.

To wow a client
Bella Vista (see above) if it's on the expense account. If it's on your dime, **Chuck's Waterfront** (pg. 132) will wow them with spectacular harbor views, steaks, seafood and cocktails.

To take the family
Wiggle your toes in the sand at **Shoreline Beach Café** while you munch on great burgers, seafood and salads, or dine on the lawn at **Beach Grill at Padaro**, just a pebble's throw from the ocean. See pages 139 and 130.

For seafood on paper plates
Order at the counter at **Santa Barbara Shellfish Company** and take your simply cooked, fresh-off-the-boat shellfish, chowder and cioppino to a picnic table – or opt for full service in the bustling little restaurant at the end of Stearns Wharf. See page 146.

A few more choices...

Beachside Bar Café
5905 Sandspit Rd., Goleta
805.964.7881
American. L & D daily. Full bar. $$$
Just down the street (or the beach) from UCSB and the airport, this is an on-the-beach spot at the foot of the Goleta pier for a good lunch or dinner. You'll see Gauchos galore, especially on Parents' Weekend or graduation. Stick with the seafood: seared ahi, crab cakes, oysters, seafood skewers, clam chowder and a great Caesar salad loaded with shrimp. Service can be spotty and slow, so don't be in a hurry – just relax, sit on the patio and watch the sunset.

East Beach Grill
1118 E. Cabrillo Blvd., Santa Barbara
805.965.8805
American. B & L daily. Beer & wine. $
It's nothing fancy at this cafeteria-style eatery, where you take your burgers, burritos and sandwiches to sit on plastic tables. But the beach is literally a five-foot stumble from the patio, and a fun playground is nearby, too. The grill is best known for breakfast, and the crowd on Sunday mornings proves it. Get there early and watch out for the birds.

Emilio's
324 W. Cabrillo Blvd., Santa Barbara
805.966.4426, emiliosrestaurant.com
Italian. D nightly. Full bar. $$$
This intimate Italian boîte is just across Cabrillo Boulevard from the harbor, so it's in the thick of the tourist district, but it's not a tourist trap. Locals come for its consistently good, if a bit pricey, Italian cooking, like grilled bone-in beef rib chop with crisp rosti potato pancake or swordfish with caramelized corn, fava beans and sweet peppers. Bread is baked from the owner's grandmother's recipe, and the kitchen makes its own mozzarella and ricotta. After dinner, take a stroll around the harbor to work off the warm chocolate cake with vanilla bean ice cream and hazelnut praline.

Our Favorite Restaurants

Ahi Sushi
3631 State St., Santa Barbara
805.687.6942, AhiSushi.net
Japanese. L Mon.-Sat., D nightly. Beer & sake.
$$-$$$
The strip-mall entrance belies the superb delicacies within this casual Japanese eatery: melt-in-your mouth sushi and sashimi, savory noodles and crispy tempura. The Japanese owners worked previously at other sushi restaurants, including a very popular one downtown (we don't need to name it), and decided to venture out on their own. The chefs make more than twenty rolls and many, many combinations of sushi, sashimi, udon, tempura, you name it. Nearly everything is made from scratch, and it also serves fresh, organic salads, fruits and veggies. Ahi doesn't take reservations on weekends, so go early or prepare for a wait.

Arigato Sushi
1225 State St., Santa Barbara
805.965.6074
Japanese. D nightly. Beer & wine. $$-$$$
This wildly popular, urban-chic restaurant attracts trendsetters and wannabes hoping to see and be seen. Line up early on weekends (no reservations) or expect to wait for a table; you might get seated faster at the sushi bar, where you can try to convince the chefs to customize a roll. While opinions regarding quality vary (some complain about small portions), nearly everyone lauds Arigato's creative menu, with wacky items like the sushi pizza with seaweed crust. Order sake and, for stellar people-watching, get a table on the patio or second-story alcove overlooking the main room.

Arnoldi's Cafe
600 Olive St., Santa Barbara
805.962.5394, arnoldis.com
Italian. D nightly. Beer & wine. $$-$$$
One of the oldest restaurants in Santa Barbara, Arnoldi's has been ladling its marinara sauce and sprinkling its Parmesan since 1937. We love coming here for a good, traditional Italian dinner and a fun night out. The dining rooms, one with enclosed wooden booths, are warm and welcoming, as all good Italian places are, but the spacious heated back patio is where the action is, with two bocce courts and an outdoor fire pit. Sure-fire entrees are the milanese di pollo and the lasagne … and where else can you play bocce between your bruschetta and your bolognese?

Ballard Inn Restaurant
2436 Baseline Ave., Ballard (near Los Olivos)
805.688.7770, 800.638.2466, BallardInn.com
French-Asian/Californian. D Wed.-Sun. Beer & wine. $$$-$$$$
Set within the Ballard Inn in the wee town of Ballard, this intimate place serves exceptional French-Asian meals in one of the Valley's most romantic dining rooms. Chef-owner Budi Kazali grew up in Santa Barbara County, graduated from the California Culinary Academy, then worked at a series of famed restaurants, including with Ming Tsai at Blue Ginger. In 2004 he and his wife, Christine, acquired the Ballard Inn, the perfect showcase for his talents. The small menu changes often, depending on the season and Budi's creative inspirations. Appetizer examples include honey-tamarind-glazed quail with arugula-coconut salad, and Asian-style ceviche with shrimp, calamari and hearts of palm. Entrees usually reflect interesting spice combinations, as with the pan-seared scallops with achiote risotto and tomatillo sauce. There's both a wine-tasting room and an extensive list. Not sure what to drink? Just ask Budi – he's a genius at pairing local wines with his culinary creations.

Beach Grill at Padaro
3765 Santa Claus Lane, Carpinteria
805.566.3900, BeachGrillPadaro.com
American/pizzeria. B Sat.-Sun., L & D daily. Beer & wine. $
Through several ownership changes, the Beach Grill has remained Santa Barbara's most unique – and iconic – dining experience. Place your order for burgers, salads, sandwiches, pizza and wine at the counter, then enjoy your meal in an Adirondack chair or at an oversize picnic table on a half-acre beachside lawn. The food is good, but the ambience is better. Leashed dogs are welcome, and kids love playing in the huge toy-filled sandbox and watching as the Amtrak trains whoosh past – at a safe distance. The beach is on the other side of the tracks, but you have to walk a bit to cross.

Bella Vista
Four Seasons Biltmore, 1260 Channel Dr., Montecito
805.565.8237, fourseasons.com/santabarbara
Modern American/Californian. B Mon.-Sat., L & D daily, brunch Sun. Full bar. $$$-$$$$
Want to impress someone? Take him or her to Bella Vista at the grand Biltmore. Painstakingly

Rack of lamb, Bouchon-style.

with a lively mix of locals and tourists who try to snag a seat at the long cocktail and oyster bar or on the patio with that to-die-for view. The clam bar menu includes such classics as beer-boiled shrimp, oysters Rockefeller, oysters and clams on the half shell and shrimp cocktail; the thick, creamy clam chowder is some of the best this New England girl has slurped. Fresh fish (mostly local) are all perfectly grilled, with simple sauces, served with chowder or salad, rice pilaf or fries, and cole slaw. If you have to wait (and you probably will), the hostess will give you a pager, so you can stroll around the harbor to work up an appetite.

Bouchon
9 W. Victoria St., Santa Barbara
805.730.1160, bouchonsantabarbara.com
Californian/Modern American. D nightly. Beer & wine. $$$-$$$$
Hidden behind a curtain of greenery just off State Street, this is the place to go when you want a romantic dinner or a really nice evening with friends. The heated, covered garden patio is lovely year-round, and the airy dining room is elegant without being stuffy. Owner Mitchell Sjerven's goal is to celebrate the food and wine of the Central Coast, and he achieves that goal night after night. All ingredients are as fresh and local as possible, with fish from the Santa Barbara Channel, produce from the farmer's markets and meats and poultry from local micro-ranches. Of course the menu changes often, but there are a few signature dishes, like the seared Pacific ahi with white bean purée and grilled asparagus, bourbon- and maple-glazed duck breast, and warm chocolate molten lava cake. An impressive wine list always includes at least 40 Santa Barbara choices by the glass. Servers are friendly and professional, and they win bonus points for graciously accommodating even picky-eater, entree-modifying dining companions.

restored to reflect the elegance of the original 1927 room, this is one of the fanciest dining rooms on the South Coast, with bubbling fountains and crackling fireplaces. Stunning views of the Pacific and the Channel Islands unfold from nearly every seat – ask for a table near the oceanside windows, or on the patio (warmed by radiant tiles); on fair-weather days, the staff cranks back the retractable glass roof. The seasonal menu centers on local and regional ingredients. Main courses might include a vegetable sampler, a free-range chicken breast filled with pistachios and goat cheese, or a grilled local fish. You can also mix and match – choose your grilled entree and pick from various sauces and sides. (We like the grilled salmon with lobster sauce, creamed spinach and braised artichokes.) Everyone needs to try the famous brunch at least once in a lifetime. The stations are staggering in their variety, beauty and quality. Fast (and save) to prepare – it's worth it.

Brophy Bros. Restaurant & Clam Bar
119 Harbor Way, Santa Barbara
805.966.4418, brophybros.com
Seafood. L & D daily. Full bar. $-$$$
This wildly popular queen of Santa Barbara's seafood restaurants has been reigning over the harbor for more than twenty years. A second-floor place with spectacular harbor and mountain views, Brophy Bros. sticks with what it does best – fresh seafood and chowder – and plenty of it. The place is nearly always crowded

Brothers' Restaurant at Mattei's Tavern
2350 Railway Ave., Los Olivos
805.688.4820, matteistavern.com
American. D nightly. Full bar. $$$-$$$$
Chef/owners and brothers Matt and Jeff Nichols renovated this 1886 stagecoach stop, respecting the original character while morphing it into one of the best restaurants in the Valley. The warm, homey dining rooms, with their red-velvet wallpaper, historic photos and crackling fires, make you want to get out

Mattei's Tavern (aka Brothers) in Los Olivos.

your hoop skirt. The menu changes frequently but often includes spicy fried calamari, prime rib, steaks and salmon. We dream about the jalapeño cornbread and the oven-roasted rack of lamb with goat cheese mashed potatoes. And you'll need dessert before you hit the dusty trail: warm mocha truffle cake or mud pie.

Cabernet Bistro & Wine Lounge
Frederik's Court, 485 Alisal Rd., Solvang
805.688.8871, CabernetBistro.com
Basque/French. D Wed.-Sun. Beer & wine.
$$$-$$$$
Jacques Toulet's family ran a restaurant in St. Gaudens, a village in the Pyrenees, and when the family eventually moved to America, he and his brother opened and ran the acclaimed Les Pyrenees in Santa Monica. Now Jacques and his wife, Diane, call the Santa Ynez Valley home, and their first Basque-French restaurant earned widespread fame for its outstanding duck dishes. When the restaurant closed, fans mourned, but now everyone's happy again, because Jacques and Diane have reopened in a delightful second-floor space with a wine bar and patio lounge with a retractable roof. Try the escargot, duck confit with port and berries, veal chop with black truffles and foie gras, and ladyfingers with Belgian chocolate mousse. Jazz piano often livens up the place.

Ca' Dario Ristorante
37 E. Victoria St., Santa Barbara
805.884.9419, cadario.net
Italian. L Mon.-Sat., D nightly. Full bar. $$$
Ebullient chef-owner Dario Furlati flung his downtown doors open in 1997 and has been energetically welcoming locals and visitors to his "house of Dario" ever since. Fans return for the consistently good northern Italian food and a true trattoria atmosphere – convivial and noisy, with conversation and laughter mingling with the clink of glasses and clank of plates.

Try one of the housemade pastas, such as the pasta pillows filled with spinach and ricotta with browned butter and sage. Dario also does a nice job with the fresh fish of the day, and the osso buco with risotto is divine.

Carlito's
1324 State St., Santa Barbara
805.962.7117, carlitos.com
Mexican. B Sun., L & D daily. Full bar. $$
The food at Carlito's is good, from the traditional mole chicken and pozole to more modern rock shrimp tacos with papaya salsa. And the margaritas are fantastic. But what you're paying for (and the prices are steepish) is the atmosphere – the tiled patio with its fountain and view of State Street is quintessential Santa Barbara. Across the street from the Arlington Theatre, this is a perfect pre-show dinner spot – and Sunday breakfasts of machaca, chilequiles and even Belgian waffles are *muy delicioso*.

Chuck's of Hawaii
3888 State St., Santa Barbara
805.687.4417, chuckssteakhouse.com
Steakhouse/American. D nightly. Full bar. $$$
Walk past the tiki torches, open the heavy wooden doors and step (carefully) into the dark recesses. You might feel like you're stepping back in time to when you were a kid going out for a special dinner with your parents. But this throwback works – steaks, chicken and fish are cooked just right, without any fancy-schmancy sauces (teriyaki doesn't count), and the salad bar is fresh and plentiful. We have friends who swear that a Chuck's mai tai and rib-eye will cure whatever ails you.

Chuck's Waterfront Grill
113 Harbor Way, Santa Barbara
805.564.1200, chuckswaterfrontgrill.com
Steakhouse/American. D nightly. Full bar. $$$
Located in the Santa Barbara Maritime Museum building at the harbor, this is the more touristy and nautical version of Chuck's of Hawaii. But don't get us wrong – plenty of locals are regulars, thanks to the simple grilled seafood and great views. Sunset dinner specials, served between 5 and 6:30 p.m., are a good value – choose from Hawaiian chicken, fresh Idaho trout, grilled salmon or Angus steak with teriyaki rice, vegetables and salad, all for about $16. Don't expect the best meal you've ever had, but, hey, take a look at that view....

Cold Spring Tavern

5995 Stagecoach Rd., Santa Barbara
805.967.0066, ColdSpringTavern.com
American. L & D daily, brunch Sat. & Sun.
Full bar. $$$

You can almost hear the rumble of stagecoach wheels as you drive up the oak-shaded road to Cold Spring Tavern. Just a fifteen-minute drive from Santa Barbara on San Marcos Pass (Highway 154), the rustic tavern was established as a stagecoach stop in 1865, and not much (thankfully) has changed since. You can still sit near one of four stone fireplaces in romantic, wood-paneled rooms and dine by lamp light. The food may be a bit more high-falutin' than it was back then – dinners include sautéed breast of duck with roasted shallot demi-glace, grilled steaks, barbecued baby-back ribs and charbroiled New Zealand rack of venison. It's famous for its traditional Texas-style chili, but live a little and instead try the black-bean chili with venison, rabbit and buffalo. Pull up a log on a Sunday afternoon and enjoy tri-tip sandwiches and music under the oaks. Bring your leather jacket – this is a popular biker spot on weekend afternoons.

Downey's

1305 State St., Santa Barbara
805.966.5006, DowneysSB.com
French/Californian. D Tues.-Sun. Beer & wine.
$$$$

We've been going to Downey's for its entire 26 years, and we can honestly say that it just keeps getting better and better. John Downey's skill in the kitchen has always been superb, and he keeps coming up with deliciously creative dishes that wow us every time. His menu changes seasonally, but you're likely to find a succulent grilled duck dish and, for dessert, the signature fresh raspberry and white chocolate millefeuille. John's wife, co-owner Liz Downey, keeps the front of the house running like a top,

Woodsy warmth at Cold Spring Tavern.

overseeing the impeccable service, which tiptoes that fine line between attentive and overzealous. The dining room is small, elegant and serene, with Liz's plein-air paintings adorning soft sage-green walls. Drink a toast with your choice of more than 150 wines from the usual California suspects, along with many boutique vintners. This is a great spot to start your evening before a show at the nearby Arlington.

Elements Restaurant & Bar

129 E. Anapamu St., Santa Barbara
805.884.9218, elementsrestaurantandbar.com
Californian. L Mon.-Sat., D nightly, brunch Sun.
Full bar. $$$-$$$$

This place has all the right elements for success: a location across from the Courthouse and its sunken gardens; terrific, creative food; and friendly, efficient service. It's been a big hit since its opening in 2004; its award-winning wine list and specialty martinis attract a jovial happy-hour crowd that frequently overflows onto the outdoor terrace. But Elements can also be romantic if you snag one of the couches in the back and snuggle in for dinner. The menu changes seasonally; if they're available try the grilled ahi tuna wrap with wasabi mayo for lunch or, for dinner, the lemongrass and panko-crusted sea bass with Thai green curry-coconut sauce and gingered basmati rice.

Waiting for a Table

At press time the much-anticipated **Sly's** in Carpinteria was about to open at 686 Linden Avenue (805.684.6666, slysonline.com). Chef James Sly, formerly at Lucky's in Montecito, has worked at the Hotel Ritz in Paris, Michel Guérard's in the south of France and L'Orangerie in L.A. Also coming is the **Boathouse at Hendry's Beach** (sbfishhouse.com) in the space where the old Brown Pelican perched, just above the rocks at Arroyo Burro Beach (Hendry's to the locals) on Cliff Drive. This new spot promises a glassed-in patio, fire pit, indoor/outdoor bar and seafood fresh off fishermen's boats. In Solvang, **Bradley Ogden** is prepping his new place at the Royal Scandinavian Inn (805.688.8000, royalscandinavianinn.com), owned by the Santa Ynez band of Chumash Indians.

The chalkboard menu at Giannfranco's invites passersby to develop an appetite.

Endless Summer Bar-Café

113 Harbor Way, 2nd floor, Santa Barbara
805.564.4666, EndlessSummerBarCafe.net
American. L & D daily. Full bar. $-$$
Want great views, a cold beer or cocktail, decent food and the chance to wear shorts and an aloha shirt? Head to the Endless Summer, perched above the Maritime Museum and sister restaurant Chuck's Waterfront Grill. The touristy, surf-themed place is named for Bruce Brown's iconic film, and Bruce himself stops by occasionally. Vintage and modern surfboards hang from the ceiling, and historical surf photographs and memorabilia adorn the walls. The fresh seafood typically comes right from the boats you're looking at, turning up in such comfort foods as clam chowder in a sourdough bread bowl, beer-battered fish and chips with cole slaw, popcorn shrimp with chipotle-lime mayo and fish tacos. You and the kids can also feast on burgers (the half-pound Rincon burger rocks) and other land-based entrees.

Enterprise Fish Co.

225 State St., Santa Barbara
805.962.3313, EnterpriseFishCo.com
Seafood. L & D daily. Full bar. $$-$$$
This is a fun place for a hungry crowd after a day at the blocks-away beach. The anchors-away décor keeps up the ocean spirit, and a convivial atmosphere prevails, with large fish tanks providing aquatic entertainment for the kids. The glass-surrounded kitchen is amus-

ing – every once in a while a ginormous flame leaps up from the grill, lighting up the place in a golden flash. Crusty bread and thick chowders are terrific comfort foods, and we can't get enough of the crab cakes and mixed seafood grill. Though it's pricey for the low-fuss nature of the food, the fish is fresh off the boat and the place is fun. The bar is popular for shooters and sashimi.

Fresco

3987 State St., Santa Barbara
805.967.6037, FrescoSB.com

Fresco North

5940 Calle Real, Goleta
805.692-8999, FrescoNorth.com
Italian/Californian. B, L & D Mon.-Sat. (North open daily.) Beer & wine. $
Despite its location in the Five Points shopping center – where parking is abominable – the original Fresco is the default lunch spot for girlfriends and couples of all ages. Also a booming catering business, the eatery itself is a master of balance, serving comfort food that feels healthy (thanks to good ingredients), and offering counter service and affordable dishes in an upscale-looking dining room. We love the warm goat cheese salad, caprese sandwich on toasted ciabatta and daily calzone specials. The new Goleta location may help with lunchtime congestion. If you can leave without diving into a monstrous cupcake or gooey lemon bar, you're a better person than we are.

Giannfranco's Trattoria

666 Linden Ave., Carpinteria
805.684.0720
Italian. L & D Wed.-Mon. Beer & wine. $$-$$$
Devout regulars make a beeline to this bustling little Carp trattoria, where owners Anna Sherwyn and Franco Contreras give you a warm welcome and their son, chef Giovanni Sherwyn, turns out southern Italian dishes with a contemporary spin. Highlights are the grilled calamari and tiger shrimp; seafood risotto; homemade lobster ravioli; cioppino; and herb-marinated grilled rib-eye steak. To complement all this good Italian comfort food, choose from a small but well-thought-out list of Santa Barbara County and Italian wines or a beer from Carpinteria's own Island Brewing Company. The tree-shaded back patio with fountain is a lovely lunch spot. Prices are not as high as the food and presentation would suggest.

Harry's Plaza Café

Loreto Plaza, 3313-B State St., Santa Barbara
805.687.2800
American/Italian. L & D daily. Full bar. $-$$
Harry's is a Santa Barbara institution. Since 1968, locals have plunked themselves into its shiny red leather booths to enjoy old-fashioned American/Italian food. New owners recently remodeled but remained faithful to the original décor and menu. Thousands of framed historical photos hang on the walls, and moose and steer heads gaze over the crowds. As soon as you're seated, your server will bring fresh bread along with salsa and sour cream to dip it in. We usually order the Omaha sandwich (tri-tip on sourdough) or a daily special, perhaps meatloaf and mashed potatoes. Kids and teens love the hefty pastas and the ice cream sundaes and splits. It's not all meat-and-potatoes, though – there are plenty of veggie dishes, salads and seafood items. Beware: The noise, especially near the bar, can overwhelm conversation. Perhaps that's because Harry's pours some of the stiffest drinks in town.

Hitching Post II

406 E. Hwy. 246, Buellton
805.688.0676, hitchingpost2.com
American. D nightly. Full bar. $$$-$$$$
The Hitching Post roots go back to Frank and Natalie Ostini's Casmalia Hitching Post, which opened in 1952 and earned regional fame for its first-rate Santa Maria-style barbecue. Four of the Ostini kids continue to operate the original eatery near Santa Maria, while young Frank owns this offshoot, where much of the food cooks slowly on an oak grill. *Sideways* fans will recognize the bar and restaurant – it's where Maya worked. The menu combines traditional steaks, chicken, pork and lamb with such less-common meats as duck breast, ostrich, turkey and quail. Don't miss the grilled artichoke with spicy smoked tomato mayo or the famous fries. Entrees come with an old-fashioned fresh vegetable tray and garlic bread; rice, baked potato or their famous fries; and a choice of organic mixed-green salad, soup or shrimp cocktail. Frank also makes Hartley Ostini Hitching Post wine; his Highliner Pinot Noir drew acclaim even before *Sideways* launched it into stardom – order a glass and you'll find out why.

The Hungry Cat

1134 Chapala St., Santa Barbara
805.884.4701, thehungrycat.com
Modern American/seafood. D nightly, brunch Sun. Full bar. $$$
Hip, happening, and red-hot, this downtown seafood spot may be small in size, but it's big in talent and creativity. Close quarters add to the energy and appeal of this sleek outpost of the original Hollywood Cat, run by chef David Lentz and his wife, A.O.C. and Lucques chef/owner Suzanne Goin. Seafood, both local and flown in daily, is the main event. Sea urchin, an occasional offering and rare restaurant find, is harvested just off the Santa Barbara coast. A must-try is the peel-and-eat shrimp – betcha can't eat just five! The only land-lubbing entree is the delicious Pug burger (named after the couple's dog). Check out the raw bar and luscious cocktails made with farmer's market fruits and veggies. This hep cat doesn't take reservations, so come early or be prepared to wait.

Hungry Cat's Pug burger.

The wine room at Olio e Limone.

Los Arroyos
14 W. Figueroa St., Santa Barbara
805.962.5541, LosArroyos.net
Mexican. B Sat.-Sun., L & D daily. Beer & wine. $
1280 Coast Village Rd., Montecito
805.969.9059
Mexican. L & D daily. Full bar. $
Owned by a husband-and-wife team who met while working at another local restaurant, this pair of convenient *cocinas* serves flavorful, authentic Mexican food based on family recipes. We love the homemade sopes, chile relleno burrito and tacos al pastor – seasoned pork and grilled onions with pineapple (just trust us). You have to pay extra for chips, but they're hot, salty and light-as-air, and they come with a trip to the salsa bar. The Montecito location has a tequila bar with more than 90 varieties.

Los Olivos Café
2879 Grand Ave., Los Olivos
805.688.7265, LosOlivosCafe.com
Modern American/Californian. L & D daily. Beer & wine. $$-$$$
If you've seen the film *Sideways*, you've been to this low-key, contemporary locals' social hub, a combination wine store, gift shop, café and tasting bar – it's where the four main characters have their first date and drink their way through several bottles of wine. If you like, you can order the same meal and shop for similar bottles (it carries more than 300) displayed on

the wall. The Cal-Med menu features wine-friendly dishes made from mostly local ingredients: fish, pastas, lamb, salads, rustic individual pizzas and grilled burgers. For appetizers, best bets include the baked brie with honey-roasted hazelnuts and the artisanal cheese plate. For dinner, try the paella (for two), chicken marsala or braised pot roast with whipped potatoes.

Louie's California Bistro
Upham Hotel, 1404 De la Vina St., Santa Barbara
805.963.7003, uphamhotel.com
Californian. L Mon.-Fri., D nightly. Beer & wine. $$$
We feel oh-so-civilized when we dine at Louie's at the Upham Hotel. A warm greeting at the door and a helpful, friendly wait staff make you feel right at home – if home was a meticulously restored 1871 Victorian, that is. Perhaps the civilized feeling comes from the casual sophistication of the décor – polished wood floors, soothing colors, flickering sconces – or the fact that the dining room is quiet enough to encourage conversation. All of this, in addition to the wraparound heated porch, makes this one of our favorite spots for a birthday celebration, business lunch or romantic dinner. And, ah yes, the food: Chef Tony Manzanares has been turning out consistently delicious dishes here for more than twenty years. We're partial to the seafood, such as the sautéed Alaskan halibut with wild mushroom risotto, but we wouldn't turn down the grilled filet mignon with sautéed mushrooms and shallots, Cabernet sauce and gorgonzola over a potato pancake. The wine list is managed by someone who obviously knows a thing or two about the subject, especially local wines. Save room for the peanut butter pie or the warm brownie with vanilla gelato.

Lucky's
1279 Coast Village Rd., Montecito
805.565.7540, luckys-steakhouse.com
American/steakhouse. D nightly, brunch Sat.-Sun. Full bar. $$$$+
Your average person doesn't want to pay six dollars for a baked potato. But these are not your average people – this is the rarefied atmosphere of Montecito, as you can see from the Maybachs and Maseratis parked outside. If Great Aunt Plentibucks is in town and wants to treat, you'll have fun here. Owner Gene Montesano (of Lucky jeans fame) and his partners have created a sleek, stylish chophouse with

great steaks, natch, seafood and, if they do say so themselves, "damn fine martinis." It's a bright and contemporary place, with black-and-white photos of Hollywood stars and a pervasive aura of glamour; you might even see a real-live celebrity. If you've got the $69 it costs, order the excellent porterhouse (a 24-ounce cut that's good for two), but even the humble $44 steaks are good. If you don't get weak in the knees at the cost of a couple of these steaks, then you probably won't faint from the prices on the A-list wine menu. But if you haven't hit it big yet, not to worry – for the price of a martini, you can stop by the bar and soak up the scene.

The Natural Café
508 State St., Santa Barbara
805.962.9494, TheNaturalCafe.com
361 Hitchcock Way, Santa Barbara
805.563.1163
5892 Hollister Ave., Goleta
805.692.2363
American/vegetarian. L & D daily. No booze. $
It's the rare place that can dish up health food that, as one 9-year-old we know says, "actually tastes better than normal food." Here grub lovers can learn to love tofu, tahini and tempeh. It's no surprise that the salads and fruit smoothies are amazing, but we're almost surprised how much we like the wholesome pesto pasta, tamales, turkey burger, chicken-stuffed baked potato and scrumptious stir-fries. Keep in mind healthy doesn't necessarily mean low-cal; the thick and creamy milkshakes will leave you feeling as happy – and full-bellied – as the Buddha statue near the door.

The Nugget
2318 Lillie Ave., Summerland
805.969.6135.
American L & D daily. Full bar. $-$$
A popular watering hole for more than twenty years, this saloon-style bar and restaurant changed hands a few years ago and got a much-needed menu makeover. But though you'll now find such upscale entrees as grilled ahi, the burgers, chili, sandwiches and salads are still kickin'. The place oozes personality: Wood-paneled walls are adorned with neon beer signs and photos of celebrities who have bellied up to the bar or into the red-vinyl banquettes. A sign under a hanging saxophone reads "For the use of President Clinton only." Apparently, Bill stopped in for a cheeseburger fix with Hillary and Chelsea while staying with

friends on nearby Padaro Lane in 1992. In a show of bipartisanship, there are also signed photos of President Reagan during his Western White House years. The chili has a good kick – try it on the chili cheese fries or a burger. A lighter option is the terrific grilled wild salmon salad on a bed of fresh greens.

Olio e Limone Ristorante
17 W. Victoria St., Santa Barbara
805.899.2699, olioelimone.com
Italian. L Mon.-Sat., D nightly. Full bar.
$$$-$$$$
We've begun inventing occasions to go to Olio e Limone.... "Well, it was my birthday exactly two months ago"... or ... "Are you sure it's not our anniversary?" It's that good – and, of course, it's not cheap. Owned by Sicilian chef Alberto Morello and his wife and general manager, Elaine Morello, the elegant little ivory and sage restaurant runs like clockwork, serving such sumptuous, authentic dishes as thinly sliced veal cutlets with fresh artichoke hearts and lemon sauce, and housemade ravioli filled with roasted eggplant and goat cheese. The wine cellar, on view through glass, stocks more than 230 selections. This gem is in a quiet spot just around the corner from the Arlington, so it's a lovely pre-show dinner choice. Just don't even think about leaving until you try the pear in puff pastry with a heavenly caramel sauce.

Opal Restaurant & Bar
1325 State St., Santa Barbara
805.966.9676, opalrestaurantandbar
Californian. L Mon.-Sat., D nightly. Full bar.
$$-$$$
We like to go to Opal, next to the Arlington Theatre, for dinner before the show, after the show or even instead of the show. For some twenty years this was the home of the beloved Brigitte's; in 2000, Tina Takaya and Richard Yates bought the place and made it their own. Locals flock here for the warm greeting at the door, the sophisticated yet comfortable ambience, the great food, the efficient team-style service and the reasonable prices (considering the quality and creativity in the kitchen). We love the shredded phyllo-wrapped tiger prawn appetizer, the chile-crusted filet mignon and the lemongrass salmon with Thai curry sauce. Save room for "Like Water for Chocolate," a dark chocolate shell filled with white and dark chocolate mousse and paired with a fresh raspberry coulis. We also like to sit at the lovely

Paradise Café.

bar and sip a fresh ginger-mandarin cosmo or a glass of wine from the well-thought-out list.

The Palace Grill
8 E. Cota St., Santa Barbara
805.963.5000, PalaceGrill.com
Cajun. L & D daily. Full bar. $$$
The Palace may well be Santa Barbara's most beloved restaurant, a festive grill with a Mardi Gras atmosphere, impeccable service and a menu swamped with richly spiced Cajun and Creole dishes: gumbo ya-ya, crawfish etouffée, blackened filet mignon and New Orleans barbecue shrimp sautéed in Dixie beer. On weekends, make a reservation for the 5:30 seating or prepare to wait outside with live music and free nibbles. Inside, everyone sings along to Louis Armstrong's "What a Wonderful World" – the stiff Caribbean rum punch and Cajun martinis help loosen everyone's vocal cords. Order your Louisiana bread pudding soufflé in advance, as it takes a while to cook.

The Palms
701 Linden Ave., Carpinteria
805.684.3811, thepalmsrestaurant.com
American/steakhouse. D nightly. Full bar. $$
Don't like the way your steak is cooked? You have no one to blame but yourself! For four decades, folks have been bellying up to the lava-rock gas grills at this family-owned hangout and cooking their steaks and chicken themselves. If you're not in a cooking mood, you can ask the chef to prepare it for you. Here's the grill-drill:

You order your teriyaki chicken breast, rib-eye, New York strip or fish, then the server brings it and you cook it, using the seasonings and sauces at the grill. One of our grill-mates once said, "We've been coming here since the steaks were $1.50!" – it's that kind of place. The salad bar, which includes beans, potatoes, bread and salsa, is a separate charge. You won't find a drop of chanterelle-mango reduction sauce here – just good, honest cooking (mostly yours) in a family-friendly atmosphere. Check out the bands on Thursday, Friday and Saturday nights.

Paradise Café
702 Anacapa St., Santa Barbara
805.962.4416, paradisecafe.com
American/Californian. L & D daily, brunch Sun. Full bar. $$-$$$
If there is a quintessential Santa Barbara place, this is it. Housed in a 1915 brick-and-stucco house a block from State Street, the Paradise has been welcoming locals, often with out-of-town visitors in tow, for 25 years. The kitchen's claim to fame is taking top-notch ingredients, grilling them over Santa Maria oak, and getting out of the way. Everything is simple and good; try the salmon chowder, the oak-grilled prawns and the juicy signature Paradise burger – it's not unusual to see one being washed down with a good bottle of Bordeaux. Speaking of wines, at least a dozen are offered by the glass, and the list is constantly changing, so this is a good place to try different local producers. Sit on the brick patio if you can to soak up that

comfortable, casual Santa Barbara vibe. The separate bar is a popular but not-too-crazy after-work or after-show cocktail spot.

Pascucci
729 State St., Santa Barbara
805.963.8123, pascuccirestaurant.com
Italian. L & D daily. Full bar. $-$$
The casual, hip atmosphere is the main draw of this busy restaurant fronting Paseo Nuevo. Choose from various seating areas, including booths, a bar overlooking the open kitchen, and two main dining rooms, and chow down on free garlic bread while you peruse the menu, which lists individual pizzas, dozens of pastas (we like the ravioli sampler), salads and a slew of traditional Italian entrees. Service can be spotty, but many people put up with it because of the setting, the food and the reasonable prices.

Pierre Lafond Bistro
516 State St., Santa Barbara
805.962.1455, PierreLafond.com
Californian. B, L & D daily. Beer & wine. $$-$$$
Recently transformed from a bakery and deli into an upscale bistro, Lafond has kicked it up a notch with a new menu of Californian cuisine with a focus on organic, sustainable food. It now harvests produce from its own organic garden on a plot at Lafond Vineyard. Some recent creative and delicious highlights include seared pepper-crusted ahi, eggplant cannoli and a surprisingly scrumptious banana-shrimp tamale. Try the fabulous wine cake made with late-harvest Riesling. This is a terrific lunch spot when you're out shopping 'til you drop.

Roy
7 W. Carrillo St., Santa Barbara
805.966.5636, RestaurantRoy.com
Modern American. D nightly (until midnight). Full bar. $$
Just off State Street, an easy walk from the arts and culture district and lower State's nightlife, Roy is a fun, bohemian-chic place that serves tasty, healthful food at exceptionally good prices. Long before the locavore life became trendy, chef/owner Leroy Gandy was shopping for organic produce at the farmer's markets, buying fish and meats from local purveyors, cranking out pasta by hand and baking his own breads with organic flours. Choose from a number of entrees on the prix-fixe-style menu – along with the main course, you get Roy's famous house-baked wheat bread, the soup

du jour and a salad of mixed organic greens, all for $25 (a couple of options may cost $20 or $30). Choices change, but the bacon-wrapped filet mignon with a sherry-portabello sauce and the chicken marsala with mushrooms have anchored the menu almost since the get-go (Roy says fans won't let him take them off). Light eaters can order smaller dishes (crab cakes or spinach salad with chicken scaloppini) from the appetizer menu. Try not to leave without trying the flourless chocolate torte, crème brûlée or homemade ice cream.

Santa Barbara FisHouse
101 E. Cabrillo Blvd., Santa Barbara
805.966.2112, sbfishhouse.com
Seafood. L & D daily. Full bar. $$-$$$
The Chart House that occupied this space for years died, but the location came back to life as the FisHouse, with local owners who know their fish, a varied, something-for-everyone menu, a lively atmosphere (especially during happy hour) and that same great location across from East Beach and Stearns Wharf. Sit inside or out on the dining terrace around the fire pit and belly up to some good, fresh seafood, from macadamia-crusted sea bass to crab cakes, with chicken, steaks and ribs for the land-lubbers. Splurge on juicy, sweet lobster during the season, and make a reservation – this House gets crowded, especially in summer.

Shoreline Beach Café
801 Shoreline Dr., Santa Barbara
805.568.0064
American. B, L & D daily. Full bar. $-$$
There aren't many restaurants where you can sit at your table and wiggle your toes in the warm sand while munching on a great burger or

Art and color at Roy.

fish taco, but this is one of them. At this locals' favorite located just down the cliff from Santa Barbara City College, you can choose from covered deck seating or the aforementioned sand-side tables. The kids can play in the sand, you can drink in the gazillion-dollar view of the sparkling Pacific and sailboats leaving the harbor, and you can all enjoy a good meal. If you're lucky, a free parking spot might be open in front. If not, there is a large pay lot next door.

Sojourner Café
134 E. Canon Perdido St., Santa Barbara
805.965.7922, sojournercafe.com
International/vegetarian. L & D daily. Beer & wine. $
When it opened in 1978, the Sojourner (aka the Soj) quickly became a beloved coffee shop where vegetarian, vegan, liberal-minded people could count on healthy, affordable natural food and good conversation. Chef Edie Robertson (and a partner) bought the place in 1997 and expanded the repertoire to focus on world cuisine, including dishes with fish, chicken and turkey (but still no beef). Order from her globe-trotting list of specials, perhaps Thai seafood curry over organic linguine or gingered salmon cakes with papaya-kiwi salsa, or choose a Sojourner classic, like the "Low Rent" soup and salad. You'll feel as if you've just sat down with old friends in someone's home.

Stonehouse
San Ysidro Ranch, 900 San Ysidro Lane, Montecito
805.565.1700, SanYsidroRanch.com
Modern American. D nightly. Full bar. $$$$
With the cheapest room going for more than $600 a night at "the Ranch," dinner at the Stonehouse is a relative bargain and well worth the price to spend a couple of hours on this gorgeous property. A recent $150-million restoration of this Rosewood Resort owned by Beanie Baby mogul Ty Warner included this restaurant, which is located in a 19th-century stone citrus packing house. The dining room is the picture of rustic elegance, with high, beamed ceilings, stone walls, a fireplace and wrought-iron chandeliers. We like to sit on the Plexiglass-enclosed deck set among the oaks with views of the ocean, creek and Santa Ynez Mountains – it's cozy year-round, thanks to the heated stone flooring, wood-burning fireplace and portable heaters. Chef John Trotta empha-sizes top-notch local ingredients and even har-

vests herbs and veggies from his onsite garden. His menu runs toward things like a Dungeness and jumbo lump crab cake with mango relish or Parmesan-crusted halibut. The wait staff is attentive but never stuffy or intrusive – the epitome of decorum, just like the restaurant.

The Tee-Off
3627 State St., Santa Barbara
805.687.1616, TeeOffsb.com
American. D nightly. Full bar. $$-$$$
Some people come for the generous cocktails. Others can't get enough of the slow-roasted prime rib, served au jus with creamed horse-radish sauce. But nearly everyone, from young families to octogenarians, heads to the Tee-Off for the traditional, old-school atmosphere, with vinyl booths and down-home American food: steaks, chops, shrimp cocktail, onion rings, po-tato skins and the like. The smaller club menu has burgers, fish and chips, salads and prime rib pot pie (guess where last-night's leftovers went?!). The restaurant welcomes kids, but bear in mind that the sometimes-rowdy bar scene is happening either right in front of them or right around the corner.

Trattoria Grappolo
3687-C Sagunto St., Santa Ynez
805.688.6899, TrattoriaGrappolo.com
Italian. L Tues.-Sun., D nightly. Beer & wine. $$-$$$
Grappolo's family-style tables fill with locals from all walks of life (ranchers, movie stars, winemakers, landscapers) who come to meet friends and feast on robust, delicious Tuscan food in a fun, lively atmosphere. Chefs (and brothers) Leonardo and Alfonso Curti are known for their veal scaloppini, homemade tortellini, cioppino, spinach salad, pork ten-

Rustic Italian charm in the Santa Barbara wine country.

derloin with balsamic sweet onion and crostini with artichoke paste and ricotta, as well as their excellent risotti and thin-crust pizzas. This place can be NOISY on the weekend, since everyone's usually having a blast conversing over numerous bottles of wine.

Tre Lune
1151 Coast Village Rd., Montecito
805.969.2646
Italian. L Mon.-Sat., B & D daily. Full bar.
$$$-$$$$
If you're in Montecito and eat only Italian food, you're in luck – there are a lot of terrific trattorias here, and this is one of our favorites. Breakfast is one of the best-kept secrets in town; try the poached eggs on toasted olive bread with artichoke spread or traditional American fare like French toast and waffles, and accompany either choice with a great cappuccino. Come back for dinner and sample the succulent veal scaloppini, thin-crust pizzas or pasta dishes. Service is engaging and efficient, but you'll still have time to gaze at the black-and-white photos of old-time Hollywood stars and pretend you're on your own Roman holiday.

Tupelo Junction
1218 State St., Santa Barbara
805.899.3100, TupeloJunction.com
Southern/Cajun. B, L & D. Full bar. $$
There's much to become addicted to here. Cinnamon apple beignets. Tangy fried pickles. Cheddar and gouda mac 'n' cheese. And sweet pear cider with a kick. But it's the fried chicken salad that leads us to dream about this Southern-style café, where fruit-crate labels deck the walls and fresh-squeezed lemonade is served in jelly jars. The salad blends dried cranberries, mixed greens, fried chicken, pumpkin seeds and chunks of crumbly cornbread with an herb buttermilk dressing – a sweet dream, indeed.

Via Vai Trattoria & Pizzeria
1483 E. Valley Rd., #20, Montecito
805.565.9393, paneevino-viavai.com
Italian. L & D daily. Beer & wine. $$$
Every neighborhood should have one of these: a casual, easy spot for great Italian food with no attitude and friendly service. In the corner of an Upper Village strip mall, Via Vai always has a crowd on its covered patio, with its spectacular views beyond the parking lot to the Santa Ynez Mountains. Try any of the paper-thin, crisp-crusted pizzas from the wood-burning oven.

We like every pasta dish we've met here, along with the rib-eye steak and lamb chops with rosemary, sage and garlic. And desserts are not the usual Italian-restaurant afterthought – we can never escape without having the dreamy bignè al cioccolato, cream-filled pastry puffs drizzled with warm chocolate sauce.

Vineyard House
3631 Sagunto St., Santa Ynez
805.688.2886, thevineyardhouse.com
Modern American/Californian. L Mon. & Wed.-Sat., D Wed.-Mon., brunch Sun. $$
The family-owned Vineyard House is a good choice for a quiet wine country meal with neither hype nor hooplah. It occupies a Victorian building in historic downtown Santa Ynez – ask for a table on the verandah if weather permits. The menu focuses on typical wine country/Cal-Mediterranean dishes: pastas, salads, seafood, steaks, rack of lamb and chops, and a number of chicken choices. You can also order simple fare like burgers and fries. Check out the daily specials and order a glass or bottle from the mostly local list of wines.

Wine Cask
813 Anacapa St., Santa Barbara
805.966.9463, winecask.com
Modern American. L Mon.-Fri., D nightly. Beer & wine. $$$$
Found inside the historic, Spanish-Moorish El Paseo complex downtown, the sophisticated Wine Cask held the honor of being one of the county's finest restaurants for nearly two decades. In spring 2007, longtime owner Doug Margerum sold the place, as well as the adjacent wine shop and bistro, Intermezzo, to an out-of-towner, who caused a local uproar when he commenced his "makeover" by chopping down a shade tree in the romantic garden courtyard. The new Wine Cask has drawn mixed reviews since then. Still, it has one of the prettiest dining rooms in Santa Barbara, with high, beamed ceilings, a huge stone fireplace and original art. It's also one of the best destinations for wine-and-food pairing, since the staff just heads over to the wine shop to get your bottle. The extensive list includes pages of wines from around the world and more than 40 by the glass. As for eating, we must warn you that portions are on the small side and prices are high for what you get. It's a better value at lunch, when you can have a Kobe beef burger or filet mignon enchiladas.

World Cuisine

Some international cuisines – notably Mexican and Japanese – are as common in California as palm trees, so they're found in Our Favorite Restaurants. Santa Barbara doesn't have the global range that its giant neighbor L.A. does, but we do have a few great spots serving (relatively) exotic cooking.

Café Buenos Aires
1316 State St., Santa Barbara
805.963.0242, cafebuenosaires.com
South American. L & D daily. Full bar. $$
Close to the Arlington and Granada theaters, this romantic, casually elegant restaurant with a courtyard patio serves a Latin American fusion cuisine that blends Argentinean, Italian, Spanish and Cuban influences. Founders Wally and Silvia Ronchietto showcase traditional foods from their Argentine home towns, including a delicious pie filled with ground sirloin, olives, sweet corn and basil, plus empanadas, tapas, pastas, fish and grilled steaks (imported from Argentina, of course). On Wednesdays a live tango milonga quintet plays, and couples are welcome to dance from 7 to 10:30 pm. Fridays bring Latin-American folkloric music with an Andean emphasis, and on Saturdays a Latin jazz quartet enlivens the space.

Chef Karim's
Victoria Court, 1221 State St., Santa Barbara
805.899.4780, chefkarim.com
Moroccan. D Wed.-Sun. Beer & wine. $$-$$$$
Enter Chef Karim's and step into another world – upholstered banquettes, warm Moroccan hospitality and leisurely, delicious feasts. But

CARDIGANS KNIT SHOP

FLAVOR OF INDIA

Indian Cuisine

Colorful outdoor dining at Flavor of India.

perhaps the best thing is the owner/chef himself, Casablanca-raised Karim Chhibbane, who makes everyone feel like his long-lost friend. Take your time and order one of the feasts, which include Moroccan lentil soup, salads, fresh bread and b'stilla, a phyllo pastry filled with chicken, almonds, eggs, cinnamon and sugar. (He also makes b'stillas vegetarian and vegan upon request.) We like the Marrakesh, a dish of stewed lamb with honey and prunes. Honey-dipped sesame cookies, fresh fruit, nuts and mint tea top it all off. A new à la carte menu is also available, but the feast, although it may seem pricey, is the way to get the full experience. Wednesday is family night; Sunday is student night. This place is a hoot with a group, but it also makes for a perfect romantic evening.

Flavor of India
3026 State St., Santa Barbara
805.682.6561, flavorofindiasb.com
Indian. L & D Mon.-Sat. Beer & wine. $-$$
You'll be drawn in by the tantalizing aromas of Indian spices wafting out of this family-owned upper-State locals' favorite. But you'll stay for the warm, friendly atmosphere and traditional northern Indian dishes. Repeatedly chosen in local readers' polls as the best Indian in town, Flavor of India makes food that is richly flavorful but not spicy – let your server know if you want it kicked up a notch or two. Try the tandoori chicken, lamb vindaloo or any of the curries. Everything is made from scratch, including the cheese for the saag paneer (spinach cooked with cheese and herbs), and the $8.95 lunch buffet is one of the best deals in town.

Saigon Noodle House
6831 Hollister Ave., Goleta
805.968.5116
Vietnamese. L & D daily. Beer only. $
Say you're driving to or from Costco or K-Mart, you're hungry and you have a light wallet. This little pho house in the K-Mart shopping center is the place for you. The bright, contemporary café ladles out great noodle and rice dishes and egg rolls. Slurp up the pho bo vien (beef

Café Buenos Aires.

meatballs in rice noodle soup), munch some crispy fried shrimp, spring rolls or egg rolls, and you'll be ready to hit the bargain shopping.

The Taj Café
905 State St., Santa Barbara
805.564.8280, thetajcafe.com
Indian. L & D daily. Beer & wine. $-$$
The Taj feels like a traditional home in a northern Indian village, with imported furnishings, art and authentic cooking at reasonable prices. Most dishes originate from northern India, including Agra, but some represent other parts of the country. They're all made with natural spices and fresh ingredients. Try a Bombay Frankie, a burrito-like wrap filled with chicken, lamb or veggies. If you find it difficult to choose an entree, go for one of the combination plates: chutneys, curries, tandooris. Save room for the housemade mango ice cream or carrot pudding with raisins and almonds. The all-you-can-eat lunch buffet costs only nine bucks and includes curries, tandoori dishes, salad, bread, rice, chutneys, fruit and desserts.

Zaytoon
209 E. Canon Perdido St., Santa Barbara
805.963.1293, cafezaytoon.com
Middle Eastern. L Mon.-Sat., D nightly. Beer & wine. $$
Zaytoon is a refreshing change in a town that doesn't exactly boast the falafel-stand-on-every-corner kind of restaurant diversity of the big city. Although the dining room in an old converted house is perfectly fine, sit outside on the patio to get the full experience: tables with built-in fire pits, fountains, lively Persian music and a few folks smoking fruit-infused tobacco from a hookah. On Saturday nights there's live belly dancing. Try the house special, the Mashawi Combo, to sample marinated chicken, lamb and a kefta kebab (ground lamb sausage with pine nuts and rice) with tabbouleh, hummus, baba ganouj and garlic sauce.

Zen Yai Thai Cuisine
425 State St., Santa Barbara
805.957.1102
Thai. L Tues.-Fri., D nightly. Beer & wine. $-$$
More than a straight Thai restaurant, Zen Yai serves food "reminiscent of things Thai" with a bit of '60s California style blended into both the atmosphere and the sassy, spicy sauces. John Lennon's image looks over the tables in the tiny, funky dining room – the tantalizing scents of duck, grilled massaman salmon, pumpkin curry and other dishes made from local ingredients probably drive him crazy. The creative menu includes lots of vegetarian dishes, and you can ask for milk-free sauces. Call for a reservation or expect a wait, especially on weekends.

Breakfast & Lunch Cafés

Arts & Letters Café at Sullivan Goss
7 E. Anapamu St., Santa Barbara
805.730.1463 sullivangoss.com/cafe
Modern American. L daily. Full bar. $$-$$$
This place is an art aficionado's dream. Head straight through the Sullivan Goss gallery and discover this sophisticated bistro in a quiet Spanish-Mexican walled courtyard with a stone fountain – a lovely setting for a romantic lunch or quiet meeting. Order a cocktail or glass of wine from an extensive selection and explore the California wine-country cooking: chilled crab and corn pudding, pumpkin soup, duck confit salad, grilled ostrich burgers and a local cioppino. If you want to take in the street scene on gallery row, ask to sit on the front porch; for a real treat, reserve a table during the regularly scheduled Opera Under the Stars, where you can listen to operas, arias and theatrical music while savoring a three-course prix-fixe meal.

Barcliff & Bair
1112 State St, Santa Barbara
805.965.5742
American. B & L daily. Beer & wine. $
There's something ever so civilized about a repast taken at Barcliff & Bair, where an order of sticky oatmeal comes with a little silver pitcher of milk and a dish of brown sugar for sprinkling. Sit outside, if you can, surrounded by the brick-and-tile architecture of La Arcada courtyard, and watch people pass on State Street. The morning menu boasts omelets, waffles and big, steamy cappuccinos; lunch offers soups, salads and sandwiches.

Cajun Kitchen
1924 De la Vina St., Santa Barbara
805.687.8062
901 Chapala St., Santa Barbara
805.965.1004
K-Mart Plaza, 6831 Hollister Ave, Goleta
805.571.1517
865 Linden Ave., Carpinteria
805.684.6010, cajunkitchensb.com
Southern. B & L daily. Beer & wine. $
The sign outside the original Cajun Kitchen on De la Vina, which first opened more than twenty years ago, says it all: "If you're in a hurry and can't wait for the best, go somewhere else and settle for less." And regulars happily wait to get some of the best homecooked Louisiana grub in the region. For breakfast, consider the New Orleans omelet, the jambalaya topped with eggs, and such sides as biscuits, grits and gra-

vy. Spice-phobic folks can order "regular" stuff like pancakes and poached eggs with toast (or a tortilla, if you prefer). Lunch guests feast on po'boys, gumbos, red beans and rice, blackened prime rib and the famous Cajun burger. As for us, we're partial to the Creole jambalaya, crawfish etouffée and Bourbon Street chili.

Ellen's Danish Pancake House
272 Ave. of the Flags, Buellton
805.688.5312
American. B & L daily, D Tues.-Sun. Beer only. $$
In 1947, intrepid souls Ellen and Carlo Hansen came from Denmark and opened Ellen's Danish Pancake Hus in Solvang. Sixty years later, Ellen's thin, golden Danish pancakes are still a hit. John Oltman bought the restaurant in 1980 and several years later moved it to this spot. The décor is old-style coffee shop meets grandma's house, and the service is friendly and efficient. Breakfast is served all day: ample plates of American pancakes, eggs with sausage and hash browns, French toast and of course those Danish pancakes, paired with fresh fruit or homemade jam. For lunch you can get a sandwich or a salad, but lots of people revel in the pancakes no matter the hour. Comfort food at its calorie-laden best.

Jeannine's Bakery & Café
3607 State St., Santa Barbara
805.687.8701
1253 Coast Village Rd., Montecito
805.969.7878
American. B & L daily. No booze. $
A purveyor of heavenly scones, coffee cakes, cakes, brownies and all things caloric and wonderful, Jeannine's is the friendly go-to café to meet a friend for breakfast or lunch, or just

The courtyard at Arts & Letters Café

Buellton's shrine to pancakes, Ellen's.

sit by yourself with a newspaper. Both locations are packed on weekend mornings with locals who like to start their day with, say, a fresh-baked raspberry scone, an omelet or breakfast burrito, and a cup of Peet's coffee. Lunches bring salads and sandwiches, and if you can get out without ordering a piece of carrot cake, you have more willpower than we do. Jeannine's also has an outpost just inside Gelson's in Loreto Plaza.

Montecito Coffee Shop
1498 E. Valley Rd., Montecito
805.969.6250
American. B & L Mon.-Sat., brunch Sun. Beer & wine. $
Aka Tom's Place, or the Pharmacy, this tiny, unassuming space in the Upper Village attracts upper-crust Montecito folks seeking basic, down-home food. The breakfast menu includes scrambles, homemade muesli, huevos rancheros and eggs Benedict. Lunch centers on salads, sandwiches and burgers; our favorites are the turkey-walnut-cranberry and chicken-apple salads and the roasted turkey sandwich. Remember to bring cash (no credit cards) and turn off your cell phone so you don't bother your neighbors (who just might be billionaires and/or celebrities – shhh).

Montecito Deli
1150 Coast Village Rd., Montecito
805.969.3717
American/Italian. B & L Mon.-Sat. No booze. $
This bustling little store on the west end of Coast Village Road is known for its grilled piadina sandwiches, a specialty of the Emilia-

Romagna region of Italy, made with housemade flatbread. Try the Montecito pollo: house-roasted chicken breast, tomatoes, ranch dressing, provolone, bacon and lettuce. We also like the barbecue tri-tip with salsa, hot pepper jack cheese, tomatoes and spicy homemade tomato sauce. Salads range from Greek to Chinese-style chicken, and if they've made tortilla soup, order it. Enjoy your feast at a modest table inside or out on the sidewalk.

Paula's Pancake House
1531 Mission Dr., Solvang
805.688.2867,
American/Scandinavian. B & L daily. No booze. $-$$
Locals and visiting celebrities alike frequently come to this cozy, family-friendly café for some of the best breakfasts in the North County. Waitresses in traditional Danish garb serve mouthwatering plates of thin pancakes sprinkled with powdered sugar, glazed strawberries and whipped cream, as well as crispy waffles, omelets and eggs Benedict. Ask for a table on the patio so you can watch the tourist parade. For lunch, Paula's serves homemade soups, salads, sandwiches, burgers and daily specials.

Pierre Lafond Montecito
516 San Ysidro Rd., Montecito
805.565.1504, pierrelafond.com
American. B, L & D daily. Beer & wine. $
This café/deli/gourmet market in Montecito's Upper Village is a haven for foodies and a hangout for folks who just want to sip an excellent cappuccino and see who else is there. Our morning fave is the breakfast burrito; for lunch try the popular Santa Rosa sandwich with grilled organic free-range chicken breast, provolone, applewood-smoked bacon, basil and tomato on a toasted French roll. Wraps (like the blackened ahi), salads (like the Thai mango), panini and the extensive salad bar each have their devoted following. While you're there, hit the market and pick up some goodies: local wines (including Lafond Winery & Vineyards, of course), cheeses and Santa Barbara olives, pistachios and olive oils.

Plaza Deli
La Cumbre Plaza, 140 S. Hope Ave., Santa Barbara
805.682.4410
American. B & L daily. No booze. $
This is a quintessential friendly neighborhood

deli, but with a twist – or a fizz. More than 300 hard-to-find bottled sodas fill the refrigerator cases and line the walls. The owner, Larry, says many of his retro sodas come from back east and are made with cane sugar instead of the dreaded high-fructose corn syrup. Larry clearly loves his work, greeting most of his customers by name and chatting up regulars. Sandwiches are fresh, delicious, ample and reasonably priced (try the Italian hoagie), and the tomato-basil soup is terrific. During the week, breakfast sandwiches are offered starting at 9 a.m.

Santa Barbara Shellfish Co.
230 Stearns Wharf, Santa Barbara
805.966.6676, sbfishhouse.com
American/seafood. L & D daily. Beer & wine. $
Sometimes we like to pretend we're on vaca-tion and head down to Stearns Wharf to drink in the ocean breezes and carefree vibe – and to eat some seriously good fresh seafood at this friendly little paper-plate spot on the end of the wharf. Santa Barbara Shellfish Co. started in 1979 as a buying station for local lobster and abalone, later evolving into the area's expert on all things crustacean … and they're all on the menu. It's a perfect place to admire the views, people-watch and dig in to chowder bread bowls, shrimp tacos, steamed clams, fried calamari, crab cakes and cioppino. And it's the cheapest vacation we've ever had.

South Coast Deli
185 S. Patterson Ave., Goleta
805.967.8226
1436 Chapala St., Santa Barbara
805.560.9800, southcoastdeli.com
Modern American. B Mon.-Fri., L Mon.-Sat. Beer & wine. $
Since 1991 Jim and Darlene St. John have provided a loyal following with fantastic healthy sandwiches and salads made from super-fresh ingredients. Everything has a creative, California-ish twist, including the unusual mayos and made-from-scratch salad dressings, like chipotle ranch. Favorites include the flank steak panini with sun-dried tomato mayo, cara-melized onions and cambozola cheese; Asian greens with chicken salad; smoked turkey sam-mie with basil mayo, cheddar and provolone cheese, and the roast beef "Hottie 88," with melted hot-pepper jack and garlic-Tabasco mayo. Fans stop by for a breakfast sandwich or to pick up a bag lunch. You can also get coffee, smoothies and desserts.

Sambo's
216 W. Cabrillo Blvd., Santa Barbara
805.965.3269, sambosrestaurant.com
American. B & L daily. Beer & wine. $-$$
Back in 1957, Sam Battistone, longtime owner of downtown diner Sammy's Grill, and his pal, Newell Bohnett, decided to open a pancake restaurant. They combined their nicknames, Sam and Bo, and called their new venture Sambo's. Pancakes were all the rage at the time, and serving a short stack made with farm-fresh eggs, buttermilk and sour cream (cost 40 cents) and a bottomless cup of coffee for ten cents sounded like a great business idea. Sam and Bo discovered *Little Black Sambo*, a storybook written by Helen Bannerman in 1899 about a little boy in India who ventures into the jungle and loses his clothing to bullying tigers. The boy regains his clothes, and the tigers turn into melted butter, which Sambo's dad brings home. Sambo's mom made pancakes, and little Sambo ate 169 of them with tiger butter on top. Sam and Bo thought the story matched just fine and used it to develop a theme. Later, the restaurant expanded into a huge chain that eventually disappeared after a complicated series of financial and political events.

Today, Sam's grandson, Chad Stevens, and his wife, Michelle, own the one-and-only original Sambo's in the same location. Prices have risen a tad but are still reasonable considering the prime waterfront location across from West Beach. (Ask for a patio or bay window table.) You can still order a short stack (can you eat 169?) and French toast, plus specialties like the salmon omelet, California eggs benedict and huevos rancheros. Lunch fare includes burgers, salads and tacos. Save room for dessert: root beer float, hot fudge sundae or banana split. If you're a longtime Sambo's fan, stock up on memorabilia in the "souvenir jungle."

Eat 'n' Run: Fast Food, Pizza & Takeout

Fast Food

All American Surf Dog
Hwy. 101 & Bailard Ave., Carpinteria
No phone
L daily. Cash only.
This is a one-man fast-food institution, just off the 101 in Carpinteria – you'll know when Bill Connell's conducting business when you see his big American flag waving near the Carpinteria Bluffs Nature Preserve. For about fifteen years, Bill has been serving up juicy hot dogs along with juicy philosophical tidbits from his shiny red trailer to travelers driving up or down the coast and to devoted regular locals. Try the Dodger dog – and don't forget the mustard.

Lettuce B. Frank
413 State St., Santa Barbara
805.965.7948
L & D daily.
Any place with a name like this has to have a sense of humor, and this lower State Street hot dog joint certainly does. Service is friendly, the atmosphere is casual, and prices are reasonable. In addition to hot dogs, it has easy-eatin' sliders – in burger, veggie, fish and pulled-pork versions – and light, crispy sweet potato fries.

Minnow Café
9 Breakwater, Santa Barbara
805.962.6315
B & L daily.
Tucked between buildings down at the harbor, this outdoor-only café is definitely no frills. You'll get a salty dose of harbor life with your great burger, fish and chips or, best of all, fish tacos. Breakfasts are hearty enough to sustain you through a long morning on the high seas: breakfast burritos, huevos rancheros, pancakes, omelets and French toast.

Santa Barbara Chicken Ranch
2618 De la Vina St., Santa Barbara
805.569.1872, sbchickenranch.com
163 N. Fairview Ave., Goleta
805.692.9200
L & D daily.
Although this qualifies as fast food because you order at the counter and it's served speedy-quick, it's not junk food – this chow is good and fresh. You'll smell the come-hither aromas of grilling meat way before you walk through the door. The menu is simple: burritos or perfectly seasoned grilled tri-tip and/or chicken (get the combo!), served with such sides as rice, beans, salsa and cole slaw. You can eat here on an indoor picnic table or outdoor umbrella table, or take it home.

Pizza

Dean-o's Pizzarama
1950 Cliff Dr., Santa Barbara
805.965.1077, deanospizzarama.com
L & D daily. Beer & wine.
Good times prevail at this old-school pizza joint, where a young crowd enjoys a good old-fashioned pinball machine, video games and TVs (let's just say usually not tuned to Fox News). Some nights there's a crowd of post-game softball players refueling with pizza and beer. Although pizza is the thing to get here, oven-baked sub sandwiches and spaghetti and meatballs are on offer for the renegades.

Giovanni's
3020 State St., Santa Barbara
805.682.3621, giovannispizzasb.com
6583 Pardall Rd., Isla Vista
805.968.2254
L & D daily. Beer & wine.
For more than 25 years, Santa Barbarans have flocked to Giovanni's for good, dependable pizza made with fresh ingredients. Northside

Bill Connell and a surf dog.

and San Roque families frequent the upper State Street location, especially on Friday nights, filling their tables with pizza pies, pasta, salads and oven-baked sub sandwiches, playing the video games and watching sports on TV. At press time, a new Giovanni's was about to open at 1905 Cliff Drive on the Mesa.

Marty's Pizza Delivery
2733 De la Vina St., Santa Barbara
805.682.6955, martyspizza.com
L & D daily, for takeout & delivery only.
For more than 22 years, Marty's has been zipping all over town, delivering piping-hot, thin-crust pizzas; since delivery is all they do, they've now perfected it by creating a convenient online ordering system. We like to kick back and await the prompt arrival of a white pizza – olive oil, chopped garlic and five white cheeses – and a crisp salad. Mmmmm….

Pizza Mizza
104 S. Hope Ave., Santa Barbara
805.564.3900, pizzamizza.com
L & D daily. Beer & wine.
Plop yourself down here after a buying spree at Tiffany & Co. down the mall. Though La Cumbre Plaza has undergone an upscale-ification of late, Pizza Mizza has, thankfully, remained. It offers a mind-bending selection of good gourmet pizzas, fresh salads, sandwiches and pastas, you can sit inside or out on the now-more-lovely mall, and the service is always friendly and efficient.

Rusty's Pizza
15 E. Cabrillo Blvd., Santa Barbara
805.564.1111, rustyspizza.com
L & D daily. Beer & wine.
Rusty's newest location across from the beach and Stearns Wharf is hard to miss – it's a stucco faux lighthouse. Happy tourists and locals flock like seagulls to sit outside in the ocean breeze (there's indoor seating, too) and dig into pizzas, sub sandwiches and salads. Rusty's has seven other locations from Carpinteria to Goleta.

Taffy's Pizza
2026 De la Vina St., Santa Barbara
805.687.3083, taffyspizza.com
L & D Mon.-Sat. Beer & wine.
A great family pizza-night-out place, this is one of the few pizzerias that has a pleasant outdoor patio. It can get noisy (what pizza place can't?),

especially during soccer season, with end-of-season team parties. When we're feeling virtuous, we get the whole-wheat crust veggie pizza.

Woodstock's Pizza
928 Embarcadero Del Norte, Isla Vista
805.968.6969, woodstocksislavista.com
L & D daily (to midnight or later). Beer & wine.
A block away from the UCSB campus, Woodstock's has been catering to a fun-lovin' college crowd since 1982. Its kitchen team makes the dough and sauce daily, loads on the toppings and lets the crowds come. And they do: Word has it that on Halloween (a particularly, shall we say, festive evening in Isla Vista) in 1992, Woodstock's achieved a personal record of making 1,000 pizzas in one night. Enterprising customers have been known to roll in empty beer kegs for extra seating when the crowds push the limits. Woodstock's has college-town sister locations in Chico, Davis, San Luis Obispo and San Diego. Free delivery.

Fruit tarts at Fresco.

Takeout

Fresco
3987 State St., Santa Barbara
805.967.6037, FrescoSB.com
Fresco North
5940 Calle Real, Goleta
805.692.8999, FrescoNorth.com
See listing page 134.

Garden Market
3811 Santa Claus Lane, Carpinteria
805.745.5505, thegardenmarkets.com
American. L & D daily. Beer & wine.
A favorite stop for Summerlanders and Carpinterians in a hurry, many of whom are on their

way to or from the steps-away beach, this friendly market/boutique/café carries fresh sandwiches, salads and a deli case stocked with entrees, some prepared in the market's own kitchen and some prepared by Rincon Catering down the lane. Try the tri-tip on sourdough and one of the irresistible desserts: tiramisu, chocolate mousse cake, lemon squares and apple cobbler bars. Grab a smoothie or espresso drink or a bottle of wine from the small but thoughtful selection and you're ready to go. But come back when you have time to enjoy the sweet garden patio in back.

Lazy Acres
302 Meigs Rd., Santa Barbara
805.564.4410, lazyacres.com
Californian. B, L & D daily. Beer & wine.
Are you out of luck for a potluck because you had no time to make a dish to share? Or just need something to eat for dinner tonight? Stop by high-end market Lazy Acres, near the intersection of Cliff Drive on the Mesa, and pick up a good-for-you gourmet meal. You'll have to fork over the dough for this takeout, but it's made with high-quality organic produce, grains and dairy products, as well as free-range, hormone-free poultry and meats. While you're at it, stop by the bakery and grab a chocolate muffin or lemon pound cake, baked onsite with organic ingredients, and then head to the coffee bar for a cappuccino. You're good to go … and there are tables if you don't have to go.

Montecito Deli
1150 Coast Village Rd., Montecito
805.969.3717
See listing page 145.

Norton's Pastrami
18 W. Figueroa St., Santa Barbara
805.965.3210, nortonspastrami.com
American. L & D Mon.-Sat. until 8 p.m. Beer & wine.
Just because of the name, this place always makes us think of Ed Norton on the *Honeymooners*, and Ed would have approved of the great, straightforward sandwiches here. Norton's does have other sandwich choices, along with hot dogs, but we can't get away from the PLT: crispy pastrami with lettuce, tomato and spicy mayo on sourdough. Or go with a classic pastrami or corned beef on rye or a reuben. The seasoned shoestring fries are tasty but don't travel well – opt for the cole slaw or potato

salad instead. This is a popular place for downtown workers to grab a lunch for the office, but table and counter seating is available. There's a minuscule extra charge for takeout orders.

Panino
2900 Grand Ave., Los Olivos
805.688.9304, paninorestaurants.com
Italian/Californian. L daily. Beer & wine.
With locations in downtown Santa Barbara, Montecito, Goleta and Solvang, there is usually a Panino near you. And thank goodness, because these are consistently voted the best sandwiches in the area by local polls. If you're in the Valley for wine tasting or gallery hopping, stop in right next to the flagpole in downtown Los Olivos and order, say, a turkey with brie or a curried chicken salad sandwich – it has about 30 delicious sandwich possibilities, as well as a Cobb or a Stilton, Asian pear and chopped walnut salad. You can sit a spell at a table inside or out, or take your panino to a picnic spot at your next wine-tasting stop.

Plaza Deli
140 S. Hope Ave., Santa Barbara
805.682.4410
See listing page 145.

Savoy Café & Deli
24 W. Figueroa St., Santa Barbara
805.966.2139, savoytruffles.com
Californian. B, L & D Mon.-Sat. until 8:30 p.m. Beer & wine.
Originally called the Savoy Truffle after a Beatles song, this gourmet market and deli has won local raves for its amazingly varied and fresh salad bar, which changes daily but might include wild salmon, tofu and roast beef. Hot prepared foods are consistently good and range from stuffed chicken breast to seared salmon, roast turkey to mac 'n' cheese. And how about some oven-roasted veggies with that? If that's not enough, you'll find about four soups, along with sandwiches and organic salads. Don't forget the baked-daily cookies and cakes and the Jessica Foster truffles for dessert. If you're not in a hurry, have a seat on the back patio.

South Coast Deli
1436 Chapala St., Santa Barbara
185 S. Patterson Ave., Goleta
See listing page 146.

Tacos, Burgers & Barbecue

Big Tom's Backyard BBQ at the Maverick Saloon
3687 Sagunto St., Santa Ynez
805.688.6904, mavericksaloon.org
Barbecue. L Mon.-Wed. & Fri.-Sun., D Mon.-Wed. & Fri.-Sat. Full bar at the saloon. $
A great place to hang out, mingle with ranchers and vintners and eat perhaps the best barbecue in the Valley. Choose from tri-tip, burgers, chicken breast or pulled-pork sandwiches, cheese steaks, hot dogs and chicken wings (ask for spicy for a little more kick). Want some chili cheese fries with that? Grab a cold Firestone Walker pale ale at the saloon, kick up your cowboy boots and enjoy.

The Burger Barn
3621 Sagunto St., Santa Ynez
805.688.2366
American/burgers. L daily, B Sat. & Sun. Beer & wine. $
Valleyites swear that the best burgers are found in this barn-like building on Santa Ynez's historic main drag. Sit inside or on the inviting patio (it's full service) or get your burgers to go. What makes 'em so good is the freshly ground local meat. Not in the mood for a burger? Try a salad, sandwich or homemade soup (the potato-leek is delicious). And it isn't every burger barn that offers some top-notch wines from vineyards just down the road.

Derf's
2000 De la Vina St., Santa Barbara
805.687.5437
American/burgers. B, L & D daily. Full bar. $
This busy corner pub is known for its good burgers, although it also serves breakfasts like scrambles and breakfast burritos. Most devotees sit on the spacious sunny deck; the inside is a relatively small, wood-paneled space, but it does have two TVs at the lively bar if you want to catch the game. There are times when nothing but a Derf's bacon burger with pepper jack and guacamole will do, but you can get a salad if you're feeling more virtuous. The fries are crispy and delicious and the prices reasonable. For dessert, walk across the street to McConnell's for great ice cream.

Freebirds
879 Embarcadero Del Norte, Isla Vista
805.968.0123
Mexican. Daily 24 hours. Beer. $
A wee-hours spot for UCSB students who have been, shall we say, busy studying all night, this is also a good place at any hour. Unless you haven't eaten for days, the ginormous burritos are enough for two meals. Here's the drill: You move down the cafeteria-ish line and watch as your burrito is assembled, so you control what goes in it. Freebirds is also known for its tacos and addictive chicken nachos, to which you can add beans, extra cheese, guacamole, salsa, you name it, and eat while sitting outside and watching the I.V. parade.

The Habit
628 State St., Santa Barbara
805.892.5400, HabitBurger.com
5735 Hollister Ave., Goleta
805.964.0366
216 S. Milpas St., Santa Barbara
805.962.7472
Hamburgers. L & D daily. No booze. $
Once upon a time, a local teen got his first job flipping burgers at an old-fashioned stand. A few years later, he bought the place with his brother, and they've been charbroiling burgers ever since. The Habit's the genuine article: thick-cut french fries, crumbly onion rings and delicious malts. At lunchtime, everyone from beachgoers to business folks in fancy suits line up for their guilty pleasures. The Milpas location is the only one with indoor seating; the original Goleta stand is the only one that still serves chili burgers. Go for the grilled onions. Slurp.

La Super-Rica Taqueria
622 N. Milpas St., Santa Barbara
805.963.4940
Mexican. L & D Sun.-Tues. & Thurs.-Sat. Beer. Cash only. $
It's easy to spot La Super-Rica – just drive up Milpas and look for a line on the sidewalk and a bright turquoise zigzag roof. This unassuming little taco stand with a vinyl tarp for a patio roof was opened by Isidoro Gonzalez (see Q & A at the end of this chapter) in 1980 and has been serving up authentic Mexican dishes to adoring locals and tourists ever since. If the place wasn't popular enough already, it was catapulted into international fame when Julia

Child started coming by for her favorite tacos and some of the fresh, grainy corn tortillas. You can watch the tortillas being made in the tiny kitchen as you place your order at the window. Isidoro or his brother and partner, Martín, might take your order ("Long time no see! Where have you been?!"); his mom helps make the salsas, and his dad runs the errands. A Santa Barbara melting pot, La Super-Rica is a hit with everyone from local housepainters and plumbers to Montecito mavens and celebs. Some Super tips: Get there early, check the daily specials, don't ask for a burrito (they don't make 'em) but do ask for extra tortillas. We recommend the Especial, a roasted pasilla chile stuffed with cheese and served with marinated grilled pork.

Everything's fresh at La Super-Rica.

Rincon Alteno Taqueria
115 E. Haley St., Santa Barbara
805.962.9798
4414 Via Real, Carpinteria
805.684.7764
Mexican. B, L & D daily. Beer. $
This is one of those off-the-beaten-path joints that you only know about by word of mouth. And we know many a local who has wrapped his or her mouth around one of its tacos or burritos and will never go anywhere else. Good homemade chips and salsa; tacos al pastor; breakfast, carne asada or veggie burritos; huevos rancheros and aguas frescas. It's all fresh, good and cheap.

Super Cuca's Taqueria
626 W. Micheltorena St., Santa Barbara
805.962.4028, supercucas3.com
2030 Cliff Dr., Santa Barbara
805.966.3863
6547 Trigo Rd., Isla Vista
805.961.0020
Mexican. B, L & D daily. Beer. $
Just saying Super Cuca's makes us smile. And eating here makes us smile even more. Voted best burrito in Santa Barbara for years, Super Cuca's is not resting on its cilantro. Each loca-

tion attracts devoted regulars, and of course the Isla Vista location is heavy on the UCSB students, who come for the hefty burritos, pudgy taquitos and tacos, filling tortas and cheesy quesadillas. For a change of pace from the burritos, we like the shrimp tacos.

Woody's Bodacious Barbecue
Magnolia Center, 5112 Hollister Ave., Goleta
805.967.3775, woodysbbq.com
Barbecue. L & D daily. Beer & wine. $
Good barbecue is hard to come by in these parts, so we're grateful for Woody's, which has been stoking a hot wood pit for more than 25 years. There's something here for every carnivore, from ribs to brisket to slow-smoked prime rib dinners. For sandwiches, we like the tri-tip or "the Porker," Texas-style pulled pork. Pair these with a trip to the salad bar or some sides (cowboy beans, potato salad, onion rings or, heaven forbid, steamed veggies) and a cold beer and you're set. This is a convivial, noisy, family-friendly place with memorabilia-decked walls, a kids' menu and celebrating soccer teams or groups watching sports on TV. Don't forget to wash your hands in the dining room's bathtub before you leave.

Good Eats: Bakeries, Caterers & Specialty Markets

Bakeries

Andersen's

1106 State St., Santa Barbara
805.962.5085, anderssenssantabarbara.com
For more than 30 years, Andersen's has been a genteel European oasis in the La Arcada building. With its black-and-white linoleum floor, lots of pink and filigree, you'll be transported to Copenhagen, especially when you gaze into the cases filled with such gorgeous creations as Danish kringle, a buttery apple strudel served warm. Marzipan is a specialty; try the Sarah Bernhardt, a marzipan cookie with chocolate mousse dipped in dark Ghirardelli chocolate. Not many places in town serve high tea, but this place does, every day from 2 to 5 pm. You can also get breakfast, lunch and dinner, with everything from smörgaasbord to schnitzel.

Anna's Bakery

7018 Camino Real Marketplace, Goleta
805.968.5590, annas-bakery.net
Anna's has been baking up a satisfying storm of goodies for more than 35 years. Originally in the Fairview shopping center, it's now found among the row of restaurants in Goleta's big-box mall. In the morning, try the muffins, croissants, doughnuts and scones; at lunchtime, sandwiches are made on Anna's fresh breads and include a cookie … sweet deal.

Crushcakes

1315 Anacapa St., Santa Barbara
805.963.9353, crushcakes.com
Cupcakes might be a fad, but in this case we're happy to be faddists. The 2008 opening of this tiny downtown shop was eagerly awaited by cupcake fans who watched as the trend spread like batter from New York to Los Angeles. Owner Shannon Feld and crew use high-quality ingredients like Nielsen-Massey vanilla and Scharffen Berger chocolate to make such creations as chocolate bliss, strawberry blush, crazy carrot and lemon drop. We love the peace cake, a cool vanilla-bean cake topped with wild tie-dye frosting and a chocolate peace sign. It usually has the signature crushcake, a red velvet cake topped with a chocolate heart dipped in sour cream frosting. If you don't want to be crushed, arrive early to get your favorite.

D'Angelo Bread

25 W. Gutierrez St., Santa Barbara
805.962.5466
If you're on a low-carb diet, avoid this place like the plague. Shelves of rustic breads, golden pastries and buttery croissants (save an almond one for us) call to you when you enter. Third-generation baker Dietmar Eilbacher, born and raised in Germany, uses natural leavens, which take more time to rise but result in a richer flavor. Breakfast is great – granola and jams are made in-house, and egg dishes are perfectly prepared. Come back for lunch, sit inside or at a sidewalk table, and try the mozzarella, tomato and roasted-pepper sandwich.

Jeannine's Bakery & Café

3607 State St., Santa Barbara
805.687.8701
1253 Coast Village Rd., Montecito
805.969.7878
See listing page 144.

Olsen's Danish Village Bakery

1529 Mission Dr., Solvang
805.688.6314, olsensdanishbakery.com
Owned by fourth-generation Danish baker Bent Olsen and his wife, Susie, this European-style bakery is a standout in a town where baked goods rule. Try the apple strudel, Danish pastry (duh!), homemade breads, almond-custard kringle or Danish butter cookies, which make great hostess gifts or take-home treats to remind you of your day among the windmills and clogs.

Our Daily Bread

831 Santa Barbara St., Santa Barbara
805.966.3894, ourdailybread.net
Our Daily Bread has been baking seven days a week since 1981, and the folks here aren't tired yet. They keep turning out everything from challah and ciabatta to Sicilian olive and sourdough breads, along with muffins, crois-

Panini are made on house-baked breads at Our Daily Bread.

Heaven in a glass case at Renaud's.

sants, scones, cakes and cookies. And ODB gets bonus points for using unbleached flour and organic whole-wheat flour before it was fashionable. It's a popular breakfast and lunch spot, so be prepared to wait in line. Stop in C'est Cheese a couple doors down for some fromage to go with your bread.

Renaud's Patisserie & Bistro
Loreto Plaza, 3315 State St., Santa Barbara
805.569.2400, renaudsbakery.com
Ooh la la, we'd like to offer a kiss on both cheeks to Renaud Gonthier, pastry chef extraordinaire, and the owner (with his wife, Nicole) of this French bakery and café. Since opening in early 2008, Renaud has been waking in the wee hours to fill his cases with flaky croissants and mouthwatering brioches, chocolate éclairs, raspberry charlottes and opera cakes – works of art that look too beautiful to eat, but we force ourselves.

Tuttini
10 E. Carrillo St., Santa Barbara
805.963.8404
This tiny place just off State Street reminds us of those neighborhood spots in New York where you get killer baked goods and feel as if you've won the lottery if you can snag one of the handful of tables – here we're lucky to have a few tables on the sidewalk, too. Come early and try the chocolate croissant – that and a latte in a bowl will make you glad to be alive. Though service can be spotty, breakfasts and lunches are excellent.

Xanadu French Bakery
1028 Coast Village Rd., Montecito
805.969.3550
This European-style bakery in the plaza across from Vons is worthy of a big city but has a small-town feel. Locals in the know gather for breakfast (fluffy omelets, egg sandwiches on croissants) or stop by to pick up a black forest cake, cream puffs or fruit torte to take home.

It's also a popular lunch spot, serving delicious sandwiches. Sit out on the patio, and you'll indeed feel like you're in Xanadu.

Caterers
Needless to say, in a town where nonprofit events abound and everyone loves a party, there are dozens of caterers to handle any type of event, from intimate to huge, in every style and price range. Here are a few favorites.

Duo Catering & Events
110 Santa Barbara St., Santa Barbara
805.957.1670, duoevents.com

Country Catering Company
5925 Calle Real, Goleta
805.964.3811, countrycateringcompany.com

Michael's Catering
805.568.1896, michaelscateringsb.com

Mondial Catering & Events
201 W. Carrillo St., Santa Barbara
805.884.0885, mondialsantabarbara.com

New West Catering
P.O. Box 596, Buellton
805.688.0991, newwestcatering.com

Pure Joy Catering
710 E. Haley St., Santa Barbara,
805.963.5766, purejoycatering.com

Rincon Beach Club & Catering
3805 Santa Claus Lane, Carpinteria
805.566.9933, rinconcatering.com

Specialty Markets

C'est Cheese
825 Santa Barbara St., Santa Barbara
805.965.0318, cestcheese.com
Opening this place in 2003 was a dream come true for Michael and Kathryn Graham, who returned from study abroad programs in Europe with a bad case of cheese lust. They based their little shop on the European model and now offer more than 100 varieties (cut fresh from the wheel), along with artisanal salamis, fine-cured hams, pâtés, and other goodies.

Kanaloa Seafood
618 E. Gutierrez St., Santa Barbara
805.966.5159, kanaloa.com
These people know their fish: Owners Don

Cheesy comestibles at C'est Cheese.

Disraeli, a biologist, and Randee Disraeli, a former researcher at Scripps Institute of Oceanography, were trained by a Japanese family that had been seafood processors for three generations. Kanaloa combines Japanese tradition with current scientific knowledge, sourcing wild and farm-raised seafood from Alaska to New Zealand. Trying a new mahi-mahi recipe? This is your first stop.

Los Olivos Grocery
2621 Hwy. 154, Santa Ynez
805.688.5115, losolivosgrocery.com
As charming as a grocery can be, this 1930s-era red-and-white building is a welcome stop on the way to or from wine country. Whether you're outfitting your picnic basket or your pantry, you'll find everything you need: hearth breads, artisan cheeses, charcuterie, Santa Barbara County and hard-to-find wines and local produce. Breakfast, lunch and dinner are served on the covered porch with views of vineyards and the Figueroa Mountains. Choose from homemade soups, rotisserie meats, hearty sandwiches and decadent desserts – and hit the espresso bar before you hit the road.

Mediterra Café & Market
5575A Hollister Ave., Goleta
805.696.9323, mediterracafe.com
Looking for black olive paste, grilled eggplant salad or a nice aged kashkaval? Stop in at this friendly market in Old Town Goleta and pick up these and many more Middle Eastern and Mediterranean foods. It stocks a variety of hummus, baba ganouj, tabbouleh, herbs, spices and olive oils. While you're there, pick up a gyro, pita wrap, panini or salad for lunch or dinner – and don't forget the baklava.

Metropulos Fine Foods Merchant
216 E. Yanonali St., Santa Barbara
805.899.2300, metrofinefoods.com
This market/deli/wine shop in the Funk Zone has become the go-to gourmet grocery. Pro-

prietors Craig and Ann Addis have created one of the best cheese, charcuterie and olive selections in town, and the wine stock, including hard-to-find releases from Greece, Spain and Italy that pair well with the market's Mediterranean foods, reflects the expertise gleaned from Craig's years in the local wine business. (The Wine Gems rack has amazing bargains for under $10.) Stop by for breakfast or lunch, or get a picnic to enjoy at nearby Chase Palm Park.

Santa Barbara Fish Market
117 Harbor Way, Unit F
805.965.9564, sbfish.com
When this fish market says its wares go "From the Boat to You," it's not kidding – fish doesn't get any fresher than this. Located in the heart of the working harbor, the retail and wholesale market sells the local catch every day, along with seafood from around the world. The selection depends on the catch and the season, so go with an open mind.

Shalhoob Meat Company
220 Gray Ave., Santa Barbara
805.963.7733, shalhoob.com
The name Shalhoob is synonymous with meat in this town. Family owned and operated since 1973, it is a locals' favorite for premium tri-tip or steaks for a backyard barbecue. It also offers chicken and gourmet beef jerky from a three-generation-old family recipe.

Tri-County Produce
335 S. Milpas St., Santa Barbara
805.965.4558, tricountyproduce.com
Did you sleep in and miss the farmer's market? Just head to Tri-County, a wholesaler-turned-retailer selling quality local produce, as well as fish, chicken, meats and cheeses. And sshhh … it's a great secret spot to buy wines.

Tri-County Produce in Santa Barbara.

The Chocolate Box

Chocolate Gallery
5705 Calle Real, Goleta
805.967.4688, ChocolateGallery.com
These are quality chocolates that won't break the bank and that you can eat every day – believe us, we know. Owners Karen Kegg and her husband, Tim Johnson, have run this mom-and-pop shop for more than 27 years, making everything here. They're known for their molded items (everything from little chocolate tools to surfboards), Texas crunch (bits of toffee in a chocolate bark) and chocolate explosion (soft chocolate center with cacao nibs). They also make custom chocolate bars and gold-foil coins. Try the melt-in-your mouth mochas.

Chocolate Maya
15 W. Gutierrez St., Santa Barbara
805.965.5956, ChocolateMaya.com
Closed Sun.
Go ahead and step into Maya Schoop-Rutten's diminutive den of decadence – you won't be sorry. You'll find chocolate creations from around the world, including some made by local Tirtza Goldman, that are almost as lovely to look at as they are to eat. Beautiful chocolate gems with everything from thyme to candied lime call out to you from the case. Maya is passionate about chocolate education, and she leads trips to such places as Venezuela and Java to learn more about it. You'll find organic chocolate, chocolate tea, Mexican and Spanish hot chocolate and Belgian and French powders and flakes, as well as sauces and pure cocoa powder. Need a pick-me-up? Try the chocolate-covered roasted cacao seeds.

Chocolats du CaliBressan
4193 Carpinteria Ave., Ste. 4, Carpinteria
805.684.6900, ChocoCaliBressan.com
Closed Sun.
This is not your grandmother's chocolate shop. Hidden in a business park just off the 101 is this quiet oasis of confectionary alchemy – candles flicker, chocolate works of art beckon from gleaming display cases, and you'll see chocolatier Jean-Michel Carré at work in the spanking-clean kitchen. Carré and his wife and co-owner, Jill, named their shop after their roots in California and Bresse, France. Jill presides over the 22 artisanal truffles infused with exotic flavors, and she's happy to guide you: perhaps the praline and milk chocolate rolled in caramelized diced almonds and milk chocolate?

Ingeborg's Danish Chocolates
1679 Copenhagen Dr., Solvang
805.688.5612, ingeborgs.com
Owner Bent Pedersen took over Ingeborg's in 1976 and has been busy ever since, making decadent chocolates and truffles with original Danish recipes. Try the dark-chocolate-covered marzipan and chocolate-covered orange slices, along with the mint sticks. These are great souvenirs, if they make it back home.

Jessica Foster Confections
805.637.6985,
JessicaFosterConfections.com
Jessica Foster prowls the farmers' markets for ingredients for her creative truffles. Two of our faves (and we're proud to say we've tried

Truffles galore at Jessica Foster.

them all) are the Meyer lemon and the extra-bitter single-origin Tanzanian truffle with local wildflower honey dipped in dark chocolate and sprinkled with bee pollen. These little bombs of chocolate heaven are sold online, as well as at a few shops around town (including Lazy Acres and Pierre Lafond in Montecito) or by appointment for local pickup; they're popular as wedding and party favors and corporate gifts.

Robitaille's
900 Linden Ave., Carpinteria
805.684.9340, robitaillescandies.com
You'll feel like a kid in a 1960s candy store, which is exactly what this is. Located on the main drag in Carpinteria, it's the perfect sweet stop after a day on the beach. Known for making the official mints of President Reagan's 1985 inauguration, Robitaille's also handcrafts a full line of chocolates, truffles, fudge, mints and brittle.

See's Candies
205 Paseo Nuevo, Santa Barbara
805.965.5745, sees.com
3849 State St., Santa Barbara
805.687.4800
Let's not forget our dear old friend Mary See – she has two locations in Santa Barbara, and See's is just the thing for last-minute gifts. Everybody loves See's. How can you not?

Farmer's Markets, Farm Stands & Food Festivals

The Lowdown on the Farmer's Markets

Every day of the week except Monday (and who likes Mondays anyway?) you'll find home cooks, A-list chefs and those who just want a really good peach loading up baskets, canvas bags and strollers with fresh veggies and fruit, while getting advice and even recipes from growers. Each market has its own personality, but the mother of them all is the big one on Saturday downtown, which has music and sometimes a balloon-animal maker. Besides produce, you'll find nuts, cheeses, fresh-baked pies and breads, olive oils, lavender products, honey, even seafood and sometimes chicken. And if your haul is heavy, carry-out service is available – just ask at the information desk. On our last visit, we saw a woman in a jean skirt with these words written on it in colorful letters: "Life I love you … all is groovy." It sure is.

Farms & Farm Stands

Apple Lane Farm
1200 Alamo Pintado Rd., Solvang
805.686.5858, applelanesolvang.com
A longtime favorite seasonal apple farm run by the Lane family, Apple Lane Farm offers you-pick or picked-for-you Golden and Red Delicious, Granny Smith, Fuji and Gala apples. The farm usually opens the second or third week of August and closes when it runs out of apples, usually just before Thanksgiving. During that time it's open every day from 10 a.m. to 5 p.m. The apple varieties on offer change during the harvest season. Get out your pie recipes!

Fairview Gardens
598 N. Fairview Ave., Goleta
805.967.7369, fairviewgardens.org
An oasis of agriculture in the middle of suburban sprawl, Fairview Gardens is a well-stocked, high-quality farm stand – but it's also much more. Located on the site of one of the oldest organic farms in California, the Center for Urban Agriculture at Fairview Gardens, a nonprofit established in 1997 to preserve and operate Fairview Gardens, is an internationally respected model for small-scale urban food production, agricultural preservation and farm-based education. On twelve and a half acres, the gardens produce a remarkable variety of

Late-fall produce at the Santa Barbara Farmers' Market.

fruits and vegetables to sell at their stand and farmer's markets, as well as to feed families through its Community Supported Agriculture program. CSA members support a portion of the crops through a season-long commitment, prepaying all or part of the cost so Fairview's farmers can purchase seeds and prepare fields for the next harvest. The farm offers popular cooking and gardening classes, farm festivals, lectures, apprenticeships and outreach programs. The gardens are open for self-guided tours from 10 a.m. until sunset; guided tours are by arrangement.

La Loma Orchard
Carpinteria
805.684.8536
Ninety-five-year-old farmer Lee Talbert and his wife, Fawzia, grow figs, including brown turkey and black mission varieties, cherimoyas, avocados and passion fruit on their fertile six-acre spread. Call for directions and let the Talberts know when you're coming – they'll make sure your fruits are freshly picked.

Lane Farms Green Stand
308 Walnut Lane, Goleta
805.964.3773
San Marcos Gardens
4950 Hollister Ave., Goleta
805.964.0424
Five generations of the Lane family have farmed in Goleta, and John and Ruth Lane are carrying on the tradition in style. Their well-stocked farm stand showcases a wide variety of beautiful, tasty produce grown on their properties, along with some non-local stock to fill in when items aren't in season here. Tomatoes, corn and strawberries are some of the best in the area. In fall, everyone comes to the pumpkin patch, famed for its huge pumpkin selection, hay rides and corn maze (we've gotten lost more than we care to admit). The Christmas tree lot, complete with carriage rides, is a great place to visit to kick off the holiday season. A few blocks away is their San Marcos Gardens organic produce stand, with the backdrop of precious growing fields, which are rapidly vanishing in the face of residential development.

Farmer's Markets

Preserves, produce and more at the Montecito Farmer's Market.

Saturday
Downtown Santa Barbara,
8:30 a.m.-12:30 p.m. year-round.
Corner of Santa Barbara St. & Cota St.

Sunday
Camino Real Marketplace, Goleta, 10 a.m.-2 p.m. year-round. Corner of Storke Rd. & Hollister Ave.

Tuesday
Old Town Santa Barbara,
4-7:30 p.m. in summer, 3-6:30 p.m. in winter. 500 & 600 blocks of State St.

Wednesday
La Cumbre Plaza Shopping Center, 2-6 p.m. in summer, 1-5 p.m. in winter. State St. between La Cumbre Rd. and Hope Ave.

Solvang Village,
2:30-6:30 p.m. in summer,
2:30-6 p.m. in winter. Copenhagen Dr. & 1st St.

Thursday
Calle Real Shopping Center, Goleta, 3-6 p.m. year-round. 5700 block of Calle Real.

Carpinteria, 4-7 p.m. in summer,
3-6 p.m. in winter. 800 block of Linden Ave.

Friday
Montecito, 8-11:15 a.m. year-round. 1100 & 1200 blocks of Coast Village Rd.

Shoppers buy right from the boats at the Saturday Fish Market.

Fishermen's Market

Santa Barbara Harbor
Sat. 7:30 a.m.-noon
This small dockside market sells seafood right from fishermen's boats. The size of the market depends on ocean conditions; offerings may include live crab, a variety of rockfish, halibut and, during fall and winter months, spiny lobster. Try to get there early: The market closes when the seafood runs out, which is usually before noon.

Morrell Nut & Berry Farm

1980 Alamo Pintado Rd., Solvang
805.688.8969
From June through September you can pick fresh, juicy raspberries and blackberries; in October and November, treat yourself to crunchy sun-dried walnuts. The Morrells also operate a seasonal farm stand (call for hours) and sell their berries and nuts at the Solvang farmer's market on Wednesdays.

Food Festivals

California Avocado Festival

October, downtown Carpinteria
805.684.5479, ext. 40, AvoFest.com
Three days of all things avocado, from guacamole to ice cream to an avocado climbing wall; one of the best food-related festivals in California.

California Lemon Festival

October, Girsh Park, Goleta
805.967.4618, CaliforniaLemonFestival.com

Two days of games, activities, entertainment and everything from lemon bread to lemonade – pucker up!

French Festival

July, Oak Park, Santa Barbara
805.564.7274, FrenchFestival.com
Usually held over Bastille Day weekend, it's the largest French festival in the Western states, with French food galore and entertainment. Free admission and parking.

Greek Festival

July, Oak Park, Santa Barbara
805.683.4492, SaintBarbara.net
Fans of Greek food come here to get their fix of gyros, spanakopita, dolma and baklava.

Harbor & Seafood Festival

October, Santa Barbara Harbor
805.897.1962 sbmm.org
A one-day celebration of the sea, with boat rides, games and fishermen casting their nets and lines, bringing their catch to the pier to be prepared by local chefs.

Old Spanish Days – Fiesta

Late July/early August, throughout Santa Barbara
805.962.8101, OldSpanishDays-Fiesta.org
Two of the most popular venues of the five-day Fiesta are the Mexican marketplaces: El Mercado de la Guerra at De La Guerra Plaza across from City Hall, and El Mercado del Norte at MacKenzie Park (at Las Positas Street and State). Del Norte is terrific for families, and both offer tons of tasty Spanish and Mexican-American food and entertainment.

Santa Barbara County Vintners' Festival

April, North County park or a winery estate
805.688.0881, SBCountyWines.com
Wine tastings, live music, silent auction and wine-country cuisine by local chefs.

A Taste of Solvang

March, Solvang
805.688.6144, SolvangUSA.com
Entertainment, wine and food that celebrate Solvang's Danish heritage and its wine-country location: the culinary fun includes a dessert showcase, a walking smörgaasbord and a tasting-room tour.

The Drinking Life

Remember when you're exploring Santa Barbara County's watering holes to appoint your tee-totaling BFF as the driver (keep those Shirley Temples comin'!) or call a taxi. There's a veritable rainbow to choose from: Santa Barbara Yellow Cab (805.964.1111), Blue Dolphin Taxi (805.966.6161) and Lucky Cab (805.968.5020, luckycab.net), with their distinctive green clovers on hybrid vehicles, are three good ones. Rockstar (805.882.9191, rockstarsb.com) is great for a special night out on the town.

Cool style at Blue Agave.

Blue Agave
20 E. Cota St., Santa Barbara
805.899.4694, BlueAgaveSB.com
Blue Agave may be located in a beach town, but it exudes a sophisticated big-city vibe. It's a two-level space that combines a romantic restaurant with a happening bar, complete with leather sofas, flickering fireplace and private booths. The downstairs bar pours more than 35 tequilas and several mezcals, and the bartenders are acclaimed for their excellent martinis, mojitos and inventive cocktails. The bar fills up quickly during happy hour, 4:30 to 6:30 p.m. every day, when you'll get a buck off on all drinks, a six-dollar chicken taquito and margarita combo special, and free chips and salsa.

Dargan's
18 E. Ortega St., Santa Barbara
805.568.0702, dargans.com
Can a place be laid-back and lively at the same time? It must be possible, because that's what Dargan's is like. This friendly restaurant and pub boasts four pool tables, a great selection of draft beer and Irish whiskeys and a full menu of traditional Irish dishes, from potato skins to Irish stew. Serious about its Emerald Isle heritage – or perhaps just looking for an excuse to have a good party – Dargan's celebrates St. Patrick's Day every month on the 17th into the wee hours with live music and drink and food specials. Explore your inner Idol at the Wednesday open-mike nights beginning at 10 p.m., and revel in the fiddle and flute every Saturday night at 6:30, when Irish musicians play.

The James Joyce
513 State St., Santa Barbara
805.962.2688, TheJamesJoyce.com
This warm and welcoming Irish bar, known to regulars as the Joyce or J.J., is one of the most popular spots in town to kick back, have a cold Guinness and listen to live music: rock on Wednesdays, jazz on Fridays, Dixieland on Saturdays and Irish music on Sundays. The crowd is on the young side and more down-to-earth than glam. It's the kind of place where you can chat with the friendly bar staff, munch some free peanuts and, what the heck, go ahead and throw the shells on the floor.

Joe's Cafe
536 State St., Santa Barbara
805.966.4638
Old-school style meets happening nightspot at this lower State Street institution. Joe's has been the go-to restaurant and cocktail spot in town since 1928. Known for its friendly atmosphere and good, stiff drinks, Joe's is a terrific place to begin your evening with a cocktail and a couple of hearty appetizers (steak bites, anyone?) or end up for a late-night snack. Don't plan on driving after a couple of Joe's cocktails, though – a typical vodka tonic is just that: vodka with a splash of tonic. The later the hour, the more people are prone to sing along with the jukebox.

Hollister Brewing Company
Camino Real Marketplace, 6980 Marketplace Dr., Goleta
805.968.2810, hollisterbrewco.com
If you want a good craft-made beer and food that's a few notches above typical pub grub – along with a lively setting and a chance of catching the game on TV – you've found the

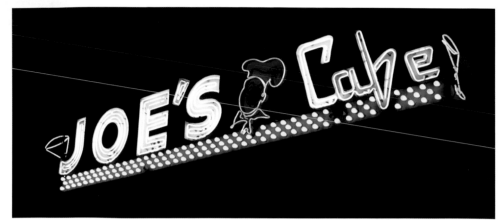

Retro neon at old-school Joe's.

right place. You'll have your choice of several TVs in this large, colorful, contemporary dining room and bar, but better still, you'll discover as many as fifteen freshly brewed beers on tap. Brewmaster Eric Rose is constantly creating new brews, so check out the chalkboard to see what's available (perhaps a subtle lemon brew during Goleta's Lemon Festival?). Both the restaurant and bar are a hit with locals, including families and students and staff from nearby UCSB. Stop by during happy hour on weekdays from 2 to 6 p.m., when most house beers are $3 a pint and $2.25 for a ten-ounce glass. Prices are also reduced on selected wines, well cocktails, pizzas and chicken wings.

Quiet luxury, Santa Barbara style, at the Biltmore's Ty Lounge.

Santa Barbara Brewing Company
501 State St., Santa Barbara
805.730.1040, sbbrewco.com
This friendly lower State Street spot attracts an eclectic group of locals of all ages – many of them regulars – along with visitors looking for a good meal and a cold microbrew while prowling the shops. The Santa Barbara Blonde is a locals' fave (and not just because of the name), along with the Rincon Red, which surfers named after the world-famous spot just down the coast. Happy hour runs from 3 to 6 p.m. on weekdays, with $3 pints and deals on such brew-friendly fare as garlic fries and chicken tenders. And there's pool during the weekdays and free WiFi most afternoons and evenings if you need a break from all the frivolity.

Ty Lounge
Four Seasons Resort the Biltmore Santa Barbara
1260 Channel Dr., Montecito
805.969.2261, fourseasons.com
When you've had enough of flip-flops and noisy brew pubs and want to dress up a bit and have a civilized conversation over a martini, head to this gorgeous bar in the equally gorgeous Biltmore. It's typically easy to find a cozy spot under the Spanish-style beamed ceiling, perhaps even by the fireplace; on balmy evenings, try to snag a table on the oceanview terrace. Excellent service and live jazz on Friday and Saturday nights.

4 Hot Happy Hours

Elements
129 E. Anapamu St., Santa Barbara
805.884.9218, elementsrestaurantandbar.com
Both a popular restaurant and elegant bar,
Elements packs them in during happy hour
(weekdays from 4:30 to 6:30), but in a classy
way – folks spill out onto the front porch that
overlooks the Courthouse's sunken gardens,
and the mood is celebratory but not raucous.
The main attraction (aside from the fetching
crowd) is the $4 discount on its signature cock-
tails, Elementinis. Make sure to try the Firetini,
with its intriguing juxtaposition of habañero-
infused vodka, passionfruit purée and simple
syrup – don't knock it 'til you've tried it. Also
during happy hour you'll find reduced prices
at the bar on such chic appetizers as Chinese
chicken salad, tuna tartare, jumbo Mexican
white shrimp cocktail and an artisanal cheese
plate.

Enterprise Fish Co.
225 State St., Santa Barbara
805.962.3313, enterprisefishco.com
A lively seafood restaurant and bar, this place
rocks during happy hour, especially during
the summer. Happy hour stretches from 4 to
7 p.m. on weekdays and from 8 to 10 p.m. on
Sundays, when well drinks are $3.25 , house
wine is $3.50, draught beers (including Fat Tire,
Firestone, Bass Ale and Widmer Hefeweizen)
are $4 and oyster shooters are $1.50. And
oysters are good for you, right?

Left at Albuquerque
700 State St., Santa Barbara
805.564.5040, albuquerque-bluechalk.com
The primo location of this Southwestern-style
restaurant and bar on lower State Street allows
for great people-watching and easy access to
other fun nightspots nearby. At last count, the
bar stocked 128 tequilas; most of them served
in groups of three so you can try them as you
would a wine flight. Needless to say, margaritas
are a specialty, but be careful – they can get
quite pricey as you venture into the high-end
tequilas. For happy-hour deals, come during
the week from 4 to 7 p.m. – house margaritas
and wines, and select well drinks, beers and
appetizers are all just $3.

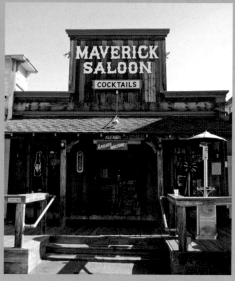

Wild West hokum at the Maverick.

Maverick Saloon
3687 Sagunto St., Santa Ynez
805.686.4785, mavericksaloon.org
This place is a hoot and a refreshing change
from the "big city" nightlife of Santa Barbara.
Put on your cowboy boots and head over the
hill to hear great concerts on the deck every
Saturday and Sunday from 3 to 6 p.m. at this
authentic country bar, and stay into the evening
when things really get hoppin'. A wildly popular
locals' spot as well as a tourist destination,
the Maverick is famous for its décor: a proper
saloon front porch, cattle brands on the bar, old
photos, a wagon wheel hung with red lanterns
and dollar bills plastered to the ceiling. Soak up
the country charm at happy hour every week-
day from 4 to 7 p.m. – all drinks are $1 off.

14 Coffeehouses That Aren't Starbucks

If this list doesn't give you enough of a jolt, you'll find even more great hometown coffee-houses in the Literary chapter under Bring Your Laptop: Where to Write.

Bulldog Café
1680 Mission Dr., Solvang
805.686.9770, bulldogcafesolvang.com
Daily from 6 a.m.
Local flavor, bulldog-strong coffee and house-made pastries are served here. You'll notice the autographed Lance Armstrong poster and cyclist photos galore – the Bulldog became the early-morning hangout for Lance and his fellow Postal Team (and later Discovery and other teams) cyclists when they held a winter training camp nearby a few years ago. Owners Greg and Barbara Meeks recall the first day Lance and company came in for coffee – they got to talking, and the next thing the Meekses knew, the crew was showing up every morning for a pre-ride round of cappuccinos and carrot cake.

Café Luna
2354 Lillie Ave., Summerland
805.695.8780
Daily from 7 a.m.
Summerlanders come here for coffee and a catch-up – maybe before or after picking up their mail at the post office, as there is no mail delivery in this teensy town. Owners Carolina Pierpont and her daughter, Nicole, source their own shade-grown Costa Rican beans from Nicole's dad. Nicole makes good panini, salads and a habit-forming egg bagel sandwich. Sit on the patio or in front of the stone fireplace, or browse through Carolina's adjoining antiques and garden shop, Méditerranée.

Cajé
1007 Casitas Pass Rd., Carpinteria
no phone
Mon.-Fri. from 6 a.m., Sat.-Sun. from 7 a.m.
This strip-mall place is easy to overlook, but don't. It's a convenient stop for coffee or a smoothie before hopping on the freeway.

Coffee Cat
1201 Anacapa St., Santa Barbara
805.962.7164
Mon.-Fri. from 6 a.m., Sat.-Sun. from 7 a.m.
This might be the best location in town for a coffee break – big picture windows look on the kitty-corner Courthouse, and the central library is across the street. Of course there's terrific coffee, but how about to-die-for crèpes, from pesto, goat cheese, tomato and chicken to Nutella and banana? Other pluses are housemade sandwiches, pastries from Arlington Bakery, free WiFi, courtyard seating and easy parking at the new city-owned Granada garage next door.

Daily Grind
2001 De la Vina St., Santa Barbara
805.687.4966
Daily from 5:30 a.m.
Daily Grind's motto could easily be: We're all in this grind together, so we might as well drink good coffee. And it is good, as well as both organic and fair trade. The housemade, Frisbee-size scones and moist muffins (try the ollalieberry) are irresistible, sandwiches, salads and smoothies are delicious, and the WiFi is free. The place attracts mostly the young and hip, some with babies or kids.

Java Jones
6560 Pardall Rd., Ste. C, Isla Vista
805.968.7441
728 State St., Santa Barbara
805.962.4721, javajonescoffeehouse.com
Daily from 7 a.m.
UCSB student Brett Winslow opened the original in I.V. in 1992, and it became such a hit that he opened another location in Santa Barbara and a couple in San Diego. His roasting facility in San Diego helps fulfill the quest to source, roast and brew organic, fair-trade coffee. The coffee drinks are fabulous, the service friendly, and the WiFi free – and at the State Street location, your four-legged friend can have a drink and a biscuit from the "dog butler" outside.

Java Station
4447 Hollister Ave., Santa Barbara
805.681.0202
Daily from 6 a.m.
This locals' fave always has a steady stream of customers, but you rarely have to wait in line. (We're not sure how they do it – it must be some kind of caffeinated voodoo.) The java is Green Star organic, and the atmosphere invites lingering, which is what many do: studying students, wired workers (free WiFi) and meeting moms hang out on cozy couches or at tables in front of the fireplace. We know one native who, when she returns from college back east,

hustles right over here for a chewy-gooey bagel melt (cheddar and cream cheese on a bagel with tomato, onion and lemon pepper). High-quality muffins, Danish and Homey comfort at the NorthStar. croissants come from Arlington Bakery; the chocolate chip cookies are made in-house.

Muddy Waters
508 E. Haley St., Santa Barbara
805.966.9328
Mon.-Fri. from 6 a.m., Sat. from 8 a.m.
Off the beaten path in more ways than one, this friendly, funky spot reminds you of that eccentric aunt you have who doesn't care what she looks like but has a heart of gold. Furnished in flea-market style with edgy local art, Muddy has good coffee, pastries, sandwiches and soups, along with live music a couple times a week – you can even sip a glass of Love Potion vino or locally made Telegraph beer.

NorthStar Coffee Company
918 State St., Santa Barbara
805.965.5593, northstarcoffee.com
Mon.-Sat. from 8 a.m., Sun. from 10 a.m.
Have a seat in front of the fireplace and you'll feel as if you're in a good friend's living room. Along with free WiFi, a friendly vibe and foam-art lattes, this downtown favorite peddles light meals and treats, including addictive gelato. We're also fans of the Mexican hot chocolate. Live music on Friday and Saturday nights.

Peet's Coffee & Tea
3905 State St., Santa Barbara
805.687.9952, peets.com
Daily from 5 a.m.
Okay, so it's a chain, but with just one location in town it's not nearly as omnipresent as Starbucks, and the coffee's really good. Many folks have adopted the place as their office, some starting from the ungodly hour of 5 a.m.

Red's
211 Helena Ave., Santa Barbara
805.966.5906
Mon.-Fri. from 6:30 a.m., Sat. from 7 a.m.
Resplendent in red in the Funk Zone, the industrial area off lower State Street, Red's has a definite artistic vibe. Owner Dana Walters

displays artists' works, hosts openings and holiday art sales, and books local and touring bands to play. The cup of joe here is Green Star organic, and pastries hail from the wonderful D'Angelo Pastry & Bread.

Roasted Bean Coffee House
3558 Sagunto St., Santa Ynez
805.688.7194
Mon.-Sat. from 6 a.m., Sun. from 7 a.m.
Larry and Linda Saarloos, along with son Keith, run this Valley favorite in their "spare" time – they are also grape growers and winemakers. Folks drop in as much for local news as for the coffee – one group shows up just about every morning to talk vineyards, politics and the economy. Extras include free WiFi, comfy seating and a great carrot cupcake from Pattibakes.

Santa Barbara Roasting Company
321 Motor Way, Santa Barbara
805.962.0320, sbcoffee.com
Mon.-Fri. from 5:30 a.m., Sat. from 6 a.m., Sun. from 6:30 a.m.
607 Paseo Nuevo, Santa Barbara
805.962.2070, sbcoffee.com
Mon.-Sat. from 7:30 a.m., Sun. from 8:30 a.m.
RoCo, as locals fondly call this place, roasts and air-cools its beans in small batches – you can see the process at the Motor Way location. That location, popular with surfers and workers, is two doors from Chocolate Maya, so you can satisfy two vices with one stop.

Vices & Spices
3558 State St., Santa Barbara
805.687.7196
Mon.-Sat. from 7 a.m., Sun. from 8 a.m.
For 33 years, this homey hangout has been a Northside fave for top-notch coffee and friendly conversation. Most mornings, the large

Vices & Spices.

communal table by the window overflows with regulars solving the world's problems and playing checkers. You can pick up specialty coffees and teas, old-fashioned candy, dried spices and cool gifts from around the world.

Q & A: Isidoro Gonzalez

Since opening the door of his humble taco stand on Milpas Street in 1980, owner Isidoro Gonzalez has barely had a chance to shut it – the orderly line of hungry taco-cravers usually flows out onto the sidewalk and sometimes around the corner. Sporting a vinyl tarp for a roof over the patio, this less-than-auspicious-looking joint has packed in everyone from foodie celebs Julia Child and Ruth Reichl to Ronald Reagan's Secret Service guys, who would pick up the President's order when in residence at the Western White House, Rancho del Cielo. Nancy Ransohoff chatted with Isidoro between bites of chiles rellenos and tamales ... yes, it's a tough job, but....

How did you get started?
I grew up in Santa Barbara, went to UCSB, majored in Spanish with a minor in French and was planning to be a teacher. I went on a UC Education Abroad Program and while I was studying and traveling I started to think about food in a way that made me appreciate the value of wonderful, delicious food. In Paris I signed up for a ten-week cooking class for foreign students – I was the only guy. It opened my eyes – the sauces! A year later I went to Mexico City on an Education Abroad Program. It was there that friends took me to a taco place. I instantly felt this bond with the taco – tacos al carbon – soft tortillas with wonderful salsas. There was a definite connection with me and the food.

Did you know then that you wanted to open a restaurant?
When I got back, I thought, "It would be so nice if someone in Santa Barbara would open a place where I could get this food." I got into a master's program in Spanish Linguistics at UCSB, and I was teaching at Santa Barbara City College. When I finished the program, I thought, "It's now or never – I'm going to Mexico City." I went to all the taco places. I was there for three months working as a cook's helper, a waiter, doing everything. Back in Santa Barbara, I had no idea what I was doing – I was no businessperson – but I knew that I liked the food and had faith that other people would like it, too. I rented this place and was eventually able to buy it.

Tell us about your experience with Julia Child.
In 1982, Julia came in with her husband and a friend. They said, "We want one of everything." They ate everything. Julia came to the window and said, "I want you to know that until now I didn't think Mexican food was for me." Three years later, she came in and asked if I would be on Good Morning America – they were going to visit three places in Santa Barbara – I was one! I just have this little place and she likes my tacos! She came frequently during the last four years of her life – she insisted on waiting in line.

Have you ever thought of moving somewhere else to a bigger place... maybe even one with a roof?
I really love this little place. This is my home base – it's got to be here. Go elsewhere? Never! People have been good to me. They seem to forgive my mistakes.

Do you ever eat at any of the other restaurants in town?
No (smiling) ... I don't have time.

Wine Tasting

Santa Barbara County has taken off as a world-class wine producer. It's become the hot spot (well, actually, the perfectly temperate spot) for grape growing and winemaking, and the cork-popping good news is that this wine country is right in our backyard. After a 40-minute drive through oak-studded rolling hills and aah-inspiring scenery, you can taste everything from Albarino to Zinfandel in tasting rooms ranging from rustic converted barns to lavish Mediterranean-style villas.

From Serra to Syrah:
Santa Barbara's Wine Roots

Santa Barbara County's grape-growing and winemaking industry started in 1782 when Father Junípero Serra carried some very important cargo – grapevines – from Mexico to Santa Barbara to establish vineyards to make sacramental wine. The padres were solo vintners for about a hundred years until French immigrant Justinian Caire, longing for the vinous pleasures of the old country, planted 150 acres on wild Santa Cruz Island. By the time Prohibition shut down all winery operations in the area, grapes were thriving on about 250 acres. It took more than 30 years, but the industry finally came back with grapey gusto. In the early 1960s, researchers at the University of California at Davis discovered that the unusual topography, geography (paying attention during those geography lectures paid off) and climate of the northern valleys of Santa Barbara County were ideal for growing certain varieties of premium grapes. Specifically, the unusual east-west orientation of the San Rafael and Santa Ynez mountain ranges creates valleys that funnel cool ocean air and fog inland during the late afternoon and evening. The resulting hot sunny days and cool nights are a winning combination for both wine grapes and wine tasters.

Wild turkeys are a common sight in the Santa Barbara wine country.

Several pioneers were already on the wine case in the 1960s, having figured out that this was a pretty good place to plant some vines. Pierre Lafond arrived from Quebec and in 1962 opened the Santa Barbara Winery downtown – the first commercial winery in Santa Barbara County since Prohibition. Stearns Wharf Vintners followed soon after, offering its wines with an ocean view. Richard Sanford zeroed in on a 430-acre ranch along the Santa Ynez River in Lompoc as the perfect spot to plant the first Pinot Noir vines in the region (now the Sta. Rita Hills AVA or American Viticultural Area), and with a partner he established Sanford & Benedict Winery. Several more wineries, including Firestone, Rancho Sisquoc, Zaca Mesa and the Brander Vineyard, sprouted up in the 1970s.

During the 1980s and '90s, the siren call of Santa Barbara's ideal growing conditions lured clusters of vintners to the area. The industry was now quietly growing great grapes, experimenting with new techniques and making award-winning wines, but it was as yet undiscovered by the hordes of wine tourists who flocked to Napa and Sonoma. Then the movie *Sideways* hit like a vinous tsunami. The 2004 movie, which chronicles the road-trip high jinks of longtime friends Miles and Jack, shone a bright (some might say blinding)

Getting There

From Santa Barbara you have a couple of options. Our fave is the scenic route along Highway 154 (San Marcos Pass), the twisty-turny road that drops into the Santa Ynez Valley. To get to the 154, take the 101 to the State Street/Highway 154 exit, then take 154 up the mountain. As you descend into the valley, you'll have spectacular views of the Santa Ynez Mountains, Los Padres National Forest and Cachuma Lake. After about 40 minutes you'll hit the 154 intersection with Highway 246. Turn left for Santa Ynez or Solvang, or continue on about five miles to Los Olivos. The second option is the coastal route north along Highway 101, which offers unspoiled California coastline views that remind us why we live here. Continue north about 45 miles to Highway 246 in Buellton. Head west for the Santa Rita Hills loop or east for the Santa Ynez Valley Wine Trail. For the Foxen Canyon Wine Trail, continue north on 101 past Buellton up to the 154 turnoff. Turn right and go east a few miles to Foxen Canyon Road.

Walkin' down a country road in the Santa Ynez Valley.

Hollywood spotlight on the Central Coast wine scene. The movie was a bane or a boon, depending on who you talk to, but there's no denying that it brought tremendous attention to the region. Tourism and demand for local wines shot up, and formerly tranquil tasting rooms buzzed with activity. Though the Hollywood lights may have dimmed a bit, the movie has had a lasting effect – on warm-weather weekends, tasting rooms can get crowded at peak times, but overall there's still plenty of room at the county's more than 120 wineries.

No matter what varietal your palate prefers, you'll probably find it here, due to the variety of microclimates and soil types. Nearly every winery grows and produces Chardonnay, but Santa Barbara County has also become known for its sublime Syrahs and its world-class Pinot Noir, a finicky grape that demands ideal growing conditions and expert treatment. Other popular local wines include Sauvignon Blanc, Riesling, Merlot, Cabernet Sauvignon and Gewürztraminer, along with some intriguing blends. The county includes three designated AVAs: Santa Maria Valley, Santa Ynez Valley and Sta. Rita Hills, along with the Los Alamos Valley growing region.

Before hitting the wine trails, pick up an up-to-date touring map at pretty much any tasting room, visitor center, wine-friendly restaurant or hotel, or call the Santa Barbara County Vintners' Association (805.688.0881, 800.218.0881) or get a PDF version of the map at sbcountywines.com. Be sure to check tasting-room hours and find out about tours before you head out – several wineries offer tours of their facilities and even their *caves*. Some have lovely picnic areas; pick up supplies on your way in Solvang, Santa Ynez or Los Olivos. Most wineries charge a tasting fee, which often includes a logo wine glass. If you're going in a group of ten or more, call ahead to make arrangements.

So let's hit the wine trails – most Santa Barbara County wineries sit happily (and conveniently) along three scenic wine loops: the Foxen Canyon Wine Trail, the Santa Ynez Valley Wine Trail and the Santa Rita Hills loop.

The Hunt for Good Wine

Foxen Canyon Wine Trail
This trail connects two wine-growing regions: the Santa Ynez and Santa Maria valleys. It begins on Foxen Canyon Road just north of Los Olivos and meanders through twenty miles of sage-green or golden hills and vineyards, depending on the time of year, until it reaches Santa Maria. Here are just a few of the top-notch wineries along the way.

Cambria Winery & Vineyard
5475 Chardonnay Lane, Santa Maria
805.938.7318, cambriawines.com
Some of the vines here are part of the original Tepusquet Vineyard, which produced high-quality grapes from the early 1970s to the mid '80s. Purchased in 1986 by Barbara Banke and her husband, Jess Jackson, of Kendall-Jackson wine fame, Cambria makes distinctive Chardonnay, Pinot Noir and Syrah.

Fess Parker Winery & Vineyard
6200 Foxen Canyon Rd., Los Olivos
805.688.1545, 800.841.1104, fessparker.com
He may have been "king of the wild frontier," but Fess Parker, who starred as Davy Crockett and Daniel Boone in the 1950s and '60s, makes some decidedly smooth and luscious Chardonnay, Viognier and Syrah. Though still a driving force, Fess has turned over the day-to-day reins to his son, daughter and son-in-law. The expansive tasting room is surrounded by 700 acres of vineyards, lawns and rose gardens. And, yes, you can buy a coonskin cap in the gift shop.

Firestone Vineyard
5000 Zaca Station Rd., Los Olivos
805.688.3940 ext. 31, firestonewine.com
Santa Barbara County's first estate winery (founded in 1972), Firestone produces a veritable wine list from its estate vineyards, including Chardonnay, late-harvest Reisling, Sauvignon Blanc, Merlot, Syrah and Cabernet Sauvignon. The recently remodeled tasting room and great picnic facilities sit on a hilltop with gorgeous views of the valley and vineyards. Tours are offered at frequent intervals throughout the day.

Foxen Vineyard
7200 Foxen Canyon Rd., Santa Maria
805.937.4251, foxenvineyard.com

If the tasting room looks familiar, it's because a scene from *Sideways* was filmed in this charming former blacksmith shop. It sits on the 2,000-acre Rancho Tinaquaic, which has been in Richard Doré's family since 1837. Although only a few acres are planted to grapes, Doré and Bill Wathen (known as "the Foxen boys") work wonders with grapes grown elsewhere in the county. You can't miss with any of the Chardonnays, Syrahs or Pinot Noirs.

Rancho Sisquoc Winery
6600 Foxen Canyon Rd., Santa Maria
805.934.4332, ranchosisquoc.com
Rustic and welcoming, Rancho Sisquoc positively oozes Old West charm. The 308-acre estate vineyard, one of the oldest in the county, is a bucolic blip on the 37,000-acre cattle ranch that makes up the rest of the property. In the rustic wood tasting room, you can sample such citified offerings as Sauvignon Blanc, Chardonnay, Sylvaner (the only one in California), Riesling, Merlot, Cabernet Sauvignon, Pinot Noir and a dreamy Meritage blend.

Zaca Mesa Winery
6905 Foxen Canyon Rd., Santa Maria
805.688.9339, 800.350.7972, zacamesa.com
You may not immediately notice the environmentally correct, barnlike buildings tucked unobtrusively into a canyon, but you can't miss the tall metal windmill out front. The winery is known for its Rhône varietals, including Syrah, Viognier and Roussanne, as well as such unique blends as the Z Cuvée, a blend of Grenache, Mourvèdre, Syrah and Cinsaut. This is a peaceful picnic spot – head for the grassy courtyard or the nature trails.

It's hard to spot the proper French-style *cave* at Sunstone (hint: look on the left).

Santa Ynez Valley Wine Trail

This loop takes you to all the major wineries in the Santa Ynez Valley. You can start in Buellton, then head over to Santa Ynez, up to Los Olivos and back through Ballard to Solvang (don't forget to stop for *aebleskivers*, those yummy pancake balls). Or follow the route in reverse. Here are some of the wineries you should visit, whichever way you travel.

Beckmen Vineyards

2670 Ontiveros Rd., Los Olivos
805.688.8664, beckmenvineyards.com
Family-owned Beckmen focuses on estate-grown Rhône varietals and is perhaps best known for its superb Syrah. After also sipping its Grenache, Marsanne and Cuvée Le Bec (a blend of Grenache, Mourvèdre, Syrah and Counoise), you can relax in one of the picnic gazebos overlooking the duck pond.

The Brander Vineyard

2401 Refugio Rd., Los Olivos
805.688.2455, brander.com
One of the original vineyards in Santa Ynez Valley, Brander was established by Argentina-born Fred Brander in 1975. You can taste world-class Sauvignon Blancs in a variety of styles – as well as small quantities of hand-crafted Bordeaux-style reds – in an adorable pink château.

The Gainey Vineyard

3950 E. Hwy. 246, Santa Ynez
805.688.0558, gaineyvineyard.com
This user-friendly winery offers drop-dead gorgeous views, exquisite wines and information-packed tours. Sip Sauvignon Blanc, Chardonnay, Pinot Noir, Merlot, Cabernet Sauvignon and Cabernet Franc in the lovely Spanish mission-style tasting facility or picture-perfect picnic spots overlooking the vineyards. We love the September crush party.

Rusack Vineyards

1819 Ballard Canyon Rd., Solvang
805.688.1278, rusackvineyards.com
A beautiful, low-key setting and standout wines make this one of our favorite wineries to visit. Sit a spell on the redwood deck over-

The impossibly charming tasting room at Alma Rosa played a part in the movie *Sideways*.

looking the vineyards and oak-studded hills and enjoy award-winning wines that might include Sauvignon Blanc, Chardonnay, Rosé, Pinot Noir, Syrah, Sangiovese and Rusack's flagship Anacapa, a velvety Bordeaux-style blend. Bring a picnic and linger under the ancient oaks.

Sunstone Vineyards & Winery
125 N. Refugio Rd., Santa Ynez
805.688.9463, sunstonewinery.com
You might think you took a wrong turn on the 246 and ended up in Provence. No such luck, but you've found an equally beautiful spot, even though this lavender- and rosemary-studded courtyard is very much rooted in Santa Ynez, with the distinctive wines to prove it. Using only organically grown grapes, Sunstone makes a renowned Merlot, along with excellent Cabernet Franc, Port-style Syrah, Syrah Rosé, Viognier, Sauvignon Blanc and Eros, a Bordeaux-style blend. Lovely tasting bar, arbored porch and two stone barrel-aging *caves* built into the hillside.

Santa Rita Hills Loop
Santa Barbara's newest and coolest (we mean in the temperature sense) AVA, the Sta. Rita Hills region is tucked behind the coastal mountains where a cooler micro-climate nurtures world-class Pinot Noir and Chardonnay. Starting from Highway 101, take either Santa Rosa Road west and loop back on Highway 246, or do the reverse. Either way, you'll find some wonderful spots, including the following.

Alma Rosa Winery & Vineyards
7250 Santa Rosa Rd., Buellton
805.688.9090, almarosawinery.com
Richard Sanford came to the valley 35 years ago with the intention of creating great Burgundy-style wines ... and he did just that, developing a stellar reputation along the way. His latest venture, with his wife, Thekla, combines his winemaking expertise with organic farming and sustainable agriculture. Although they are known for their award-winning Pinot Noir

and Chardonnay, they also make superb Pinot Gris and Pinot Blanc. The tasting room is in a beautifully rustic converted dairy barn on the 738-acre Rancho El Jabali, part of the original Santa Rosa land grant.

Babcock Winery & Vineyards
5175 E. Hwy. 246, Lompoc
805.736.1455, babcockwinery.com
Its Chardonnay makes us weak in the knees, but this family-owned winery also crafts highly regarded Sauvignon Blanc, Pinot Noir, Pinot Gris, Syrah, Cabernet Sauvignon and a Bordeaux-style blend called Fathom. The recently remodeled tasting room invites you to sit down and enjoy, especially with those weak knees.

Foley Estates wine.

Foley Estates Vineyard & Winery
6121 E. Hwy. 246, Lompoc
805.737.6222, foleywines.com
Owned by businessman and vintner William Foley II, this Rancho Santa Rosa property (once a thoroughbred horse farm) is now home to a 3,500-square-foot stone and stucco tasting room and event center. Highly regarded Chardonnay, Pinot Noir and Syrah are made from estate-grown Sta. Rita Hills grapes.

Lafond Winery & Vineyards
6855 Santa Rosa Rd., Buellton
805.688.7921, lafondwinery.com
In 1962 the visionary Pierre Lafond opened the first commercial winery in the county since Prohibition, Santa Barbara Winery, in downtown Santa Barbara. In 2001 he opened his lovely estate winery and vineyard to visitors, who can take a Pinot-fueled peek at the working areas of the property before bellying up to the picnic tables on the lawn with their Pinot, Syrah or Chardonnay.

Melville
5185 E. Hwy. 246, Lompoc
805.735.7030, melvillewinery.com
Winemaker Greg Brewer has earned rave reviews for both his earthy Pinot Noir (be still my heart!) and his Chardonnay. And we also love the setting – the tasting room is in a romantic Mediterranean villa surrounded by expansive vineyards, lavender and poplar, and oak and sycamore trees. Quaff the estate-grown Pinot Noir, Chardonnay and Syrah while overlooking the gorgeous gardens and courtyard, then nibble lunch on the lawn or patio.

Mosby Winery & Vineyards
9496 Santa Rosa Rd., Buellton
805.688.2415, 800.70.MOSBY, mosbywines.com
Mosby sits just off the 101, and although it's not technically in the Sta. Rita Hills AVA, it's an easy stop and a unique opportunity to sample premium Cal-Ital wines from estate-grown fruit. Drink in the rustic ambience of the restored 1860s carriage house/tasting room as you try the Pinot Grigio, Sangiovese and brandies, along with an award-winning Dolcetto, which Bill Mosby describes as "a good quaffing wine … it's a wine you'd find on most family dinner tables in the Piedmont region."

Oak-barrel aging.

Tasting Around Town

Los Olivos

You can almost picture some Old West types sashaying into the saloon or threatening a duel here, but this tiny, historic town is now home to more galleries and tasting rooms than bars and cowboys. Sip a variety of civilized wines with one ramble up and down Grand Avenue, and you'll find a few off the avenue as well.

Andrew Murray Vineyards
2901-A Grand Ave., Los Olivos
805.693.9644, andrewmurrayvineyards.com

Consilience
2933 Grand Ave., Los Olivos
805.691.1020, consiliencewines.com

Daniel Gehrs Wines in Los Olivos.

Daniel Gehrs Wines
2939 Grand Ave., Los Olivos
805.693.9686, 800.275.8138, dgwines.com

Longoria
2935 Grand Ave., Los Olivos
866.759.4637, 805.688.0305, longoriawine.com

Los Olivos Tasting Room & Wine Shop
2905 Grand Ave., Los Olivos
805.688.7406, losolivoswines.com

Los Olivos Wine Merchant & Café
2879 Grand Ave., Los Olivos
805.688.7265, santabarbarawine.com

Solvang

Over the past few years, tasting rooms have popped up like quick-rise dough among the bakeries and gift shops in this touristy Danish town. Here are a few to duck into when you need a break from the windmills and clogs.

Lucas & Lewellen Vineyards & Winery
1645 Copenhagen Dr., Solvang
805.686.9336, llwine.com

Stolpman Vineyards
1659 Copenhagen Dr., Solvang
805.688.0400, stolpmanvineyards.com

Tastes of the Valleys
1672 Mission Dr., Solvang
805.688.7111, tastesofthevalleys.com

Trio Tastings
1557 Mission Dr., Solvang
805.688.3494

Downtown Santa Barbara

For an off-the-beaten-path tasting adventure, hit Santa Barbara's urban wine trail. Some are in the industrial area known to locals as the Funk Zone, with its artists' studios, coffeehouses and hip boutiques. A map of the Urban Wine Trail is available at most locations.

Carr Vineyards & Winery
414 N. Salsipuedes St., Santa Barbara
805.965.7985, carrwinery.com

Cellar 205/Oreana Winery
205 Anacapa St., Santa Barbara
805.962.5857, oreanawinery.com

Jaffurs Wine Cellars
819 E. Montecito St., Santa Barbara
805.962.7003, jaffurswine.com

Kalyra Winery
212 State St., Santa Barbara
805.965.8606, kalyrawinery.com

Santa Barbara Winery
202 Anacapa St., Santa Barbara
805.963.3633, sbwinery.com

Whitcraft Winery
36 S. Calle Cesar Chavez, Santa Barbara
805.730.1680, whitcraftwinery.com

Carpinteria & Summerland
Corktree Cellars
910 Linden Ave., Carpinteria
805.684.1400

Summerland Winery Boutique
2330 Lillie Ave., Summerland
805.565.9463, summerlandwine.com

Tours, Events & Shops

Wine Country Tours

There are about as many ways to tour the wine country as there are varietals of vino. Either use your own designated driver (a lavish gift would be in order) or choose a touring company – you can hop on a bike or in a Jeep, pretend you're a limo-ridin' rock star, focus on organic vineyards or combine winery visits with horse farm tours.

Breakaway Tours
800.799.7657, breakaway-tours.com

Cloud Climbers Jeep Tours
805.646.3200, ccjeeps.com

Coastal Concierge
805.265.6065, sbcoastalconcierge.com

Limousine Link
805.564.4660, santabarbaralimousinelink.com

Rockstar Transportation
805.882.9191, rockstarsb.com

Santa Barbara Wine Country Cycling Tours
888.557.8687, winecountrycycling.com

Sustainable Vine Wine Tours
805.698.3911, sustainablevine.com

Wine and Horse Tours
805.688.5984, wineandhorsetours.com

Wine EdVentures
805.965.9463, welovewines.com

Our Favorite Wine Events

April
Santa Barbara County Vintners' Festival
Lompoc, sbcountywines.com

June
Santa Barbara Wine Festival
Museum of Natural History, Santa Barbara
sbnature.org/winefestival

July
California Wine Festival
Chase Palm Park, Santa Barbara
californiawinefestival.com

October
Celebration of Harvest
Santa Barbara County Vintners' Association
sbcountywines.com

Easygoing tasting at the Santa Barbara County Vintners' Festival.

Wine Shops We've Known & Loved

Whether you have a novice nose or pro palate, you'll find great selections, guidance, advice or just local grapevine gossip at the following emporiums of the vine. Many host tastings, so give them a call or check web sites for events.

Carpinteria Wine Co.
4193 Carpinteria Ave., Carpinteria
805.684.7440, carpinteriawineco.com

East Beach Wine Company
201 S. Milpas St., Santa Barbara
805.899.1535, eastbeachwine.com

Liquor & Wine Grotto
1271 Coast Village Rd., Montecito
805.969.5939

Renegade Wines
417 Santa Barbara St., Santa Barbara
805.568.1961, renegadewines.com

Vino Divino
2012 De La Vina St., Santa Barbara
877.834.8466, vinodivinosb.com

Wine Cask
813 Anacapa St., Santa Barbara
805.966.9463, winecask.com

Wine Country
2445 Alamo Pintado Ave., Los Olivos
805.686.9699

The Winehound
1221 Chapala St., Santa Barbara
805.845.5247, thewinehound.com

Q & A: Richard & Thekla Sanford

For more than 30 years, Richard and Thekla Sanford have been in the vanguard of wine-making in Santa Barbara County. Richard was the first to plant Pinot Noir vineyards in the region at his Sanford & Benedict Vineyard in 1970. The couple married in 1978, started Sanford Winery in 1981, and for the next 25 years produced award-winning wines sold in 50 states and sixteen countries. They separated from their namesake winery in 2005 and embarked on a new enterprise, Alma Rosa Winery & Vineyards, located just outside Buellton, where they make highly acclaimed wines from grapes grown on their 100-plus-acre certified organic vineyards in the Santa Rita Hills. Nancy sat down with Richard and Thekla and a glass of Pinot in the converted dairy barn that is the former Sanford, now Alma Rosa, tasting room – which also, by the way, was Miles and Jack's first stop in *Sideways*. Fans of the movie will be glad to know that Chris Burroughs, the cowboy-hat-wearing tasting-room manager of Sanford Winery in the film, has followed Richard and Thekla to Alma Rosa.

You were pioneers in local winemaking. How did you get started?
Richard: *I had studied geography in college and was interested in the geography of wine. I had been introduced to the wonders of Burgundy and wanted to find the ideal location to plant Pinot Noir and Chardonnay. At the time, Pinot Noir was being grown in climates in California that were too warm, and it was burning out some of the beautiful raspberry fruit of the grape. But our unusual east-west mountain range jumped right out at me. I started driving up and down the valleys with a thermometer in my car – people thought I was nuts. In 1970, after putting together a group of investors, I started Sanford & Benedict Vineyard in Lompoc with my college friend Michael Benedict.*

When did you two meet?
Thekla (with a sly smile): *We met in 1976 sailing in the Santa Barbara harbor during a Wet Wednesday race.*
Richard: *It was a really good year – we also had our first vintage!*

How long have you been farming organically?
Richard: *For 23 years. All the vineyards that we own are CCOF [California Certified Organic Farmers] certified. We're totally committed to sustainable agriculture, environmental responsibility, ecologically responsible packaging and green building.*

How did the new Sta. Rita Hills American Viticultural Area come about?
Richard: *The original Santa Ynez Valley appellation covered such a vast area that it wasn't very meaningful as an appellation. As a founding member of the Sta. Rita Hills Winegrowers Alliance, I was an advocate for a new appellation that would better represent this area west of Buellton. It was the first time vineyardists had gotten together to determine the boundaries without regard to any special interests.*

What effects have you seen from *Sideways*?
Richard: *It has been incredibly good. It introduced Pinot Noir to a broader audience and introduced the region to the largest wine market in the world: Los Angeles.*
Thekla: *It's pretty exciting – we're happy that people are starting to understand Pinot Noir.*

What do you do when you need a break?
Thekla: *We go down to the river. And if it's a hot day, we jump into the swimming hole.*

Entertaining

Do you live to lambada? Are you bonkers for Beethoven? Have you sold your soul to the silver screen? Never mind our restful ocean air and quaint shops and cafés. Commit your eyes and ears to soaking up the area's slew of shows, from sing-alongs to *Swan Lake* to cinema.

Fresh-Air Fun

In a postcard-perfect world, the only thing better than top-notch entertainment is top-notch entertainment al fresco. If you can catch a show under the California sun — or under the Central Coast's spate of stars — then you absolutely should.

Outdoor Concert Venues

Cold Spring Tavern
5995 Stagecoach Dr., Santa Barbara
805.967.0066, ColdSpringTavern.com
Sun. 1:30-4:30 p.m.
Usually when people say, "It's like another time and place," they're exaggerating. But not at Cold Spring Tavern, a 140-year-old former stagecoach stop that presents live music and barbecue outdoors on Sunday afternoons. In a canyon down a winding road off Highway 154, you can buy a tri-tip sandwich, pull up a log and listen to great down-home music. Local "blues ambassadors" Tom Ball and Kenny Sultan are regulars. This is a biker hangout, so bring your chopper if you've got one.

Concerts in the Parks
805.897.1982, SantaBarbaraCA.gov
Thurs. evenings at Chase Palm Park, north side of E. Cabrillo Blvd.; & Sun. afternoons at Alameda Park, 1400 Santa Barbara St.
June-Aug.
Provided by the city, the free park concerts have become one of the town's most beloved summer traditions. Bearing blankets, picnic baskets and lawn chairs, folks swarm the grass an hour before show time to get a spot near the stage. Bands perform salsa, rockabilly and everything in between. Concerts begin at 3 p.m. at Alameda Park and 6 p.m. at Chase Palm Park, where kids can play in the Shipwreck playground.

El Capitan Canyon Concerts
11560 Calle Real, Santa Barbara
866.352.2729, ext. 714, ElCapitanCanyon.com
Sat. 6 p.m., May-October
Families, friends and fans of the great outdoors escape on summer Saturday nights to this posh campground for live blues, soul, rock and bluegrass music beside a mountain creek. It's not cheap: Admission is $10, and a barbecue dinner, while yummy, is $18 ($12 for kids). You can bring your own picnic, though. We suggest you pack fixings for s'mores; there's a raging bonfire that begs to roast marshmallows.

Santa Barbara Bowl
1122 N. Milpas St., Santa Barbara
805.962.7411, sbbowl.org
Spring through fall seasons
Many music-world giants swear there's no better place in California to play. We wouldn't know, but we think there's no better place in California to see a concert than this outdoor 4,500-seat amphitheater — a mini-Hollywood Bowl hidden in the trees. Built in 1936 as a WPA project, it's hosted David Bowie, Sting, Pearl Jam, Steely Dan, the Cure, Tom Petty and Sheryl Crow. Tip: Park on the street or at Santa Barbara High. A free shuttle spares you the long, steep trek to the Bowl. A noise ordinance requires all concerts to shut down by 10 p.m., so this is a great night out for early birds.

Tom Ball and Kenny Sultan at Cold Spring Tavern.

Festivals & Parades
Pamplona has its running of the bulls. Manhattan has its New Year's Eve. Santa Barbarans wonder why those places party just once a year, when we seem to take to the streets every weekend.

Big Dog Parade
805.963.8727, BigDogs.com
First Sat. in June
Santa Barbara-based retailer Big Dog sportswear sponsors this four-legged extravaganza, in which people parade their 1,200 costumed pooches down State Street, vying for awards

like Most Humorous. The largest dog event in the country, it ends with live music, food and vendors at Chase Palm Park, and it benefits the Big Dog Foundation for needy dogs and kids.

Old Spanish Days/Fiesta
805.962.8101, OldSpanishDays-Fiesta.org
First Wed.-Sun. in August
The *madre* of all Santa Barbara festivals is Old Spanish Days, commonly known as Fiesta. A celebration of the area's Spanish and Mexican heritage, the five-day party — consider it our Mardi Gras — takes place in August, flooding parks, plazas and even city streets with mariachis and flamenco dancers. Major events include the dancing shows Fiesta Pequeña on the steps of the Mission and Noches de Ronda on the steps of the County Courthouse; a rodeo; marketplaces and entertainment in De La Guerra Plaza and at Mackenzie Park; and two parades on State Street, El Desfile Historico and the children's parade.

Parade of Lights
Santa Barbara Harbor
805.564.5520, santabarbaraharbor.com
A Sun. evening in December
One of the few must-see traditions that doesn't take place in the summer, the Parade of Lights is a procession of 30 boats, from dinghies to superyachts. Owners decorate their vessels in holiday lights and float through the harbor competing for prizes. The best place to watch the twinkling flotilla — and the fireworks that follow — is Stearns Wharf and the Breakwater at the Harbor, both of which can be downright chilly. Bring a jacket. And a thermos of hot cocoa.

Welcoming summer at the Summer Solstice Parade.

Ethnic Festivals
Shady Oak Park (300 West Alamar Street, Santa Barbara) hosts numerous free summer festivals, each celebrating a different culture. Revelers can hear steel drums at the Caribbean Festival, purchase tin whistles and Celtic scarves at the Irish festival and covet kugel at the Jewish Festival. Here are two of the longest-running and best-attended festivals:

French Festival
805.564.PARIS, FrenchFestival.com
Taking place on the weekend closest to Bastille Day, July 14, this is the largest French celebration in the western United States. More than 20,000 Francophiles come to frolic amid baguettes, guillotines and cancan dancers. Best bets are the Poodle Parade, which is exactly what it sounds like, and the Femmes Fatales Drag Revue. *Sacre bleu!*

Greek Festival
805.683.4492, SaintBarbara.net
Also in July, this has been the loud, lively heart of the local Greek community for more than 30 years. Fans of Greek food, sadly, don't find much in town, so they come here to stock up on gyros, spanikopita, dolma and baklava. The entertainment would make Bacchus himself shout "Encore!" We saw a guy dancing with a table between his teeth once. No joke.

Summer Solstice Parade
805.965.3396, SolsticeParade.com
First Sat. after June 21
Since its humble beginnings in 1974 as a birthday celebration for a local artist, the Solstice Parade draws more than 100,000 spectators, who clamor to set up lawn chairs along the parade route hours before the event begins. At high noon, more than 1,000 whimsically costumed people march, dance and cartwheel up State Street from Cota to Micheltorena. There's a different theme each year, but it's more a celebration of oddball artistry than anything else. There are dancers and drummers, people blowing bubbles and pushing floats. It ends at Alameda Park with a festival of food and music.

Classical & Modern Music & Dance

Camerata Pacifica
P.O. Box 30116, Santa Barbara
805.884.8410, CamerataPacifica.org
This ensemble features what the *L.A. Times* called "chamber music luminaries" playing a repertoire from baroque to of-the-moment. Founded in 1990 by Irish flute player Adrian Spence, the group is known for its regularly broadcast performances on NPR's "Performance Today." Especially innovative is its Lunchtime Series, condensed Friday-afternoon concerts designed as a sort of workday break with Bach.

Community Arts Music Association (CAMA)
111 E. Yanonali St., Santa Barbara
805.966.4324, CAMAsb.org
Since its 1919 formation, CAMA has been bringing orchestras from around the world to perform in our town, from the St. Petersburg Philharmonic to the State Symphony of Mexico. Over the years, guest musicians have included Sergei Rachmaninoff, Igor Stravinsky, Isaac Stern and Marian Anderson.

Music Academy of the West
1070 Fairway Rd., Santa Barbara
805.969.4726, MusicAcademy.org
Founded in 1947, this music conservatory on a spectacular ten-acre estate in Montecito invites the nation's top young classical musicians to study — with full scholarship — in an eight-week summer program. Those of us who are not oboe or bassoon prodigies should care, because the place opens its doors for free or low-cost master classes, at which the public can watch these young wonders at work. Former academy students include songwriter Burt Bacharach and mezzo-soprano Marilyn Horne.

Opera Santa Barbara
123A W. Padre St., Santa Barbara
805.898.3890, OperaSB.com
A relative newcomer to the local arts scene, Opera Santa Barbara recently adopted a festival format that allows fans to see two fully staged operas by the same composer in a single weekend, or on consecutive weekends. Led by maestro Valery Ryvkin, the company produces cool stuff, like vignettes in the gardens of Lotusland and a VIP opera tour to Italy.

Santa Barbara Dance Theatre
University of California, Santa Barbara
805.893.4527, SantaBarbaraDanceTheatre.com
In residence at UCSB, the professional contemporary dance company is known for its visually stunning and imaginatively rendered performances. The group is led by artistic director Jerry Pearson, a dance professor at the university who has danced and choreographed throughout the world.

Santa Barbara Symphony
1900 State St., Ste. G, Santa Barbara
805.898.9626, TheSymphony.org
The half-century-old symphony recently underwent some major changes: moving to the newly remodeled Granada Theatre after years of calling the Arlington its home, and appointing big-shot international conductor Nir Kabaretti as its maestro. The symphony, however, will do well to keep a few things the same – the amazing outreach to schools, the cool preconcert "Music Behind the Music" discussions and the beloved New Year's Eve pops concert.

State Street Ballet
322 State St., Santa Barbara
805.965.6066, StateStreetBallet.com
Company director Rodney Gustafson worked with such esteemed choreographers as Alvin Ailey and Rudolf Nureyev while dancing with the American Ballet Theatre. His local company stages and tours gorgeous shows and performs works by Agnes de Mille and George Balanchine. But it is best known around these parts for its crackling Christmas *Nutcracker*.

The Santa Barbara Symphony performing at its former home in the Arlington.

On Stage & Screen

On Stage

Arlington Theatre
1317 State St., Santa Barbara
805.963.4408, TheArlingtonTheatre.com
Santa Barbara's largest indoor theater, the Arlington seats 2,200 for blockbuster movies, symphony concerts and touring dance and theater productions. Built in 1930 to look like a Spanish castle, the theater draws "oohs" and "aahs" for its interior's trompe l'oeil effect: a ceiling that twinkles like the night sky and walls fashioned to look like a Spanish villa, with faux balconies, windows and staircases.

Boxtales Theatre Company
P.O. Box 91521, Santa Barbara
805.961.3906, Boxtales.org
A favorite of local kids, the Boxtales guys have developed their own big, bold brand of theater that spotlights dramatic world myths and folktales. Using handmade masks, live drumming and exaggerated, dancelike movement, they hunker, pounce and flail across stages throughout California for more than 160 performances every year, including a number in Santa Barbara.

Center Stage Theater
751 Paseo Nuevo, Santa Barbara
805.963.8198, CenterStageTheater.org
This nonprofit black-box theater overlooks the Paseo Nuevo Mall from the tiled second-story balcony it shares with the Contemporary Arts Forum. Some of Santa Barbara's award-winning stage shows have sprung to success from this intimate and flexible space, which seats about 130 and can be configured as a traditional theater, thrust stage or even cabaret-style venue with surrounding tables. It's a great place to see small companies do interesting work, from experimental modern dance to provocative and up-close theater.

Ensemble Theatre Company
914 Santa Barbara St., Santa Barbara
805.965.5400, EnsembleTheatre.com
The longest-running professional theater company in town, the Ensemble stages ambitious plays, and even readings by important and up-and-coming playwrights. Its home is the historic Alhecama Theatre, whose 140 seats squeak with age, and which took its name from the first two letters of the landowners' daughters' names: Alice, Helen, Catherine and Mary.

The Arlington is one of the last of the ornate, old single-screen movie theaters in California; it also hosts concerts, dance and theater.

The group's Storybook Theatre stages original plays for thousands of school kids each year.

Granada Theatre
1214 State St., Santa Barbara
805.899.2222, GranadaSB.org
Fresh from a $50-million renovation, this grand 1924 theater reopened in 2008 with refined acoustics, a bigger stage and eight new audience side boxes, in which posh patrons can enjoy privacy. The closest thing Santa Barbara has to a skyscraper, the eight-story Granada has hosted such legends as Fred Astaire and Ginger Rogers on its stage. It's the area's premier venue for touring Broadway-style shows.

Lit Moon Theatre Company
Westmont College, 1052 Westmont Rd., Montecito
805.565.6778, LitMoon.com
Based at Westmont College, Lit Moon is an experimental, Shakespeare-tweaking theater company led by boundary-nudging artistic director John Blondell, a Westmont professor. We saw a performance of *Hamlet* in which the "band" was one guy with — we're not kidding — a saw. Beloved by critics, Lit Moon has taken its avant-garde act on the road to fringe theater festivals the world over.

Lobero Theatre
33 E. Canon Perdido St., Santa Barbara
805.963.0761, Lobero.com
Namesake José Lobero was an Italian trombonist and tavern owner who went bankrupt and died from a suicidal gunshot wound. But the theater itself has a much happier history. Rebuilt in 1924 by George Washington Smith, the 680-seat venue opened the same time

Christian McBride lets loose during a performance with the McCoy Tyner Trio at the Lobero.

that the city's first-ever Fiesta celebration took place. It's known these days for its ornate tiled ceiling, its ability to draw performers like Mikhail Baryshnikov and the so-cool-it's-hot Sings Like Hell music series — concerts and backstage shindigs with singer-songwriters from Tracy Chapman to Randy Newman. Local resident David Crosby not only played the series – he bought season tickets.

Marjorie Luke Theatre
721 E. Cota St., Santa Barbara
805.884.4087, LukeTheatre.org
Tucked in the halls of Santa Barbara Junior High, between lockers and classrooms, the Marjorie Luke is named for one of the school's beloved drama teachers from the 1960s and '70s. Renovated to its stunning high-tech state in 2003, the theater serves local students — with the goal of fostering self-esteem by encouraging creative expression — and hosts shows by major music studs like Rufus Wainwright and KT Tunstall.

PCPA Theaterfest
800 S. College Dr., Santa Maria
805.922.8313, PCPA.org
Okay, let's just say it. Santa Maria is the last place we'd expect to find hotshot live theater. But the Pacific Conservatory of the Performing Arts at Allan Hancock College — better known as PCPA — is a resident theater company that has trained Robin Williams and Kathy Bates, among others, and puts on incredible produc-

tions of huge shows like *Ragtime* and *Grease*, as well as works by Shakespeare and Molière. Plays are staged at the Marian and Severson Theatres on campus or, in summer, at Solvang's 700-seat outdoor Festival Theatre.

Santa Barbara City College Theatre Group
721 Cliff Dr., Santa Barbara
805.965.5935, SBCC.edu
The affordability of the tickets belies the professionalism of the shows at SBCC, where the theater group's season subscriptions have been rising steadily for years. Expect fun fare as well as challenging stuff: *Six Degrees of Separation*, *The Rocky Horror Show*, the *Laramie Project*. The steep rake of the 400-seat Garvin Theatre means you can always see over the guy in front of you. We suggest a matinee so you can ogle the jaw-dropping ocean view from the campus' surrounding greenbelts.

Speaking of Stories
924 Anacapa St., Santa Barbara
805.966.3875, SpeakingofStories.org
Actors of stage and film are invited to read great works of literature at the Lobero Theatre. It's like storytime for grown-ups, a chance to close your eyes and let the nuanced voices of trained storytellers go to work on your imagination. Each show's readings relate to a theme: baseball, wedding cake, ghost stories. Readers have included Christopher Lloyd, Robert Guillaume and Jane Seymour; authors have included Truman Capote, Anne Sexton and Dave Barry. We like to sip coffee beforehand, as the act of being read to — no matter how engaging the reader — tends to trigger the sleepies.

UCSB Arts & Lectures
University of California, Santa Barbara
805.893.3535, ArtsandLectures.UCSB.edu
Nobody but *nobody* brings the big names to our small town like Arts & Lectures. Perhaps the hottest tickets around belong to this group, whose lofty goal is to supplement the university's academic instruction with exposure to important cultural phenomena. Hence appearances by such world-class performers as Queen Latifah and Arlo Guthrie, readings by Anne Lamott and David Sedaris, lectures by Tom Brokaw and Stephen Sondheim and screenings of human-rights documentaries. Most events are at Campbell Hall on campus, but some are in downtown Santa Barbara.

The Cannes of California

Santa Barbara International Film Festival
Various locations, Santa Barbara
SBFilmFestival.org
For eleven days every January, locals stop bragging about Santa Barbara's red roofs and start bragging about red carpets. Continually drawing the hands-down hottest names in Hollywood, the Santa Barbara International Film Festival briefly turns our otherwise low-key hamlet into Tinseltown North, where filmmakers come to schmooze.

From humble beginnings, when C-list actors and no-name directors were the best the fest could get, the 24-year-old event is now among the top twelve film festivals in the United States. What makes it so great?

Celebs. Boatloads of 'em.

Festival director Roger Durling, a former playwright and longtime film geek, says there are two reasons that stars like Angelina Jolie and Javier Bardem flock to the Santa Barbara festival. One is timing: The event is strategically scheduled for late January, right after Academy Award nominations are announced. Stars and producers hope that taking part in the festival will raise their showbiz profiles, and thus the likelihood of taking home a statue on Oscar night. Location is the festival's other secret weapon. The proximity to L.A., and the appeal of spending a glitzy weekend in paradise, makes it hard for invited guests to say no. To that end, such cinematic bigwigs as Will Smith, Helen Mirren, George Clooney, Cate Blanchett and Al Gore happily make the trek north.

Fans wait by the red carpet for the action to begin at the Santa Barbara International Film Festival.

Beyond stargazing, though, the festival has quite a spate of offerings for true cinemaphiles. It screens a couple of hundred films, including world premieres, from many nations. It honors a "guest director" each year with a retrospective of his or her work. Fans can attend the always-sold-out panels where of-the-moment screenwriters, directors and producers answer questions about their craft. And there are always fun clusters of screenings based on a theme: surfing, horror, musicals.

Audiences usually can buy tickets to individual films and events, but priority is given to folks who shell out for pricey inclusive festival passes. If you've got the cash and can't stand waiting a whole year for your film fix, we recommend the festival's exclusive Cinema Society, which invites members to star-studded screenings of not-yet-released buzz films all year long.

On Screen
Santa Barbara's movie theaters represent a monopoly – they're all owned by Metropolitan Theatres. Below are addresses; for times, call 805.963.9503 or go to MetroTheatres.com.

Arlington Theatre
1317 State St., Santa Barbara
805.963.4408

Camino Real Cinemas
7040 Marketplace Dr., Goleta

Fairview Theatre
225 N. Fairview Ave., Goleta

Fiesta 5 Theatre
916 State St., Santa Barbara

Metro 4 Theatre
618 State St., Santa Barbara

Paseo Nuevo Cinemas
8 W. De La Guerra Pl.

Plaza de Oro Theatre
371 S. Hitchcock Way, Santa Barbara

Riviera Theatre
2044 Alameda Padre Serra, Santa Barbara

The Gig Guide

Live Music

Chumash Casino
3400 E. Hwy. 246, Santa Ynez
800.CHUMASH, ChumashCasino.com
Next door to rural Santa Ynez, the Chumash
Casino Resort, with its giant hotel and 2,000
slot machines, looks weirdly out of place. But
if you're looking for a close-up view of country
stars like Brooks and Dunn, comedians like
Kathy Griffin, and where-are-they-now acts like
KISS and the Go-Go's, the Casino's 1,300-
seat Shamala Showroom is a sure bet. Which
is more than we can say of the bingo tables.
Show tickets typically range from $25 to $195.

Dargan's
18 E. Ortega St., Santa Barbara
805.568.0702, Dargans.com
The James Joyce
513 State St., Santa Barbara
805.962.2688, TheJamesJoyce.com
The sweet sounds of the Emerald Isle pour
forth from both of these popular and atmo-
spheric downtown pubs every week. Dargan's
hosts live traditional Irish music on Thursday
and Saturday evenings. The James Joyce has
Irish music on Sunday evenings, live rock and
roll on Wednesdays and jazz bands on Friday
and Saturday nights. Pull up a stool, order up a
Guinness and let your ears do a little jig.

The Maverick Saloon
3687 Sagunto St., Santa Ynez
805.686.4785, MaverickSaloon.org
Live country bands perform Friday and
Saturday nights beneath the antlers at this
cowboy bar in the heart of dusty-chic Santa
Ynez. Western dance lessons before the show
help you perfect your two-step or "horseshoe
shuffle" before the tunes get twangin'. Jeans
and a big ol' hat are appropriate attire.

The Mercury Lounge
5871 Hollister Ave., Goleta
805.967.0907
A true "lounge" with funky couches and coffee
tables, the Mercury has live music every Thursday night, and often on other evenings as well.
The bands are eclectic, from folk and country
to guys called, um, Zohn Shotir and his Cult
of Goat-Eye'd Gypsies. John Doe and Exene
Cervenka, both formerly of the punk icon band
X, have played here.

SOhO
1221 State St., Ste. 205, Santa Barbara
805.962.7776, SOhOsb.com
A locals' favorite to see live bands, SOhO has a
more sophisticated feel than some of the downtown dance clubs. With brick walls, wood floors
and a full dinner menu, it's the only nightspot
with live music seven nights a week. You'll hear
it all: funk, blues, singer-songwriter, reggae,
Latin and rock.

Stateside Restaurant & Lounge
1114 State St., Santa Barbara
805.564.1000, StatesideSB.com
The newest entry to the nightclub scene, the
Stateside took over the space long occupied by
Acapulco Restaurant at the back of La Arcada.
The place boasts a giant fountain out front, an
ultramodern bar inside and live entertainment
most nights of the week, from comedy to live
dance bands to ticketed concerts.

Velvet Jones
423 State St., Santa Barbara
805.965.8676, Velvet-Jones.com
A hard-rocking, hip-hopping nightspot for
college-age and twentysomething music lovers, Velvet Jones features local and national
bands Thursday through Sunday. The stage
has welcomed Dishwalla, Frank Black and the
Catholics, Alien Ant Farm and local heavy-metal
quartet Nogahyde.

Dancing

eos Lounge
500 Anacapa St., Santa Barbara
805.564.2410, eosLounge.com
With whitewashed booths, cobalt-blue accents
and a rock bar, eos Lounge aims for a Mediter-

Regulars play darts in between music sets at
Dargan's.

Party time at the Wildcat Lounge.

ranean ambience — that is, if the Mediterranean were a hard-thumping, see-and-be-seen dance floor with state-of-the-art sound equipment. Eos has DJs most nights, and it draws an older-than-college crowd for dancing and lingering on the outdoor patio.

Q's Sushi a-Go-Go

409 State St., Santa Barbara
805.966.9177, QsBilliards.com
You can't miss Q's: It's got one of the coolest facades on State Street. Inside the swank building, built in 1885, there are four full bars, and a full sushi menu, as well as an always-bustling dance floor. On the downside, it can get seriously crowded. On the upside, there's free pool on the second floor if you get bored — or tired — of boogeying.

Sandbar

514 State St., Santa Barbara
805.966.1388, SandbarSB.com
A tequila bar with an indoor-outdoor tropical feel, the Sandbar blasts reggae on Tuesdays and hosts DJs every Friday and Saturday night for shaking your thing on the palm-shaded patio or in the south-of-the-border-style interior. Once a month, if you'd rather do the buck than the bump, there's a mechanical bull.

Wildcat

15 W. Ortega St., Santa Barbara
805.962.7970, WildcatLounge.com
Some places ooze "cool." This place just drips "hip." Sparkly red vinyl booths and a jeweled canopy over the bar give the Wildcat a retro-

kitsch ambience, and go-go dancers give it a flirtatious prrrrsonality. This hot spot is known for its DJs, who spin everything from hip-hop and house to alternative and '80s pop.

Zelo

630 State St., Santa Barbara
805.966.5792
One of the longer-running dance clubs in town, Zelo is known for its California and seafood menu by day and its eclectic mix of danceable sounds at night. Cha-cha in this narrow but popular dance spot to Brazilian sounds, jazz, house and pop.

Karaoke

Madison's Grill & Tavern

525 State St., Santa Barbara
805.882.1182, MadisonsSB.com
Madison's is your typical brick-wall sports pub with three dozen TV sets — that is, until somebody busts out the Donna Summer. On Sundays and Tuesdays at 9 p.m., you can belt out your Journey, Skynyrd or Madonna between swigs of beer and bites of hickory-smoked ribs.

Tiburon Tavern

3116 State St., Santa Barbara
805.682.8100, TiburonTavern.com
This neighborhood watering hole isn't big, or fancy, but karaoke fans consider it an ideal venue for testing their pipes. Whether you hope to catch the show — or avoid it — the singing starts at 9:30 p.m. on Fridays.

Q & A: Roger Durling

From his earliest memories of growing up in Panama, Roger Durling has been a self-described film geek, loitering at the cinema, handicapping the Oscars and sneaking off to film festivals in his spare time. Now he heads up the 23-year-old Santa Barbara International Film Festival, one of the country's fastest-growing movie fests. Drawing Angelina Jolie and Will Smith in recent years, the late-January festival screens hundreds of new films, from world-premiere studio flicks to locally made surfing documentaries. Roger took his eyes off the screen to talk to Starshine Roshell.

What's a big-city guy like you doing in a small town like this?
It feels like a small town, but it has the heart of a big city. Culturally, it's so diverse. We get lots of great touring shows because we're a nice stop between Los Angeles and San Francisco. I hear people every once in a while saying it's provincial here and that there's nothing going on, and I just think, "You're out of your mind." There's actually not enough time to do all the stuff going on.

How does our festival compare with the biggies, like Cannes and Toronto?
We're in the top twelve in the U.S. and the top 50 in the world. That's not a bad place to be.

How'd it get so big? What's your secret?
It's the timing, the geography and the accessibility to Hollywood. It's not hard to twist the arms of, say, Angelina and Brad to come up for the weekend. Most of our honorees want to stay longer than one night because it's so idyllic.

What do celebs say about our town after visiting for the first time?
They find it very warm, and they're impressed with how educated and sophisticated our audiences are. They like the town's laid-back charm.

Best place in town to see a show?
I go to the Jazz Series at the Lobero Theatre, and I see plays at the Ensemble Theatre and Santa Barbara City College. But there's nothing like the Arlington Theatre. I see even bad movies there. It reminds me of the Ziegfeld Theatre in New York. The fact that we still have this grand movie palace here says a lot – that we value tradition and history.

What's your favorite local hangout?
I always go to Palmieri's on the westside. It's this great, laid-back neighborhood bar. You can have drinks inside and then order pizza from Paisano's next door. It's one of the best pizzerias in town, and they'll deliver to the bar next door.

Outdoorsy

Few places in the world have the bounty of natural settings that Santa Barbara boasts, from palm-lined beaches to oak-forested mountains, with stunning cliffs, serene lakes, sprawling ranches and mesmerizing creeks in between. Whether hiking or biking, strolling or galloping across the landscape, our residents have a passion for the outdoors that knows neither walls nor ceilings.

6 Great Hikes

With the Pacific Coast in our frontyard and Los Padres National Forest as our backyard, there's almost nowhere you can tread in Santa Barbara that isn't gorgeous. And colorful, too: From Red Rock to Blue Canyon, and from the top of White Mountain to the bottom of Tangerine Falls, the names of local hiking trails promise a broad spectrum of vibrant views and flashy flora along the way – and they deliver on the promise. The hikes listed here offer more than just an al fresco workout; they bring you face to face with the area's natural wonders. You'll see seals and butterflies, waterfalls and swimming holes. These six routes are just a few of our favorites. For more of the dozens and dozens of spectacular hikes from Carpinteria up through Santa Ynez and the forest's backcountry, pick up a local trail guide at Pacific Travelers Supply (12 West Anapamu Street, 805.963.4438). For hikes within the forest, you'll need to purchase the controversial Adventure Pass, a $5-per-day permit that allows one carload of adventurers to park within forest areas all day and overnight. You can get it at the Los Padres National Forest headquarters (6755 Hollister Avenue, Suite 150, Goleta, 805.968.6640), and often at kiosks near hiking trailheads. And note that you needn't go it alone: The Los Padres Chapter of the Sierra Club leads social and conditioning hikes every week, and you don't have to be a member to join them. See santabarbarahikes. com/hikes/sierraclub for the most up-to-date schedule.

Carpinteria Bluffs
About 2 miles round-trip; easy

Just south of Santa Barbara in sleepy, seaside Carpinteria, craggy bluffs run parallel to the Pacific. It's a pretty place for a peaceful stroll with lots to see along the way — particularly the full-grown and baby harbor seals that hang out on the beaches below. From December through May, the area is a protected seal sanctuary, but you can observe the barking and sunbathing mammals from the 100-foot-high cliffs, which also afford fabulous views of the Channel Islands.

Harbor seals hang out on the beach below the Carpinteria Bluffs.

Follow any of the paths through the wildflower meadow out toward the ocean. Turn right when you reach the cliff's edge and amble along the eucalyptus-lined trail. When you reach the edge of a flower farm, where bright orange and purple petals sprout before your eyes, bear left and (carefully!) cross the railroad tracks. The rookery lookout is just up ahead on the left. Volunteers there will tell you that dogs and even, no kidding, large sticks can scare the seals below, so tie your canine to a nearby post.

Turn around to complete the two-mile walk, or continue a bit farther past the oil pier and through another parking lot to check out Tarpits Park. The eight-acre blufftop park was once the site of a village for Chumash Indians, who sealed their canoes and cooking bowls with the tar that seeps up naturally from the earth here. You can still see the stuff oozing down the cliffs, so watch your feet! If you get goo'ed, we recommend baby oil for removing the tar.

Driving Directions: From Highway 101, take the Bailard Road exit in Carpinteria and turn toward the ocean. The road dead-ends into a free parking lot.

The wall of green at Nojoqui Falls.

Nojoqui Falls
Half-hour round-trip; easy

Niagara it ain't, but after a good rain, the towering waterfall at the edge of Nojoqui Falls County Park (just outside of Solvang) is a dazzling streak of white against a moss-covered sandstone wall. Even in drier months, visitors find the shady walk to its base enchanting. Pronounced "no-HO-ee," the falls stand at the end of a lush and secluded sylvan canyon canopied by oaks and sycamores. This is a terrific walk for kids because it's less than fifteen minutes to the falls, the incline is subtle, and the payoff is so cool.

Make your way through the picnic areas to the start of the forested trail, which carries you over wooden bridges and up stone steps along the way. Take time to stop and plop on a bench to watch for acorn woodpeckers and purple martins. If the season's right, you'll hear it before you see it: water rushing (or else, well, trickling) over a vertical rock wall and down into a pebbly pool surrounded by ferns. Nearby boulders are fun for climbing, or just perching and soaking up the spectacle of this cascade — which looks much taller than it actually is. Dogs are welcome on leashes.

Driving Directions: From Santa Barbara, take Highway 101 north through the Gaviota tunnel. Turn right onto Old Coast Highway. Turn left onto Alisal Road, then right into the county park. You'll find the parking lot and trailhead two miles down the road.

Ellwood Grove
1 to 4 miles round-trip; easy

Nestled between the beach and surrounding Goleta suburbs stands a eucalyptus thicket where thousands of Monarch butterflies come to stay warm in the winter. On cool days they hang in dense orange and black clusters from the highest branches; on sunny days they flutter freely throughout the enchanting grove, surrounding visitors in silent movement. Prime viewing time is December through February.

From the streetside sign marking the Coronado Butterfly Reserve, walk up the small hill, down the other side and across a bridge over Devereux Creek. Turn right at the juncture and head through the ravine until you come upon the eucalyptus forest — almost a chamber unto itself with sunlight streaming through the treetops. Hike through the hilly and sometimes muddy woodland, being careful not to step on butterflies!

From here you can go back to the car, or head up and out of the grove to an open meadow with a network of trails leading straight ahead to 80-foot-high ocean bluffs. Take one of two access trails down to the beach, or head right for more meadow romping.

Another fun side trip leads you left to Coal Oil Point Reserve, an enclave of dunes, grasslands, a salt marsh and the 45-acre Devereux Lagoon. If you haven't seen enough winged creatures for the day, the lagoon is a popular spot for bird-watching.

Driving Directions: From Santa Barbara, take Highway 101 north to the Glen Annie/Storke Road exit in Goleta. Turn left off the freeway and right onto Hollister Avenue. Turn left onto Coronado Drive and park near the end, where you'll see a sign for the Butterfly Preserve.

Monarch butterflies warming themselves at Ellwood Grove.

Rattlesnake Canyon
5 to 6 miles round-trip; strenuous

Named for its winding shape, not for any venomous trail residents, Rattlesnake Canyon is a favorite hike for locals because it's shady and follows alongside Rattlesnake Creek. Pools, waterfalls and a series of rock-hopping creek crossings make this trail especially lovely. Stay on the path, though: Rattlers may not necessarily lurk in the bushes, but poison oak does.

Start out with your first creek crossing just after the lovely old stone bridge, and head up the wide trail that was once a buggy road. After you reach the second crossing, you'll head into switchbacks that lead you out of the canyon. Between the last two crossings is a peaceful spot where the stream cascades over rocks, creating waterfalls and pools — look for trout in the water, if no dogs are romping through it. Next you'll come upon a triangular meadow called Tin Can Flat, named for the tin roof of a cabin that once stood there. Past the meadow, the trail leads another three-quarters of a mile up to the turnaround point: Gibraltar Road, a gain of 1,500 feet overall.

Driving Directions: From the Santa Barbara Mission, take Mission Canyon Road north to Foothill Road and turn right. Make a quick left back onto Mission Canyon Road. Bear right at the fork and hang a sharp right onto Las Canoas Road, following it to Skofield Park. The trailhead is just over a mile up the winding road near a stone bridge over Rattlesnake Creek.

Heading down Rattlesnake Creek toward the stone bridge.

Cold Spring Canyon
3.5 miles round-trip; moderate

Another shady jaunt, this forested trail takes you up along a creek that always has water in it, even in the dry months. The east fork leads to an overlook of Montecito with panoramic views of the mountains, Pacific Ocean and Channel Islands.

Start out on either side of the creek; they join together soon enough. The first pool is just twenty yards upstream with a bench and a fork to the western trail. Continue on the east fork up the canyon on

One of the pools and waterfalls on the Cold Spring Canyon trail.

the right side of the creek. After two more crossings, past waterfalls and pools, switch-backs take you up the hill away from the creek. (Be sure to stay on the zigzagging trail; if you head straight, you'll find yourself on a loop back to where you started.) When the trail meets up with a road, turn right and catch your breath — before the Montecito Overlook steals it away again.

Driving Directions: From Santa Barbara, take Highway 101 south to the Hot Springs Road exit in Montecito and head toward the mountains. Turn left onto Hot Springs Road. Two miles later, go left on East Mountain Drive. You'll find the trailhead a mile up on the right, where the creek runs over the pavement. Park on the street.

Red Rock
6 to 7 miles round-trip; moderate

Some hikes pay off with a refreshing swim, others with a rewarding view. The Red Rock loop has both. Winding up alongside the Santa Ynez River, this trail leads you past sweeping meadow views to a breathtaking overlook of Gibraltar Dam before heading back down for a number of river crossings. The cool, blue destination: a series of irresistible swimming holes surrounded by towering red-hued rocks.

Look for a dirt road at the back of the parking area. Proceed past the metal gate along what locals call the "High Road." The trail is steep and windy at first but finally levels off at a plateau overlooking the river. After your first view of Gibraltar Dam, it heads down to the river trail that will take you back — frequently sloshing through the water — to the popular and inviting Red Rock pools, which can get populous in the hot months.

We recommend wearing sneakers you don't mind getting wet, being very careful crossing the river when the water is high and NOT jumping off the 40-foot-high rocks into the pools below; someone gets hurt or killed doing that every year.

Driving Directions: From Santa Barbara, take Highway 154 for 10 miles to Paradise Road and turn right. Head another 10 miles to the trailhead parking area at the end of the road, after the last river crossing. You need an Adventure Pass to park here; they can be purchased for $5 at kiosks along Paradise Road.

Out for Adventure

You may think Santa Barbarans are as mellow as they come. After all, what's there to get edgy about in this placid paradise by the sea? Turns out that there's a wild streak running through some of our outdoor enthusiasts, who sometimes enjoy taking fun to, well, extremes.

Rock Climbing
Up Mountain Drive off Gibraltar Road, Gibraltar Rock is a popular climbing face with sweet views. But the best area for boulder scrabbling is up Highway 154 off Painted Cave Road and West Camino Cielo. Here, a vast outcropping of sandstone slabs provides an almost alien landscape — and lots of places to find footholds. Lizard's Mouth, the Brickyard, Fire Crags and the Playground are but a few.

Hang-gliding & Paragliding
Geography makes Santa Barbara one of the nation's premier spots for hang-gliding and paragliding. Beachside cliffs make for spectacular launching spots, and sea breezes give gliders a nice lift, while tall mountains keep winds from getting too gusty. Expert gliders may want to join the flock of foot-launched pilots that soar from La Cumbre Peak to Elings Park every New Year's Day during the Hang Gliding and Paragliding Festival. Newcomers can take lessons from Fly Above All (FlyAboveAll.com) at Elings Park's world-class training hill.

Skateboarding
Sidewalk surfers are stoked to have their own free skate park at Skater's Point, where Cabrillo Boulevard meets Garden Street. Even if you don't ollie, the skaters are wicked fun to watch. You'll see riders from tykes to old dudes shredding on the ramps, half pipe, grind rails and taco bowl (if you have to ask ...). The park's open from 8 a.m. to just after sunset, with weekend mornings reserved for younger and less-experienced skaters. It's free to skate, but helmets and elbow and kneepads are required.

Lizard's Mouth draws rock-climbers from all over the Central Coast.

Adventure Tours
Thrill-seekers who don't like that whole pesky planning part can sign up for a series of wild adventures arranged down to the last harness and helmet. The Santa Barbara Adventure Company (SBAdventureCo.com) leads surfing, kayaking, rock-climbing and mountain-biking tours. Captain Jack's (CaptainJacksTours.com) will take you horseback riding, beer-tasting and soaring through the sky in a glider. Cloud Climbers Jeep Tours (CCJeeps.com) goes off-roading, hiking and even trap-shooting.

Surfing
It's not the North Shore. But Santa Barbara's known for having surfable waves year-round, peaking in February and typically small and accessible in summer. Leadbetter Beach (at the base of Santa Barbara City College just west of the harbor) provides nice swells for beginners; experts flock to Rincon, at the Santa Barbara/Ventura county line. You can learn to surf with world-traveled Greg Lewis, who coaches all ages through the Santa Barbara Surf School (805.745.8877, SantaBarbaraSurfSchool.com); also good are Santa Barbara Seals (805.687.9785, SantaBarbaraSeals.com) and Surf Happens (805.966.3613, SurfHappens.com). Forgot your board? You can rent one on Leadbetter Beach.

Kayaking
Some say the best view to be had in Santa Barbara is from sea level. Rent a kayak or canoe from Paddle Sports (805.899.4925, KayakSB.com) in the Santa Barbara Harbor, paddle out to sea and turn around for a stunning vista of the twinkle-lit town and the Riviera hills that cradle it. You can glide under Stearns Wharf and out to see the sea lions that lounge on the harbor's bell buoy. Or take a kayak tour through the caves and inlets of the Channel Islands. Never been on a kayak? No problem — they teach you. Good guided outings, too, including the monthly full-moon Santa Barbara Harbor by Moonlight.

5 Walks Around Town

The beach path tops the breakwater that demarcates Santa Barbara Harbor.

West Beach & the Harbor

West of State St. on Cabrillo Blvd., Santa Barbara
Route: Wooden pier and paved sidewalk
Park along Cabrillo Blvd. or at the end of Stearns Wharf

For us, this is the town's quintessential trek. It's flat. You can't get lost. There's uniquely Santa Barbara stuff going on at every single juncture. And at just over two miles round-trip, it's long enough to burn off some of the burrito you gobbled down for lunch.

Start off at the end of salty, scenic Stearns Wharf and make your way back down the wooden pier toward dry land. When you hit the iconic Dolphin Fountain, go left onto the bike path along Cabrillo Boulevard past sleepy West Beach. When the path juts left to the Santa Barbara Harbor, follow it to the water, then turn right and head past the boat-launching ramp to the sidewalk that runs alongside the harbor slips.

You'll see everything from yachts to dinghies among the 1,100 vessels bobbing in the marina — and always a smattering of homeless folks enjoying the views (and showers) the harbor provides. As you pass the final slip, turn left and follow the sidewalk past the stately Santa Barbara Maritime Museum and bustling Brophy Bros. seafood restaurant.

As you head out toward the sea, the pathway bends left, leading down the long, flag-lined breakwater. At high tide, waves spray over the sea wall, showering pedestrians in cool — and sometimes surprising — blasts of saltwater. At the end of the walkway, scramble over the rocks onto the manmade beach, or sandbar, for panoramic views of the wharf, sparkling hills, harbor and Channel Islands.

East Beach & the Bird Refuge

East of State St. on Cabrillo Blvd., Santa Barbara
Route: Wooden pier and paved sidewalk
Park along Cabrillo Blvd. or at the end of Stearns Wharf

A longer but equally picturesque waterfront promenade begins at the far tip of the wharf and leads walkers east, rather than west, from the Dolphin Fountain. (Take note that east might appear to be south, since you might assume that the ocean is west, but the shoreline here is angled.) Follow the bike path past the noisy but highly entertaining skate park, or stay on the sidewalk where, on Sundays, you can peruse the ceramics, watercolors and jewelry of art-show vendors.

Cross Cabrillo Boulevard at Garden Street and walk through Chase Palm Park, whose antique carousel, Chumash bridge, duck pond, shipwreck playground and music pavilion make it a whimsical thoroughfare.

Staying on the inland side of the palmtree-lined boulevard, continue heading east past oceanfront hotels and artist Herbert Bayer's hard-to-miss rectangular rainbow sculpture, the "Chromatic Gate." You'll meet up with the bike path again (beware of cranky bikers!) as it heads under a shady stretch of trees. To the right, you'll see tanned, leaping hard-bodies at beach volleyball courts. To the left, if you listen carefully, you might hear the roar of the Santa Barbara Zoo's proud lions.

Follow the path around to the left, where it will lead you to the peaceful and vast Andree Clark Bird Refuge, once a tidal salt marsh and now a freshwater lake. Time it right and you'll see the dusk sky reflecting off the water as songbirds take wing above.

Twilight on the bike path at East Beach.

Douglas Family Preserve
Oceanfront open space above Arroyo Burro Beach, Santa Barbara
Route: Dirt path through natural setting
From Shoreline Dr., turn onto Mesa Lane toward the ocean. Go right onto Medcliff Rd., follow it to the end, park on the street and proceed through the gates

The biggest chunk of undeveloped oceanfront in Santa Barbara, this 70-acre blufftop preserve is a favorite with dog walkers, as pooches can scamper off-leash so long as their humans pick up after them. There's even a spigot and communal water bowl partway through the trail that unfussy canines like to slurp from as they pass.

Open from sunrise to 10 p.m., the park allows you to amble along the coastal cliff through mature oaks, Monterey pine, cypress and eucalyptus trees to a bird's-eye overlook of Arroyo Burro Beach, known to locals as Hendry's. Head back along the same path, or continue through the loop for a slightly longer walk. Either route is less than a mile, and along it you'll see folks parked in beach chairs, admiring the soul-churning view. Kids will love climbing over logs and watching hang-gliders launch from the cliff.

Long known as the Wilcox Property for Roy Wilcox, who ran a plant nursery here until the 1950s, the space nearly fell to developers in 1996. But the community rallied, raising nearly the $3.5 million required to buy it back. When the locals came up short, actor and Santa Barbara resident Michael Douglas chipped in the last $600,000, earning him naming rights.

Carved into a stone on the site is a verse by local poet Perie Longo: "Here you may walk in peace. Here you may walk in time and history...."

The view to Arroyo Burro Beach from the Douglas Family Preserve.

Just one of the several appealing offshoot pathways near the Veterans Memorial Walk high up in Elings Park.

Elings Park

1298 Las Positas Rd., Santa Barbara
Route: Paved path or dirt trail
Park in the uppermost lot for Memorial Walk or near the soccer fields for Sierra Club loop

Visitors to this vast spread of more than 230 hilltop acres have two choices when it comes to hoofing it: The short and paved Santa Barbara County Veterans Memorial Walk, with a few unpaved side routes for added interest, or the longer and more rustic Sierra Club loop.

The 1,500-foot Memorial Walk is a surprisingly moving pathway past marble and sandstone plaques honoring county residents who perished in the Vietnam War. Midway through, a Terrace of Remembrance pays tribute to those who lost their lives in battles as far back as the Civil War. The loop continues to a pavilion with stunning city overlooks. If you arrive before 10 a.m., you can drive all the way up to the Memorial Walk area; if you arrive later, you'll have to park a little lower down, by the ranger station, and walk up a short but steep paved road.

More popular with hikers is the 1.3-mile Sierra Club loop, which begins just past the softball fields. On the right side of the road, signs mark the trail's entrance. Follow it up to the right through a series of switchbacks and hop off onto any side paths that strike your fancy, they all lead to the same place: a plateau with 360-degree views of Santa Barbara's ocean, harbor, red rooftops and majestic mountains. When you've had your fill — and do take your time! — head left for more switchbacks that lead you back down the hill.

Early evening on Lake Los Carneros.

Lake Los Carneros Park
304 N. Los Carneros Rd., Goleta
Route: Dirt path around lake
Park in the free lot for the Stow House and the South Coast Railroad Museum

Hidden in the center of this quiet county park is a 25-acre manmade lake that birds, frogs, fish and turtles call home. Meandering pathways lead around the reservoir for about a mile of serene strolling, with benches for resting and scenery scoping along the way.

At the trailhead stands the quaint South Coast Railroad Museum and historic Stow House, a charming Victorian home built in 1872 by Sherman Stow (open for tours; see entry in Architectural chapter). His family farmed on the property for decades before giving it to the county in 1967. The lake began as a small duck pond and was built into an irrigation system for the surrounding lemon orchards. These days, it's a popular lunchtime getaway for employees of nearby office parks.

A favorite feature is a narrow, zigzagging wooden footbridge at the north end of the lake that leads you over tall, marshy grasses and reeds. It's a super vantage point for spotting ducks and egrets, and for soaking up views of the Santa Ynez Mountains.

Our Favorite Campgrounds

From Boy Scouts and college kids to families on holiday and couples jonesing for a weekend escape, Santa Barbara's mountain and beach campgrounds are blanketed in sleeping bags every night of the year. Los Padres National Forest welcomes overnighters in ten campgrounds in its Santa Ynez Recreation Area. Cachuma Lake is popular with both tent and RV campers; now the recreation area has cabins, too. But the following are our very favorites for rugged tent camping, beachfront car and RV camping, and luxury cabin camping.

El Capitan Canyon
11560 Calle Real, Santa Barbara
866.352.2729, ElCapitanCanyon.com
$125-$350 per night; reservations recommended
This is roughing it for royalty. As rustic as a Ralph Lauren ad, El Cap houses guests in creekside safari tents and cedar cabins with fine linens, bent-willow headboards and — hallelujah! — private bathrooms. There are even circular canvas yurts for group meetings. Further amenities include a pool, general store with gourmet deli, a hiking trail to the beach and even the option of a massage. Saturday nights from May through October there's a live concert, bonfire and barbecue. We may never pop a tent again.

A tent cabin at El Capitan Canyon.

Carpinteria State Park
5361 Sixth St., Carpinteria
805.684.2811, ReserveAmerica.com
$16-$44 per night; reservations recommended
Drive up and park in one of 200-plus campsites close enough to the beach to hear the ocean waves at night, but still within walking distance of this quaint town's grocery store and charming eateries. All sites have a fire pit and picnic table, and a couple of quarters will buy you a hot shower after a day in the sand and surf. The tide pools full of sea stars, crabs and prickly anemones are so captivating that they make up for the whistle and roar of the train as it passes by the campsite in the wee hours.

Channel Islands National Park
Off the coast of Santa Barbara
877.444.6777, recreation.gov
$15 per night; reservations required (accepted up to 5 months in advance)
Primitive tent camping is available year-round on all five Channel Islands off the coast of Santa Barbara. This is hardcore camping with little more than picnic tables and pit toilets for your conveniences. You have to book a boat across the channel through Truth Aquatics (805.963.3564), haul your own gear on foot to the primitive campsite and pack out your trash when you leave. But believe us: Nothing says "getting away" like staring back at the mainland from a remote, uninhabited island. We particularly recommend Scorpion Ranch on the east end of Santa Cruz Island.

Refugio State Beach Campground
10 Refugio Beach Rd., Goleta
805.684.2811; ReserveAmerica.com
$16-$44 per night; reservations recommended.
Twenty miles north of Santa Barbara is one of our favorite California campgrounds, set in a small cove with grass, palm trees, picnic tables and a mile and a half of downright beautiful beach. Thanks to this location, not to mention the bike path leading 2.5 easy miles to neighboring El Capitan State Beach, this campground is hugely popular with families and school camping trips, so reserve early. The lack of hookups makes this a tent-camper's paradise. You'll hear the trains from the nearby tracks, but they're not nearly as loud as they are at El Capitan down the road.

On 2 Wheels & 4 Legs

Mountain biking at Elings Park.

Mountain Biking

Here, as everywhere, an ongoing rivalry exists between those who enjoy treading trails on foot and those who like to tear down 'em on two wheels. Trail damage, personal safety and equal access are among the issues at stake. But Santa Barbara mountain bikers — and there are lots of them — have found ways to have fun on local trails without raising hikers' hackles.

First, they follow trail etiquette: Responsible dirt bikers wear bells so others know they're coming. They avoid skidding or riding on the outside edges of trails, which can damage them. And they yield to hikers and horses, and slow down at blind corners.

Those in the know recommend the following trails: Romero Road for scenery and fitness; east and west along Camino Cielo for sweeping views; and from Knapp's Castle down Snyder Trail for a bit of history and distance. Join in regular group rides found at RideSB.com or by calling Mike Hecker at 805.569.0616. CentralCoastCycling.com provides details for two terrific rides in the North County to Point Sal and through Colson Canyon.

Or stay in town and fly off the groomed jumps at the Elings Park BMX track, which has open rides on Tuesdays and Thursdays. Check out SBBMX.com or call Dale Bowers at 805.564.8859 for more information.

Road Riding

Santa Barbara's streets are super cycle-friendly, with bike lanes on many of the downtown and crosstown avenues. The bike path along Cabrillo Boulevard is prime riding territory — but watch for strollers! For the safest and most popular routes around town, download detailed views of the Santa Barbara County Bike Map at TrafficSolutions.org. The Santa Barbara Bicycle Coalition also suggests more than a dozen scenic rides ranging from four miles to 26, from Montecito Village out to Santa Ynez's wine country. Check out SBBike.org for routes, descriptions and maps of each.

Everyday cyclists can follow the route taken each year by the Amgen Tour of California, which comes through Santa Barbara; here they are heading up Casitas Pass.

You can rent road bikes by the day or week at Open Air Bicycles in the Amtrak station parking lot (805.962.7000). Alternately, take a guided tour through vineyards, horse ranches and lavender farms with Santa Barbara Wine Country Cycling Tours (888.557.8687). Or rent mountain bikes, tandem beach cruisers, family-size four-wheeled surreys — and even GPS-equipped, open-air electric cars — at Wheel Fun Rentals, with three beachside locations (805.966.2282).

Heading out for a morning ride in the Santa Ynez Mountains.

Horseback Riding

Since Santa Barbara's 19th-century rancho period, when Mexico ruled the land, horses have galloped across its beaches, through its foothills and within its ranches. Former President Ronald Reagan liked to play cowboy at his Rancho del Cielo, aka his Western White House. Here's where you can hop in the saddle, too.

Circle Bar B Riding Stables
1800 Refugio Rd., Goleta
805.968.3901, horsebackridingsantabarbara.com
Located on 1,000 acres of Gaviota coastline, the Circle Bar B is an upscale guest ranch whose stables are open to the public year-round. Horses take riders through canyons and past waterfalls to a ridge with views of the ocean and islands. Reservations are recommended.

Rancho Oso Riding Stables
3750 Paradise Rd., Santa Barbara
805.683.5110, rancho-oso.com
Up Highway 154 in a rustic mountain setting sits a Western-style guest ranch complete with bunkhouse cabins and covered wagons. You needn't be an overnight guest to sign up for a

trail ride through Los Padres National Forest. Beginners are welcome for tours lasting from one to four hours, but kids must be 8 years or older to ride.

El Capitan Ranch
10920 Calle Real, Santa Barbara
805.685.1147, ElCapRanch.com
The ranch leads daily tours through the Santa Ynez Mountain foothills, from a one-hour trot through a secluded avocado grove to a three-hour trek to a mountaintop picnic. Horse-drawn carriage rides are offered on Friday and Saturday evenings.

Q & A: John McKinney

The author of fifteen books on hiking and the outdoors, John McKinney is known as the Trailmaster. A longtime hiking columnist for the *Los Angeles Times*, John grew up hiking the mountains around Los Angeles and moved to Santa Barbara 25 years ago for, ahem, the superior surroundings. A father of two, he spends weekends traversing local trails with his family and crusading against what he jokingly calls NDD, or Nature Deficit Disorder. John took a rare sit-down to shoot the breeze with Starshine Roshell.

How did your love of the outdoors develop?
I was a super Boy Scout growing up in L.A., so I got to know the local mountains. As a broadcast journalism major at USC, I started helping out on nature documentaries. The more I got into it, the more I wanted to make my avocation — a love of nature — into a vocation. Now my current crusade is against Nature Deficit Disorder.

What's the appeal of hiking? Why bother?
Either you get it right away or you don't get it. People who are out there get it: the joy, the experience of being in nature, and the fun of sharing it with friends and family.

You've traveled and hiked all over the world. What's unique about Santa Barbara?
There are a lot of places on earth that have beautiful mountains or shorelines or a vast backcountry — but really only Santa Barbara has all of that together. Also, unlike other places in California, the mountains and shoreline don't go north-south, they go east-west. That translates into this beautiful, soft light.

Is there a scent that defines the Santa Barbara mountains to you?
The trails are so aromatic because there are several kinds of sage: black sage, white sage and hummingbird sage.

What's the wildest thing you ever saw on a local trail?
I had some very proper British friends with me on Cold Spring Trail and one day, there was a gentleman hiking stark naked. He didn't even have car keys. I don't know where he was going, but I just nonchalantly exchanged "good afternoons" with him. It confirmed everything my friends ever thought about California.

Any advice for first-time hikers?
What's ruined many a visitor's trip is poison oak. It's everywhere. If you stay on the trail, it's no problem. But people want to go off it, and they run into those three sticky leaves. All parts of the plant, all year round, are toxic. That can turn anyone's hike into a bummer.

We're lucky to have great weather most of the year but ... what do you do when it rains?
Get wet! We hike rain or shine. I think it's really fun to walk in the rain. Naturally, my children have no choice in the matter.

Besides hiking, what's another way to explore our surroundings?
Kayaking. You're looking out at islands in one direction, the shoreline in the other. That, to me, is really a cool way to look at Santa Barbara.

Athletic

We know, we know, saying that Santa Barbara is athletic is like saying the pope is Catholic. Around here, you can feel out of place if you *don't* train for triathlons, bike to work, surf or play beach volleyball all weekend, or go to Pilates six days a week. In SB, relaxation means walking a 5K instead of running a 10K.

The good news is that there are so many opportunities for getting out and working out that you have few excuses not to. The scenery can't be beat, either. It doesn't seem like hard work when you're running along the bluffs or riding on the bike path, with the ocean and islands on one side and the mountains on the other. Here's how to get in touch with your athletic side, Santa Barbara style.

Working Out: Gyms, Yoga & Pilates

Santa Barbarans can't always be out in the sun, or so say our dermatologists, but that doesn't prevent us from staying in shape. We head for the gyms, yoga and Pilates studios, and fitness classes – and the hardest part is narrowing down our choices from the multitudes of options.

Cabrillo Bathhouse
1118 E. Cabrillo Blvd., Santa Barbara
805.897.2680, sbparksandrecreation.com
This unbelievably affordable public gym sits right on East Beach – the perfect place to start and end a run, bike ride, ocean swim or volleyball match at one of the many beach courts. The city-managed facility offers warm showers, weight room and lockers. No memberships are required; just pay $4 for a daily pass ($3 if you're a city resident). Or you can buy a multiple-visit pass at a discounted rate. It also rents beach wheelchairs and equipment (umbrellas, volleyballs and the like).

Cathedral Oaks Athletic Club
5800 Cathedral Oaks Rd., Goleta
805.964.7762, wcaclubs.com
With twelve tennis courts, two outdoor heated pools, a full menu of classes for kids, teens and adults, and a fully equipped fitness area with state-of-the-art machines, Cathedral Oaks is the family-friendly version of its urban sibling, Santa Barbara Athletic Club. Parents can check their kids into the Kids' Club, then take a yoga or Pilates class, sign up for a massage or relax in the spa. Membership will cost you a hefty fee, however.

Channel Islands YMCAs
ciymca.org
Santa Barbara Family YMCA: 55 Hitchcock Way, 805.569.1103
Montecito Family YMCA: 591 Santa Rosa Lane, 805.969.3288
Stuart C. Gildred Family YMCA: 900 N. Refugio Rd., Santa Ynez, 805.686.2037
The three local Ys are the people's gyms of Santa Barbara County. They're all part of a broader association called the Channel Islands YMCA, headquartered in Santa Barbara. Most families sign up for children's swim lessons, sports classes and childcare, then stick around for years, taking advantage of the aqua aerobics, yoga, Pilates, martial arts and exercise machines. Membership at one YMCA allows you to visit others for a limited number of times per month. Day passes are also available.

Community Parks & Recreation Classes
Santa Barbara Parks & Recreation Programs
805.564.5418, sbparksandrecreation.com
Carpinteria Parks & Recreation Program
805.566.2417, 805.684.5405, carpinteria.ca.us
Solvang Parks & Recreation Program
805.688.7529, cityofsolvang.com
It's the best deal in town – the city of Santa Barbara organizes a full slate of recreation

Cabrillo Bathhouse has an enviable location right on the sand at East Beach.

Club-Team Athletics

Santa Barbara is so athletic that it has spawned a couple of hybrid organizations for exercise buffs who like to socialize while they're training. Some of these have grown into international networks with home bases right here – in one of the world's most beautiful places to get, and stay, in shape.

Momentum 4 Life

momentum4life.com

Dawn Schroeder created Momentum 4 Life (M4L) in the early 2000s. M4L forms teams of men, women, children (and combinations thereof) who want to challenge themselves and give back to the community. Teams train for triathlons, biathlons, 5K and 10K runs and half or full marathons. Members receive coached group workouts, training plans, discounts on team uniforms and access to a national web-based community. M4L also raises money to donate to charitable organizations.

Moms in Motion

momsinmotion.com

Jamie Allison founded Moms in Motion here in 1999 (see the Q & A at the end of this chapter), hoping to encourage women to carve out time for themselves by combining three things that typically pull them in mutually exclusive directions: fitness, fun and philanthropy. It started with a small group of local moms who wanted to train together for a triathlon. Now it's an international network that counts more than 4,000 members across the United States and other nations. Groups encourage participants to set personal goals, and participants also can join and form teams for women of all ages and

abilities. Groups and teams vary depending on location, but they cover just about every type of activity you can imagine — 5k, 10K, half-marathon, marathon and ultra-marathon running and walking groups; sprint, Olympic and half-Ironman triathlon teams; and metric, half- and full-century cycling teams. Other groups focus on hiking, trail running, cross-country skiing, dance, mountain biking, Pilates, yoga, surfing and cross training. A trainer, instructor or coach leads some teams; others function more like a moms' club, with members sharing leadership and operational roles.

Santa Barbara Triathlon Club

c/o Hazard's Cycle Sport, 110 Anacapa St., Santa Barbara
805.966.3787, sbtriclub.com
If you like to swim, bike and run, this group is for you. It doesn't matter whether you've ever completed a sprint triathlon or have crossed the Hawaii Ironman finish line – you'll be able to train and have fun with other athletes at your level. The club meets the second Thursday of each month from February through November. It also organizes year-round group rides and seasonal coached track workouts.

classes, programs and sports leagues for all ages and all seasons for affordable (by Santa Barbara standards) fees. There's dance, Pilates, yoga, soccer, swimming, skateboarding, ceramics, you name it. Anyone can enroll as long as you meet the respective age/skill level requirements, and if you live within the city limits, you get discounts. Just contact Parks & Rec to apply for your card. The cities of Carpinteria and Solvang also offer programs, especially in the summer months.

Goleta Valley Athletic Club

170 S. Los Carneros Rd., Goleta
805.968.1023, gvac.net
Many companies in the Goleta high-tech and business hub near the university offer GVAC memberships to their employees. Hence, this spacious facility is often filled with professionals on their lunch breaks or before or after work. It features personal training, massage, cardio equipment, a café and wellness center, massage and indoor cycling. Outdoors, there's a climbing wall, narrow lap pool and whirlpool.

The pool and second-floor weight-training area at Santa Barbara Athletic Club.

Santa Barbara Athletic Club
520 Castillo St., Santa Barbara
805.966.6147, wcaclubs.com
Well-heeled professionals and serious exercise
buffs head for this luxe downtown club, with all
the state-of-the-art equipment you'd expect,
along with more than 80 Pilates, Spinning, NIA
and yoga classes. Outdoors you'll find a four-
lane, 25-yard lap pool, with an adjacent weight
room and Spinning studio. The club is famous
for its squash facilities and programs (a rarity
in these parts), and regularly hosts local and
national championships. Membership includes
childcare, but children aren't allowed to use the
facility, except the pool on weekends.

Santa Barbara Yoga Center
32 E. Micheltorena St., Santa Barbara
805.965.6045, santabarbarayogacenter.com
Since 1992, this gorgeous downtown place has
offered excellent-quality instruction representing many different styles. Light pours into the
studios, which occupy a historic building with
twenty-foot ceilings. You can choose from more
than 100 classes every week, and attend workshops, special events and retreats.

Spectrum Athletic Clubs
spectrumclubs.com
Goleta: 6144 Calle Real,
805.964.0556
Uptown: 3908 State St., 805.563.8700
Downtown: 21 W. Carrillo St., 805.965.0999
The three local Spectrum clubs are good all-
around gyms – and the fees are very reasonable for what you get. They have plenty of
exercise machines, so there's hardly ever a
wait. They also have lots of classes, from yoga,
kickboxing and dance to conditioning, spinning
and aerobics. The facilities include women's-
only areas, and the Goleta and uptown locations have excellent kids' clubs. The downtown
location is not as spacious as its siblings, but
it's a great place for people who like to exercise
before or after work, or at lunchtime.

Yoga Soup
28 Parker Way, Santa Barbara
805.965.8811, yogasoup.com
It's only been around for a couple of years, but
Yoga Soup already has established itself as a
local favorite. It adds a unique ingredient to the
traditional yoga recipe: a vibrant, lighthearted
yet serious space for introspection. The charis-
matic center is growing and transforming by the
minute, adding classes like "Integrating Pilates"
to the simmering pot to meet its fans' requests.
The menu includes many types of yoga classes,
plus workshops and special events.

Playing Around

Outside of the gyms and yoga studios, here's how Santa Barbarans stay in shape. For more information on hiking, cycling and horseback riding, see Outdoorsy.

Beach Volleyball

Santa Barbara can't technically claim to be the world's beach volleyball capital — but it sure seems that way. Legendary v'baller Charles F. "Karch" Kiraly grew up here playing on East Beach. Dr. Laszlo Kiraly, Karch's dad and a skilled player himself, taught his son how to play at age 6. Karch went on to win three Olympic gold medals and 148 pro beach-volleyball titles. Other pros who started here as young scruffs (and still live here) include 2004 Olympian Dax Holdren and his former San Marcos High partner Todd Rogers. At press time, local duo and reigning world champions Todd Rogers and Phil Dalhausser were atop the 2008 AVP tour rankings and had just earned a spot on the U.S. Olympic Team heading to Beijing.

It's not something in the salt air that explains why so many great volleyball players come from here; it's because Santa Barbara provides outstanding support for the sport. East Beach, with fourteen courts, is the main venue for practice and watching. These are usually first-come, first-served, though some are reserved for parks and recreation programs. You'll also find courts at Toro Canyon Park in Carpinteria, Lookout Park in Summerland, Santa Barbara's West Beach, Leadbetter Beach and, in Goleta, at Goleta Beach, Stow Grove Park and Tucker's Grove. Contact the Parks and Recreation Department (805.564.5418, sbparksandrecreation.com) for information on programs, leagues and venues. Other good resources for youth

Volleyball players in action at East Beach.

programs are the Santa Barbara Boys Volleyball Club (sbbvc.com) and the Santa Barbara Volleyball Club for girls (sbvballclub.com).

Even if you don't play, set up a chair and watch the best. The AVP tour usually stops here during the season. In 2008 the Crocs AVP Santa Barbara Open took place in early September.

Bowling

Zodo's Bowling & Beyond (5925 Calle Real, Goleta, 805.967.0128, zodobowl.com) is pretty much the only bowling show in town. It's a lively one, though, with 24 lanes, bumper bowling and a light show; on Thursday, Friday and Saturday nights, they add fog and haze to colorful lights while a DJ spins songs. Bring your laptop and you can surf (or work, ha ha) at Z's Taphouse and Grill or in the arcade while you're hanging around the lanes.

Golf

Residents with plenty of cash and connections can play at such exclusive enclaves as La Cumbre Country Club and Birnam Wood, but there are plenty of places for the rest of us. The public, 50-year-old **Santa Barbara Golf Club** has affordable greens fees ($37 to $47), with discounts for city and county residents. It's right in town, off Las Positas Road, and even though it's in a prime real estate zone, it's the

Paradise with a putt: Sandpiper Golf Course.

Glen Annie Golf Club
405 Glen Annie Rd., Goleta
805.968.6400,
glenanniegolf.com
18 holes, par 71

Hidden Oaks Golf Course
4760 Calle Camarada, Santa
Barbara
805.967.3493,
hiddenoaksgolfsb.net
9 holes, par 27

**Rancho San Marcos Golf
Course**
4600 Hwy. 154, Santa Barbara
805.683.6334, 877.776.1804,
rsm1804.com
18 holes, par 72

River Course at the Alisal
150 Alisal Rd., Solvang
805.688.6042, rivercourse.com
18 holes, par 72

Sandpiper Golf Course
7925 Hollister Ave., Goleta
805.968.1541,
sandpipergolf.com
18 holes, par 72

Santa Barbara Golf Club
3500 McCaw Ave., Santa
Barbara
805.687.7087, sbgolf.com
18 holes, par 70

longest short course (6,037 yards from the back tees) you probably will ever play. Serene **Hidden Oaks Golf Course**, near the More Mesa bluffs and beach just east of Goleta, is a secret spot where you can fit in a quick nine holes without breaking the pocketbook – greens fees are just $13 to $15. Environmentally sensitive **Glen Annie Golf Club**'s eighteen holes straddle the foothills above Goleta, making for challenging play with to-die-for views.

Sandpiper Golf Course is our Pebble Beach – six of its eighteen holes edge the cliffs above the ocean on the outskirts of Goleta. It's pricey but still affordable, when you consider the awesome location. Part of the Alisal Guest Ranch in Solvang, the **River Course** flanks the Santa Ynez River and Mountains – a stunning setting. Wild turkeys, deer and mountain peaks surround posh, oak-studded **Rancho San Marcos**

Golf Course, set on a former 1860s ranch near Cachuma Lake. The natural environment and classy services make it worth the drive.

Running
Runners rule in Santa Barbara. They're everywhere, jogging or racing on the bike paths, trails, bluffs and beaches. **Santa Barbara Running Company** (805.899.8802, sbrunningco. com), a community hub and store for runners, maintains a web site detailing loads of road and trail routes, including distances. **RunSantaBarbara.com** is a resource for running and walking events in the area and hosts a number of favorite races, including the Thanksgiving 4-Miler and the grueling, thirteen-mile Pier to Peak race, which climbs nearly 4,000 feet from Stearns Wharf to La Cumbre Peak.

Skateboarding
Skater's Point, next to the beach on Cabrillo Boulevard, is a free, 14,600-square-foot paradise for skateboarders, with bowls, ledges, ramps, rails and a palm-lined beachfront setting. Helmets, elbow and kneepads are required. It's open daily from 8 a.m. to sunset. Saturday mornings are reserved for the 12 and under set, so they have a chance to skate without fearing for their lives when the big folks whoosh in. In the summer months, the popular Parks and Rec youth skateboard clinic takes over until 11:30 a.m. on weekdays. For information, call 805.564.5418 or visit sbparksandrecreation.com. In the North County, skaters rock at **Solvang Skatepark** in Hans Christian Andersen Park in Solvang, 805.688.7529, cityofsolvang.com/skatepark.html. It's a fun ride, with areas for advanced and beginner skaters.

Swimming
We consider ourselves lucky to have a free, if a bit chilly, natural swimming pool right in our front yard. Kids grow up playing in the ocean, and lots of them learn how to swim there safely through Junior Lifeguard and other programs. To swim with other mer-people, contact **Ocean Ducks** (805.637.8331, oceanducks.com), which Emilio Casanueva originally founded in South America but is now based in Santa Barbara. It organizes weekly ocean swims, clinics, competitions and events. He also founded the Santa Barbara Channel Swimming Association, which sponsors the annual Santa Barbara Channel Relay Swim (santabarbarachannelswim.org) to benefit the Channel Islands Marine Sanctuary Foundation and Heal the Ocean.

If you prefer warmer, calmer water, you have plenty of options. Built in 1914 and recently renovated, **Los Baños Del Mar** (805.966.6110, sbparksandrecreation.org) at the harbor offers lap swimming and aquatic programs. The outdoor 50-meter pool is also home to Santa Barbara Swim Club (sbswim.org), with teams from novice to national and master's levels. The **Carpinteria Valley Community Swimming Pool** (5305 Carpinteria Avenue, 805.566.2417) has lap swimming, aqua aerobics and lessons. In the summer, when most students are gone, the fab **UCSB Recreation Center** pool is open to the public. Pay a day-use fee or get a summer family membership (essr.ucsb.edu).

Los Baños Del Mar.

Mark Warkentin
Open-water Race Olympian
Local swimming phenom Mark Warkentin competed in the pool with Santa Barbara Swim Club, then switched to distance swimming in the ocean. He's now one of the top open-water swimmers in the country, finishing in the top ten at the 2008 World Open Water Championship in the 10K and becoming the first American to qualify for the Olympics in open-water swimming. He also won a silver medal in the 25K event at the same event. At press time, the entire community was wishing him luck in Beijing.

Tennis
While many avid players join private clubs, it's easy to find a public court. The Parks and Rec Department (805.564.5573, sbparksandrecreation.com) operates public courts at three sites (see below). Day permits are $5; you usually can buy them at the courts or at the Parks and Rec offices at 620 Laguna Street during business hours (closed every other Friday). You also can buy annual permits. Lighted courts stay lit until 9 p.m. on weeknights.

Las Positas Tennis Courts: 6 lighted courts at 1002 Las Positas Road, near Elings Park.

Municipal Tennis Center: 12 courts (3 lighted, 9 unlighted) at 1414 Park Place at Old Coast Highway, at the edge of Montecito.

Pershing Park Tennis Courts: 8 lighted courts at 100 Castillo Street, across from the harbor. Open after 5 p.m. on weekdays and all day on weekends and City College holidays.

Spectator Sports

We're lucky to have a UC campus, because we get to watch fantastic collegiate sports in our own backyard. UCSB Gauchos fans are a rowdy bunch, known to fling tortillas on the courts and fields while cheering. When the Gaucho men's soccer team won the NCAA championships in 2006, wildly exuberant spectators stole a goal cage and tried to haul it to the beach. Fans also crowd the Thunderdome for top-level men's and women's basketball games. Kids can become Little Gauchos and get lots of perks for supporting their local teams. For details, visit ucsbgauchos.cstv.com.

The Santa Barbara Breakers basketball team debuted in 2007 (805.685.5600, breakers-basketball.com). It's part of the newish men's International Basketball League (iblhoopsonline.com) with teams from the U.S.A., Canada, People's Republic of China and Japan. Special rules in this league make for fast-paced, high-scoring games. The season runs from March into July, and home games are played at Santa Barbara City College.

Baseball fans adore the **Santa Barbara Foresters**, a collegiate summer-league team (805.684.0657, sbforesters.org). The Foresters were the national champs in 2006 and runners-up in 2003 and 2005. More than 170 former Foresters have signed professional contracts, with more than twenty becoming major leaguers. The team has no owners save its supporters; it's a nonprofit with amateur players and a volunteer staff. And everyone has a good time – kids can compete in hula hoop, bat spin and pie-eating contests. Home games are held at Caesar Uyesaka Stadium at UCSB.

The **Santa Barbara Polo and Racquet Club** (805.684.6683, sbpolo.com) has been around since 1911 – it's one of the oldest polo facilities in the nation. From May through October, its three world-class fields host matches, tournaments and high-level championships, which are open to the public. We know many locals who pack a picnic and watch the ponies play on sunny Sunday afternoons during the season. If the polo bug nips, you can sign up for lessons at the club. The club also houses a tennis center, swim club, fitness facilities, social clubhouse and horse-boarding facilities, but you have to snag a membership (and pay!) to enjoy the privileges.

Athletes hit the water for the Santa Barbara Triathlon.

Triathlons

We're not sure if there are as many triathletes as palm trees here, but it often seems that way. Many folks train through clubs (see Club-Team Athletics above); others do it on their own. The biggest event, drawing elite international athletes, is the **Santa Barbara Triathlon** (santabarbaratriathlon.com), held on the third weekend in August and including a long course and women's, coed and parent-child sprints. Late June brings the **Breath of Life Ventura Triathlon** (triforlife.com), with Olympic, sprint, youth and junior courses, as well as a beer garden and food fair to help you recover. And in late September, look for the **Carpinteria Triathlon** (carpinteriatriathlon.com), with Olympic and sprint courses on downright beautiful routes.

Water Polo

This sport's popularity is growing by the month here, largely due to the media coverage of our rising young stars and world-class coaches. In 2008, the girls' teams from Dos Pueblos and Santa Barbara high schools blew away their competition. The CIF championships were supposed to be held in Irvine, but since both teams vying for the title hailed from Santa Barbara, they were allowed to move the final match to home turf. Local youth teams are often considered among the top ten in the nation. The 2008 men's U.S. Olympic Team coach, Terry Schroeder, grew up in Santa Barbara, and UCSB's men's and women's coach, Wolf Wigo, is a three-time Olympian. For information on playing or watching water polo, visit the Santa Barbara Water Polo Club web site, sbwaterpolo.com. Programs are available for all ages, from teeny novices to masters.

The Sports Shopper

Carpinteria Sports
1060 Casitas Pass Rd., Carpinteria
805.566.1800, carpsports.com
Head here for one-stop shopping in downtown Carpinteria: boogie boards, bikes, junior life-guard swimsuits, tennis rackets, skim boards, gym equipment, golf clubs and more.

Goleta Sports
Calle Real Center, 5738 Calle Real, Goleta
805.964.8703, goletasports.com
This locally owned shop packs friendly service (it will special order for you) and character into a tiny space in a strip mall. It specializes in team-sports stuff: uniforms, balls and cleats, as well as swimming and water polo gear.

Hazard's Cyclesport
110 Anacapa St., Santa Barbara
805.966.3787, hazardscyclesport.com
One of the oldest bike shops in the state, Hazard's can set you up on a cool cruiser or fit you on a triathlon race bike. It also builds custom bikes and wheels and does repairs.

Mountain Air Sports
14 State St., Santa Barbara
805.962.0049, mountainairsports.com
This well-stocked store sells everything for hikers, backpackers, skiers and snowboarders, as well as clothes for people who like to look sporty. In the winter, it rents ski and boarding equipment; we advise reserving your gear early.

Santa Barbara Outfitters
1200 State St., Santa Barbara
805.564.1007, sboutfitters.com
This small, locally owned store specializes in equipment and clothing for outdoor adventurers. Looking for a hand-sewn sleeping bag for snow camping near Mt. Whitney? No problem. Items can be pricey, but the quality and service are usually exceptional. Kids and beginning climbers clamber up and down the indoor climbing wall, which is open every day for a fee.

Santa Barbara Running Company
110 Anacapa St., Santa Barbara
805.899.8802
129 N. Fairview Ave., Goleta
805.964.6700, sbrunningco.com
This highly specialized store focuses on all things related to road and trail running, racing and walking. The folks here also will analyze your treadmill stride and gait, organize weekly training programs and update you on local-running-community news.

Sports Authority
Camino Real Marketplace, 7035 Marketplace Dr., Goleta
805.968.8551, sportsauthority.com
Part of a nationwide chain, this giant store houses equipment, gear, clothing and accessories for many sports and outdoor activities, from golf and skiing to camping and snorkeling.

Velo Pro Cyclery
633 State St., Santa Barbara
805.963.7775
5887 Hollister Ave., Goleta
805.964.8355, velopro.com
Serious mountain, BMX and road bikers come here for the staff's expertise in choosing equipment, repair and trail knowledge. It also carries comfort and cruiser bikes.

Semana Nautica Sports Festival
805.897.2680, semananautica.com
This is (we're pretty sure) the largest festival of its kind in the nation. Its roots date to 1933, when five U.S. Navy battleships were moored outside the harbor. The locals invited the crews to come on over and engage in Fleet Week, a series of contests on the beach. They had so much fun that the city council made it an annual event series surrounding the 4th of July, renaming it Semana Nautica to honor Santa Barbara's Spanish roots. Seventy years later, thousands of participants from California and beyond come to take part in ocean swimming, age group and masters' swimming, fishing, volleyball, a beach biathlon, a 15K road race, cycling, sailing, lawn bowling, spearfishing, adaptive paddling, tennis, water polo, inline hockey, basketball, gymnastics, softball, semipro baseball, tug-of-war and a hilarious cardboard kayak race. Spectators attend free of charge.

Hit the Surf

When the surf's up – which is often – hundreds, sometimes thousands, of Santa Barbarans head for the coast. Winter months typically bring the best waves, but serious swells do arrive at other times of year. Here we provide cut-to-the-punch info for surfers trying to decide where to go. Refer to the Beachy chapter for details on the beaches themselves, including how to find them. By the way, bring your wetsuit or spring suit – the water's usually cold (frigid in winter) except during the late summer months. The breaks below are listed from south to north.

Santa Barbara native Chris Keet, who runs the annual Rincon Classic surf contest, rips it up at his home break.

Rincon Point

Affectionately called "The Queen of the Coast," this world-class right point break with a famous cobblestone bottom has no rivals on the South Coast. Legendary local surfers, including Kim Mearig, Tom Curren and Bobby Martinez, cut their teeth here. Rincon breaks on west and northwest swells, which bring waves from two to twenty feet. Medium to low tide is the best time for a session. The place draws surf stars like a neodymium magnet and is therefore insanely, aggressively crowded – but even the best of the pros will tell you it's worth it. Catch one good Rincon wave and you're hooked for life. This is not a place for beginners – and if you surf here, make sure you know all the "rules" about the wave-catching pecking order. To get there, exit Highway 101 at Bates Road, southeast of Carpinteria at the Ventura County line. It's easiest to park in the State Park lot on the lower left and walk out to the point; you can also park in the Rincon Beach county park lot up the hill on the right.

Hammond's

This longtime locals' hangout has a long, right-hand reef break that can generate a rippable wall. The waves are inconsistent, but the small-ish surf, scenic backdrop and peaceful vibe make it a fun place to practice.

Sandspit

The end of the long breakwater at the Santa Barbara Harbor does more than just protect the local yacht fleet. During certain rare conditions, it also creates a serious dredging right-hand barrel. This doesn't happen often, but when

Sandspit is on, it defies description. Pros – including Kelly Slater, Tom Curren and Bobby Martinez – go out of their way to surf the near-perfect tubes here when it's good. Prepare for a humbling experience during those times. The intense, ruthless crowd and steep waves are both likely to bounce you (it's happened to the best of them). At least the bottom's sandy.

Leadbetter
"Leds" is the bunny slope of Santa Barbara surfing, a good option for beginners and families who want to hang out. It has a shifty and soft C-grade right break. The waves peel off the point at the west end of Leadbetter Beach, just below Shoreline Park. Longboarders can usually count on a fun ride.

Arroyo Burro
Old-timers know this as "the Pit," and locals also call it Hendry's Beach. It favors a west wind swell but can manage a ground swell with a bit of tide. It has lefts and rights on an uneven rock-and-sand bottom. The surf is often quirky and shifty but has its moments.

Campus Point – UCSB
Locals and students love to chill at this classic Santa Barbara right point break fronting the UCSB campus. Shortboarders and boogie boarders rule the top of the point. Midpoint and down into the cove (aka Poles) is longboard heaven – the top is generally bigger but gets warbled by the surge ricocheting off the tide rock. Half-mile and longer rides are not uncommon. The waves here aren't tubey, but they're super playful. This break loves a low west swell and a minus tide. The path to the beach starts near the Marine Sciences building. You have to pay for parking at the meters or kiosks in the nearby lots; we recommend getting a $12 weekend/evening 30-day permit if you can.

Sands
When every other place is flat, Sands will have something to ride; in fact it's generally the biggest place around. Situated at the western edge of Isla Vista, near UCSB, Sands picks up just about any swell except a south swell. The break ranges and shifts, going from round to mushy in the same wave. No two waves in

Surf Lessons
Surf Happens! Surf School (805.966.3613, surf-happens.com) and A-Frame Surf Shop (3785 Santa Claus Lane, Carpinteria, 805.684.8803, aframesurf.com) both provide quality instruction for all ages and abilities. The Adventure Company of Santa Barbara (805.898.0671, sbadventureco.com) specializes in introductory surfing lessons, focusing on the fundamentals, for ages 7 and older. See Beachy chapter for additional instructors.

the same set break alike or in the same spot. Sands does best on a west or a northwest swell with a bit of wind swell mixed in, and it likes a fuller tide. The scenic walk from the bluffs down to the beach is one of the prettiest rambles on the South Coast.

El Capitan State Beach
When it comes to surf, El Capitan (aka El Cap) is a rare bird. But when it's on, it's one of the best waves on the South Coast, with speedy, insane barrels. El Cap will break on a northwest swell, but it really likes a straight west and an ultra-low tide. Watch out for the rocky, barnacle- and mussel-clad bottom. El Cap has a beautiful right point break and a nice meadow with giant sycamore trees. In the winter the creek flows straight out into the lineup.

Refugio State Beach
Down the road from El Cap, Refugio is another classic Santa Barbara right point. It breaks on a northwest swell but loves a straight west. It even picks up a south swell occasionally. Again, watch out for the rocky bottom. Refugio is a killer longboard wave and great for beginners.

Jalama Beach County Park
In between points Conception and Arguello an hour's drive north of Santa Barbara, Jalama feels like the edge of the Earth. It has both beach and reef breaks, and decent surf rolls in here most of the year. However, northwest winds prevail and can wreak havoc on the surf. Bring your wetsuit — these waters are always chilly.

Q & A: Jamie Allison

Jamie Allison has always been on the move, as a triathlete, entrepreneur, wife and mom. A competitive runner since age 7, she fell in love with the triathlon as a high school senior. A few years later she started the UCSB Triathlon Team and an intercollegiate triathlon circuit that became the national model. Jamie's not just an athlete, though – she earned both teaching credentials and a master's degree in education from UCSB, and she's taught at all levels. In 1999 she founded Moms in Motion (see Club-Team Athletics earlier in this chapter) to help women set and achieve fitness goals in a supportive, all-female environment. It's now an international continually growing network. Cheryl Crabtree (huffing and puffing) caught up to Jamie during a rare break in her full-speed schedule.

Why did you start Moms in Motion?
Athletics has always been part of my life. I was the last of my friends to get married and the last to have babies. The fact that women struggle to find time for themselves was an obstacle I was determined to overcome. I was looking for time where I could focus on just me – time to set new fitness goals, meet other women who shared the same interests, and do something positive for the community. Women have embraced our unique niche, because they feel comfortable and supported, no matter what their age or ability level. It has certainly been an amazingly rewarding journey!

Are all the groups for women only?
Yes, but we do have a handful of male coaches, which works really well, too. They don't have any problem wearing pink.

Why is philanthropy an important part of each group?
Because it is not just about ourselves – it is about the greater good. And we all are at the stage of life where it is our turn to contribute. Yes, we are crazy busy, but that's the beauty of Moms in Motion: You can get your social, fitness and philanthropic needs met all in one place.

What's your favorite sport?
I love to run. Swimming is second. Running is like meditation for me. Both running and swimming eliminate stress, so whenever I am grouchy, my sweet husband lovingly pushes me out the door, knowing that I haven't had my exercise fix.

After you've had a really good workout, where do you go refuel and celebrate?
Because I typically work out in the morning, my favorite places to treat myself are Blenders in the Grass if it is super hot, Peet's Coffee if it is super cold, and, if I am really hungry, breakfast at Jeannine's Bakery. As a family, we love eating at the Natural Café, an easy place to accommodate hungry kids, and it serves organic foods to boot.

Do you have a favorite place to run?
This is a tough one. Put me on any Los Padres National Forest trail – Jesusita, Romero, Rattlesnake or Hot Springs – and I am in heaven. I feel like a kid again, hopping rocks and getting dirty. But I'm also rejuvenated on our bluffs, my favorite being Ellwood. We really are quite fortunate to live and run in Santa Barbara.

Materialistic

You don't need a compass to explore Santa Barbara's charming retail districts. You don't even need a car. In fact, there's only one thing you do need: your wallet. From outdoor crafts fairs and antiques alleys to chic boutiques that cater to its famous clientele, the area's dinging cash registers are said to nearly drown out the mission bells. Pick up a Dolce & Gabbana gown, Mexican candelabra or hibiscus tattoo right here in town – the home of Lucky Brand Jeans, Big Dogs sportswear and hip Simple Shoes.

Please note that there are more shops to be found in this book – bookstores in Literary, kids' stuff in Childlike, surf shops in Beachy, nurseries in Horticultural, food and wine shops in Hungry & Thirsty and Tasting Wine, and athletic gear in Athletic.

Where the Locals Shop

Santa Barbarans believe strongly that when you *can* be outside, you *should* be outside. Therefore, all our shopping districts are outdoors, intended to be strolled in the sunshine – or meandered under a marine layer. If you consider shopping to be the perfect rainy-day activity ... well, you're sort of out of luck here.

State Street, the main drag through downtown Santa Barbara, is the No. 1 choice for both browsing and buying. From the 400 block, where State crosses under the freeway, up through the 1300 block, the pedestrian-friendly street is positively packed with retail pleasures: high-brow chains like Juicy Couture and Betsey Johnson, local shops like Yellowstone Clothing and Mi Casa Imports – and plenty of java dens and juice bars to keep you fueled in between.

In the 1100 block of State Street lies **La Arcada**, arguably Santa Barbara's most beautiful shopping plaza. The Spanish-style courtyard is home to quirky fountains, lifelike statues, art galleries, a sumptuous consignment boutique, a modern furniture store, an old-fashioned barber shop and a couple of top-notch cafés. Don't miss Lewis & Clark, a beloved boutique full of nostalgic knickknacks and whimsical gifts. A sixteen-foot-tall clock with Westminster chimes marks the State Street entrance to this tiled paseo.

No city should be without its own hip, four-letter neighborhood. Manhattan has SoHo, Denver has LoDo, and Santa Barbara has **SoCo**, a five-block area south of Cota Street where art galleries and artsy shops invite in shoppers-with-an-edge. Take time to shuffle along the area's grid of sidewalks, but if you're short on hours, head straight to East Haley Street between Laguna and North Quarantina streets for seriously stylish clothing at Taka-Puna, ethnic textiles and pottery at Kilu World and high-quality used furniture at the Opportunity Shop. No groovy neighborhood would be complete without a boho coffeehouse percolated into the mix; Muddy Waters is SoCo's.

It's hard to sniff snobbily at international retail chains when they're tucked into an architectural beauty like **Paseo Nuevo**. Two city blocks in the heart of the State Street retail district, the inviting mall leads shoppers along winding, tiled pathways past fountains and balconies. Built in 1990, it features a movie theater, art gallery, live theater and copious underground parking. Anchored by Macy's and Nordstrom, it is also home to such specialty shops as Aveda, Sephora and L'Occitane, as well as local children's boutique This Little Piggy Wears Cotton. Plus there's a Ben & Jerry's. We're just saying.

Even the shopping-phobic can't resist a stroll along State Street.

La Cumbre Plaza is an uptown mall anchored by Macy's and Sears off upper State Street between Hope Avenue and La Cumbre Road. A recent revamp welcomed such upscale retailers as Tiffany, Coach and Yves DeLorme. Fountains, seating areas and a lack of crowds make this a great spot for taking a latte-fueled rest between purchases.

An 1872 wooden pier at the foot of State Street, **Stearns Wharf** draws mostly tourists to its myriad souvenir shops, fish-and-chips dives and fortune-teller. But locals know it's a great place to score a killer beach hat, talking toy parrot or pound of sticky-good fudge. Nearby, the **Santa Barbara Arts & Crafts Show** is a beachside phenomenon that's been taking place weekly along Cabrillo Boulevard since 1965. More than 100 vendors peddle their oil seascapes, stone sculptures, fused-glass jewelry, leather handbags, crocheted booties and hand-thrown pottery from 10 a.m. to dusk on Sundays (and on Saturdays of three-day holiday weekends).

Coast Village Road is a tree-lined lane that runs from Olive Mill Road to Hot Springs Road in Montecito. In addition to countless Mercedes SUVs parked along the curb, you'll see some of the best upscale shopping the county has to offer: haute couture boutiques, eclectic home-furnishing shops, high-end jewelry stores and exclusive day spas. Mixed in is the occasional pizza joint or old-school eatery. The farmer's market on Friday mornings is not to be missed.

Tucked back into the locals-only foothills of Montecito is a crossroads that residents call the **Upper Village**. Bustling despite its off-the-beaten-path location, the village occupies the corners of San Ysidro and East Valley roads. You might spot a celebrity here, where the denizens of this exclusive zip code shop for hardware, stop for coffee and pop into the library (wait until you see this adorable library) for a good read.

Old Santa Barbara style meets modern upscale-chain shopping at Paseo Nuevo.

The single-square-mile town of **Summerland** rests quietly between Montecito and Carpinteria, a vertical village where brightly colored bungalows dot the hillside, looking out over the 101 to the glistening Pacific beyond. Long has the area been known as an antiques haven, but main drag Lillie Avenue has of late become a draw for all kinds of shoppers. Its eclectic offerings include the amazing flower shop Botanik, the bird hub McLeod Parrot Menagerie and the relaxing Sacred Space for its world treasures.

Once a sleepy beach town, **Carpinteria** is developing into quite the hot spot. Armed with a wallet and some curiosity, one can easily spend a day marveling at the shops along Linden Avenue (off Highway 101). Here you'll find world-famous Robitaille's candy shop, Magpie antiques, Rincon Designs surf shop, Dandelion Blues garden shop and the outlet store for This Little Piggy: the Snoutlet. Buster's is a CD store that sells hot dogs. What's not to love?

Between its looming windmills and countless pastry shops, the Danish town of **Solvang** boasts great book dens, toy stores, needlework shops and leather vendors. A Disneyland-like village off Highway 246 (take Buellton exit off Highway 101), Solvang is sprinkled with cute retailers like the Jule Hus (pronounced *yule hoose*), where you'll find Christmas decorations year-round. The Solvang Vintage Motorcycle Museum alone is worth the day trip.

Made in Santa Barbara

Big Dogs
136 State St., Santa
Barbara
805.963.8728,
BigDogs.com
The famous sports-
wear line is head-
quartered in Santa
Barbara, where it
opened its first retail
store in 1984. Best
known for baggy
shorts and graphic
T-shirts bearing slo-
gans like "Bite me!"

Big Dogs HQ.

and "If you can't run with the big dogs, stay on
the porch," the company was conceptualized
during a river-rafting trip among friends and
has grown into a Saint Bernard-size chain with
more than 100 stores across the country. Big
Dogs hosts the annual Big Dog Parade down
State Street, attracting more than 1,200 dogs
and their owners to raise money for charities
that help dogs and kids.

Deckers Shoes
805.967.7611, deckers.com
The company that makes UGG Boots, Teva
sandals and groovy-cool Simple shoes began
in 1973 when UCSB student Doug Otto began
making sandals under the name Deckers. Over
the years, the company acquired water-friendly
Tevas, cozy Australian UGGs and green-minded
old-skool sneaker makers Simple – a brand that
includes an illustrated map of Santa Barbara in
its shoeboxes. The Deckers Corporation operates out of Goleta; its shoes are sold locally at
Nordstrom, Urban Outfitters and Santa Barbara
Outfitters (1200 State Street).

Horny Toad
888.865.8623, HornyToad.com
Santa Barbara–based Horny Toad makes
casual, outdoorsy clothes and apparently has
a good time doing it – the company is listed
in *Outside* magazine's best places to work.
The "Toadies" support myriad local causes,
especially environmental ones. You can try on
some Toadwear and feel the Toad love at Santa
Barbara Outfitters, 1200 State Street; Paddle
Sports, 117B Harbor Way; or The Tin Roof,
2982 Grand Avenue, Los Olivos.

Lucky Brand Jeans
805 State St., Santa Barbara
805.962.5539, LuckyBrandJeans.com

Lucky Kid
740 State St., Santa Barbara
805.966.0272
Barely adults at the time, Gene Montesano
and Barry Perlman opened their first clothes
shop in Florida in 1972, selling jeans that
they'd washed in bleach at a local laundromat.
Montesano eventually launched the Bongo
jeans line, popular in the 1980s. In 1990 the
duo regrouped to create Lucky Brand Jeans, a
vintage-style denim and T-shirt line known for
its killer fit and irreverent style – a label sewn
into every zipper says "Lucky You." The brand's
got major Hollywood caché; celebs from Brad
Pitt to Ellen DeGeneres swear by the stuff.
It's sold in more than 150 stores nationwide,
including two in Santa Barbara, where Montesano now lives.

Magellan's
110 W. Sola St., Santa Barbara
805.568.5402, magellans.com
Widely regarded as the nation's best travel-
supply catalog, the Santa Barbara–based
Magellan's has a retail store here in town (and
another in Santa Monica). Founded by former
Pan-Am exec and world traveler John Mc-
Manus, the store stocks everything a jet-setter
could need, from luggage tags and jet-lag pills
to money belts and electronic sixteen-language
translators.

The Territory Ahead
515 State St., Santa Barbara
Outlet: 400 State St., Santa Barbara
805.962.5558, TerritoryAhead.com
"I reckon I got to light out for the territory ahead
of the rest," says Huck Finn in the last para-
graph of Mark Twain's classic adventure tale.
Since 1988, this Santa Barbara–based clothier
has been manufacturing men's and women's
clothing with a laid-back style – the kind of
easygoing duds in fine fabrics you'd expect
to see on well-heeled vacationers (think Eddie
Bauer with more personality). The company's
got nine retail stores and four outlets from Palo
Alto to Massachusetts, but it maintains its flagship store in the heart of State Street, with an
outlet located the next block over.

The Goods

Antiques

Brinkerhoff Avenue
Several antiques shops operate out of Victorian homes on a short but absurdly cute residential block just west of State Street between Cota and Haley streets. The grandfather of the neighborhood is Robert Livernois Art & Antiques, having been at 533 Brinkerhoff Avenue for 40 years. It's open by appointment only and specializes in California landscape paintings.

State Street
In between State Street's sparkling new chain retailers, you'll find deep-rooted antiques shops where collectibles can be hunted and snatched up for a bargain. There are traditional antiques malls like Antiques Etc. (521 State Street) and Antique Alley (706 State Street), with cases lined with jewelry, boxes full of crate labels, racks hung with hats and shelves packed with well-preserved teacups. More treasures abound a block off the thoroughfare at the Antique Marketplace (26 East Ortega Street).

More exotic are the Far East antiques at Mingei Oriental Antiques (736 State Street) and Antica Furnishings (1117 State Street).

Summerland
This tiny hillside town is truly a haven for antiques shoppers, with more than a dozen shops peddling pieces of the past. And they're all within walking distance. Forty dealers display their mirrors, statues, linens and architectural elements at Summerland Antique Collective (2173 and 2192 Ortega Hill Road). Mary Suding Antiques (2240 Lillie Avenue) sells American and European furniture, fine art, quilts and pottery. You'll find Persian rugs, crystal lamps and 18th-century sculpture at Lifestyle Antiques (2264 Lillie Avenue).

Summerland Antique Collective.

Arts & Crafts

Art Essentials
32 E. Victoria St., Santa Barbara
805.965.5456, SBArtEssentials.com
For two decades, Art Essentials has been providing fine and graphic artists with a broad spectrum of paints, brushes, easels and everything they need to channel their inner Chagall.

Art from Scrap
302 E. Cota St., Santa Barbara
805.884.0459, artfromscrap.org
At this clever reuse store, you'll find bins overflowing with colorful, squiggly skateboard-wheel shavings, beads and burlap, picture frames and paper, fabric and film canisters – all treasures donated by local businesses and individuals to keep these items out of the landfills. It's a great low-cost option for art projects, holiday decorations, costumes and Solstice Parade floats.

Beads Santa Barbara
137 E. De La Guerra St., Santa Barbara
805.966.1138, BeadsSantaBarbara.com
Two blocks off State Street downtown sits this little treasure shop full of carved bone pendants, shells, glass, Swarovski crystal and freshwater pearls from all around the globe. Make your own, or pick out a piece of finished beaded jewelry.

Craft Essentials
187 S. Turnpike Rd., Goleta
805.681.3115
The crafty sister of downtown's Art Essentials, this expansive space has a huge selection of yarns, frames, children's crafts, toys and games, sewing supplies, party favors, scrapbooking materials and holiday decorations. A must-go when your child has a diorama due. It's also one of the few remaining stores in the area that sells fabric.

Loop & Leaf
536 Brinkerhoff Ave., Santa Barbara
805.845.4696, LoopAndLeaf.com
This delightful escape might as well be called Knit 'n' Sip for its colorful array of yarns, fibers and – that's right – loose-leaf tea. Pick up

cashmeres or glittery alpaca yarns and black, green or herbal teas, then sign up for felting, crocheting and lacework classes.

California style at Blue Bee.

Clothing & Accessories

becca:christian
432 State St., Santa Barbara
805.884.4700, beccachristian.com
Newcomer becca:christian carries its own line of hip 'n' sexy men's and women's clothes, plus pieces by other designers, including Gwen Stefani's L.A.M.B., Michelle Mason and the Santa Barbara Jean Company – with its insider names like the Butterfly Beach Skinny Jean.

Blue Bee
923 State St., Santa Barbara
805.897.1137, BlueBee.com

Blue Bee Jeans
913 State St., 805.882.2468

Blue Bee Kids
9 E. Figueroa St., 805.966.6734

Blue Bee Luxury
1100 State St., 805.965.1956

Blue Bee Shoes
1102 State St., 805.965.1956

Blue Beetle (men's store)
925 State St., 805.897.1137

Beginning with one boutique in 2000, the Blue Bee guys have fashioned no less than a retail empire with six stores carrying designer tank tops, killer suits and one-of-a-kind runway couture, from such names as Twisted Heart, Paul Smith, Burning Torch, Marc Jacobs and Moschino Cheap & Chic (hint: it's not cheap). Women (teens and up) line up around the block for the megasales in September and January.

Bryan Lee
802 State St., Santa Barbara
805.963.0206
Rock 'n' roll *riche* is the defining style at long-standing fashion staple Bryan Lee, where hipsters go to buy their duds.

Carroll & Co.
1273 Coast Village Rd., Montecito
805.969.0500, CarrollandCo.com
With stores in Beverly Hills and Pasadena, it was a logical step for Carroll & Co. to open an outpost in the upscale enclave of Montecito. The company has been in business since 1949, and styles remain as classic as they were back then. Private-label clothing in quality fabrics and tailoring comes from Italy, England, Scotland, Switzerland and the United States; you'll also find Robert Talbott shirts and ties.

DIANI
1324 State St., Santa Barbara
877.342.6474, DianiBoutique.com
Simple-but-elegant is the theme of this trio of women's boutiques. Tent-like dressing rooms harken to owner Stephanie Diani's native Kenya at the flagship store. Diani Essentials highlights the season's top sellers for shoppers who like to cut to the chase. And Diani Shoes carries high-fashion footwear from such designers as Tashkent and French Sole.

dressed
1253 Coast Village Rd., Montecito
805.565.1253, dressedonline.com
Uber-stylish, New York–rooted Susan Pitcher opened her friendly, high-fashion women's boutique in 2003, and it's become a must-stop shop for locals and celebrity visitors alike.

Browse Balenciaga and Stella McCartney, Pucci and Valentino – plus vintage jewelry and clutch-worthy handbags. The edgier **ready**, two doors down, flaunts sophisticated streetwear by such hot young designers as Parker Blue and Maggie Coulombe.

Also in the neighborhood:
kate
1137 Coast Village Rd., Montecito
800.454.1554, kateboutique.com
Simple, luxurious women's styles.

Drishti
130 E. Canon Perdido St., Santa Barbara
805.963.0222, DrishtiYoga.com
There's a peaceful vibe inside Drishti, which sells everything a yoga fan could need: camis and tank tops, stretchy pants and capris, mats and music – even incense and "om" symbol pendants.

Natasha
1231 State St., Santa Barbara
805.965.4542
This low-key shop brims with colorful, casual-chic women's styles, typically made from natural fabrics. Locals know it as the place where

Haute couture, Montecito-style, at dressed—and yes, those are Hank Pitcher paintings on the wall.

you can't *not* find something cute, whether it's a summer sundress or playful silk jacket.

Patty Montana
Calle Real Center, 5726 Calle Real, Goleta
805.683.1816
Jeans are the foundation of all everyday fashion, or so says owner Betty Ann Denier, who carries the serious names in denim: True Grit, Big Star, Johnny Was and more. You'll also find tees, handbags and fun gifts, including gorgeous silk chiffon scarves made by local designer Caron Miller. Unfussy, personal service.

Santa Barbara Outfitters
1200 State St., Santa Barbara
805.564.1007, sboutfitters.com
For many Santa Barbarans, style grows out of what you do, not what you wear – and when they need stuff to wear for stuff they do, they come here. Clothing, footwear and accessories for kayakers, hikers, runners, yogis, cyclists and other active sorts are what you'll find, from such homegrown companies as Patagonia, Simple and Horny Toad, and some national names, too. Take a break from the stress of trying on clothing by climbing the indoor wall.

Taka-Puna
428 E. Haley St., Santa Barbara
805.963.4848, TakaPuna.com
Named after a seaside New Zealand town, Taka-Puna draws customers from L.A. for its Clacton & Frinton menswear. Its retro two-tone, button-down shirts were a wardrobe mainstay of Chandler on the TV series *Friends*. John Malkovich is also a big fan.

Wendy Foster
833 State St., Santa Barbara
805.966.2276, WendyFoster.com
516 San Ysidro Rd., Montecito
805.565.1506, WendyFoster.com
World-traveled Wendy Foster opened her first store in 1977 and truly is the grande dame of Santa Barbara fashion. Montecito's boutique is the epitome of elegance. Its sportswear store next door carries Foster's casual looks; the State Street store is a mix of modern styles and jewelry. With urban and beach looks, Angel, at 1221 Coast Village Road in Montecito, appeals to a younger buyer.

Just a hint of the color-intense goods at Italian Pottery Outlet.

Furniture & Housewares

Indigo
1323 State St., Santa Barbara
805.962.6909, IndigoInteriors.com
Born from a love of Japanese antiques, Indigo
offers Asian-inspired and custom furnishings,
including Chinese and Indonesian antiques. Its
staff members are also known for their interior
design work.

Italian Pottery Outlet
19 Helena St., Santa Barbara
805.899.9170, ItalianPottery.com
You honestly won't believe the colors when you
duck into the warehouse where these importers
display their cobalt-and-gold, orange-and-ver-
million platters, pitchers, planters and pots, all
handmade in the Italian countryside. Collectors
go nuts here.

Livingreen Store & Gallery
218 Helena Ave., Santa Barbara
866.966.1319, livingreen.com
1275 Coast Village Rd., Montecito
805.565.4103, livingreen.com
Dedicated to providing eco-friendly building

materials without sacrificing design, Livingreen
sells bamboo and cork flooring, recycled teak
tables, organic cotton sheets and nontoxic
paints. All products are ranked by "shades of
green," showing just how earth-conscious each
item is.

Maison K
1253 Coast Village Rd., Montecito
805.969.1676, MaisonKInc.com
Kimberly Phillips fills her Montecito boutique
with unique treasures from around the world
– sumptuous textures from shell to silver,
glass to cashmere, leather to clay. Drool over
the Venetian pillows (only, don't really) and a
Moroccan metal-and-bone mirror.

Mi Casa Imports
929 State St., Santa Barbara
805.564.8323, MiCasaImportsDeSB.com
Just stepping into this shop full of rustic-style
banquet tables, iron candelabras and Mexican
pottery makes you want to plop down on a
carved wooden bench and sip a margarita. We
love the folk-art accents and handsome cabi-
nets from India, Spain and Indonesia, too.

Porch
5065 Carpinteria Ave., Carpinteria
805.684.0300
An oasis amid ornamental grasses and suc-culents, Porch peddles garden pieces plus furnishings and lots of interesting gifts. The shop's indoor-outdoor style melds modern with Mediterranean and comes up with a decidedly Californian flair.

Rooms & Gardens
2330 Lillie Ave., Summerland
805.565.4877
924 State St., Santa Barbara
805.965.2424, roomsandgardens.com
It's all in the details here – a few softly worn shells on a woven table from Thailand, a hand-cast bronze bowl for a garden corner, richly col-orful Chinese fortune balls atop an old armoire. Chosen by owners Jami and Eric Voulgaris and partner Mary Steenburgen, the new upholstered furniture, antiques, framed prints and maps, and accessories all ooze a relaxed but carefully considered look that evokes a Colonial–West Indies feel – and yet is totally Californian, too. Good for redoing a room or picking up a gift.

Mi Casa Imports: armoires and tables and benches, oh my!

Hemp hats at Marcel Hemp.

Retail on the Edge

Energy Tattoo
33 Parker Way, Santa Barbara
805.564.6779, energytattoo.com
Husband-and-wife Nic and PJ Ferrante (he also goes by the name Poop Jr.) have the rare ability to make you feel safe even when they're com-ing at you with a needle. Their off-the-beaten-path tattoo and body piercing studio has a stellar local rep – and PJ's magna cum laude degree from Rutgers University may make him the smartest ink-slinger in town.

Fuzion
3120 State St., Santa Barbara
805.687.6401, FuzionSB.com & Fuzionart-SB.com
Opened by college students, this upper State Street boutique peddles both urban fashion and modern art, as its name implies. Word is there's a head shop in the back, but, well, we wouldn't know.

Marcel Hemp
531 State St., Santa Barbara
805.963.8387, MarcelHemp.com
Marcel, whose baby picture graces all his clothes, designs and manufactures his own T-shirts, hats and hoodies out of strong, sus-tainable hemp.

Sage

1095A Edison St., Santa Ynez
805.688.0955
You easily could get sucked into browsing for hours in this enchanting cottage, packed with sideboards and armoires, candles and soaps from Provence. If you like the style, make sure to check out the owner's clothing shop, Tumbleweeds, just around the corner at 3532 Sagunto Street.

Santa Barbara Home Improvement Center

415 E. Gutierrez St., Santa Barbara
805.963.7825, SBHICAce.com
Everyone's favorite family-owned home store sprawls over two acres with hardware, tools, knickknacks and an impressive nursery, plus a surprisingly inspiring collection of housewares: pots, place mats and picnic supplies.

Jewelry & Gifts

Bryant & Sons, Ltd.

812 State St., Santa Barbara
805.966.9187
1482 E. Valley Rd., Montecito
805.565.4411, bryantandsons.com
When your ship comes in, this is where you'll want to come to splurge on a diamond-and-sapphire necklace or a pair of pavé-set diamond huggie earrings. Exuding classic taste and quiet wealth, Bryant & Sons has been meeting the jewelry needs (or wants) of Santa Barbara and Montecito denizens for more than 40 years. Choose from a large selection of high-end watches (Breitling, Cartier, Patek Philippe, Ebel, Baume & Mercier, Chopard); pearls by Mikimoto; crystal by Lalique and Baccarat; and engagement and wedding styles by Scott Kay and Tacori ... and if you don't find anything that suits your fancy, they'll make you a custom piece.

Fibula

2 E. De La Guerra St., Santa Barbara
805.962.8851, fibulajewelry.com
Founded in Maine, where the only other Fibula store exists, this jeweler surprises with regal-but-modern designs: clean, striking settings for Tahitian green pearls, yellow sapphires – and the $8,600 Gold Kick-Ass Bracelet.

Imagine

11 W. Canon Perdido St.
805.899.3700
1470V E. Valley Rd., Montecito
805.695.0220
If you can't find something you like here, it means they're closed. This inspired gift shop is the kind of place where you need to do several laps to make sure you've seen every quirky notecard, artsy word sculpture and fabulous bracelet.

Folk-art fun at Just Folk.

Just Folk

2346 Lillie Ave., Summerland
805.969.7118, justfolk.com
Look for the eye-catching new building with a tin roof, capacious front porch and pig weather vane. This whimsical shop, owned by former television producers Marcy Carsey and Susan Baerwald, displays unique American folk art, including antique, contemporary and outsider works. It's a great place to find something original for your home or as a very special gift.

Lewis & Clark

1116 State St., Santa Barbara
805.962.6034
1286 Coast Village Rd., Montecito
805.969.7177
The loose brick flooring in here makes a soothing clinking sound as you wander through
the Provençal tablecloths, bracelet charms,
clever gift books, nostalgic posters and dishes.
Gentlemen are well advised to grab a bench
outside and be prepared to wait....

Santa Barbara Gift Baskets

1221 State St., Santa Barbara
805.965.1245, SBGiftBaskets.com
Wanna boast about how great Santa Barbara is
to someone who can't experience it first-hand?
This place will send a gorgeous package filled
with local wine, tortilla chips, olives, honey, coffee, salsa and the latest issue of *Santa Barbara
Magazine* anywhere in the country. You can also
browse the store and pick out the ingredients
for your own custom brag-basket.

Silverhorn

1155 Coast Village Rd., Montecito
805.969.0442
Four Seasons Resort The Biltmore Santa
Barbara
1260 Channel Dr.
805.969.3167, silverhorn.com
Since 1976, Silverhorn has been hand-crafting
exquisite pieces of jewelry from rare and
unusual gemstones and planting jewelry lust in
many a local's heart. These are one-of-a kind
pieces, many of which have won awards for
creativity, design and craftsmanship – and we
want them all.

Upstairs at Pierre LaFond

516 San Ysidro Rd., Montecito
805.565.1502, upstairsatpierrelafond.com
Yes, that's the actual name. Perched almost
secretly above the Pierre LaFond Market & Deli
in Montecito's Upper Village, this serene and
homey loft carries kids' clothes from France,
Calleen Cordero leather goods, hurricane lanterns, lingerie, bright woven baskets, bedding
from Matteo in L.A., lovely gift books and the
homegrown scent called Montecito.

Personal Care

Bellezza Vita

2410 Lillie Ave., Summerland
805.969.7300, BellezzaVita.com
In addition to being a full-service spa, Bellezza
Vita peddles make-you-feel-good goodies,
from snuggly bathrobes and silk sachets to soy
candles and herbal teas. Pick up a bottle of
organic shampoo, or a beauty buy from these
hometown Santa Barbarans: the Jacqua gals.

Skin Deep

3405 State St., Santa Barbara
805.687.9497, SkinDeepSalon.com
Opened by three sisters and their mom nearly
30 years ago, Skin Deep is a mainstay for
beauty buys – and gifts for girlfriends, too. In
addition to getting yourself waxed and tinted,
check out the vast hair-care, skin-care and nail-
care product lines.

Soap

910 Linden Ave., Carpinteria
805.684.6695
In an adorable retail space that was once a
geologist's office, Soap owner Fran Puccinelli
sells everything from European hand soaps and
shampoos to silk jammies and bath towels.
How can you not relish a place that displays its
wares in the basin of an antique pedestal sink?

sumbody

920 State St., Santa Barbara
805.568.1552, sumbody.com
Featured in *Lucky*, *O* and *In Style* magazines,
this all-natural skin-care line boasts ingredients
like fresh mango, sea salt and honey. Browse
the bath "fizzers," sugar scrubs and the Baby
Butt Salve in this apothecary-style store, one of
five in California.

Treat

1324 State St., Santa Barbara
805.966.2336, TreatThyself.com
The owners of this luxury "beauty boutique"
and spa want it to feel like a candy shop for
grown-ups. To that end, it is stocked with
deliciously scented candles, cute French soaps
and flavored body butters. Not sweet enough
for you? Try the Royal Honey Facial.

Secondhand flair at Cominichi's.

Skivvies

Bikini Factory
2275B Ortega Hill Rd., Summerland
805.969.2887
For more than 30 years, this swimwear shop
has prided itself on making the bathing-suit-
buying process as painless as possible. They
have all manner of sizes, and they'll even do
alterations for a custom fit.

Intimo
1046 Coast Village Rd., Montecito
805.565.5606, shopantoinette.com
This chic lingerie shop shares space with high-
fashion clothing store Antoinette, so maybe
you'll find just the right bra for that perfect little
black dress. It carries everything from Italian
lace bustiers to silk-and-lace chemises, with an
emphasis on La Perla.

Purrmission
18 W. Calle Laureles, Santa Barbara
805.898.1241, purrmission.net
Owned and run by a saucy local mom who
goes by the name of Miss Kitty, Purrmission
sells classic and sensible underthings, special-
izing in complimentary bra fittings from size A

to H – but it also offers naughty lingerie and
toys from feathers to, um, handcuffs. If you
need a portable stripper pole, not to worry –
Miss Kitty has one.

A Tropical Affair
12 E. Cota St., Santa Barbara
805.730.1625, ATropicalAffair.com
In downtown Santa Barbara, this chic but
discreet shop is ready to outfit you in bikinis by
Diane Von Furstenberg and Michael Kors, lingerie by Dolce & Gabbana and La Perla – and,
of course, a pair of fab fluffy slippers to polish
off the look.

Stationery

Letter Perfect
1227 Coast Village Rd., Santa Barbara
805.969.7998, letterperfectstationery.com
Old-fashioned in its extraordinary level of service but stocked with modern designs by Vera
Wang and Kate Spade, Letter Perfect is the
kind of shop where it's fun to linger, fingering
the elegant papers and cards. It offers calligra-

phy, engraving, embossing, in-store printing… the works.

Check out its sister store, too:
Paper, Ink.
3325 State St., Santa Barbara
805.687.3580

folio
4437 Holllister Ave., Santa Barbara
805.964.6800
We love this little store *and* the alliteration in its subtitle: paper, print and post. Need a gift? It's one-stop shopping: choose from an array of beautiful stationery and cards, some printed by hand on antique letterpresses, as well as gifts from Murano glass bottle stoppers to marquetry boxes. Then you can mail your gift and card right on the spot from its handy mail station. Folio also offers offset printing and graphic design services.

The Stationery Collection
1470 E. Valley Rd., Montecito
805.969.3414, stationerycollection.com
You'll feel like writing that long-overdue letter to Grandma after checking out the selection of catchy cards and lovely stationery from the likes of Crane's and William Arthur. Pick up a fine writing instrument, too, while you peruse the invitations, clever party favors and table accessories.

Thrift & Resale

The Closet
1213 State St., Santa Barbara
805.963.8083
UCSB student Johanna Melamed opened this downtown resale-clothing boutique in 2003. Its specialty: secondhand couture, vintage accessories and barely worn designer jeans. Check in often to find bargains in such labels as Marc Jacobs, True Religion and Ella Moss.

Cominichi's Flea Market
421 E. Cota St., Santa Barbara
805.962.1413, Cominichis.com
Talk about a bright idea: This place has an annual Festival of Ugly Lamps. The beloved shop displays a hodgepodge of utterly lovable stuff, from funky furniture and art to vintage Halston dresses and clawfoot tubs. Prepare to wander for a while.

The Rack and Treasure House
1070 Fairway Rd., Montecito
805.969.0190, MusicAcademy.org
Situated on the enchanting campus of the Music Academy of the West, these two shops resell donated clothing and furniture to raise money for the academy's remarkable full-scholarship summer program. Open only from noon to 3 p.m. Tuesday through Saturday, the Rack houses outfits, jewelry, shoes and handbags, and the Treasure House carries antiques, china, silver and linens.

Victorian Vogue & the Costume Shoppe
4289 State St., Santa Barbara
805.967.4626, VictorianVogue.com
Pitchforks and pirate hats. Flapper frocks and Edwardian gowns. Whether renting or buying, this sizable store has the duds and accessories (white go-go boots, anyone?) to outfit you in the finery of your favorite era. And the salesfolks know *everything.*

Dapper duds at Yellowstone Clothing.

Yellowstone Clothing Co.
527 State St., Santa Barbara
805.963.9609
Owned and operated by husband-and-wife team Stephanie and Paul Haugen, Yellowstone has a cool retro vibe and racks of stylin' bowling and cowboy shirts, plus vintage skirts and jackets.

Q & A: Marty Bebout & John Doucette

Originally from Texas and Massachusetts, respectively, Marty Bebout and John Doucette came to Santa Barbara in 2000 with a plan to open a single clothing shop. Now they have half a dozen high-style Blue Bee boutiques, where local nobodies and L.A. celebs alike line up to get their mitts on Rich and Skinny jeans, Nicole Miller frocks and Marc Jacobs boxer briefs. From menswear to kidswear and pumps to tees, Bebout says the key to their retail success is carrying fashions that their high-profile clientele can't find just anywhere. Though Blue Bee shoppers are hot on "going out" clothes, this couple likes nothing more than hanging out at the renovated downtown bungalow where they live with their dogs, including 12-year-old Daisy, (below). Starshine Roshell sat down to talk with Marty and John, and Marty (on the left) did all the talking.

What's your perfect Friday night?
Going home and relaxing after a really great day in the store.

What's your favorite breakfast spot?
Lazy Acres market, because it's healthy and you can get fresh fruit. And Moby Dick's on Stearns Wharf for the view.

What do you make of the truism that "dressing up" in Santa Barbara just means wearing shoes?
That's the exact reason that casual luxury is successful in Santa Barbara, because it is a casual environment – and yet you need to look good.

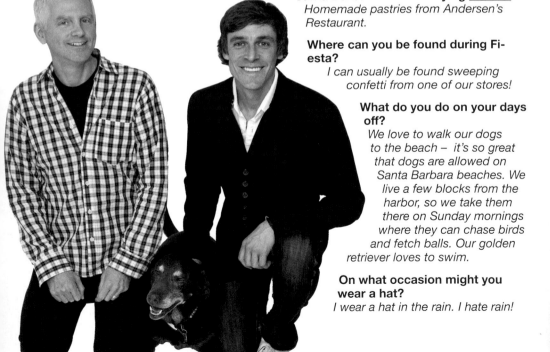

Fill in the blank: No tourist should leave Santa Barbara without buying _____?
Homemade pastries from Andersen's Restaurant.

Where can you be found during Fiesta?
I can usually be found sweeping confetti from one of our stores!

What do you do on your days off?
We love to walk our dogs to the beach – it's so great that dogs are allowed on Santa Barbara beaches. We live a few blocks from the harbor, so we take them there on Sunday mornings where they can chase birds and fetch balls. Our golden retriever loves to swim.

On what occasion might you wear a hat?
I wear a hat in the rain. I hate rain!

Childlike

How could a kid not love Santa Barbara? For starters, you've got some 100 miles of beaches, each with its own personality and pleasures. Add to that the beautiful parks, kid-friendly hiking trails, kid-scaled zoo, bike paths, skate park, parades and festivals, and you're still just scratching the surface of life here in Southern California's kid heaven.

The Outdoor Life

Santa Barbara offers a plethora of parks to choose from. An all-age favorite is **Chase Palm Park** on both sides of Cabrillo Boulevard, near West Beach. The mountain side boasts fountains, creeks, an old-fashioned carousel and a Shipwreck Playground modeled after an ocean schooner from the turn of the century. The large grassy area hosts **free outdoor concerts** every Thursday night in the summer. Visit sbparksandrecreation.com for the schedule.

Riding the rim at Skater's Point.

Just across the street, the ocean side of Chase Palm Park is home to the **Sunday/Holiday Arts and Crafts Show**, a good place to pick up hand-crafted gifts, including toys, kites and games made by locals. Also along the waterfront is **Skater's Point**, a free, state-of-the-art skate park with a half-pipe, rails, fun boxes and ramps. Weekends before noon are reserved for younger, less experienced skaters; in the afternoon, older kids – and many adults – work on mastering ollies, alley-oops and kick flips. The park always gets raves for its **summer skateboard clinics**; call 805.564.5495 for details.

Alameda Park (1400 Santa Barbara Street), one of Santa Barbara's oldest parks, fills two city blocks and has rare trees, a gazebo, lawns, picnic tables and **Kids' World**, an 8,000-square-foot paradise of a playground built by local residents, with a castle, swings and slides.

Kids love to run laps down the long fishing pier at **Goleta Beach** (off Highway 217 at Sandspit Road). With 29 acres of public space, including an expansive playground and areas for volleyball, horseshoes, barbecues and picnics, this is a perfect place to spend a day with the family. If you don't have energy to pack a picnic, the **Beachside Restaurant** is casual and kid-friendly. Bring bikes if you can – the paved bike path leads right to UCSB.

Surfers, skimboarders and boogie boarders can hit the waves at **Arroyo Burro Beach** (2981 Cliff Drive), known as Hendry's Beach or "The Pit" to longtime locals. A beach favorite for families and dog lovers, it allows off-leash frolicking to the east of the estuary.

Surf Happens is a cool local program that teaches the fundamentals of surfing to people of all ages and abilities through clinics, camps and private lessons; it also fields surf teams for locals and organizes the Rincon Classic surf contest every spring. And kids don't get to have all the fun – Surf Happens Family Camp is held every summer at El Capitan campground, just 20 minutes north of Santa Barbara. Call 805.966.3613 or go to surfhappens. com for details.

Parents will appreciate the ocean views at **La Mesa Park** (295 Meigs Road) while kids enjoy the large play structure and sandbox area, as well as the lawns and picnic area – the perfect spot for no-fuss birthday parties. **Lazy Acres**, the natural-foods market across the street, is the place to go for picnic provisions.

Lookout Park (Evans Avenue at Highway 101) in Summerland is a hidden gem, with a sandy beach and calm ocean swimming. On the bluff above the beach, there's a grassy play area, playground, horseshoes, volleyball courts, picnic tables and hiking trails, and all are within easy access to the parking lot.

Bring your hiking shoes and your bathing suits to visit **Seven Falls**. Kids love to watch Mission Creek plunge down seven waterfalls in steps, each waterfall splashing into a small, rock-lined pool. The trail is about a mile and a quarter and is easy to negotiate from the parking lot. For the more ambitious, another steep mile will take you to **Inspiration Point**, where you can enjoy a jaw-dropping view of the Pacific Coast. To reach this trail from the Santa Barbara Mission, drive up Mission Canyon Road to Foothill Road, turn right, then turn left back on to Mission Canyon Road. Follow Mission Canyon Road to Tunnel Road. Here the Santa Barbara Botanic Garden sign directs you to continue up Mission Canyon Road, but turn left instead, continuing another mile to the Seven Falls parking area on your right.

One of the most wonderful things about the Santa Ynez Mountains is its hidden places, like the **Playground**, an off-trail route (moderate in challenge) that meanders through a magical maze of rock formations. School-age kids love to explore and find their own way through this trail. To get there from Santa Barbara, take Highway 154 over the Santa Ynez Mountains to West Camino Cielo Road. Then drive approximately 2.5 miles to a point where a power line crosses the road, and look for this hidden trail on the left side of the road.

Another family favorite hiking area is **Rattlesnake Canyon**, so named because the gently curving canyon has the shape of a sunbathing rattler. Getting there involves a beautiful drive up the back side of the Riviera, where thick oaks dot the shady hillsides, in contrast to the wildflower- and grass-covered slopes of the sunny side of the mountains. To get there from the Santa Barbara Mission, drive up Mission Canyon Road to Foothill Road, turn right, turn left back on to Mission Canyon Road. Continue past Tunnel Road to Las Canoas, where you'll turn right and continue a mile and a half to an open area and a large sign noting the start of the trail. Here you'll find lots of side trails leading to breathtaking waterfalls and pools, but stay on the trail – and watch out for poison oak.

Noa Mahoney, the youngest member of the Surf Happens Elite Team, rips it up at a summer-camp session.

Kids & Culture

Voted Best Children's Theater Troupe by the *Santa Barbara Independent*, **Boxtales Theatre Company** (805.961.3906, boxtales.org) uses an exciting mix of storytelling, music, masks and movement to present world myths and folktales to audiences of all ages. Make sure to check them out.

Run by longtime locals Radu and Marian Azdril, **Showstoppers Theatre Productions** (805.682.6043, ShowstoppersTheatreProductions.com) gives children ages 5 to 18 the chance to take part in musical theater as performers, crew and audience members through its year-round programs.

At **Yellow Bird Music** (805.898.9070, YellowBirdMusic.com), children from three months up to 12 years can explore the world through music, movement and art classes. Owner Alexandra Adams-Arreguin combines a kindermusik-based curriculum with innovative additions, resulting in engaging classes in musical exploration, art, yoga, piano, choir and drum. Summer camps, too.

Santa Barbara Dance Arts (805.966.5299, sbjda.com), formerly known as the Santa Barbara Jazz Dance Academy, offers classes for all ages in jazz, hip-hop, lyrical, tap, ballet technique and Pilates for everyone for tiny tots to adults. Ballerinas in training can also practice their pliés at **Gustafson Dance** (805.965.6690, GustafsonDance.com), the official school of the State Street Ballet Company. Preballet classes are available for ages 2 1/2 and up, tap for ages 3 to 10, and jazz for ages 4 and up. Students of the **Santa Barbara Ballet Center** (805.966.0711, SantaBarbaraBalletCenter.com), home of the Santa Barbara Festival Ballet Company have been performing *The Nutcracker* at the Arlington for more than 30 years – a beloved hometown tradition, and one of the few productions in California performed with a live orchestra. Classes are offered for the tutued tiniest to preprofessionals.

The **Santa Barbara Public Library** system – with branches downtown, and in Goleta, Montecito, on the eastside and in Carpinteria – can't be beat for its knowledgeable librarians and free children's programs. Local storyteller Michael Katz is always a crowd pleaser, and don't miss the bilingual storytelling hour and preschool storytimes, which usually include music and puppets. Check sbplibrary.org for complete schedules. The web site also offers free live homework help for 4th graders through first-year college students from 1 p.m. until 10 p.m. every day. Just log on with a library card to connect to well-trained tutors.

Families enjoy exploring the 5,000 years of world art on display at the **Santa Barbara Museum of Art** (1130 State Street, 805.963.4364, SBMuseart.org), which provides activity guides and interactive family tours. The Museum Store is full of creative gifts for all ages. Up the street at the museum's Ridley-Tree Education Center at McCormick House (1600 Santa Barbara Street), kids from 3 to 5 partake in parent-child art classes; the after-school ArtVenture program is geared to kids 6 and up. ArtVenture Camps are offered over spring, summer and winter breaks.

Masks, music and movement are part of the inventive productions at Boxtales Theatre Company.

It's All Happening at the Zoo

You must visit the zoo, even if you have to borrow a kid – or go without one. Known to old-timers as the Child Estate because it was once owned by Lillian Child, the **Santa Barbara Zoo** is truly a local jewel. Its formal name is the Santa Barbara Zoological Gardens, and for good reason – this is no city zoo. Most of the 500 animals are housed outside in natural habitats, in a well-maintained, 30-acre gardenlike setting overlooking the Pacific. The zoo is also known for having been the home of Gemina, the beloved crooked-necked giraffe, who lived a long and healthy life until she died in January 2008 due to complications from old age.

Santa Barbara Zoological Gardens
500 Niños Dr., Santa Barbara
805.962.5339, SantaBarbaraZoo.org
Open daily 10 a.m.-5 p.m.; admission $11, kids 12 & under and seniors over 60, $8; kids under 2 free

When you arrive, be sure to check out the visitor kiosk just inside the front entrance to check for special events, feedings and keeper talks. Don't-miss exhibits include Eeeww!, the aptly named collection of environmentally important but often overlooked invertebrates and creepy-crawly animals, including snakes and lizards (very little ones may need a hand-hold in this area); Gibbon Island, where you might catch these show-offs performing a noisy trapeze act; the colorful Tropical Aviary; Lorikeet Landing, where you can sometimes join in on feeding these chatty birds; a "contact area" with domestic animals; and a soon-to-come kids' marketplace with a conservation theme, featuring environmentally friendly merchandise. Stroll through the African savannah where the Cats of Africa include meerkats (hey, isn't that Timon?)

Suzi gives herself a shower at the Santa Barbara Zoo.

to lions and black-footed domestic-looking cats. The recently arrived Humboldt penguins are a big hit, as are the snow leopards, gorillas, giraffes and elephants. And stay tuned – California condors will be the majestic centerpieces for the upcoming California Trails exhibit. A well-designed playground and pathways throughout the zoo help kids burn off energy between animals. And don't miss a ride on the train that circles the perimeter of the zoo. Young ones will relish a spin on the carousel, a Dentzel original with fanciful hand-carved animals, built especially for the zoo.

When you're ready for a break and some sustenance, stop in at the Ridley-Tree House restaurant, in a lovely garden courtyard, for a sandwich, burger, salad or some dino-shaped chicken nuggets. Or the large grassy hilltop overlooking East Beach is a great spot for a picnic – it's so picturesque that it's also a popular spot for weddings and corporate barbecues. Zoovies are shown here in the summer (generally Wednesday nights in July), for which you can bring your blanket and popcorn and take in a family-friendly film under the stars. And if your kids fantasize about a sleepover at the zoo, here's their chance – the occasional ZooSnooze is offered, so check the web site to see when the next one is on tap.

The zoo also hosts one of the best summer camps in town (it was voted Best Summer Camp by both *Independent* and *Santa Barbara News-Press* polls) for kids 3 to13, with themed programs, games, behind-the-scenes visits, up-close animal introductions and hands-on science and crafts.

Age to Age:
Fun for Little Kids, Bigger Kids & Teens

Little Kids

Energetic little ones love to hop aboard the miniature train and handcar at **Goleta's historic train depot** (300 North Los Carneros Road, 805.964.3540, GoletaDepot.org). Part of the **South Coast Railroad Museum**, which is dedicated to the history and adventure of railroading, it's surrounded by the 25-acre **Lake Los Carneros Park**, where you can watch the ducks, comb through the cattails, explore the historic 1872 **Stow House** (304 North Los Carneros Road, 805.964.4407) and maybe even catch a cowboy replacing his horse's shoes at the blacksmith shop.

Hilda Ray Park (1400 Kenwood Drive) on the Mesa is a great one for toddlers, with a spider web to climb, a sandbox to explore and a completely fenced-in grassy hill to run around on, while parents can sit at a picnic table, relax and perhaps enjoy lunch. **Hidden Valley Park** (Calle de Los Amigos at Torino Drive) is similarly structured, so there's no escape for little ones, and there's a great toddler playground as well. But there are no bathrooms, so plan accordingly.

For parents wanting to cool off on hot days without the stress of watching the kids in a swimming pool, both **Oak Park** (300 West Alamar Avenue, 805.564.5418) and **West Beach Park** (401 Shoreline Drive) have 18-inch-deep wading pools for children up to age 7, with lifeguards on duty from May to September.

Santa Barbara Botanic Gardens in Mission Canyon has more than five miles of hiking trails and dirt paths meandering through 65 acres of gardens bursting with native plants in natural settings. Kids love exploring the banks of Mission Creek, which flows through the gardens and includes a rock dam (now a State Historic Landmark) that was built in 1806 by local Native Americans. Children's programs include a class called Little Sprouts: Mommy, Daddy and Me, as well as a summer camp, where kids hike, play games and participate in science activities, nature crafts and outdoor investigations. More outdoor explorations can be made at the **Mission Rose Garden** just down the canyon and across from the Santa Barbara Mission. The expanse of grass here calls out to kids to run, play catch and try a few impromptu cartwheels.

If you've had enough sun, or on that rare rainy day, check out **My Gym** (3888 State Street, 805.563.7336, my-gym.com), an award-winning program designed to help children from three months to 13 years develop strength, balance, coordination, flexibility and social skills through music, dance, games and gymnastics.

Santa Barbara City College Continuing Education (805.964.6853, sbcc.edu) offers fun mommy-and-me classes for infants, toddlers and preschool-age kids – our favorites are the ones that meet in various parks around town.

The best **farmer's market** for little ones is the Saturday morning downtown Santa Barbara Market – it has lots of musical entertainment and crazy balloon creations.

Kids can work a real-live handcar at the South Coast Railroad Museum.

Holy cow, that's one big skeleton! Kids love the blue whale at the Santa Barbara Museum of Natural History.

School-Age Kids

Watch and grin at the googly-eyed wonder in your children's eyes as they walk under and around a life-size 72-foot blue whale skeleton to enter the **Santa Barbara Museum of Natural History** (2559 Puesta del Sol Road, 805.682.4711, sbnature.org). Once inside, your kids will make a beeline to such hits as the interactive space lab; a sparkling-new gem and mineral display; the recently remodeled bird diversity room, complete with amazingly alive-looking stuffed specimens, nests and eggs; and Mammal Hall. The Chumash culture display is a fascinating snapshot of Santa Barbara history. Sometimes in summer, you can see 1,000 butterflies up close as they flutter around you in the Butterfly Pavilion. Other summers you might have a chance to roam with life-size dinosaur replicas and dig for fossils. The Nature Trail along Mission Creek is a beautiful walk for kids and grown-ups – kids love playing in the authentic Indian canoe they'll find along the trail. Picnic tables under the oaks are perfect for a snack break. If you have time, take in a celestial show at the Gladwin Planetarium – ask for the schedule at the museum entry. Shows range from Chumash Skies, which relates astronomical events and stories told by the Chumash, to Twinkle, Twinkle for Little Stars, an introduction to the stars, planets and constellations geared toward preschoolers and parents. Admission is free every third Sunday; also note that the Santa Barbara Nature Pass allows unlimited access to both the Natural History Museum and the satellite Ty Warner Sea Center for two days (excluding planetarium shows). Summer camps, classes and weekend workshops here and at the affiliated Ty Warner Sea Center are some of the best in town.

Your kids will start the day smiling if you begin at the harbor with pancakes at the **Breakwater Restaurant** (104 Harbor Way, 805.965.1557). Then take a stroll along the breakwater, where you can see the harbor, the beach, Stearns Wharf, the Santa Barbara Riviera, the Channel Islands and boats sailing by. On your way, stop by the **Santa Barbara Maritime Museum** (113 Harbor Way, 805.962.8404, sbmm.org) to explore a working submarine periscope, then hop on **Lil' Toot** (6 Harbor Way, #117, 805.896.6900, sbwatertaxi.com) where Captain Fred lets the kids drive the boat over to the wharf. Then they can touch real sharks at the **Ty Warner Sea Center** (211 Stearns Wharf, 805.962.2526, sbnature.org), fish off the pier, walk around the stores and maybe even buy some candy or an ice cream.

If you've had just about enough of that pesky sunshine and great outdoors, duck inside to the **Susan Quinlan Doll & Teddy Bear Museum & Library** (122 West Canon Perdido, 805.730.1707, QuinlanMuseum.com), located near Paseo Nuevo mall, which offers plenty of parking. This is one of the largest displays of dolls and teddy bears in the world, as well as the largest known research library of related books. About 3,000 pieces – many limited

Ty Warner Sea Center, atop Stearns Wharf.

Feeding time at Ostrich Land.

edition or one-of-a-kind – from around the world are displayed in three galleries. You'll find book-character dolls and teddy bears, from Pooh to Paddington, and ones that represent the ethnic groups that settled California, historical figures, movie stars (who knew there were Leonardo DiCaprio and Kate Winslet bears?) and so much more.

It's not every day that kids get the opportunity to get up close and personal with ostrich and emu. Fine feathered friends rush up to the fence to greet you at **Ostrich Land** (610 East Highway 246, Buellton, 805.686.9696, OstrichLandUSA.com), a 33-acre breeding farm with a small roadside shop that sells fresh eggs, meat, feathers and egg art. Also nearby is **Quicksilver Miniature Horse Ranch** (1555 Alamo Pintado Road, Solvang, 805.686.4002, syv.com/qsminis), where 34-inch horses prance around the grassy meadows of this twenty-acre high-tech training facility, one of the largest miniature-horse facilities on the west coast. Originally bred in Europe as pets for royalty, the horses were imported to the United States in the 1930s to work the coal mines, and now they're bred as pets.

If the family has had a little too much togetherness, **Whiz Kidz** (189 North Turnpike Road, 805.696.9449, WhizKidz.net) is a great place to drop your kids (ages 3 to 18) off to explore the latest and most popular computer programs and games under the guidance of professionals. "My favorite time is when the kids are all playing a game together," says owner Paige Shields. "Ten kids all playing the same game at the same time, and they're screaming, 'You killed me! I'm gonna get you!' It's almost like playing chase in your backyard, but on computers. They have so much fun."

For another type of creative outlet, check out **2000 degrees** (1206 State Street, 805.882.1817), a ceramics workshop that encourages novices and experts alike to paint pottery and glass or create a tile mosaic. Kids (and adults) can choose from a vast array of objects – say, a piggy bank, picture frame or cartoon character – and let their imaginations and paintbrushes run wild. The studio will fire the creations; they'll even ship it, or you can pick it up five days later. You pay for the item you paint, plus a workshop fee for each person.

Middle School & High School Kids

The **Santa Barbara Parks & Recreation Department** offers a wealth of year-round affordable or free teen programs – from sports teams and classes to Guitar Hero tournaments and karaoke nights – as well as dances, parties and excursions to such popular places as Six Flags Magic Mountain and Disneyland during the summer. Visit SantaBarbaraCA.gov/teens for a schedule.

Teens also like the **TWELVE35 Teen Center** (1235 Chapala Street, SantaBarbaraCA.gov/teens/twelve35.htm), which hosts open-mike nights, video-game tournaments and a variety of classes. Teens also get to use the recording studio, snack bar, arcade, HDTV PS3, Xbox 360, pool and air-hockey tables.

Santa Barbara's two versions of the mall – that ubiquitous teen hangout – are both outdoors and upscale. **La Cumbre Plaza** (Highway 101 at Hope Avenue, 805.687.6458, ShopLaCumbre.com) has more than 60 shops and eateries to choose from, while **Paseo Nuevo** (651 Paseo Nuevo, 805.963.2202, sbmall.com) has more than 50 shops and eateries, as well as the **Paseo Nuevo Movie Theatre** (805.963.9503, MetroTheatres.com).

Goleta's **Camino Real Marketplace** (home of the big-box stores), with its **Metropolitan Camino Real** theater complex (805.963.9503, MetroTheatres.com), is also a good place for teens to hang out, hit the movies and maybe grab a pizza at **Gina's Pizza** or a cone at locally made **McConnell's Ice Cream**.

Wildly popular with this age group is **Skater's Point** (see The Outdoor Life, in this chapter. For other outdoor activities, from rock-climbing to kayaking, see the Outdoorsy, Athletic and Beachy chapters).

The historic **Los Baños del Mar pool** (401 Shoreline Drive, 805.966.6110) offers year-round outdoor swimming, with lap and open swim daily. This is also the home of the Santa Barbara Swim Club.

Disc golf (Frisbee golf to the uninitiated) does require skill, but plaid knickers are optional; it's popular with a certain crowd of older high school and college kids. Check out Evergreen Open Space in Goleta and the Isla Vista Peace Course near UCSB.

The **Metropolitan Transit District** (MTD) in Santa Barbara is a lifeline for nondrivers. And the electric, open-air Waterfront-Downtown Shuttle, which quietly cruises along State Street and the waterfront, is a great option for both shopping and beach-going teens – and a bargain at 25 cents. See the Home Away from Home chapter for bus routes.

For Kids of All Ages
Touring Santa Barbara is fun for the whole family, especially if you jump on the **Land Shark** (805.683.7600, out2seesb.com), Santa Barbara's original amphibious tour vehicle, for a narrated 90-minute land and sea adventure. From Stearns Wharf, you'll wind your way through the enchanting streets of Santa Barbara, then splash into the pacific waters of the harbor, without ever leaving the comfort of your original seat.

Whale watching and **island excursions** on the **Condor Express** (805. 882.0088, CondorCruises.com) will also appeal to the whole family. The Santa Barbara Channel is home to more than 30 species of whales, dolphins and seals and sea lions that visit throughout the year, making these waters among the best anywhere to view a variety of marine mammals. It's a great way to enjoy the ocean together.

For a mellow day, head over to **Cachuma Lake Recreation Area** (805.686.5054, sb-parks.org/docs/Cachuma.html). This small lake is a fishing paradise, stocked with trout, bass and catfish. Pack a lunch, buy some bait, rent a boat, and enjoy a leisurely afternoon. Also highly recommended is the two-hour naturalist-led cruise on the ***Osprey***, which delivers views of seasonal wildlife and eagles; call 805.686.5050 for reservations. Younger children in particular will get a giggle out of the **Nature Center's** free "everybody poops" exhibit (805.693.0691). Tent campsites are available, and they have a few yurts for rent as well.

Zodo's Bowling & Beyond (5925 Calle Real, Goleta, 805.967.0128, zodos.com) has something for everyone to enjoy, with a tricked-out new arcade, bowling, including glow bowling and rock and bowl nights – and kid-friendly food. Not to mention a parent-friendly assortment of brews from **Z's Taphouse and Grill**. Plus, kids bowl their first game free all summer long, so the price is hard to beat.

Lake Cachuma is a serene lake with boat rentals and plenty of fish.

Parades & Parties

Santa Barbarans love to celebrate. It seems like every time you turn around there's a parade, a festival or a celebration of some sort going on. Here are our favorites, roughly in calendar order.

Big-ticket amusement-park rides are a big draw at the annual Santa Barbara Fair.

Santa Barbara Fair & Expo

April, Earl Warren Fairgrounds, 3400 Calle Real, Santa Barbara
805.687.0766, sbfairandexpo.com
The Santa Barbara Fair & Expo showcases local livestock, as well as agricultural, crafts and cooking talents. It also includes a carnival and petting zoo for little ones, as well as a full array of rides, games, concerts and attractions for older kids and teenagers.

Children's Festival

May, Alameda Park, Santa Barbara
805.965.1001, fsacares.org
On a Saturday in May, sprawling Alameda Park in downtown Santa Barbara becomes kid heaven, with games, art projects, sporting events, food, pony rides and entertainment galore, ranging from concerts to puppet shows. Free to the public, the festival is sponsored by the Family Service Agency of Santa Barbara.

Fourth of July

July 4th, various locations
Independence Day events abound all over the Santa Barbara area, with downtown, Montecito and Goleta all hosting their own celebrations of our nation's founding. Start with pancakes at the Montecito Firehouse (595 San Ysidro Road), and then enjoy the Village Fourth Parade down Coast Village Road, followed by fun and games at Lower Manning Park on San Ysidro Road. Or head to Goleta for a hayride or a ride on a vintage fire truck at the Stow House Old-Fashioned 4th of July (304 North Los Carneros Road), followed by the Goleta Fireworks Festival at Girsh Park (7050 Phelps Road). In Santa Barbara itself, check out the Spirit of 76 parade down State Street, the free symphony concert at the Santa Barbara Courthouse (1100 block of Anacapa Street) and the spectacular nighttime fireworks show at West Beach, along Cabrillo Boulevard.

Scrap for making art at Art From Scrap.

Old Spanish Days Fiesta
August, various locations
805.962.8101, OldSpanishDays-fiesta.org
In the first week of August, savory smells, sombreros and cheers of "Viva la Fiesta!" announce the celebration of Santa Barbara's Spanish history and strong Hispanic community. We could easily fill an entire chapter with the traditions of Fiesta, but for now we'll say that children especially love La Fiesta Pequeña, the opening night's entertainment at the Mission; the delicious food, live music and carnival rides at El Mercado del Norte (MacKenzie Park, State Street and Los Positas Road); and El Desfile de los Niños, the charming children's parade on State Street, for which young people don traditional costumes and celebrate Santa Barbara's rich Latin culture.

Sandcastle Festival
September, East Beach, Santa Barbara
SandcastleFestival.com
Back-to-school season finds East Beach dotted with grand castles, far-out sand sculptures and whimsical structures as far as the eye can see. Live music and food make this a great day for the family to enjoy the beach – and the remarkable properties of damp sand.

California Lemon Festival
October, Girsh Park, 7050 Phelps Rd., Goleta
CaliforniaLemonFestival.com
This small-town festival invades Girsh Park every fall with lemon food fun and festivities. A petting zoo, amusement-park rides, a classic-car and motorcycle show, arts and crafts and the fabled lemon-pie-eating contest make this event mouth-puckeringly fun.

Santa Barbara Harbor & Seafood Festival
October, Santa Barbara Harbor
805.564.5531, santabarbara.com/events/harbor_festival
This fun family festival serves up a taste of Santa Barbara's seafaring history, including boat rides, live entertainment, goings-on at the Maritime Museum and, oh yes, plenty of fresh seafood.

Downtown Holiday Parade
December, downtown Santa Barbara
805.962.2098, SantaBarbaraDowntown.com
Kicking off the holiday season is this good old-fashioned Christmas parade, complete with elementary and high-school marching bands and drill teams, the cast of *The Nutcracker* pirouetting, and Santa and his sleigh as the grand finale.

Harbor Parade of Lights
December, Santa Barbara Harbor
805.897.1962, santabarbaraca.gov
Every December Santa Barbara's waterfront plays host to a lovely holiday celebration, in which boats dress up in colored lights and parade around the harbor. The fun starts in the afternoon, when Santa arrives at the city pier, escorted by his elves – and the Harbor Patrol. The area is transformed into Santa's Village with snow from the North Pole, holiday carolers and lots of treats. Then comes the boat parade, with fireworks immediately following. Dress warmly, come early to get a good spot, and don't forget the cocoa.

Shopping Like a Kid

Art from Scrap
302 E. Cota St., Santa Barbara
805.884.0459, ArtFromScrap.org
This brilliantly creative art supply store sells nothing but recycled materials donated by the community. It offers environmental education on reuse and recycling, and it's a fantastic low-cost option for making holiday decorations, Halloween costumes and theater projects. Local artists hold modestly priced workshops for kids (with or without parents) every Saturday.

Bennett's Educational Materials
5130 Hollister Ave., Santa Barbara
805.964.8998, BennettsEducational.com
Kids will amuse themselves watching marbles race through a kinetic sculpture or playing with the trains while parents browse through Bennett's great selection of educational toys, art supplies, books and more.

Blue Bee Kids
9 E. Figueroa St., Santa Barbara
805.965.1956
All the necessities of the (very) young, affluent and style conscious life are here, in sizes for infants to tweens – from the tiniest True Religion and 7 For All Mankind jeans to small Splendid and James Perse tops to eensy-weensy Ella Moss dresses. We oogled over the Dolce & Gabbana bikinis and lilliputian leather loafers.

Chaucer's Books
Loreto Plaza, 3321 State St., Santa Barbara
805.682.6787, Chaucers.Booksense.com
With a massive children's section staffed by knowledgeable book lovers, Chaucer's is one of the last of the old-fashioned, locally owned bookstores. It's crammed floor to ceiling with books – more than 150,000 titles – and is staffed by a warm, well-informed cast of characters. Chaucer's motto is "No music or coffee machines, just lots of great books and great people." And they mean it.

Kernohan's Toys
5739 Calle Real, Goleta
805.964.6499, KernohansToys.com
A Santa Barbara original (albeit in a different location) since 1954, Kernohan's has a good selection of quality toys, including lots of building kits, including Legos, Tinkertoys, Mega Bloks and thinking toys that inspire creativity.

Metro Entertainment
6 W. Anapamu St., Santa Barbara
805.963.2168, metro-entertainment.com
Kids love Metro for its wealth of comic books (new and used), graphic novels, comic-related paraphernalia, board games, trading cards and more. School-age kids get credit for free merchandise if they get a good report card.

Naartjie
933 State St., Santa Barbara
805.965.9870, naartjie.com
You won't find many bargains on State Street, but Naartjie (who knows how you pronounce it) is an exception, selling soft, comfortable clothes for infants to children up to size 10.

Santa Barbara Scrapbooks
918 Chapala St., Santa Barbara
805.962.5099, sbscrapbooks.com
Packed with a wonderful selection of albums, paper, stickers, die-cuts, tools, adhesives and embellishments – all in all, more than 10,000 items. Kids go nuts over the wall of stickers. It's a fun place for craft-y birthday party, too.

This Little Piggy Wears Cotton
311 Paseo Nuevo, Santa Barbara
805.564.6982, LittlePiggy.com
Founded in Santa Barbara in 1989 by Jennifer Powell, this small chain sells its own kids' clothing and gifts that display humor, style and nostalgia. Let your child try on silly hats and play with puppets while you ooh and ah over all the darling merchandise. If you're considering having another baby, this store just might put you over the edge!

Got a Crib?
Whether you're visiting from out of town or hosting friends, the Santa Barbara Baby Company (805.275.2414, sbbabyco.com) can set you up with quality rental equipment at a reasonable price. Its gear includes cribs, toddler beds, strollers, car seats, high chairs, toys, swings, tables and even diapers. Plus, every order comes with the company's signature beach ball. The goods are delivered anywhere in town — and they'll even deliver a car seat to the car-rental agencies at Santa Barbara Airport.

Eating Like a Kid

Santa Barbara has more culinary-establishment treasures per capita than just about anywhere, but let's face it, kids' palates can be harder to please adults'. Here are some places that cater to kids and their parents — and you won't find a single Happy Meal toy buried in the minivan afterward.

Beach Grill at Padaro
3765 Santa Claus Ln., Carpinteria
805.566.3900, BeachGrillPadaro.com
American. L & D daily. Beer & wine. $
This is the perfect place to spend a lazy afternoon in the backyard you wish you had. Kick off your shoes, soak in the sun, and enjoy the breezes from the ocean that looms just beyond the tall hedges separating this half-acre site from the train tracks and the beach (there's no beach access). Order at the counter, grab one of the picnic tables, let the kids and dogs run, and enjoy your beach burger, fish and chips, California-style pizza or salad, washed down with a decent California wine or a cold beer.

Derf's
2000 De La Vina St. Santa Barbara
805.687.5437
American. B, L & D daily. Full bar. $
The patio at Derf's is the perfect place for enjoying one of those glorious Santa Barbara December mornings that makes you call your East Coast friends and gloat. The chow runs to burgers, fries, nachos, salads and basic breakfasts – the menu hasn't changed in the past few decades, and that's just the way the locals like it. Plop yourself in front of the big-screen TV on game day.

East Beach Grill
1118 E. Cabrillo Blvd., Santa Barbara
805.965.8805
American. B & L daily. Beer & wine. $
No shoes, no shirt, no problem – you can dine outside here with a sandy swimsuit and feel right at home. The lunches are what you'd expect – burgers, dogs, fries, sandwiches and a smattering of so-so Mexican food – but the breakfasts can't be beat. A few feet away are a swing set and a kids' playground on the sand.

Ellen's Danish Pancake House
272 Ave. of the Flags, Buellton
805.688.5312
Danish. B & L daily, D Tues.-Sun. No booze. $
If you're heading to Solvang, make sure to stop by Ellen's for what are, quite simply, the best pancakes you've ever had – and try them with the house-made jam. Breakfast is served all day. Kids love the mom-and-pop atmosphere.

Eller's Donut House & Thai Food
4317 State St., Santa Barbara
805.683.0838
Thai/American. B & L daily. No booze. $
Thai food and doughnuts may seem like strange bedfellows, but at this atmosphere-free strip-mall place, you'll find both the best yellow curry and chocolate crullers in town.

The sandbox at the Beach Grill at Padaro.

Farmer Boy
3427 State St., Santa Barbara
805.687.7011, FarmerBoy.com
American. B & L daily. No booze. $
A local institution since 1958, this hole-in-the-wall coffee shop serves hearty food at affordable prices in a comfortable setting. Kids love the "under 10 and over 65" specials, as well as the homemade cinnamon rolls and pancakes.

Giovanni's
3020 State St., Santa Barbara
805.682.3621, GiovannisPizzaSB.com
Italian. L & D daily. Beer & wine. $
Family-owned for more than 25 years, Giovanni's makes the best pizza in town. Everything is fresh, from handpicked vegetables to the classic toppings. Homemade pasta, sandwiches and salads are also tasty, and kids love to play video games or watch sports on TV.

Los Gallos
2009 De la Vina St., Santa Barbara
805.563.4883
Mexican. L & D daily. Beer. $
Great, inexpensive food in a very casual setting is the draw here. Walk up to the counter and order from an extensive menu, which includes zippy salsa, excellent tri-tip, all kinds of tacos, homemade tortillas and fabulous black beans.

McConnell's
201 W. Mission St., Santa Barbara
805.569.2323, McconnellsOnMission.com
Ice cream. Open daily to 11:30 p.m.
A Santa Barbara institution for more than 60 years, this friendly ice cream parlor carries a creamy, delicious, slightly less rich version of the ice cream found in supermarket freezers nationwide. Local teenage girls and their weight-conscious parents are addicted to McConnell's excellent Wow Cow frozen yogurt.

Pizza Mizza
104 S. Hope Ave., Santa Barbara
805.564.3900, PizzaMizza.com
Italian. L & D daily. Beer & wine. $-$$
An appealing assortment of gourmet pizzas, salads and pastas makes this a great choice for families. It has crayons, kids' menus and free chocolate-chip cookies for little ones. Plus it's located in La Cumbre Plaza, so if you sit outside, the kids can run around until the food comes.

Santa Barbara Chicken Ranch
2618 De la Vina St., Santa Barbara
805.569.1872, SBChickenRanch.com
163 N. Fairview Ave., Goleta
805.692.9200
Mexican/Barbecue. L & D daily. No booze. $

One scoop of McConnell's peppermint stick. please!

Owner Matt Benko keeps it simple, cheap and delicious: Tri-tip, chicken and burritos (plus a few sides) are all you'll find on the menu at the Chicken Ranch, but those are more than enough to keep the many regulars happy.

Shoreline Beach Café
801 Shoreline Dr., Santa Barbara
805.568.0064
American. B, L & D daily. Full bar. $-$$
Precious few restaurants provide the experience of wiggling your toes in the warm sand while munching on a great burger or fish taco, and this is one of them. At this cherished locals' favorite just down the cliff from Santa Barbara City College, you can choose from covered deck seating or the aforementioned sand-side tables. The kids can play in the sand, you can drink in the gazillion-dollar view of the sparkling Pacific, and you all can enjoy a good meal.

Something's Fishy
500 State St., Santa Barbara
805.966.6607, SomethingsFishyRestaurant.com
Japanese. L & D daily. Full bar. $$-$$$
Kids love to watch their food being cooked on the teppan-style grill before their very eyes. The chefs have lots of crowd-pleasing tricks up their sleeves, making this a great place for celebrations. There's also a full sushi bar.

Woody's Bodacious Barbecue
5112 Hollister Ave., Santa Barbara
805.967.3775, woodysbbq.com
Barbecue. L & D daily. Beer & wine. $-$$
Voted Santa Barbara's favorite barbecue for 24 years in a row, Woody's is a family favorite for its awesome ribs and chicken, huge burgers, full kids' menu and sawdust on the floors. And the french fries are pretty much the tastiest fries you'll find anywhere, ever.

Q & A: Rachael Steidl

Recognizing the need for a centralized place for parenting information in Santa Barbara, Rachael Steidl created SBParent.com in 2002, and it quickly became an indispensable resource for local moms and dads. Part internet portal, part calendar and part bulletin board, the site not only serves locals, it is also the model for nineteen other cities that have licensed the ParentClick.com technology. Leslie Dinaberg talked to Rachael at her Goleta home about life as a mom on the Central Coast.

Is Santa Barbara a good place to raise a family?
Absolutely. One of the biggest reasons is that you spend so little time in your car. Truly, the number of things you can do in one day in Santa Barbara compared to most cities is amazing. I also think we have so much to offer kids: great weather, great beaches, great activities and such an outdoors mentality. They get exposure to so many different types of experiences.

I know you grew up here. How has it changed?
I've lived here since I was 3. It's just incredible to think that the 101 used to have a traffic light! There's certainly a lot more traffic nowadays, with the increase over the years in residents, visitors, businesses and nonprofits. I've also watched the way Goleta has been built up and how much farther north Santa Barbara now spreads. But I'm not complaining – I don't know if I would have wanted to stay here had it not grown. We have so much going on now.

What do you really think about Fiesta?
I look so forward to Fiesta – till it gets here! It always sounds so fun, but the minute it arrives and the crowds start rolling in, I lose my desire to get in the middle of it. My family typically goes to one major Fiesta outing, like De La Guerra Plaza to try the food. I also like going to the Sunken Garden to watch the shows at night and have a picnic dinner. I so love the tradition of what Fiesta is, and so very much respect the committees that put it

together every year, but it's not as much fun as when I was young. As a teenager, and coming home from college, it was such a great place to connect with all of my peers, but now, as a mom, I look at the crowds and think, "Ugh."

You're president of the board of the Teddy Bear Cancer Foundation. Tell us about its mission.
The Teddy Bear provides financial aid to families whose kids have cancer so they can focus on being with their children and not worry about finances. It started in Santa Barbara, when Nikki Katz watched a friend care for a child with cancer. She was shocked that there was no help for parents when they had to quit their jobs to take care of sick children. When you talk to these parents who have just found out that their children have cancer ... I mean, it could be any one of us. They literally have to drop everything. So Teddy Bear works with Cottage Hospital and the Cancer Foundation to make sure these families have what they need.

Home Away from Home

In the pages that follow you'll find everything you need to make Santa Barbara and environs your home away from home: a welcoming hotel, a restorative spa, a guide to getting around, a calendar of events and all sorts of useful places to know about, from dry cleaners to florists to emergency vets.

A Comfortable Bed

The Alisal Guest Ranch & Resort
1054 Alisal Rd., Solvang
805.688.6411, 800.425.4725, alisal.com
$495-$650
You can ride horses on 50 miles of trails, play tennis, golf, fish or sail on the 100-acre spring-fed lake – or just lounge around by the pool. This serene, old-money, 10,000-acre getaway in the Santa Ynez Valley has welcomed stars and ordinary (if well-heeled) families alike since 1946. The 73 rooms and suites combine Spanish-Mexican-American-era elements like Spanish tile, fireplaces and Western art with casual-upscale ranch-style furnishings. Children can participate in various activities, including a summer youth and teen program, and adults can play in the new 5,500-square-foot fitness center and spa. There are neither phones nor TVs in the rooms, but if you get twitchy you'll find them in several public areas. Breakfast and dinner are included in the rates; note that menfolk must wear a jacket to dinner.

The Ballard Inn
2436 Baseline Ave., Ballard
805.688.7770, 800.638.2466, ballardinn.com
$225-$315
One of the most romantic lodgings in the Santa Ynez Valley, this elegant inn offers traditional bed-and-breakfast rooms in the tiny town of Ballard, two miles south of Los Olivos. It's a true getaway, with no phones or TVs in any of the fifteen rooms (although you can request these items if you wish). The top-notch onsite restaurant is one of the main draws, since chef-owner Budi Kazali serves some of the finest French-Asian food in Southern California. He whips up a mighty fine breakfast, too.

Canary Hotel
31 W. Carrillo St., Santa Barbara
805.884.0300, canarysantabarbara.com
$405-$525, suites $500 & up
In 2004 a brand-new hotel called the Andalusia, built on the site of a demolished building, opened downtown. It quickly changed owners, who spared no expense in changing the theme and décor. They also own the top-notch Casa del Mar and Shutters on the Beach in Santa Monica, and they wanted this new place to echo the casual, beachy feel of Shutters, even though it's not on the waterfront. The full-service Canary hatched in early 2008 – and no, it's not really named for a bird, but rather the Canary Islands off the coast of Spain. African masks, dark wood floors and sea-grass hues evoke a North African/Spanish/island vibe. The 77 rooms and twenty suites include four-poster beds, yoga mats, candles, DVDs, WiFi and many other amenities. Head up to the Perch on the sixth floor (one of the highest rooftops in town) for a dip in the pool or spa and for gorgeous 360-degree views. The Coast restaurant on the lobby floor serves upscale comfort food — think meatloaf and mashed potatoes and a raw-seafood bar. You can walk to cultural and arts events, shops and businesses.

Casa del Mar
18 Bath St., Santa Barbara
805.963.4418, casadelmar.com
$159-$229, suites $194-$279
We've stayed here from time to time for many years, through several remodels, and we still appreciate its comfort, value and location. Because Casa del Mar doesn't have a pool (but it does have a large spa and the beach just a block away), the tab is lower than at other neighborhood hotels. A converted 1930s Spanish-style apartment building, it has several roomy suites that are good for families; some have kitchens, and a couple even have fireplaces. Rates include a generous continental breakfast, evening wine and cheese and high-speed internet access. The beach, Stearns Wharf and State Street are an easy walk.

A guided horseback ride at the Alisal Ranch.

Fess Parker's DoubleTree Resort
633 E. Cabrillo Blvd., Santa Barbara
805.564.4333, 800.879.2929, fpdtr.com
$250-$645, suites $750-$875
Built in 1986 on the site of the city's old railway roundhouse, this fairly soulless megahotel sprawls across 23 acres across from East Beach. The seaside-themed 337 rooms and 23 suites are relatively large compared to other

The Four Seasons Biltmore puts tremendous effort into its lush and varied gardens.

beach-area hotels (rooms average 450 square feet), so there's room to spread out. Each has its own patio or balcony, and 76 open to ocean views – try to nab one on the second floor. This is a good spot for active people: You can play tennis on the lighted courts, swim, shoot hoops and practice on the putting green. The hotel also provides free airport and train-station shuttle service, seasonal children's programs and a bike and skate rental outlet. When the city agreed to let Fess build his hotel here, he was supposed to build a youth hostel close to the Amtrak station. Twenty-some years later, it's finally under construction and should open in 2009. He also agreed to landscape and maintain grassy parkland that fronts the hotel along Cabrillo Boulevard – it looks like it's part of the resort, but in fact it's a city park. We know locals who hold regular get-togethers there to remind everyone of the true state of affairs.

Fess Parker's Wine Country Inn & Spa
2860 Grand Ave., Los Olivos
805.688.7788, 800.446.2455, fessparker.com
$295-$545
This upscale inn is a good choice if you're looking for a centrally located base while touring the Foxen Wine Trail and the northeastern stretches of the wine country. It's right in the heart of Los Olivos, so you can walk to restaurants (or dine at the hotel) and the inn's spa down the street. The luxury rooms (including one suite) are spacious and have wet bars, fireplaces and WiFi.

Four Seasons Resort
The Biltmore Santa Barbara
1260 Channel Dr., Montecito
805.969.2261, 800.332.3442, fourseasons.com
$550-$850, suites $800 & up
Designed by Reginald Johnson and epitomizing Santa Barbara's Spanish Colonial style, the ultra-luxe Biltmore sits amid lush gardens across from Butterfly Beach in Montecito, where it's reigned as the queen of beachfront hotels since 1927. This is where you get married, celebrate a milestone, or just plain indulge in the setting and the first-rate service – if you can afford it. Now owned by Beanie Baby mogul Ty Warner and managed by Four Seasons, the Biltmore has been restored to its former glory – and then some. It houses 178 rooms, seventeen suites and twelve fabulous cottages, all perfectly equipped, plus a 10,000-square-foot spa with a pool and gardens; it's one of the top spas in the region. Guests also have privileges across the street at the Coral Casino Beach and Cabana Club, an historic (and super-exclusive) fitness and swim club that reopened in 2008 after a

The courtyard at Inn of the Spanish Garden.

$65-million restoration. Bella Vista Restaurant overlooks the ocean and serves seasonal California fare and a spectacular brunch; if the weather's nice, ask for a patio table overlooking the ocean. The back rooms near the train tracks are supposedly soundproof, but they still shake a bit when the engines run by. You can check out complimentary mountain bikes and beach cruisers, as well as movies and games, and hit balls at the putting green and croquet lawn. The hotel is kid- and pet-friendly – ask about babysitting, children's programs and pet rules.

Franciscan Inn
109 Bath St., Santa Barbara
805.963.8845, 800.663.5288, 805.564.3295, franciscaninn.com
$99-$185, suites $125-$295
When visitors with kids want to be close to the waterfront without breaking the bank, we often send them to this 1920s Spanish-style lodge a block or two north of the harbor. The 53 rooms range from standard kings to fireplace suites; families usually request the standard suite, with a queen bedroom, living room with queen sofa bed and a kitchenette. Amenities include a pool, WiFi, continental breakfast and laundry.

Hotel Mar Monte
1111 Cabrillo Blvd., Santa Barbara
805.963.0744, 800.643.1994, hotelmarmonte.com
$189-$400
Originally built in 1931, the Mar Monte boasts one of the best locations in town: right across from East Beach and the Cabrillo Bathhouse, and just a block from the zoo. Over the years the three-acre Spanish-Moorish property has undergone several name changes (Sheraton, Radisson, etc.) and remodels, and today it looks spiffier than ever while providing casual but quality accommodations and service. It's

an ideal place for families, with 173 rooms in four buildings, an outdoor pool and therapy spa, a restaurant/lounge and room service and doggies are welcome in some rooms for a fee. Rooms have microwaves, fridges and wireless internet. Grown-ups can escape to Spa Mar Monte.

Inn of the Spanish Garden
915 Garden St., Santa Barbara
805.564.4700, 866.564.4700, spanishgarden-inn.com
$259-$409, suites $369-$519
Step into the candlelit, fountain-splashed courtyard at this hidden downtown luxury inn and you might think you're in Spain. All 23 rooms have private balconies or patios, tile floors, fireplaces, soaking tubs and WiFi. It's less than a block from the presidio and an easy walk to downtown's restaurants, theaters and museums. This inn provides excellent service and caters more to businesspeople and travelers seeking a romantic getaway than to families.

Inn on Summer Hill
2520 Lillie Ave., Summerland
805.969.9998, 800.845.5566, innonsummerhill.com
$209-$279, suites $370-$429
Perched on a hill overlooking the ocean at the border of Montecito and Summerland, this luxury B&B, completed in 1989, looks like an historic Craftsman home and feels like an elegant English country manor. The fifteen rooms (really minisuites) have hardwood floors, canopy beds with puffy duvets, fireplaces, flat-screen TVs with DVD players, refrigerators, WiFi, whirlpool tubs and fabulous ocean views from a private balcony or patio (choose a second-floor room for the best views). The tranquil gardens include an outdoor hot tub and sitting areas. You won't go hungry – guests rave about the gourmet breakfast in the fireside dining room, afternoon appetizers with wine and cheese, and bedtime desserts. In-room massages can be arranged.

Montecito Inn
1295 Coast Village Rd., Montecito
805.969.7854, 800.843.2017, montecitoinn.com
$245-$425, suites $375-$475, apartment $725
The hotel says it was founded by Charlie Chaplin in 1928, a claim strongly disputed by the Montecito Historical Society, but nonetheless, Chaplin's image is everywhere. It's right on Montecito's main street, so it's an

Beach-cottage charm at Prufrock's.

easy walk to Butterfly Beach and posh shops and restaurants, and rates aren't bad given the upper-crust location. The latest remodel in 2003 gave the 61 small rooms an elegant Spanish-Mediterranean look; amenities include wireless internet, refrigerators, ceiling fans, flat-screen TVs and CD/DVD players (watch Charlie Chaplin movies for free). Rooms with air conditioning and fireplaces are available; you can also splurge on the two-bedroom apartment with a full kitchen. Outdoors, relax in the pool, hot tub and sauna, work out in the fitness center, or cruise the beach on complimentary fat-tire bikes. The Montecito Café serves excellent meals in a casual-chic dining room; room service delivers to your room or poolside table.

Motel 6 Santa Barbara Beach
443 Corona Del Mar Dr., Santa Barbara
805.564.1392, 800.466.8356, motel6.com
$99-$169
Location, location, location – this was the very first Motel 6 anywhere (opened in 1962), and it occupies a premium spot just a half-block from East Beach and a block from the zoo. It's pricey for a Motel 6, but the rates are a rock-bottom bargain for the area, believe us. Kids under 17 stay free in their parents' room. The 51 clean rooms are basic and have few amenities, other than access to WiFi. But who needs amenities when you're at the beach all day.

Prufrock's Garden Inn
600 Linden Ave., Carpinteria
805.566.9696, prufrocks.com
$199-$339
Jim and Judy Halvorsen restored this 1904 seaside home and transformed it into a cozy B&B in 1995. It's on Carpinteria's main street, in a quiet area near Carpinteria Beach, restaurants, shops and the Seaside Shuttle. Five country-themed rooms are in the main house, where the Halvorsens serve a scrumptious gourmet breakfast. A path in the colorful garden leads to a separate cottage with two private rooms, each with a private entrance, fireplace, spa tub and patio with porch swing. Three rooms have daybeds – great for families with kids.

Ramada Limited
4770 Calle Real, Santa Barbara
805.964.3511, 800.654.1965, sbramada.com
$100-$200, suites $160-$250
This is where we send our relatives and friends with kids. It's a step above a motel, with resort-style amenities at some of the lowest rates around, and children 17 and under stay free with their parents. It's in a peaceful residential neighborhood near Highway 101 and Turnpike Road, about six miles from downtown and 4.5 miles from UCSB and the airport. The 126 rooms and three suites surround lush, palm-studded gardens, a spacious pool and hot tub and a freshwater lagoon with waterfalls, water lilies, koi and ducks. Rates include wired and wireless internet access, refrigerators, microwaves, continental breakfast, athletic club passes and airport/train station transportation.

San Ysidro Ranch
900 San Ysidro Lane, Montecito
805.565.1700, 800.368.6788,
sanysidroranch.com
$695-$995, suites & cottages $895-$5,995
The world's movers and shakers have retreated to San Ysidro Ranch for more than a century, seeking a private, back-to-nature experience, without giving up the first-class pampering to which they are accustomed. Vivien Leigh and Sir Laurence Olivier exchanged wedding vows here, and John Huston stayed here for three months to finish The African Queen script. Other famous guests include Winston Churchill, Somerset Maugham, Bing Crosby and Audrey Hepburn. Book the cottage where John and Jackie Kennedy honeymooned; it'll cost you $3,000 a night, but what the hey, life's short and you'll probably never find as romantic and posh a mountain hideaway so close to the beach. Or do what neighbor Oprah does – send your overflow guests here when your mansion is full. The historic property edges 500 acres of open space with seventeen miles of hiking trails, and includes an 1825 adobe. The 41 rooms, suites and cottages are situated mostly along a hillside creek and tree-lined paths, amid herb and flower gardens and clusters of citrus trees.

Suites and cottages feature fireplaces, plasma TVs and sunken hot tubs on private patios with outdoor rain showers. And the historic Stonehouse is one of the most romantic restaurants anywhere (see Hungry & Thirsty chapter).

Santa Ynez Inn
3627 Sagunto St., Santa Ynez
805.688.5588, 800.643.5774,
santaynezinn.com
$325-$495
The twenty spacious rooms in this deluxe, two-story Victorian-style building in downtown Santa Ynez offer first-rate amenities and authentic historical furnishings (the owners are antiques buffs). It sits on the main street in old Santa Ynez, so you can easily walk to restaurants. Rates include a fabulous full breakfast and lavish afternoon/evening happy hour with wine and appetizers.

Simpson House Inn
121 E. Arrellaga St., Santa Barbara
805.963.7067, 800.676.1280,
simpsonhouseinn.com
$285-$475
We're not kidding – this traditional bed-and-breakfast inn ranks among the best lodgings in the nation (and that includes hotels). Here's one example: Every year for more than a decade, it has been the only B&B in North America to earn a Five-Diamond rating from AAA. An acre of manicured gardens surround the Victorian main house and its seven guest rooms, as well as a century-old barn with four junior suites and four cottages, each with wood-burning fireplaces. Rates include a gourmet vegetarian breakfast, evening appetizers and wine, WiFi, athletic club passes, bicycles and parking. You can also arrange for massages and spa services in your room. The inn is just a few blocks from the Arlington and Granada theaters, and it's an easy walk to all downtown attractions and shuttles. A two-night minimum stay is required on weekends.

Solvang Gardens Lodge
293 Alisal Rd., Solvang
805.688.4404, 888.688.4404,
solvanggardens.com
$119-$199, suites $149-$239
Colorful, carefully tended gardens with waterfalls and fountains – as well as a super-friendly staff – set this small lodge apart from nearby traditional motels. Each of the 24 rooms

The charm stops short of becoming kitsch at Solvang Gardens.

and suites boasts a different floral name and English-country décor, including antique furnishings. The owners are continually upgrading what was once a small, no-frills motel, so some of the rooms are still basic, while others have such bells and whistles as marble baths and showers. Amenities include WiFi and an onsite massage studio. The inn sits several blocks away from Solvang's main tourist hub, so it's a good bet for folks who want peace and quiet but still want to be able to walk to town.

The Upham Hotel & Tiffany Country House
1404 De la Vina St., Santa Barbara
805.962.0058, 800.727.0876, uphamhotel.com
$220-$350, suites $300-$550
Banker Amasa Lincoln (a relative of Abraham Lincoln) built this New England–style hotel in 1871. It was originally a redwood boardinghouse called the Lincoln House, and Cyrus Upham renamed it the Hotel Upham when he bought the property in 1898. Today, the Upham upholds (usually) its reputation for attentive service and homey atmosphere. The Victorian main building and cottages occupy an acre of gardens and grounds at the corner of De la Vina and Sola, near the Arlington and Granada theaters. The 50 individually decorated rooms and suites vary greatly in size and character, from small bungalow rooms to a sunny master suite with fireplace and spa tub, so be sure to check out your options carefully online or by phone. WiFi is available in all rooms and public areas. The comfy lounge and the adjacent restaurant, Louie's California Bistro, are two of our favorite places to hang out with out-of-town guests. Across the street, the affiliated, century-old Tiffany Country House (tiffanycountryhouse.com) offers eight traditional bed-and-breakfast rooms.

A Soothing Spa

Avia Spa
350 Chapala St., Stes. 101 & 102, Santa Barbara
805.730.7303, aviaspa.com
Ancient Asian philosophy meets Western technology, with custom-built Japanese massage huts, soothing music, trickling water and stress-reducing treatments for body and mind.

Bacara Resort & Spa
8301 Hollister Ave., Goleta
805.968.0100, bacararesort.com
This posh spa is almost too big – its three levels include 36 treatment rooms, a full fitness center, steam rooms, saunas, a beauty salon, a café and a shop filled with luxury potions. Still, it's a superb place to escape from the stresses of the world beyond, if you don't mind forking over lots of greenbacks.

Bellezza Vita
2410 Lillie Ave., Summerland
805.969.7300, bellezzavita.com
This charming boutique offers facials, massages and spa packages, plus a full-service hair and beauty salon.

Camille the Day Spa
1115 State St., Santa Barbara
805.899.4883
Slip in to this cozy spa in the heart of downtown's arts and shopping district for quality care for skin, hair, nails and body.

Chumash Casino Resort & Spa
3400 E. Hwy. 246, Santa Ynez
800.248.6274, chumashcasino.com
Ever had a Chumash massage? Now's your chance to try one, along with treatments that use such Santa Ynez Valley essential oils as lavender and bay laurel, in a luxurious spa that shields patrons from the casino crowd nearby.

Divine Day Spa
2971 Grand Ave., Los Olivos
805.686.9000, thedivinedayspa.com
A full range of treatments and spa services are offered in a serene, historic cottage in downtown Los Olivos.

Four Seasons Resort
The Biltmore Santa Barbara
1260 Channel Dr., Montecito
805.969.2261, 800.332.3442, fourseasons.com
The Biltmore oozes luxury from every corner

of its sleek and sumptuous spa. It's a 10,000-square-foot oasis with lush gardens and a swimming pool. Four of the eleven treatment rooms are fireplace suites with terraces overlooking the ocean. It's open to hotel guests, as well as nonguests. This is one of the nation's top resort spas, so don't let your blood pressure rise when you see the hefty price tags.

The Haven Day Spa at Hadsten House Inn
1450 Mission Dr., Solvang
800.457.5373, hadstenhouse.com
Massages, facials and body treatments are offered in a sparkling, intimate new facility at the Hadsten House Inn at the edge of Solvang's tourist town.

Le Rêve Aromatherapy Spa
21 W. Gutierrez St., Santa Barbara
805.564.2977, le-reve.com
A dreamy spa experience with featherbeds in the treatment rooms and holistic approaches to body care.

Qui Si Bella Spa
3311 State St., Santa Barbara
805.682.0003, quisibella.com
Drink Amazon spa water and rejuvenate through holistic treatments at this eco-friendly, sustainable spa in Loreto Plaza.

Sea Spa Santa Barbara – the Day Spa
1187 Coast Village Rd., Montecito
805.565.5555, seaspasantabarbara.com
This super-luxurious spa specializes in European skin care and anti-aging treatments for those of means seeking the ultimate in pampering and privacy.

Skin Deep
3405 State St., Santa Barbara
805.687.9497, skindeepsalon.com
Owner Tina Hasche opened this favorite local "spatique" with her sisters and mom in 1980. Best known for great facials, body treatments and waxing, plus quality beauty products, it's still going strong.

Walter Claudio Salon Spa
11 W. Figueroa St., Santa Barbara
805.963.7579, walterclaudio.com
An Aveda spa/hair salon with massages, makeovers and body treatments.

Stuff You Need

Animal Care – Emergency

Animal Medical Clinic
1037 Casitas Pass Rd., Carpinteria
805.684.8665
Veterinary emergency services.

CARE Hospital
301 E. Haley St., Santa Barbara
805.899.2273, carehospital.org
A full-service hospital with 24-hour emergency
services for cats, dogs, birds, rabbits, pocket
pets, wildlife and companion exotics.

Churches
See Reaching Out chapter

Currency Exchange

Paul A. Brombal
3601 State St., Santa Barbara
805.687.3641
This longtime rare coin and jewel collector also
purchases all current world currencies and
stocks all major legal tender.

Dry Cleaners & Alterations

Ablitt's Fine Cleaners
14 W. Gutierrez St., Santa Barbara
805.963.6677, ablitts.com
Neil and Sue Ablitt founded this first-rate establishment in 1984. Now their daughter Sasha
Ablitt runs the show, which includes services
from wedding-gown preservation and drape
cleaning to cobbling shoes and free pickup and
delivery – all at highly competitive prices.

American Cleaners & Laundry
Mesa: 1836 Cliff Dr., 805.564.2307
Downtown: 31 E. Victoria St., 805.962.2980
americancleanerssb.com
Known for its eco-friendly techniques and
cheery staff, this is a good choice for quick,
same-day service. It picks up and delivers for
free, and it also offers tailoring and alterations.

Martinizing
Turnpike Center: 155 S. Turnpike Rd., Santa
Barbara, 805.967.1555
San Roque Plaza: 3351 State St., Santa Bar-
bara, 805.687.7800
Coast Village Shopping Center: 1024 Coast Vil-
lage Rd., Montecito, 805.969.3880
onehourmartinizing.net

Martinizing's plant specializes in environmentally safe, odorless, 100-percent non-perc dry
cleaning. Onsite alterations, too.

Emergency Rooms

Cottage Health System (cottagehealthsystem.
org) operates three hospitals with emergency
rooms, as follows:

Goleta Valley Cottage Hospital
351 S. Patterson Ave., Goleta
805.967.3411 (hospital), 805.681.6473 (ER)

Santa Barbara Cottage Hospital
(Level II trauma center)
ER entrance at Junipero St. & Castillo St.
805.682.7111 (hospital), 805.569.7210 (ER)

Santa Ynez Valley Cottage Hospital
Alamo Pintado Rd. at Viborg Rd.
805.688.6431 (hospital), 805.686.3989 (ER)

Florists

Botanik
2329 Lillie Ave., Summerland
805.565.3831
Botanik's exotic flowers, succulents, orchids
and luxury gift items decorate many a fine local
home, including Oprah's. Browse the adjacent
shops (one's a florist, the other a boutique) to
feast on all the eye candy.

Riley's Flowers
1106 Chapala St., Santa Barbara
805.965.1187, 800.552.4944, rileysflowers.com
Maureen Riley's shop is famed for affordable
roses from local and Ecuadoran growers.

Santa Barbara Certified Farmer's Market
sbfarmersmarket.org
The markets sell an incredible variety of local
blooms. Weekly markets take place around
the region; visit the web site for the schedule.
Saturday's market has the best selection.

Victor the Florist
135 E. Anapamu St., Santa Barbara
805.965.3075, victortheflorist.com
Victor's has been taking orders for quality
floral gifts since 1930. The family-owned and
-operated business often goes the extra mile
for customers – it even offers 24-hour service
seven days a week.

Hair Salons

About Faces
2273 Las Positas Rd., Santa Barbara
805.682.5294
Good cuts, color and styling by friendly and expert stylists, who also can fix you up with manicures, pedicures, facials and waxing. The salon sells skin and hair products, including mineral makeup. The owner is known for her waxing and (bless her) anti-aging expertise.

Danny's Custom Styling
Loreto Plaza, 3337 State St., Santa Barbara
805.687.7915
Danny's is an honest-to-goodness old-time barbershop (nearly 50 years old) that clips all types of hair at fantastic prices.

Underground Hair Artists
1021 Chapala St., Santa Barbara
805.899.8820, undergroundhairartists.com
A hip European salon, Underground (think London) cuts contemporary styles at reasonable rates – from $29 to $65, depending on the stylist. You can also get cornrows, braids, facials, manis, pedis and waxes.

Walter Claudio
11 W. Figueroa St., Santa Barbara
805.963.7579, walterclaudio.com
Escape to this sparkling, light-filled Aveda salon and spa for pampering and almost excessively precise hair design. Stylists are trained in Vidal Sassoon methods; splurge and request Walter to create your new do for a hefty fee. All cut and style sessions include a consultation, scalp treatment and cleansing massage.

Jewelers

Bryant & Sons, Ltd.
812 State St., Santa Barbara
805.966.9187
1482 E. Valley Rd., Montecito
805.565.4411
Situated at the entrance to the historic El Paseo since 1965, this swank shop (and its newer Montecito sibling) dresses up the glitterati with the world's most elegant jewels and gift items. The staff members know their stuff and are the go-to folks for accurate appraisals.

Libraries
See Smart chapter

Nail Salons

Aqua Nail Bar & Boutique
Goleta: 143 N. Fairview Ave.
805.964.0282
Santa Barbara: 3455 State St.
805.687.8483
aquanailbar.com
This squeaky-clean, aqua-walled salon with an oceanic theme looks like it belongs in a mermaid movie. Both locations offer the usual manicure and pedicure options. Waxing and makeup by appointment only; mani and pedi walk-ins are welcome. Grown-up girlie birthday parties here are a hoot.

Artistic Nails & Spa
Goleta: 5801 Calle Real, Ste. F
805.964.7588
Mesa: 1964 Cliff Dr.
805.730.1737
Santa Barbara: 651 Paseo Nuevo Mall
805.560.0633
The convenient locations of this popular local chain make it easy to pop in for a quick mani-pedi. Great prices.

Santa Barbara Nails
3124 State St., Santa Barbara
805.563.0868
Fast, friendly and efficient, the manicurists here are busy but always seem able to handle a walk-in. It's open daily and is a popular pre-prom spot. Waxing and facials, too.

Pharmacies

L. M. Caldwell
1509 State St., Santa Barbara
805.965.4528
235 W. Pueblo St., near Cottage Hospital
805.682.7353, caldwellness.com
Here you get a lot more than a highly respected med dispensary – it's also a wellness center, with specialists in non-traditional approaches to maintaining health. It also carries natural and herbal medicines and homeopathic remedies. Known for great customer service since 1947, Caldwell's delivers prescriptions for free.

Long's Drug Stores
1282 Coast Village Rd., Montecito
805.565.0897 (prescriptions), 805.565.0987 (refill recorder), longsdrugs.com
Typically friendly, careful and quick to fill pre-

scriptions, this chain has pharmacies all over. The Montecito store is a nice Long's, and you can call in for refills at any time.

Post Offices

Goleta Area Post Office
130 S. Patterson Ave., Santa Barbara (just east of the Goleta city limits)
800.275.8777
Convenient to UCSB, this post office has easy parking right in front. Open 8:30 a.m. to 6 p.m. weekdays, 9 a.m. to 3 p.m. Saturday.

Santa Barbara Main Post Office
836 Anacapa St., Santa Barbara
800.275.8777
This historic 1937 Spanish-Moorish-Mission Revival building is on the National Register of Historic Places (see Architectural chapter). It's the coolest place to mail a package, since you can gawk at the architectural detail while standing in line. Open 8:30 a.m. to 6 p.m. Monday through Friday, 9 a.m. to 2 p.m. Saturday.

Public Restrooms
Restroom facilities are strategically placed along the waterfront and at the larger public beaches. You'll also find nice, new restrooms at the Visitors Center at the corner of Cabrillo and Garden, and on the 900 block of State Street.

Senior Services

Carrillo Recreation Center
100 E. Carrillo St., Santa Barbara
805.897.2519, sbparksandrecreation.com
Call or stop by the Active Adults and Classes office at this historic rec center, where seniors can sign up for everything from swing, jazz and ballroom dance to basketball and yoga.

Louise Lowry Davis Recreation Center
1232 De la Vina St., Santa Barbara
805.897.2568, sbparksandrecreation.com
Seniors congregate at this homey downtown center to hang with friends and participate in a slew of activities: lawn bowling, chess, bridge, painting, knitting, tai chi, Italian and more.

Shoe Repair

Jesse's Shoes & Repair
5915 Calle Real, Goleta
805.964.3414

People whose favorite Italian designer shoes need expert fixing entrust them to Jesse Holder, who has been repairing footwear and leather items for more than 50 years.

Step-N-Out Instant Shoe Repair
805 Paseo Nuevo Mall, Santa Barbara
805.966.2299
The quality of repairs can vary, but, hey, the service is quick and reasonably priced, and it's smack-dab in downtown's shopping district.

Travel Agent

Santa Barbara Travel Bureau
1028 State St., Santa Barbara
805.966.3116
1127 Coast Village Rd., Montecito
805.969.7746, sbtravel.com
Locals Charles and David de L'Arbre now run the firm that has arranged trips for thousands of clients and businesses since 1947. They specialize in corporate and leisure travel, but also coordinate meetings and events.

Visitor's Bureaus

Carpinteria Valley Chamber of Commerce
1056 Eugenia Pl., Carpinteria
805.684.5479, ExploreCarpinteria.com

Santa Barbara Conference & Visitors Bureau
1601 Anacapa St., Santa Barbara
805.966.9222, 800.676.1266, santabarbaraCA.com

Santa Barbara Visitor Center
1 Garden St. at Cabrillo Blvd.
805.965.3021
Stop by for info, maps and advice. Park for free in the adjacent public lot for the first fifteen minutes. Open 9 a.m. to 5 p.m. Monday through Saturday, 10 a.m. to 5 p.m. Sunday.

Santa Ynez Valley Visitors Association
800.742.2843, 805.686.0053, SantaYnezValleyVisit.com
Help with exploring the Santa Ynez Valley

Solvang Conference & Visitors Bureau
1511 Mission Dr., Solvang
805.688.6144, 800.468.6765, solvangusa.com
Here's where you can find one-stop travel help for Solvang and the Santa Ynez Valley.

Getting Around

It's easy to get around Santa Barbara. Visit Santa Barbara Car Free (santabarbaracarfree.org) to hook up with options and incentives for leaving your car in the garage or the lot. Traffic Solutions (trafficsolutions.info, 805.963.SAVE) also provides detailed information on commuter services, bike maps and more.

Airports

Santa Barbara Airport
500 Fowler Rd. (off Hwy. 217), Santa Barbara
805.967.7111, flysba.com
Next to UCSB, our cute little airport with the red-tile roof is about to expand, but it'll stay as convenient as ever. You can fly direct from SBA to Los Angeles, San Francisco, Denver, Las Vegas, San Diego, Sacramento, Dallas, Phoenix, Portland, Salt Lake City, San Jose and Seattle. Fares go up and down; sometimes we choose to drive to Burbank or take the Airbus (see below) to LAX for cheaper flights.

Airport Shuttles

Central Coast Shuttle Services, Inc.
3249 Terminal Dr., Ste. 102, Santa Maria
805.928.1977, 800.470.8818, centralcoastshuttle.com, cclax.com
Serves the Santa Barbara and Santa Maria areas; it also connects with LAX and Long Beach and San Pedro harbors.

Road Runner Shuttle & Limousine Service
800.247.7919, rrshuttle.com
Door-to-door shuttle service for Santa Barbara and Ventura counties

Santa Barbara Airbus
805.964.7759, 800.423.1618, sbairbus.com
Deluxe motorcoaches and some minicoaches run back and forth from LAX, fourteen trips a day, with stops in Carpinteria, Santa Barbara and Goleta. Buy ahead for a discount.

Bike & Skate Rental
See Outdoorsy and Beachy chapters

Buses

Santa Barbara Metropolitan Transit District
805.683.3702, sbmtd.gov
The MTD's green machines – said to be the nation's largest fleet of hybrid biodiesel/electric buses – travel more than 35 routes with 850 stops in the greater Santa Barbara region. The transfer hub is downtown on Chapala Street, between Carrillo and Figueroa. Line 22 (Old Mission) stops at many of Santa Barbara's tourist destinations, from downtown near the art museum up to the Mission, Museum of Natural History and sometimes the Botanic Garden. Adult fares are $1.25; you can also buy a 30-day pass. Express buses link Santa Barbara with Goleta/UCSB and Carpinteria. The Valley Express commuter buses connect Santa Ynez, Solvang and Buellton with Goleta/UCSB and Santa Barbara on weekdays.

Car Rental & Taxis

Avis Rent-a-Car
800.331.1212, 805.683.4715 (airport), avis.com
Downtown and airport outlets

Budget Car & Truck Rental
800.527.0700, 805.964.6792 (airport)
budget.com

Enterprise Car Rental
800.736.8222, 805.683.3012 (local)
enterprise.com
Five locations in Santa Barbara and Goleta.

Hertz Rent-a-Car
800.654.3131, 805.967.0411 (airport)
hertz.com

Thrifty Car Rental
800.847.4389, 805.681.1222 (airport)
thrifty.com

U-SAVE Auto Rental
800.272.8728, 805.964.5436 (local)
usavesantabarbara.com
Downtown and airport locations

Blue Dolphin Taxi
805.966.6161

Lucky Cab
805.968.5020, luckycab.net
Hybrid, eco-friendly cabs, vans and limos

Santa Barbara Yellow Cab
805.964.1111

The Downtown Waterfront Shuttle uses clean electric vehicles.

Parking Dos & Don'ts

The City of Santa Barbara operates twelve public lots in the downtown area near State Street, with access from Anacapa and Chapala streets, which run parallel to State. They're open 24 hours a day, every day, and the first 75 minutes are free. After that you pay $1.50 an hour. You'll find a map of the lots at santabarbaradowntown.com. Most street parking spaces within about three blocks of State Street in the downtown area are marked with fifteen- or 75-minute time limits. State itself has no street parking.

The city lots along the waterfront are a bit pricier – you start paying after you've parked for only fifteen minutes, unless you find one of the few free spaces marked with 90-minute limits. Some parking in the neighborhoods near the waterfront is limited to residents with passes.

DO: If you're a regular beachgoer or waterfront visitor, get an annual parking pass for $95 from one of the attendants in the kiosks at the lot entrance.

DON'T: Think you can outfox a meter maid (or mister). They have sixth senses and invariably show up the second your time limit expires.

DO: Try to get a waterfront, harbor or beach parking place before noon on summer weekends. They fill up fast.

DON'T: Go the wrong way on one-way streets when you're looking for parking. One-way streets are the norm downtown.

DO: Try to leave your car at home or at your hotel and use other modes of transportation. It's easy around here.

DON'T: Lose the parking lot ticket you pull from the machine when you enter a public city lot – you'll pay for a full day if you lose it.

Rail

Amtrak
209 State St., Santa Barbara
805.963.1015, amtrakcalifornia.com,
amtrak.com
Pacific Surfliner trains link San Diego and Los Angeles with Santa Barbara six or seven times a day; some travel up to San Luis Obispo and Paso Robles. In Santa Barbara County it stops in Carpinteria, Santa Barbara, Goleta, Lompoc and Guadalupe. The newly refurbished Coast Starlight stops in SB, too, on its daily trip back and forth from San Diego to Seattle.

Segway Rental

Segway of Santa Barbara
16 Helena Ave., Santa Barbara
805.963.7672
These things may look dorky, but they're sure fun to ride – and think of the gas savings and carbon-footprint reduction!

Shuttles

These cute little open-air electric buses link our most popular tourist and business areas during the most popular times of the day, and the fare is only a quarter. They typically come every ten to 30 minutes, depending on the season and time of day. Check the sbmtd.com web site for schedules.

Calle Real/Old Town Shuttle: Travels from Kellogg Avenue in Old Town Goleta up Hollister Avenue and across the freeway to the Calle Real business area and back.

Downtown Waterfront Shuttle: Cruises up and down State Street from Stearns Wharf to Sola Street, then connects with the Waterfront Shuttle, which travels up and down Cabrillo Boulevard between the harbor and the zoo.

Seaside Shuttle: Loops through downtown Carpinteria to the beach and through the neighborhoods.

Wharf Woody: This free shuttle runs on weekends from late May through late October. It starts from the public parking lot across from Chase Palm Park and goes out to the end of Stearns Wharf and back.

Calendar of Events

January
Santa Barbara International Film Festival.
805.963.0023, sbfilmfestival.org. A world-class festival that attracts some of the brightest stars in the celebrity galaxy. Attendees in 2008 included Cate Blanchett and Javier Bardem.

February
Amgen Tour of California. Solvang & Santa Barbara, tourofcalifornia.com. The world's best pro cycling teams whiz through the county. Stages and/or time trials usually begin or end in Solvang and Santa Barbara, and fans turn up in droves to cheer on their favorite cycling studs.

March
Santa Barbara International Orchid Show.
Earl Warren Showgrounds, sborchidshow.com. You saw this show already, in the film *Adaptation*. But it's better in real life, with hundreds of exotic orchids, free workshops on orchid care, and growers' open houses.

April
Santa Barbara County Vintners' Festival.
sbcountywines.com. A weekend-long celebration with wine and food tastings, winemaker dinners and open houses, usually at a North County park or winery estate.

May
I Madonnari Italian Street Painting Festival.
Mission Santa Barbara, imadonnarifestival.com. Over Memorial Day weekend, artists of all ages transform the steps of the Old Mission with more than 200 large-scale chalk paintings. Live music, Italian food, free evening concerts.

June
Summer Solstice Parade & Festival.
Downtown Santa Barbara/Alameda Park, 805.965.3396, solsticeparade.com. This two-day festival is Santa Barbara's version of Mardi Gras – a wild and whimsical celebration that draws more than 100,000 people. World music, dancing, drumming, food and a themed parade with outrageously funny floats and costumes.

Music Academy of the West Summer Festival begins. Various venues in Montecito/Santa Barbara, 805.969.4726, musicacademy.org. Rising young musicians get full scholarships to train with the masters – and wow us with a series of summer concerts at the academy and other sites around town.

July
Fourth of July Pops! Concert. Courthouse Sunken Garden, Santa Barbara, 805.898.9326, thesymphony.org. Locals gather with beach chairs and picnics for this 4th tradition. The free concert ends just in time to zip down to the waterfront to ooh and aah at the fireworks.

French Festival. Oak Park, Santa Barbara, 805.564.7274, frenchfestival.com. *Ooh la la!* Oak Park turns into a Francophile's dream over Bastille Day weekend. It's the largest French festival in the West, with *superbe* food and entertainment. Free admission and parking.

Late July/Early August
Old Spanish Days – Fiesta. 805.962.8101, oldspanishdays-fiesta.org. The first Old Spanish Days festival was in 1924. Now it's the biggest annual act in town. For five days Santa Barbara pays tribute to its Chumash, Spanish, Mexican and American heritage with music, dancing, food, drink, performances and one of the largest equestrian parades in the nation.

September
Danish Days. Solvang, 805.688.6144, 800.468.6765, solvangusa.com. A weekend celebrating Solvang's Danish heritage.

October
Santa Barbara Harbor & Seafood Festival.
Santa Barbara Harbor, 805.897.1962, santabarbaraca.gov. A day of homage to all things maritime. Pick out fresh seafood and watch chefs prepare it, cruise the harbor, listen to live music, tour the Maritime Museum and more.

California Avocado Festival. Carpinteria, 805.684.5479, ext. 40, 805.684.0038 (recording), avofest.com. One of the largest festivals in California, it's three days of food, music and family fun. Where else can you witness the world's biggest vat of guacamole – *and* the best-dressed avocado contest? Proceeds benefit more than 40 Carpinteria nonprofits.

December
Downtown Holiday Parade. State St., Santa Barbara, santabarbaradowntown.com. Santa Claus rides his sleigh through town, accompanied by nearly all the performing groups in town: school marching bands, floats, karate kids, gymnasts and dancers.

Index

Photo Credits

Author photo
Author photo by Stephanie Baker.

7 Towns in Search of One
Goleta Beach by Paul J. Click; all other photos by Matt Hormann and Colleen Dunn Bates.

Historic
Chumash couple, Hotel Californian & Sloyd School courtesy Santa Barbara Historical Society; railroad & stagecoach courtesy Santa Barbara Public Library; Painted Cave, El Presidio & El Presidio Chapel by Colleen Dunn Bates; vineyards, Casa Covarrubias & Michael Redmon by Paul J. Click.

Beachy
Mussel Rock by Carrie Rosing; Frenchys Cove by Derek Lohuis, National Park Service; Elephant Seals courtesy National Park Service; Lil' Toot by Greg Peterson; Renny Yater courtesy Renny Yater; Carpinteria Beach, Church of Skatan & Rincon Designs by Colleen Dunn Bates; Rincon, Miramar, East Beach, Leadbetter, Goleta Beach, Stearns Wharf & Kim Mearig by Paul J. Click.

Architectural
Mission Santa Barbara & Courthouse interior by Melissa Fargo; La Purisima & Presidio by Greg Peterson; Ablitt House by Wayne McCall; Solvang courtesy Solvang Vistiors Bureau; Courthouse front by Matt Hormann; Lutah Maria Riggs courtesy Montecito Historical Society; Pearl Chase courtesy Santa Barbara Historical Society; Stow House by Colleen Dunn Bates; Barry Berkus, Biltmore Hotel, Meridian Studios & Arlington Theater by Paul J. Click.

Horticultural
Wildflowers by Melissa Fargo; Lotusland garden clock by Greg Peterson; other Lotusland courtesy Lotusland; Santa Barbara Botanical Gardens courtesy the Botanical Gardens; A.C. Postel garden, Courhouse palm garden & Seaside Gardens by Matt Hormann; Moreton Bay Fig Tree, Clairmont Farms, poppies, Eye of the Day & Dan Bifano by Paul J. Click.

Smart
UCSB, Alan Heger & Walter Kohn courtesy UCSB; Brooks courtesy Brooks Institute of Photography; Pacific courtesy Pacifica; Westmont courtesy Westmont College; Montecito Library by Colleen Dunn Bates; Santa Barbara City College courtesy SBCC.

Famous
Guadalupe Dunes by David Klinger, U.S. Fish & Wildlife; Dishwalla by David Bazemore; 1969 oil spill by Robert Duncan; Flying A Studios courtesy Santa Barbara Historical Society; Los Olivos Café courtesy Los Olivos Café; Herb Peterson courtesy David Peterson; Santa Claus & cow by Colleen Dunn Bates; News-Press building by Paul J. Click; Kathy Ireland by Jonathan Exley.

Artistic
Oak Group photo by Wm. B. Dewey; Santa Barbara Museum of Art & I Madonnari by Greg Peterson; Contemporary Arts Forum by Matt Hormann; Santa Barbara Museum of Art & Monet painting courtesy Santa Barbara Museum of Art; Edward Cella courtesy Edward Cella; Sunday Arts & Crafts Show by Melissa Fargo; Wilding Art Museum courtesy the museum; It Is Raining & Hank Pitcher by Paul J. Click.

Literary
Fannie Flagg at Writers Conference courtesy Santa Barbara Writers Conference; Vedanta bookstore, Tecolote & Santa Barbara Library by Matt Hormann; Chaucer's by Colleen Dunn Bates; Marcia Meier by Paul J. Click.

Reaching Out
Girls Inc. girls courtesy Girls Inc.; Unity Shoppe & Vedanta Temple by Matt Hormann; Griffin Saxon courtesy the Saxon family; All Saints-by-the-Sea by Colleen Dunn Bates; La Casa de Maria courtesy La Casa de Maria; Thomas Tighe by Paul J. Click.

Green
Earth Day by Mattia Balsamini, courtesy the Community Environmental Council; Bren Hall by Timothy Hursley; Ellwood Mesa by Rich Reid; bus by Colleen Dunn Bates; farmland & Hillary Hauser by Paul J. Click.

Hungry & Thirsty
Shoreline Beach Café, Trattoria Grappolo, La Super-Rica food, Ellen's Pancake House, Montecito Farmers' Market, Maverick Saloon & Isidoro Gonzalez by Paul J. Click; Hungry Cat pug burger by Aaron Cook; Paradise Café by Matt Hormann; Jessica Foster truffles by Kristen Johansen, fotografik.com; Giannfranco's, Our Daily Bread, Renaud's & NorthStar by Colleen Dunn Bates; Vices & Spices by Nancy R. Ransohoff; C'est Cheese, Metropulos, Roy & Blue Agave by Melissa Fargo; Matttei's Tavern, Cold Spring Tavern, Tri-County Produce, farmers' market produce & Joe's Café by Greg Peterson; Arts & Letters Café courtesy Sullivan Goss; Sambo's by Christina B. Castro; Café Buenos Aires courtesy Café Buenos Aires; Olio e Limone courtesy Olio e Limone; Bouchon dish courtesy Bouchon; Surf Dog by Nathan Welton; Ty Lounge by Peter Vitale.

Wine Tasting

Wine Country road, Foxen sign, Foley bottles and Rusack glasses by Stephanie Baker; wild turkeys, Sunstone cave, Alma Rosa, Daniel Gehrs and Richard and Thekla Sanford by Paul J. Click; wine barrels by Melissa Fargo; wine festival courtesy Santa Barbara Vintners Association.

Entertaining

Fiesta Parade by Arthur Fisher; Christian McBride & Santa Barbara Symphony by David Bazemore; musicians at Cold Spring Tavern by Larry Sultan; Santa Barbara International Film Festival by Ray Mickshaw; Dargan's by Greg Peterson; Wildcat Lounge courtesy Wildcat Lounge; Roger Durling by Paul J. Click.

Outdoorsy

Harbor seals, Arroyo Burro Beach & beach path by Melissa Fargo; Monarch butterflies by Chuck Place/PlacePhotography.com; Nojoqui Falls by Dave Retz; Lizard's Mouth by Chuck Place/Place-Photography.com; tent cabin courtesy El Capitan Canyon; Amgen cyclists by Steve Besserman; mountain bikers by Ralph Fertig; horseback ride by Greg Peterson; Rattlesnake Creek, Cold Spring Canyon, Elings Park & Lake Los Carneros by Colleen Dunn Bates; breakwater & John McKinney by Paul J. Click.

Athletic

Cabrillo Bathhouse & Los Baños Del Mar courtesy Santa Barbara Parks & Recreation; Chris Keet surfing at Rincon by Michael Kew; triathletes by Melissa Fargo; Santa Barbara Athletic Club, volleyball players, Sandpiper Golf Course & Jamie Allison by Paul J. Click.

Materialistic

State Street & Just Folk by Colleen Dunn Bates; Paseo Nuevo, Big Dogs, Summerland Antique Collective, Italian Pottery Outlet, Marcel Hemp & Cominichi's by Matt Hormann; dressed by Gina Vaccarello; Mi Casa courtesy Mi Casa; Yellowstone Clothing by Melissa Fargo; Blue Bee & Marty Bebout & John Doucette by Paul J. Click.

Childlike

County Fair ride by Greg Peterson; handcar courtesy South Coast Railroad Museum; Ostrich Land by Greg Peterson; junior surfer by photo: keet, courtesy Surf Happens; elephant showering by David Orias; Boxtales performers by David Bazemore; Lake Cachuma by Matt Hormann; whale skeleton courtesy Santa Barbara Museum of Natural History; Beach Grill at Padaro & McConnell's by Colleen Dunn Bates; Skater's Point, Ty Warner Sea Center & Rachael Steidl by Paul J. Click.

Home Away from Home

Alisal Guest Ranch courtesy Alisal Guest Ranch; Prufrock's & Botanik by Colleen Dunn Bates; Four Seasons Biltmore courtesy Four Seasons Biltmore; Inn of the Spanish Garden courtesy Inn of the Spanish Garden; Solvang Gardens by Paul J. Click.